A HISTORY OF ENGLISH GARDENING,

CHRONOLOGICAL, BIOGRAPHICAL, LITERARY, AND CRITICAL.

TRACING THE PROGRESS OF THE ART IN THIS COUNTRY FROM THE INVASION OF THE ROMANS TO THE PRESENT TIME.

BY
GEORGE W. JOHNSON.

"Increscunt quotannis Scientiæ, emendantur quotidie, et ad fastigium suum optatum sensim sensimque, plurium virorum opera et studio junctis, feliciter properant."

THUNBERG.

LONDON:
PUBLISHED BY BALDWIN & CRADOCK, AND LONGMAN & Co. PATERNOSTER ROW; H. & W. WRIGHT, 51, HAY-MARKET; J. RIDGWAY, PICCADILLY; AND H. WICKS, 41, NEW BRIDGE STREET, BLACKFRIARS.

1829.

This scarce antiquarian book is included in our special *Legacy Reprint Series*. In the interest of creating a more extensive selection of rare historical book reprints, we have chosen to reproduce this title even though it may possibly have occasional imperfections such as missing and blurred pages, missing text, poor pictures, markings, dark backgrounds and other reproduction issues beyond our control. Because this work is culturally important, we have made it available as a part of our commitment to protecting, preserving and promoting the world's literature.

TO

THOMAS ANDREW KNIGHT, Esq.

PRESIDENT OF THE HORTICULTURAL SOCIETY,

&c. &c.

AS A

DEMONSTRATION OF RESPECT AND ESTEEM

FOR HIS TALENTS AND KINDNESS,

THIS WORK

IS DEDICATED,

BY,

THE AUTHOR.

PREFACE.

It is usual for an author, in his prefatory remarks, to dwell upon the importance of the subject of his work, but the Art of which the following pages contain a portion of the History is too highly and generally appreciated to render such remarks necessary.

To the general reader this work offers entertainment from its historical details; to the man of literature it affords notices of the authors on Gardening with statements of their various works and their editions; to the Gardener all of its contents possess some degree of interest for besides being a record of his Art in every age of which we have any history, it may serve as a guide to such authors as contain information on subjects relating to it of which he may be in search.

The chief qualifications required of the author were diligence and care, and on these points he can assure his readers that he sought his references in the original authorities but in such instances as he has otherwise specified, and where he has relied upon others, it has been on such as are known to be trustworthy.

Among his guides to such authorities he has particularly to acknowledge his obligations to *Weston's Tract's*, Professor Martyn's edition of *Miller's Gardener's Dictionary*, *Watts's Bibliotheca Britannica*, and to *Loudon's Encyclopædia of Gardening*.

The author's reasons for fixing upon the reigns of Edward the III, Elizabeth, and George the I, as eras in the History of our national Gardening are founded upon an attentive examination of our annals, and most of them will be developed in the body of the work whilst considering the literature of Gardening.

Of any critical remarks that occur in the course

of the subsequent pages, the author has to observe that they are always the result of consideration, and if upon literary subjects were not formed until after a careful perusal of the works upon which the criticisms are made. In none of such remarks has he given vent to any personal feelings of jealousy or pique, for the best of all reasons, viz. that not a shadow of such feelings exist. He has only expressed his opinions, and those who differ with him in these, will do him but justice by considering him, if really wrong, as guilty of no greater crime in such instances than an error of judgment.

The author has the ungrateful task of confessing his knowledge that his work is very far from perfect. Owing to the very numerous authorities he has had to consult, and in the extracts made, errors it is feared may have arisen; but there are none that diligence could prevent. In confessing such imperfection he follows the example of a labourer in the same field with himself, "1 see daily, says Professor Martyn, *Complete* Systems, and *Complete* Dictionaries; but 1 cannot discover this perfection in any of my performances, which after all my labour and pains, most provokingly still continue incomplete and erroneous." This confession is no affectation of humility, the author of the following pages employed his best efforts, endeavoured to be correct and perfect, and confesses that in many instances he has failed that at the same time he may express how open he is to correction; for any such whether in the form of additions or errata, he will always be grateful.

Great Totham,
Essex.

INTRODUCTION.

THERE is not in the whole of the Arts and Sciences, one link of their Circle so suitable for the occupation of man in a state of innocency, as that which embraces the cultivation of Plants; and it is an instance of the beneficent providence of the Deity, that He assigned a Garden as the dwelling of our first-created Parents. It is no consequence of the fall of Adam, that Plants require cultivation, he was placed in Paradise to till and to keep it. Then, the weed had not sprung up to render the tillage toilsome, Fruit Trees which God had "planted" were the chief objects of care, and it was an employment without labour; combining the preservation of health with amusement; pure without insipidity; constant without sameness. From that period Gardens have never ceased to engage the attention of man, and even now that their labours are manifold, they still afford "the purest of Human pleasures."

Whether as a private individual man regulates his Garden; —or with more extended benefit cultivates his Farm, still he participates in pleasure combined with utility; whilst his time is agreeably employed, he is benefitting mankind; "Nihil melius, nihil uberius, nihil libero homine dignius." When Alexander of Macedon enquired of Abdalonimus, a Sidonian Prince, who had been reduced to support himself from the produce of a Garden cultivated with his own hands, how he had endured his poverty, Abdalonimus answered, " May Heaven assist me in bearing my prosperity as well! I then had no cares, and my own hands supplied all my wants."*

For many ages after the Creation, the Arts and Sciences were chiefly confined to the Eastern Nations. In tracing the progress of the Agricolan Arts, in those early periods we must gather into one general outline the scanty information afforded by our oldest records of those times and countries.

Of the disposition of the Garden of Eden, we know nothing; to Poetic fiction it has been a fertile subject, but the Historian has no facts to relate. Horticulture being the almost sole occupation of our first Parents and their immediate descendants, and their attention being directed to those few Trees which afforded them sustenance, and perhaps the still fewer herbs that served them as medicaments, it is reasonable to conclude that in the course even of an ordinary life, one person might obtain considerable skill in their cultivation, but the practice of an existence protracted to a period embracing eight or nine centuries, and the experience of it participated in by descendants long arrived at maturity before its extinction, must of necessity have carried forward the improvement of the Art, as much nearly as now would occur in an equal number of generations. Experience soon would teach mankind those vegetables which were salutary, and the same unerring guide would speedily disclose the situations and circumstances in which those were in the greatest perfection. The Vine would be observed most vigorous in those warm climates, by the side of the stream, and thence Man would learn to carry Water to those at a distance from its banks. He would see those of its clusters first ripening which were open to the sun, and he would learn to expose them to its influence;

* Just. ii. c. 10. Q. Curtius 4. c. 1. Diodorus 17.

He would observe the rankness of vegetation where animal exuviæ were deposited, and thence would be taught the use of Manures. Thus as necessity prompted an attention to Plants, so experience would give birth to their culture. These suppositions are supported as probable by the knowledge we possess of the various nations of the World, and their various grades of improvement; they are supported by every day's experience, for this demonstrates that every Art is comprised of the results of experiments, and that is the most perfect, in illustration of which the most have been obtained. Immediately after the flood Noah planted a Vineyard, and became intoxicated with the produce of its fruit. This slender information substantiates the supposition of their rapid improvement in the Arts, for Wine though discovered by chance, would require lengthened attention and practice to manufacture, yet Noah was only the tenth descendant from Adam.

That their attention was chiefly confined to fruits is evident. In Jacob's time the Vine, the Fig and the Almond, are frequently but exclusively, mentioned as products of the Garden. As might be anticipated, considering the warmth of their climate, a Cistern or Well of Water, a Fig Tree, and a Vine appear to have accompanied every habitation. Nuts and Almonds were also reckoned among the most choice productions of the country; they are specified as " being of the best fruits of the land," in the present which Israel sent to the governor of Egypt.* By this time Man had become habituated to a stationary life; property in land became appreciable; their cultivated lands were enclosed and Trees were grown in their hedge-rows.† The laws issued on Mount Sinai extended to the protection of their Vineyards. Olives, Leeks, Onions, Garlic, Cucumbers and Melons, were among the inhabitants of their Gardens.‡ Their Vineyards were so extensive that Solomon had one which let for one thousand pieces of silver per annum.‖

* Genesis xliii. 11. † Ibid. xxiii. 9. ‡ Numb. xi. 5. ‖ Canticles viii. 12.

Of the style of laying out their most splendid Gardens, we have but two authentic accounts, which describe that of Solomon, and those of Babylon.

Solomon flourished about 1014 years B. C. In his time luxury and refinement had extended to their Horticultural establishments. Sculptured ornaments were introduced among the flowers; fountains adorned as well as refreshed the Garden; Fruit bearing and aromatic plants; the Camphor, Cinnamon, Frankincense and chief Spice Trees; the Pomegranate, Cedar, Pine, Sweet Flag, Aloe, Lily, Vine, Nut Tree, Saffron, Fig, Apple, &c. were among its products. The Area appears to have been square and surrounded by a wall; Aviaries and other buildings adorned it.* In another place Solomon tells us he made Gardens, Orchards and Vineyards; planted them with Trees of every kind, and introduced water for their nourishment.†

"The Hanging Garden of Babylon was not built by Semiramis, who founded the city, but by a later prince, called Cyrus, for the sake of a Courtezan, who being a Persian, as they say, by birth, and coveting meadows on mountain tops, desired the king, by an artificial plantation, to imitate the land in Persia. This Garden was four hundred feet square, and the ascent up to it was as to the top of a mountain, and had buildings and apartments out of one into another, like a theatre. Under the steps to the ascent, were built arches one above another, rising gently by degrees, which supported the whole plantation. The highest arch upon which the platform of the garden was laid, was fifty cubits high, and the garden itself was surrounded with battlements and bulwarks. The walls were made very strong, built at no small charge and expence, being twenty-two feet thick, and every sally port ten feet wide. Over the several stories of this fabric were laid beams, and

* Solomon's Song passim.   † Eccles. ii. 4.

summers of large massy stones, each sixteen feet long and four broad. The roof over all these was first covered with reeds, daubed with abundance of brimstone, (or bitumen,) then upon them, was laid double tiles, joined with a hard and durable mortar, and over them all, was a covering, with sheets of lead, that the wet which drained through the earth might not rot the foundation. Upon all these, was laid earth of a convenient depth, sufficient for the growth of the greatest trees. When the soil was laid even and smooth it was planted with all sorts of trees, which both for beauty and size might delight the spectators. The arches, which stood one above another, had in them many stately rooms of all kinds, and for all purposes. There was one that had in it certain engines, whereby it drew plenty of water out of the river Euphrates, through certain conduits hid from the spectators, which supplied it to the platform of the Garden.*

It is not improbable, says Major Rennel, that the trees were of a species different from those which are natives of the soil about Babylon. Curtius says, that some of them were eight cubits in girth, and Strabo states that there was a contrivance to prevent the large roots destroying the superstructure, by building vast hollow piers, which were filled with earth to receive them.

In ascertaining the state of the Horticultural practice of these early Nations we have little to guide us. Of Fruit Trees they appear to have taken the most care, and of these the Vine was preferred. They considered that it flourished best upon a hill.† Stones were removed from the soil.‡ The margin of some water was preferred. They appear to have raised varieties from seed, "I had planted thee a noble Vine, wholly a right seed, how then art thou turned into the degenerate plant of a strange Vine unto me?"‖ A reproach to the

* Diodorus Siculus, b. ii. c. 1. Curtius.—Strabo, &c. † Ps. lxxx. 10. Isa. v. 1. ‡ Ibid. ‖ Jerem. ii. 21.

Jews which would have been unintelligible to them, if they were not aware of the practice of raising the Vine from seed. That they were aware of the effects of one flower being impregnated by the pollen of another appears in the following verse. "Thou shalt not sow thy Vineyard with divers seeds, lest the fruit of thy seed which thou hast sown, and the fruit of thy Vineyard be defiled."* We may likewise conclude that they were aware, that Plants grow chiefly during the night, from the distinction which Moses made between the " fruits brought forth by the Sun," and those " put forth (or, as it may be translated, thrust forth) by the Moon."†

This early period was not without its literature relative to plants. Solomon wrote of them, "from the lofty Cedars of Lebanon, down to the humble Hyssop of the Wall."‡ It is to a still earlier period that many historians refer Zoroaster, even identifying him with Ham, Chuz, or Mizraim of the Holy writings; others place him at a much later period; a third set consider that there were several of the same name. One of these two last opinions is probably correct, since Pliny relates that Zoroaster left a Treatise upon Gardening; a work scarcely credible as existing in so early an age of the World.‖

About a Century posterior to Solomon flourished Homer. If we are to judge of the state of Gardening among the Greeks at that period, from his writings, we may decide that their Gardens were not very extensive. As with the brilliant fancy of a Poet he has given to the Garden of Alcinous an eternal Summer, and to his Palace Silver Pillars, we may reasonably conclude with Walpole, that the size of the Garden was proportionably exaggerated. This he states as being four Acres, an enclosure therefore though comprehending the Orchard and Kitchen Garden which the Grecians probably never witnessed. The Apple, Fig, Pomegranate, Pear, Olives

* Deut. xxii. 9. † Deut. xxxiii. 14. ‡ 1 Kings iv. 22.
‖ Plin. b. vii. c. 10. b. xxx. c. 1.

and various herbs were its products. The Vine was there in regular rows; the whole watered by two fountains, and surrounded by a hedge.

That vegetables and their cultivation were highly esteemed among the Grecians in their earliest days is evident from their Mythology. Minerva, their personification of Divine Wisdom, gave as the greatest blessing to mankind, the Olive Tree, and this fable is as old as the foundation of Athens, or about 1550 years B. C.; whilst Ceres, the sister of their King of Heaven, was invoked as the presiding Deity of Agriculture, and the original imparter of the Art to mankind. It may serve as an illustration of the same remark, to observe that almost every Deity had some plant held as sacred to him or her. The Oak was sacred to Jupiter: The Cypress, Narcissus, and the Maidenhair to Pluto; The Dittany, the Poppy and the Lilly to Juno: The Poppy to Ceres: The Olive to Minerva: Dog's Grass to Minerva: The Myrtle, Rose and Apple to Venus, &c. It is worthy of notice that the most admired human favourites of the God's were changed after death, or to avoid calamities, into Trees, or Flowers. Many other fables of their Mythology are poetical and beautiful. Flowers in general, they declared, sprang from the tears of Aurora. The tremblings of every leaf, the graceful waving of the grass, was attributed to the passing breath of Zephyrus; as the curl of the Waters was said to arise from the sports of the Naiads. I pass without description the Gardens of the Hesperides,* and of Adonis,† for poetical fiction must give place to more sober facts.

We are without very clear information of the skill of the Greeks in cultivating their Gardens, or of their taste in disposing them, even during the splendour of their Republics.

The Academus at Athens, which was laid out by Cimon the

* Virgils Æneid. iv. 484. Serv. ad. Æneid. Eccl. vi. 61. Pliny l. v. c. 5.
† Virg. Georg. ii. 87. Ovid. Amor. i. 10. 56. Stat. Sylv. i. 3. 81.

Athenian General, about four hundred and thirty years, before the Christian era, as well as other Gardens of which we have record, consisted of walks shaded by Plane Trees, watered by Streams, and enclosed by Walls.* The warlike manners of the people made them delight in the addition of the Gymnasium, where their exercises were performed. Fruit Trees were planted in them, not caring for the produce of which, we read that Cimon threw open his Gardens to the public.† Epicurus, the philosopher of the Garden, as he has been called, died at the age of seventy-two, B. C. 270. His Gardens were celebrated as much for their beauty as for the Lectures he delivered in them. The scite of the one he possessed at Athens cost him eighty Minæ, or about two hundred and sixty pounds, no inconsiderable sum in that age. He had it laid out around his house, being the first of the kind introduced into the city.‡ Of their Horticultural skill the Geoponick writers, give us a favourable idea, for however empirical and accompanied by gross superstitions, they were aware of practices at present adopted and recommended. Thus Anatolius says, that if you wish an Apple Tree to bear much fruit, a piece of pipe should be bound tight round the stem. Sotian recommends the same, and to sever some of the largest roots when the tree is over luxuriant. They were aware of the necessity of Caprification, and bring wild Figs upon the branches of the cultivated Trees to prevent them casting their fruit, " wherefore, says Democritus, some insert a shoot on each Tree that they may not be obliged to do that every year." The knowledge of grafting which this and other passages intimate, was the acquirement of a period coeval with the earliest age of which we have any informaton. Of manures they had a correct knowledge, and when this was deficient, they turned in green vegetable matters, and even sowed Beans, for the purpose of ploughing them in, when grown up.‖ They were very fond of flowers, which were used as ornaments

* Paussnius b. i. 29.   † Corn. Nepos in vitâ Cimon.   ‡ Pliny b. xix. c. 4.   ‖ Theophrastus viii. 9.

upon all occasions; they cultivated Violets, Roses, the Narcissus, Iris, &c.* which were extensively sold at Athens, in a Market Place appropriated to their disposal.†

HESIOD is the most ancient author on the cultivation of the earth, whose work has descended to us. His History is obscure and uncertain. The most probable incidents of his life appear as follows. He was born at Ascra, in Bœotia, and flourished about the same time with Homer. He is said to have carried off a prize in a contest of Poetry with that writer. Being murdered and his body thrown into the Sea by his slayers, it was thrown ashore, and his fate being thus revealed, the murderers were detected by the Poet's dogs.

Hesiod is to be admired both as a Poet and Philosopher, we have here however only to consider him as an Agricultural writer. His Poem entitled "the Works and Days" Pliny considered as the first positively known work that contained directions for cultivating the ground, Tzetzes, who lived in the twelfth Century, in his Scholia on Hesiod, mentions two Poems by Orpheus, entitled "Works" and "Diaries," the latter of which from its title would promise to be of more utility than Hesiod's superstitious Calendar. It admits of considerable doubt whether Orpheus ever existed, if he did, he lived about the time of the Argonautic expedition, 1263, B. C. At all events, Hesiod's work is the earliest on Agriculture that has descended to us. He wrote a Treatise on herbs now lost, and there is strong reason to believe, "The Works," is mutilated and imperfect, for Pliny (b. 15.) adverts to Hesiod's opinion of the unprofitableness of the Olive; and Manlius in his Astronomicon refers to his Treatise on Grafting, and on the situations suited to Corn and Vines, none of which passages occur in any of our copies. From what remains, we can glean but small information as to the Agricultural practices

* Theophrastus vi. c. 5.   † Aristophan. Acharn. v. 212.

of the Age, the moral reflections and instructions being by much the most lengthy. Of any of the practices of Horticulture he is still more meagre. Timber was felled in Autumn. They ceased digging in the Vineyard, when from the heat of the weather, about the season of the Pleiades, the snails left the ground for shelter upon the Plants. The vintage was in the course of November. In common with all other Heathens he had a superstitious regard to lucky and unlucky days; the thirteenth day of the Moon, he considered favourable to planting, but not to sowing; the sixteenth and ninth were also propitious to planting.

That the work as known to us is not perfect, I think is further proved by no mention being made of the Olive, or of manures, nor even of the burning of stubble, which is perhaps the most ancient mode of ameliorating the soil.

I have not followed historically the divisions of the Eastern nations. The Egyptians, the Chaldeans, the Medes, the Persians, the Macedonians, the Greeks, &c. as they successively rose into separate powers, were only off-sets of the same, or contiguous people, and practised the same Arts, and were of manners and habits modified perhaps by a slight difference of climate, but otherwise without change. Especially were there no alterations in the practices of the Arts of cultivating the soil, for these of primary importance to mankind were not subject to fickleness of taste, and were pursued in an almost unaltered climate and soil. The scattered fragments of information that have escaped to us concerning such practices have been therefore arranged in one chronological series. From them we cannot but conclude that even in those early ages, some of the most recondite practices of the Gardener were known and followed. We need not be surprised that their Gardens were not more extensive, inasmuch that the number of plants known to them as worthy of cultivation, was a very sufficient reason for the contrary being the case. When Architecture had done its best to cause a variety of positions; shade and coolness had been procured by Avenues and Fountains, and Fragrance obtained by beds of Roses, &c.; their object was obtained, for amid such they delighted to repose; and as they required in consequence of their heated climate, no extent of surface to wander over, these were secured in a very small space, and a still less sufficed to contain the few herbs they cultivated for use, though the Vineyard and other enclosures of Fruit Trees were necessarily much more extensive.

The continent of Asia we have seen rapidly became peopled and divided into various empires, and these again as the population increased, prompted by various motives, sent forth colonies into neighbouring districts. The Greeks having peopled the whole of Asia Minor, passed thence into the neighbouring country of Italy, and from thence descended the Romans, the state and progress of whose Gardening we shall now proceed to consider.

First of their Kitchen Gardens.

We are not speaking without consideration, or with too great positiveness when we declare that we know of no reason for concluding that an establishment for the cultivation of culinary plants ever existed within the walls of Rome, either separate or combined with the pleasure Garden. In an advanced period of the empire, and perhaps much earlier than we have records, there was in the city a *Fora Holitorum*, or Market Place for the sale of Garden produce, to supply the inhabitants generally. I am inclined to think that it was supplied from the Farms of the chief men of the City, and not by any persons who subsisted by such trafick

It is certain from the writings of Cato and others, that the principle inhabitants had their Horti, or country Farms, which grew all kinds of Vegetables, in some luxuriant part of the country near the City, and from them obtained their supply. Hence, in the first years of Rome, we read but of one Garden within its precincts, that of Tarquin, which was evidently one devoted to flowers and ornament; and even when the walls of the City formed a circuit of fifty miles under the Emperor Valerian,* it appears solely to have been distended by buildings and pleasure grounds. In the first ages after the foundation of the City, the Farms, which resembled our Market Gardens, were cultivated by the chief men with their own hands, as must occur in every new colony, and hence the Piso, the Fabii, the Cicero, the Lentuli, and other celebrated families derived their patronymics from ancestors distinguished for the successful cultivation of the culinary vegetables intimated by their respective names. Even their Dictators were summoned from the Field, and dropped the Plough Staff for a more extended and arduous governorship.

Of the Kitchen Garden as might be expected, we have less information in the writings that have survived to us than of any of the other Horticultural departments. Literature was confined to the higher classes, these would not condescend to record the rules for planting Cabbages, and there were none more practical, and therefore more useful authors in those days when writing materials were costly and printing unknown. Cato has glanced over the subject, and Varro, Columella, and Palladius have done no more. From the little information they do afford us, and from casual lights that break in upon us from the writings of other authors, we learn enough to assure us that their Culinary Vegetables were excellently, nd than their fruits perhaps better cultivated.

* Vopiscus in Aureliano.

About six Centuries after the foundation of Rome, or 150 years B. C. lived Cato. From his writings we learn that it was considered a Garden should have a southern aspect, and be well supplied with Water. Palladius makes a similar statement, a Garden, says this author, should be a level, gently sloping piece of ground, divided by a small current of Water.* Turnips, Coleworts, Radishes, Basil, Beans, Cabbages, Garlic, and Asparagus are mentioned by Cato. Endive, Parsley, Cucumbers, Lettuces, Beets, Peas, Kidney Beans, Carrots, Parsnips, Mallows, Onions, Mustard, Fennell and Mushrooms are mentioned by the later Writers, Columella, Varro, Pliny, Virgil, and Martial.

Asparagus is one of the very few plants, of which we have the full detail of the mode of culture pursued by the Romans; and if we are justified in considering it a fair standard by which we may estimate their proficiency in the art, we cannot but conclude that it was decidedly excellent. The directions which are given by Cato, are an Epitome of those which occur in Abercrombie, Miller or any other standard work on Horticulture: they are as follows, "You must well work a spot, says Cato, that is moist, or which has richness and depth of soil. Make the beds so that you may be able to clean and weed them on each side; let there be a distance of half a foot between the plants. Set in the seed, two or three in a place, in a strait line; cover with mould; then scatter some compost over the beds. At the Vernal Equinox, when the plants come up, weed often, and take care that the Asparagus is not plucked up with the weeds. The year you plant them, cover them with straw during the Winter, that they may not be killed. In the beginning of the spring after, dress and weed them,— The third year after you have sown them burn the haulm in the beginning of the Spring. Do not weed them before the Plants come up, that you may not hurt the stools. The third

---

* De Re Rustica, b. i. 33.

or fourth year, you may pluck them close by the Root; if you break them off they yield side shoots, and some will die. You may take them until they run to seed. The seed is ripe in Autumn. When you have gathered the seed, burn the haulm, and when the plants begin to shoot, weed and manure. After eight or nine years when the beds are old, lay out a spot, work and manure it well, then make drills where you may plant some roots; set them well apart that you may dig between them. Take care that they may not be injured. Carry as much sheep's dung as you can on the beds, it is best for this purpose; other manures produce weeds."*

It is certain they took great delight in cultivating their grounds, and not only improved under the best of masters—Practice, but consulted the ancient writers then extant upon the subject. When as the result of such attention and study the grounds of C. Furius Cresinus produced larger crops than even the more extensive ones of his less assiduous neighbours, he was publicly accused of making use of magical arts, Cresinus presented his tools before the Senate, " These, Quirites, he exclaimed, are my magic implements; but I cannot exhibit in this Forum the cares, the toils, the anxious thoughts, that employ me during the day, and over my lamp.†

It still further appears that in the time of the later Emperors, the Romans had become acquainted with the most difficult branch of Kitchen Garden practice, Forcing. A still further evidence of their Horticultural skill. Cucumbers were the principal subjects of forcing. The Emperor Tiberius was exceedingly fond of them, and by artificial means had them in perfection throughout the year. They were grown in large baskets of dung covered with Earth, and were sheltered during cold days by means of thin plates of Lapis Specularis,

* Owens Translat. of Cato's de Re Rustica. p. 143. s. 161.
† Pliny. xviii. c. 6.

which admit the passage of light nearly as well as Glass, and were transported at night to the shelter of some house.* Whether they ever employed the more transparent medium of Glass as a shelter, we are unable to determine. It is certain that in the reign of Aurelian, A. D. 273. the luxury of Glass windows was enjoyed.

It is pretty certain that in the earlier ages of the City, the Kitchen and Fruit Gardens were in one common enclosure, nor have we any direct testimony that they were divided into separate departments, until the time of the younger Pliny, who mentions in a letter to his friend Gallus, the Kitchen Garden as being separate from the Orchard and Pleasure grounds.

In those early days when the departments were amalgamated, and when from the pot-herbs and fruits produced by their joint growth, the poorer Romans and the slaves of proprietors derived their chief sustenance, it was usually under the care of the housekeeper or Steward's wife, who was lightly estimated, if it was not productive and capable of sustaining the household.† The husbandman used to deride its culture, and designate it " *a second dessert*," and " *a flitch of bacon*," always ready for cutting.‡

Of the Fruit Gardens of the Romans.

In accordance with the observation which we made at the commencement of this Chapter, that the cultivation of Fruit appears always to engage, the first Horticultural notice of every nation, we find that the Romans were much more attentive to their Orchards than their Kitchen Gardens, as is manifested by the greater number of species and varieties of their inhabitants. Cato, our earliest informant, mentions seven varieties of the Olive; six good ones of the Vine, more than

* Columella b. xi. c. 3. Pliny b. xix. c. 23. † Pliny xix. 4. s. 19.
‡ Cicero de Sen. 16.

four of the Apple, five of Pears, Pomegranetes, Services, six varieties of Fig, three of Nuts, Quinces and Plumbs. It is not alone, the number of varieties of Fruit, that demonstrates their attention to Fructiculture, the details of their practice in cultivating them, speaks as decidedly in support of that opinion. In speaking of moving the Olive among other directions, he says, " the earth that was upon the surface should be put next the roots ;" now although they knew nothing of the surface soil being most abounding in Oxygene Gas, and for that reason to be of benefit when applied to the roots of plants, it demonstrates the care and attention bestowed upon the culture of Fruits, for the benefit had been noticed. In his directions for Grafting, I find none that are omitted by modern writers ; though terse he is sufficiently explicit. If it is true, as Cato, Varro, Palladius, Virgil, Columella, Pliny, and a host of other writers, even more ancient as well as contemporary agree, that they had the Art of grafting one kind of Tree, upon others of entirely different Genera, as Apples upon Plane Trees, the Vine on the Cherry, &c. &c. they certainly excelled the Gardeners of the present age, for this branch of the Art is lost to us. They held it as a maxim generally to be relied upon, that any tree might be grafted upon another which had a bark similar in appearance ; if the Fruit also had a resemblance there was not a doubt of the success.* It must not however be forgotten that the same author in his Treatise " On Trees," has a chapter in support of this promiscuous grafting, in opposition to some ancient Authors, who denied the practicability of the Art, so that even in those days there were doubts, which needed no refutation but a practical exhibition of success. Pliny and Columella give the necessary directions for Inoculating. Cato dwells upon the importance of frequently stirring the earth about the Roots of Trees ; the various modes of raising layers, as by passing up a shoot through a hole made in the

* Columella v. 2.

bottom of a pot filled with earth. He is most explicit upon the Vine. From his writings, and those of succeeding Authors, Pliny, Virgil, &c. as full directions for its culture might be selected as any modern Gardener would require.

The assiduity of the Romans in collecting new species and varieties of Fruit may be gathered from the writings of the elder Pliny who lived A. D. 23—79. There were then cultivated in the vicinity of Rome, nearly all the Fruits with which we were acquainted at the commencement of the present Century, the chief exceptions being the Orange, and Pine Apple, the first of which however they became possesed of in the 4th Century. Very few of their cultivated Fruits were indigenous, but were introduced at the expence of no little money and trouble from distant and different climes. The Fig and Almond were brought from Syria; the Citron from Media; the Apricot from Epirus or Armenia; the Pomegranate from Africa; Apples, Pears and Plumbs from Armenia, Numidia, Greece, &c.; the Peach from Persia; and Cherries from Cerasus in Pontus by Lucullus about 73 years B.C.* Strawberries, Raspberries and others mentioned before by Cato, appear to have been natural products.† The Gooseberry and Currant are found wild in the hills of Northern Italy. As the species were increased in number, so were the varieties. Pliny mentions 22 Apples, one without kernels; 8 Cherries; 6 Chesnuts; Figs, many black and white, large and small; Medlars large and small; Large and small Black Mulberries; Filberts and Hazel-nuts; 36 Pears; Plumbs "ingens turba," black, white and parti-coloured; 3 Quinces; 3 Services; Grapes numerous; 2 Walnuts; Almonds, bitter and sweet.‡

---

* Mr. Vernon found on the borders of the Black Sea, abundance of Wild Cherries, near Cheresium, from whence the name probably arose, and is identical with the Cerasus of Lucullus. Bradleys Gen. Treatise on Husb. v. ii. p. 130. † Pliny. xv. 25. xvi. 14. Mercellin xxii. 13.
‡ Trans. of the London Hort. Soct v. i. p. 152.

There is no doubt, supported as the opinion is by Martial, Pliny and Columella, that the Romans of their age forced Fruit in a kind of Hot House, protected from the exterior cold, and heated artificially.* The Epigrams of Martial quoted in support of the above opinion are the following,

> Pallida ne Cilicum timeant pomaria brumam,
>   Mordeat et tenerum fortior aura nemus
> Hibernis objecta notis specularia puros
>   Admittunt soles, et sine fæce diem.   Ep. xiv.

> Qui Corcyræi vidit pomaria regis,
>   Rus, Eatelle, tuæ præferat ille domus.
> Invida purpureos urat ne bruma racemos,
>   Et gelidum Bacchi munera frigus edat;
> Condita perspicua vivit vindemia gemma
>   Et tegitur felix nec tamen uva latet.
> Fæmineum linet sic bombycina corpus;
>   Calculus in nitido sic numeratur aqua.
> Quid non ingenia voluit natura licere?
>   Autumnum sterilis ferre jubetur hiems.
>   Ep. lxviii.

The first, as was conjectured by Sir Joseph Banks, probably related to a Peach House, and the latter to a Vinery. Of the form or arrangement of these structures we have no information, but we have seen they were in possession of a transparent substance that would act in the place of glass, and they were well acquainted with the mode of heating apartments with flues; they positively practised the forcing of less bulky vegetables; they were better acquainted with the habits and training of Fruit Trees, especially Vines, than they were of any other department of Gardening; and we know they had ingenuity enough to compass such a desideratum of luxury as the ripening

* Martial's Epig. viii. Ep. 14 and 68. Pliny xix. 23. Columella xi. 3.

of Fruit in unusual seasons. As at present the Romans trained Trees against their houses.*

Of the Pleasure Gardens of the Romans.

Although we have a fuller account of the Roman Pleasure Gardens than of the other departments of their grounds, yet even of them it is a matter of considerable difficulty to form a correct idea from the descriptions which we possess, so much so, that if ten persons were to delineate their conceptions of the ground plot, scarcely two of them would produce plans bearing much resemblance to each other. The following is all that I have been able to collect upon the subject.

The Garden of Tarquin the Proud, within two centuries after the building of the City, is the first of which we have mention. It was within the Walls of the City, and was occupied by beds of Roses, Poppies, Lilies, odorous herbs, a stream of Water, &c.† It is certain that these were arranged in mathematical order, and without any attempt at foreign ornaments. In the time of Cato the country Villas of the Romans were accompanied by grounds compounded of fields and garden, cultivated for alimentary purposes, whose surplus produce, after the family of the Proprietor were supplied, was probably sold in the Fora Holitorum of the City. As the people became more refined, the Villa, or Country Residence of the Proprietor, was built entirely separate from his farming establishment; and often was constructed in a different part of the country. From habitations barely affording the conveniences of life, they became replete with luxuries. The beds of herbs and roots were exchanged in the neighbourhood of the Villa, for statuarized Walks and beds of flowers, and every device that pleasure could desire, fashioned according to the reigning taste. Thus in the infant days of Rome, Varro defines a Villa, as being a farm house and

* Horace. Ep. i. 10. 32. Tibullus. iii. 3. 35. † Livy. i. 54. Ovid. Fast. ii. 704. and Dionysius Halicarnassus.

its appurtenances, with accommodations for the mere husbandman*; but Cicero, in the period of the Empires most flourishing state, implies by the same title, all that is magnificent and luxurious for the lodging of an opulent Roman family. It was here they were seen in all their splendour.† Pliny is still more particular, describing the dwelling of the Proprietor as the Villa urbana; that of the mere farming establishment as Villa rustica.

This magnificence was soon displayed, being introduced by L. L. Lucullus, a contemporary of Cato. Paterculus laments so expensive and luxurious a style of living, as tending to vitiate the manners, and enervate the character of his countrymen. The example of Lucullus was soon followed by others perhaps less capable of bearing the expense, for in excuse for his profuseness he pleaded that a Roman Knight, and even a Free-man who were his country neighbours had magnificent Villas; but retorts the Historian "Non videbit ab ipso natum esse, ut illi talia cuperent—Primus auctor fuit."‡

The Pleasure grounds of Lucullus are immortalized by Plutarch. They were situated near Neapolis, on the lofty promontory of Misenum, commanding the most extensive views both inland and maritime. Phœdrus says of them,

——monte summo posita Luculli manu
Prospectat Siculum et prospicit Tuscum mare.||

From Plutarch we learn that they were formed at an unbounded expense. They contained artificial elevations of ground of great height, buildings projecting into the Sea, and vast pieces of Water formed upon land. Passages were dug under the hills of the Campanian shore, and by their means the Sea Water conducted round his house and grounds. From the style

* Varro De. Re Rus. i. 2. 14. † Cicero de Leg. iii. 13. ‡ Paterculus b. ii. c. 33. || Phœdrus ii. 5.

manifested in the above details, it is very probable that he copied models which he had seen in Asia, where a great part of his life had been passed in a situation affording every opportunity for inspecting the most splendid constructions of the kind.* The ground originally belonged to Marius, who purchased it for about two thousand five hundred pounds sterling, but it acquired a higher value during the few years he held it, for when he fell, Lucullus paid near eighty thousand pounds to acquire its proprietorship.† Lucullus had many other Villas, and so variously situated for the securing an agreeable climate at each season of the year &c. that he was accustomed to boast that " he changed his climate with the Storks and Cranes."‡

Descending in the order of time, we come next, as offording information on our subject, to the age of Cicero, who died B. C. 43.—Of the Villas of that Orator we have no particular description; but in a brief notice of the grounds surrounding his Villa of Arpinum, there is sufficient to acquaint us that the natural beauties so associated with his dwelling were not considered as misplaced. He evidently admired this Villa for its romantic Scenery; dwells with delight upon Groves which he had formed; on streams that rushed by it from the wild and craggy hills around, unshackled by Art or disfigured by false Taste.‖

Of the Gardens of Sallust, the contemporary and rival of Cicero, we have rather more precise information. That Historian returning from the government of Numidia, laden, it is to be feared, with extorted riches, built a magnificent palace and laid out very extensive Gardens on the Qurinal Hill, either of which have never been mentioned by Historians but with admiration as being the ornament and pride of Rome. M. de

* Tacitus Ann. xiv. 3. xvi   † Plutarch in vit. Mari and Lucull.
‡ Ibid. Lucull.   ‖ Cicer De Leg. ii.

Brosses a celebrated French writer surveyed them, and reports that within their vast circuit they must have contained the present scites of the Churches of Madonna della Vittoria—St. Suzanna and St. Nicholas—the street of Solaria—the ruins of the Erucinian Venus, the whole of the present Negroni, the greatest part of the Ludovisii, and the bottom of the Barberini Gardens, besides a considerable, now uncultivated space. So beautiful were they that when Rome fell beneath the sway of her Emperors, they were selected for the imperial residence. Art and nature indeed seem to have been combined to render them delightful. The beautiful prospects seduced the eye to wander, whilst umbrageous walks, open parterres and cool porticoes, interspersed with flowers and streams, and master pieces of Sculpture, invited it when weary to the most luxurious repose* Joining in the tide of fashion we may presume that the foliage of his trees, were cut into regular figures, since it was just previous to his time that Matius, the friend of Julius Cæsar, and particular favourite of Augustus, first taught his countrymen this method of distorting nature.† A practice which even the refined Pliny admired, and which continued to be practised in England until the close of the last Century. Seats were formed amid the branches of any monarch Trees that grew within their grounds. Such a seat in a Plane Tree near the imperial Villa at Velitræ, was called by the Emperor Caligula, his Nest.‡

About the period of the Christian Era, the love of Horticultural luxuries so far prevailed that every person of any consideration possessed a Country Villa. The neighbourhood of Tibur appears to have been the favourite spot for their erection. The magnificence of the attendant Architecture was not now the chief point attended to for the decoration of their Gardens, although they had not yet learnt that Nature could be improved by Art, without being completely subjugated.

* Tacit. Ann. iii. 30. xiii. 47.—Hist. iii. 82.—Stewarts life of Sallust.
† Columella xii. 44.   ‡ Pliny. Nat. Hist. xii. 3, 4 5.

Pliny the younger was born, A. D. 62. From his writings we acquire the most complete description of the Roman Gardens as regards their disposition, that is extant. His Laurentine Villa was one in which he spent some of the colder months of the year, when his professional duties allowed his absence from the City. It is therefore not surprising that the Garden does not occupy any considerable part of the narration in which he describes this estate. He merely, in an Epistle to his friend Gallus, states that the Gestatio, or place for exercise, surrounded his Garden,—" this he continues, is encompassed with a Box-tree hedge, and where that is decayed with Rosemary; between the Garden and this Gestatio, runs a shady walk of Vines, which is so soft that you may walk upon it barefoot without injury. The Garden is chiefly planted with Fig and Mulberry Trees, to which the soil is as favourable as it is averse to all others."

His description of the Gardens attached to his Tuscan Villa, is more diffuse, yet particular. It is contained in a letter to his friend Apollinaris (Ep. v. 6.—thus elegantly translated by Melmoth) " In the front of the Portico is a sort of Terrace, embellished with various figures, and bounded with a Box Hedge, from which you descend by an easy slope, adorned with the representation of divers animals in Box, answering alternately to each other: this is surrounded by a walk enclosed with tonsile evergreens, shaped into a variety of forms. Behind it is the Gestatio, laid out in the form of a Circus, ornamented in the middle with Box, cut into numberless different figures, together with a plantation of shrubs prevented by the shears from running up too high: the whole is fenced in by a Wall, covered with Box rising in different ranges to the top.—" After describing several Summer Houses, &c. he proceeds."—In the front of these agreeable buildings is a very spacious Hippodrome, encompassed on every side by Plane Trees covered with Ivy. Beneath each Plane are planted Box Trees, and, behind these,

Bays which blend their shade with that of the Plane Trees. This plantation forming a straight boundary on each side of the Hippodrome, bends at the further end into a semi-circle which being set round with Cypress Trees, varies the prospect and and casts a deeper and more gloomy shade; while the inward circular walks enjoying an open exposure, are perfumed with Roses, and correct by a very pleasing contrast, the coolness of the shade with the warmth of the Sun. Having passed through these winding allies, you enter a straight walk, which breaks out into a variety of others divided off by box hedges. In one place you have a little meadow; in another the Box is cut into a thousand different forms; sometimes into letters expressing the name of the master; sometimes that of the artificer; whilst here and there little Obelisks rise intermixed alternately with fruit Trees; when on a sudden you are surprised with an imitation of the negligent beauties of rural Nature, in the centre of which lies a spot surrounded with a knot of dwarf Plane Trees. Beyond these is a walk interspersed with the smooth and twining Acanthus, where Trees also are cut into a variety of names and shapes. At the upper end is an Alcove of white marble shaded with Vines, supported by four small Pillars of Corystian Marble. From this bench the Water gushing through several small Pipes, falls into a stone Cistern beneath, from whence it is received into a fine polished Marble Bason, so artfully contrived, that it is always full without ever overflowing. When I sup here this Bason serves for a Table, the larger Dishes being placed round its margin, while the smaller ones float in the form of little Vessels and Water fowl. Corresponding to this is a fountain, which is incessantly emptying and filling; for the Water, which it throws up to a great height, falling back again into it, is, by means of two openings, returned as fast as it is received. Fronting the Alcove stands a Summer House of exquisite Marble, whose doors project into a green enclosure; as from its upper and lower windows the eye is presented with a variety of different Verdures. Next to this is a little private closet, which though it seems distinct may be laid into the same room furnished with a Couch, and notwithstanding it has windows on every side, yet it enjoys a very agreeable gloominess by means of a spreading Vine which climbs to the top and entirely overshades it. In this place a fountain also rises and instantly disappears; in different quarters are disposed several marble seats, which serve, as well as the Summer House, as so many reliefs when one is wearied by walking. Near each seat is a little fountain; and throughout the whole Hippodrome several small Rills run murmering along, wheresoever the hand of Art thought proper to conduct them, watering here and there spots of verdure, and in their progress refreshing the whole."

From several remarks in the preceeding Epistle the most careless peruser must notice a dawning of that taste for the beauties of Nature unaltered by Art, which were only for a short time perfected about the same time under the care of the Emperor Nero, but soon enveloped and overlooked amid distorted Vegetables and mathematical walks. This transitory idea of Pliny's appears to have been the decided taste of that Tyrant who fell A. D. '68. From the writings of Tacitus we learn that aided by two Architects of the Imperial City he brought his plans to perfection. Of his Palace it would be misplaced to speak in detail; it is sufficient to state that it encircled the City; that its Galleries were a mile in length, and that the whole was adorned with Gold and precious Stones. Within the Area were spacious Fields, artificial Lakes, Gardens, Orchards and Groves. "Nero, says the Historian, availed himself of the ruins of his country, and built a house in which gems and gold, formerly of usual and common luxury, were not so much to be admired as fields and lakes; and as in uncultivated places, here were woods;—there open spaces and prospects. The masters and designers being

Severus and Celer; men possessed of genius and courage, to attempt by Art, even what Nature had denied."*

The citizen's Gardens of the age we are considering, were similar to those which now exist in the suburbs of all our great towns. The paintings lately exhumed from the ruins of Herculaneum, which was overwhelmed, A. D. 79. represent the Gardens before the townsmen's houses, as small square enclosures, girded by Trellis work and Espaliers; and ornamented with Urns, Fountains and Careatides. As now they had pots and boxes of Plants in their Windows.† To demonstrate that the splendid style of Gardening adopted by Nero, was neither singular or evanescent, I shall quote the examples of three of the later Emperors. In the reign of Hadrian, who died A. D. 138. a palace was built at Tivoli. Its grounds were of a very large extent, and included within their bounds some of the most picturesque and romantic scenery that abounds in the broken and irregular ground of that vicinity. We have records of its containing, " a Vale of Tempe,"—" the Elysian fields,"—" the Regions of Tartarus, &c."; which epithets however hyperbolical, afford decisive proof of the beauty and wildness which had been secured in its prospects, as well as of the feelings with which they were viewed.

The Imperial Brothers, Caracalla and Geta, A. D. 210. had Palaces and Gardens which equalled in extent the remainder of Rome.‡ This is easy of belief, when we recollect with Mr. Gibbon, that the opulent inhabitants of Rome had almost surrounded the City with their Villas, which these Emperors had by degrees confiscated for the most part to their own use. If Geta resided in the Gardens, which bore his name in the Janiculum, and Caracalla those of Mœcenas on the Esquiline, they were separated by a space of several miles, yet that space was occupied by Gardens which had once belonged to Sallust,

* Tacitus Ann. xv. 42.   † Pliny xix. 4. 19.   ‡ Herodian, b. iv. p. 139.

Lucullus, Agrippa, Domitian, Caius, &c. now thrown perhaps into one, and united with the Imperial Palaces by bridges over the Tibur.

At the time Alaric invaded Rome, A. D. 408. Rome contained 1780 residences of wealthy and honourable citizens,* the precincts of each palace contained not only Aviaries, Porticoes and Baths, but Groves, Fountains, Hippodromes Temples, and even markets.† A moderate palace would have covered the whole four-Acre farm of Cincinnatus‡ So little space was left for the houses of the Plebians that they built them many stories high, each inhabited by more than an equal number of families. Wealth and consequently landed property gradually accumulated in the hands of the comparatively few noble families. The Estates of the same owner stretched over a large space in Italy, as well as distant provinces. Faustinus a Roman, as Gale conjectures, possessed an Estate near the modern Bury in Suffolk, and a second in the vicinity of Naples.‖

We have thus followed the progress of Gardening among the Romans from their first existence as a colony, through their rise as a people to the pinnacle of power, and thence through their decay in effeminacy and debauchery. Nor is there any thing singular in their rise and fall, any more than in their accompanying progress in our Art. As their Arms were at first restrained to their own establishment as a people; and the Arts of cultivation to the obtaining subsistence: so as their conquests and wealth extended, to a want of the necessaries of life, they added the desire of its comforts, and when their victories carried them to those very Eastern countries from which they themselves proceeded, and who lost in luxury and effeminacy, soon fell beneath the swords of their less degenerate

* Nardini. Roma Antica. p. 89. 4 8. 500. † Claudian. Rutil. Mumatian. Itinerar. v. iii. ‡Val. Max. iv. 4. ‖ Antoninus. Itinerary in Britain. p. 92.

offspring, these last speedily caught the infection, and becoming as decidedly enervated, were punished, as it were, for their filial ingratitude, by becoming in turn the easy prey of Nations less debased by the vices of civilization.

The Roman practice of the Art we have seen in its various departments was correct, and is evidence of the most powerful encouragement. We cannot be charged with exageration if we say that in its pursuit they were little inferior to us in our present practice. We have traced the gradual advances by which they attained to such proficiency, and in the highest department, that of Garden Designing, it is apparent that if the name of George the first was inserted in the place of that of Nero, and those of Bridgeman and Kent, instead of Severus and Celer, we cannot but consent to think that the description of Nero's Garden by Tacitus, would answer for one in the reign of the English monarch.

That their progress in the Art was peculiarly rapid is certain. A Century does not intervene between the simple country Villa described by Cato; and the existence of the elaborate Gardens of Lucullus, and this, notwithstanding that the civil strife between the parties of Sylla and Marius intervened. From Lucullus to the time of the first Pliny, another Century elapsed, and when we compare the list of Fruits, &c. given by the latter, with that in the work of Cato, we receive another evidence of the rapid prosperity of the Art. From thence through the age of the second Pliny, Nero, and other Emperors, Gardening continued to advance, and we cannot be much in error if we place the summit of its rise in the reign of Tiberius. Under the subsequent Emperors, such as Galba, Otho, Vitellius, &c. when the monarchs were made and unmade as the brutal passions of the soldiers dictated, and when each differed from the other, only in the varied excess and enormity of his debaucheries and cruelties, the meanest Arts must have stagnated, much more must Horticulture have been interrupted, since its chief patrons, the patricians of the state, were scarcely for an hour secure in the possession of their properties and lives. The morals, the virtues of the people gradually forsook them—Law neglected—Philosophy perverted—the language becoming barbarous—literature nearly abandoned—foreign mercenaries admitted among the troops, and even to the civil dignities.—By such means the bonds of union; the respectability of the Empire's institutions, and the nationality of its manners were destroyed. It became a matter of indifference to the people who were their rulers—patriotism was extinct; and after a feeble opposition the Empire was overrun by the Barbarians of Northern Europe.

Alaric, general of the Goths, A. D. 410, and Gesneric, king of the Vandals, in 455, successively pillaged the City, and finally Italy was parcelled out into petty States.

However we may lament the ruin of so great a nation, with whose name is associated the excellence of all that is great in the Arts, and all that renders man ambitious;—however we may regret the ignorance that succeeded during the Middle Ages, yet it is certain that by the dispersion of the Roman people, and the increased intercourse which less enlightened nations had with them by this means, that the seeds of improvement were dispersed over Europe, and by degrees gave rise to improvements which otherwise could only have been stumbled upon by chance during the slow progress of Ages. But above all, the destruction of the Roman Empire, speaks trumpet-tongued this lesson to mankind, that wealth the most unbounded, and learning the most refined, and general, if unaccompanied by a fixed and moral Code, form but a hot bed in which the seeds of civil incapacity and dissention rapidly germinate. A fixed moral Code can alone check the rankness of such growth, and a modern example has taught us that such a Code is beyond the power of the *human* mind to invent.

ON THE STATE OF

GARDENING IN ENGLAND,

From the Invasion of the Romans, until the accession of Edward the Third.

B. C. 55.——A. D. 1327.

WHEN the conquering arms of Rome reached this almost Ultima Thule of their Geography, they found the barbarous inhabitants existing chiefly upon the produce of their herds, and of the chase, although not totally inattentive to the cultivation of the Soil. The inland inhabitants, descended from the Cimbri, lived in straw thatched Cottages, and a fixed habitation is an earnest of the existence of the Agricolan Arts among the settlers. That they were practiced in Britain at this early period is certain, for although Tacitus affirms that the inhabitants were without Corn, notwithstanding the soil was favourable to its growth,* yet this could only have been partially the case. The farms of some of their neighbours and progenitors, the Gallic husbandmen, were large,† and as most of the manners and habits of the Britons were in accordance with theirs, we are justified in including this among

* Vitâ Agricola, 12   † Pliny Hist. xviii. c. 6 & 29.

the number of their coincidences, more especially as in some of the details of Agriculture they were even superior to the Gallic cultivators. No one can read Pliny without being struck with the minute discriminations, the evident results of long, attentive practice, which were displayed by those our forefathers in the application of Marle to particular Soils; * discriminations which every Kentish Farmer at present, with very little variation, confesses to be correct by his own practice. In the practices of threshing, mowing, &c. they were confessedly superior to the Romans. Their implements were different, as were the varieties of grain cultivated by the two nations.†

Now although these demonstrations of the Britons, being attentive cultivators of the soil, do not immediately afford any illustration of the state of Horticulture among them, it certainly is an earnest that it must have partaken of the general care shewn to nutritious plants, for an attention to Plants however limited their number, as in the then infant state of Agriculture was the case; or whether directed by superstition for magical purposes; by a desire to obtain mendicaments for the removal of diseases; or by a liberal desire to ascertain their habits and relations; always tends to one effect,—the improvement of the Art of cultivating, the most useful. The Horticulture of every country will be found to date an era of permament improvement from the foundation of its Physic and Botanic Gardens. Hence we may conclude that the attention which the Druids are known to have paid to Plants was propitious to the advancement of the art of cultivating those deserving the care, although their researches were professedly confined to the ascertaining their medicinal qualities. That they noticed other Plants than those so gifted is demonstrated by the numerous names appropriated to insignificant Plants,

* Pliny b. xvii. c. 6, 7, 8. † Ibid. b. xviii. & xxxvi

which are enumerated by Gerarde as being common among the Welch, and by Threkeld as in use by the Irish.

That the southern Britons actually had Gardens disposed around their houses is stated by Strabo.* These of course were chiefly a compound of our Kitchen and Orchard departments. There are many facts on record besides those already mentioned, which justify an inference that Gardening was pursued by the Britons with attention. The Carrot grows wild in Briton as it does in France, from the latter it was imported into Italy, being only improved by cultivation.† Unless it had been employed by the natives, we can scarcely conceive so useless a weed as it is in a wild state, would have gained the attention of the Roman legionaries. Turnips were particularly abundant in Gaul, so extensively indeed were they cultivated as to be given to Cattle.‡ The idea of a Park, and the accumulation of Game, has been fancifully traced by a learned antiquary, to the ancient Britons, who particularly delighting in the breeding of Hares, as Cæsar informs us, usually kept many of those animals about the courts of their chiefs.‖

That the Apple was known and cultivated by the Britons before the arrival of the Romans, we are warranted in believing by the etymology of the name. In the Welch, Cornish, Armorican and Irish languages or dialects, it is denominated the Avall or Aball. The Hœdui, who dwelt in the modern Somersetshire, appear particularly to have cultivated this fruit, and their town which stood upon the scite of the present Glastonbury, was known when the Romans first visited it, by the name of Avallonia (Apple Orchard.)§

* Strabo's Geography p. 306. † Plin. xix. c. 5. ‡ Columella De Re Rustica. b. ii. c. 10. ‖ Whittaker's Hist. of Manchester. p. 235. § Richards, Chron. p. 19.

Another Avellana afterwards came into notice in the north of England. Other fruits as the Pear, Damson, &c. being known by names evidently derived from the Roman appellations, we, on the other hand, are induced to consider as being introduced to the Britons from Italy. The same observation may apply to the Rose, Violet and other inhabitants of the flower garden, of which there is little doubt the Britons were ignorant before their introduction by the Romans. The Kitchen Garden is similarly indebted for most, though not all, of its inhabitants. The Cabbage or Kale tribe is an example of the exceptions.

Of the Roman Pleasure Grounds, during the decline of the Empire we have the most ample accounts. Highly polished as were the citizens of the then Mistress of the World, it was in this department of Horticulture their luxury and taste was displayed, and the most poetical subject here proffered itself to the pen of the Historian and man of Letters. To the Briton, just emerging from his barbarism, that which was most useful seemed most worthy of attention, hence the Fruit Garden became his first particular care, and it is of this, in the earliest periods of which records exists, that we have the most particular, though at the same time scanty notice.

Tacitus informs us that all Fruit Trees succeeded in Britain, but the Olive and Vine, and such others as require a warmer climate, for although Vegetables were quick in shooting up, yet the moisture of the Atmosphere rendered them slow in arriving at maturity.* It is evident from this cursory remark that the Romans began immediately their endeavours to improve the place of their settlement even before they had penetrated into the southern and more mild districts of the Island; or before its climate could be ameliorated by the removal of exuberant forests, and accompanying marshes, the never failing

* Vita Agric. c. xiv.

deteriorators of the climate of the country in which they abound. That they did so is further proved by the testimony of Pliny, who informs us that they introduced Cherries into our Island B. C. 42.

But although Britain was first visited by the Romans 55 years before the Christian Era, and although it is thus evident how much they were alive to the improvement of this, in common with all other nations, over which they had spread their conquering arms, yet it was not until the time of Agricola, A. D. 78. that the devastations and turmoils attendant upon a war of subjugation, had ceased so far as to enable them to win the attention of the natives with success, to the arts of Peace. By the strenuous endeavours of that distinguished general, the natives were inspired with a love of the Roman language and acquirements, and when the Legions were finally withdrawn from the Island, A. D. 426, the Britons were left comparatively a polished, but enervated people.

The art of cultivating the ground was a principal object of improvement, and that they extended the practice of that pursuit is certain, since during their possession of the Island, large quantities of Corn were annually exported from it. About A. D. 278, the Roman settlers finding that some parts of the Island were not unfit for Vineyards, obtained permission of the Emperor Probus, to plant Vines and make Wine of their produce, a liberty which had been refused to them by the narrower-minded policy of his predecessor Domitian.* Some varieties of the Apple, Pears, Figs, Mulberries, and Almonds were also introduced. Before the third Century, the Apple, had become pretty generally an object of cultivation, for at that period large plantations of that Fruit had been made as far north as the Shetland Islands.†

* Vospiscus.   † Solinus. c. xxii.

From the remains of Roman Villas, and other records of the state to which they had brought the arts of civilization in this Island, we have every reason to believe, although particular evidence is wanting, that Gardening was likewise improved by them so as to be in every respect similar to its practice in their mother country. The Britons amalgamated with the Roman settlers, who were very numerous. The veterans even, whether they received reward of their services in land or money, usually settled with their families in the country were they had spent their youth, and in Britain far removed from the influence of the tyranny, and convulsions which shook the City, and their native land generally, there were many extra temptations to adopt this as their home.

The seeds of improvement having thus strongly germinated, no untoward circumstances were afterwards capable of entirely preventing their further growth, for though continually checked yet on a review of ages, the superior civilization of any one over its immediate predecessor is always apparent.

Immediately after the departure of the Romans, namely about A. D. 450, the Saxons formed a settlement in our Island, and a series of civil wars succeeded until the inhabitants pretty generally hailed Egbert, about A. D. 726, sole sovereign of the realm. During this stormy period, in A. D. 507, Christianity was introduced among the inhabitants, and may be reckoned as an Epoch in the Hortulan Annals of this Country. Independant of the tendancy which Christianity had to soften the manners of the people, and thus by rendering them more domestic, in an equal ratio encouraging the progress of the useful Arts, to its Ministers, in those days especially, Gardening was an Art most congenial; it helped innocently to beguile otherwise unoccupied hours, and was the means of affording luxuries to the palate, which were by no means held in contempt by the Monks and other Religieux of those times. They were persons of education when compared with the laity; and had an intercourse with foreign countries, through their brethren, which facilitated the communication of improvements; even their fasting from animal food, was of benefit to Horticulture, for it rendered them more desirous of superior vegetables, and condiments arising from their tribes. Thus Italy, Spain, Germany, France, countries always abounding in the ministers of religion, became distinguished for their culinary vegetables and fruits. It may be added as another truly valuable advantage to Horticulture, secured to it by Religious establishments, that whilst the country at large was devastated in War, their property was usually held sacred, and consequently many varieties of vegetables were preserved, which otherwise would soon have become extinct if cultivated only in less hallowed ground.

From the example of the Ecclesiastics, the higher orders of the laity acquired a similarity of taste, and from these again the fondness for the products of the Garden, and its improvements, extended in wider circles.

Gardens and Orchards are mentioned as being in the possession of the Inhabitants of Monasteries and other Religious establishments in the oldest Chartularies. Of Orchards many traces still remain. One in Icolmnkiln, or Columbkill, one of the Hebrides, is described by Dr. Walker,* as having existed there probably from the 6th Century.† Camden, and Leland also mention various other instances in England. The Vine we have seen was introduced by the Romans and was particularly admired, and attended to by the carousing population of that age, if for no other of its qualities than the liquor yielded by its Fruit. Guin-uydden, Guin-bren, Guin-ien, or Fion-ras, its names in the Welch, Cornish, Armorican, and Irish dialects, is literally, the Wine Tree. Vineyards were flourishing here at

* Essays, v. ii. p. 5.   † The Monastery of St. Columba, was founded there, A. D 566. Gibbons, Hist. of Rome. c xxxvii.

the comencement of the eighth Century, as is testified by Bede.*

During these periods, marked by a continued series of intestine broils, the continued invasions of the Danes, who finally established their power in the island, A. D. 1017, and who in their turn were succeeded by another conquering dynasty in 1066, in the person of William the Ist., Horticulture continued unimpaired and silently to advance. Nor is this a matter of surprise, for the Saxons and Danes when they won a better home, than they had left in their native land, came as students in the arts of civilization, which their successive sovereigns, (Alfred and Canute need alone be instanced,) used every means in their power to foster and improve. They came not, as did the Caliph Omar to Alexandria, to destroy those acquirements as useless which he did not already possess. That the conquest of a polished nation, by others more barbarous than themselves, is not productive of that lamentable decay of civilization that at first sight might be apprehended, is further instanced by the result of the conquest of the Roman state by the Goths. The estimable arts of civilization were prized and studied by the brave and manly nations of the North, whilst the meretricious ornaments spread over them by the effeminate Romans were despised and swept away. It is only a savage, or a bigot that conquers to destroy; the Saxons, the Danes, and the Goths conquered to improve their own comfort and condition, which alone could be effected by sustaining the superior arts pursued by the nations they overcame.

When success in Arms has established an empire as well as extended it, the reputation of superior valour and power procures to the conquerors the security that always attends a complete ascendancy; such security leaves the mind at ease and affords leisure to cultivate the arts and sciences. Such conse-

* Eccles. Hist. b. i. c. 1.

quences resulted to the Athenians after their triumph over the Persians; to the Romans after Carthage had fallen beneath their arms; and such also resulted to the Saxons and Danes in their successive conquests of Britain. The Normans were about our equals in civilization, when William acquired the throne of our Island.

At the time of the arrival of the Normans, Gardens were generally in the possession of the laity, as well as of the ecclesiastics. Even Gardens for the growth of Vegetables to supply the public demand were then in existence. Eight Cotarii and their Gardens are enumerated in the Manor of Fulham, in Middlesex, a village it is worthy of remark still celebrated for its Market Gardens. Private houses with their Gardens are in like manner recorded.* In fact there is no reason to doubt that at this period every house from the palace to the cottage, was possessed of a Garden of some size.

From the writings of William of Malmsbury, who died in 1143, we learn that Vineyards and Orchards were possessed by the Barons as well as the Monks. He remarks that the Grapes of the vale of Gloucester furnished the best Wine. Next in superiority were those in the isle of Ely. Robert of Gloucester also informs us that Worcester was celebrated for its fruit, probably Apples.

BRITHNOD, the first Abbot of Ely, A. D. 1107. was celebrated for his skill in Horticulture. "He performed another great and useful work, says the Historian of the Monastery, being skilful in the art of planting and gardening, he laid out very extensive Gardens and Orchards, which he filled with a great variety of herbs, shrubs, and fruit trees. In a few years these appeared at a distance like a wood, loaded with the most excellent fruits in great abundance, adding much to the commo-

* Domesday Book. p. 127.

diousness and beauty of the place."* At Edmonsbury, the modern Bury, in Suffolk, the Monks of the Monastery then flourishing there, planted a vineyard for their own use, in 1140. The products of the Garden at this period were by no means so restricted as some authors have estimated. Matthew Paris, in recording the ungenial seasons of 1257, says, "Apples were scarce, Pears still scarcer; but Cherries, Plumbs, Figs, and all kinds of fruits included in shells (Filberts, Walnuts, &c.) were almost quite destroyed."† So numerous were the various plants which engaged their Horticultural skill, that the different departments occupied separate enclosures. We have seen that the Vineyard was independent of the Orchard, the latter was separated from the Kitchen Garden, and the Herbary again was a distinct enclosure. The Monks of Dunstable it is recorded, were at much expence in 1294, in repairing the Walls of their Gardens, and of their Herbary. As early as the eighth Century, the list of cultivated Herbs was very numerous, as we learn from the " *Capilarium de Villis et Curtis*" in which Charlemagne details to his gardeners, such herbs as he requires them to cultivate.

As an Art of design and taste Gardening can scarcely be considered to have existed. The Gardens belonging to the castellated dwellings of the gentry were confined within the narrow space included by the Glacis, required for defence in those times of feudal broils. In the Orchards without the moats of their Castles, they however indulged their taste for ornamental Gardening, which consisted, as it continued to a much later age, in having plants cut into monstrous figures, labyrinths, &c. Henry the first, formed at Woodstock, A. D. 1123, the first Park of which we have any record. Spelman says he borrowed the idea from the Easterns. It was probably chiefly designed as a preserve for Game (habitationem

* Gale's Hist. of Ely, v. ii. c. ii. † Henry's Hist. of England, b. iv. c. 5. s. i.

ferarum.*) It contained however a laybrinth, which appears to have chiefly constituted the Bower, so immortalized by the fate of the unfortunate mistress of this monarch, Rosamond. Labyrinths were so much in unison with the taste of the age that there is scarcely a design for a garden given by De Cerceau in his " Architecture," about A. D. 1250, in which there is not a round and a square one. A Century before this last mentioned date, namely in the reign of Henry the 2nd, (1154—1189.) Fitzstevens describes the gardens around the villas of the London citizens as "large, beautiful, and planted with Trees."

We have thus traced with as much clearness as we have been enabled by the scanty materials the Chroniclers of these times afford, the progress of Horticulture in this country down to the close of the 13th Century, and from the whole it is apparent that the Art had gradually, and slowly continued, to improve, and that a love of the pursuit had become pretty generally diffused. The period was now approaching when its operations of every kind were more rapidly and eminently to be improved, for though of its own importance and merits it had continued to preserve attention and esteem, yet it is certain the manners of the period over which we have followed, it were decidedly opposed to the advance of this one of the peaceful Arts. The latter part of the Time we have been considering, embraces that period known in history as "the Middle or Dark Ages," comprising the five centuries which elapsed between the overthrow of the Western Roman Empire, about A. D. 500, to the extinction of that of the East, about A. D. 1000. Horticulture can never flourish in any country where the pleasures of life are not sought for at home; in these ages however, War and Hunting were the pursuits of the Ecclesiastics, as well as of the Laity, and even Woman, whilst in person she learnt to ride with the foremost in the Chace, was taught to love no Knight who besides being a good Lance in the Tilt Yard, had not proved

* Henry of Huntingdon's Hist. b. 7.

himself "without reproach and without fear" in some strife more deadly than that or a Tournament.

Even as late as 1321, an Archbishop of York is described, without remark of its being unusual, as making his visitations with a train of two hundred attendants, and a pack of hounds, with which he hunted from parish to parish.* Even as late as the reign of Elizabeth females sought amusement in the Chase, in Bear Baitings and Tournaments.

These habits nurtured the odious system of the Forest-Laws, which were a distinguishing mark of the Norman dynasty; and fettered the improvement of the twin, but less polished sister of our Art, Agriculture. Laws oppressive and destructive of Agriculture would only remotely be accessary to the retardation of Gardening, but the warlike propensities, and excessive passion for field sports which are features of that period, by fostering a laborious idleness, and weakening the love of home, had a proportionate tendency to discourage our Art.

Down to the conclusion of the 13th Century, England had been a strictly Agricultural country, and even the produce of her soil had been so limited, that she had little surplus to enable her inhabitants to become important as merchants, for we were also without manufactures. Now, whatever may be the cause it is not for us here to enquire, but, it is certain, that as in the abstract, in commercial, and more especially manufacturing districts, the mental powers of the people are more strong and cultivated, a greater desire and research after improvements are elicited, and that from them by far the greater number of men distinguished either in the Arts or Sciences arise; so in the aggregate it is certain that a country enriched

* Whittaker's Hist. of Craven, p. 342.

by its manufactures and commerce is always more enlightened, and more favourable to the advance of the superior arts of life, than one that is supported simply by the produce of its own soil. England did not become a manufacturing and commercial country until the reign of Edward the third.‡

* Hallams Hist. of the Middle Ages. v. 3. p. 386.

ON THE STATE OF

GARDENING IN ENGLAND,

From the accession of Edward the Third, to the accession of Queen Elizabeth.

A. D. 1327.——A. D. 1558.

During the reign of the heroic and patriotic Edward the III the commerce and manufactures of our country obtained, next to the liberty of the subject, the chief care of the parliament. Their increase was rapid and the accumulation of wealth proportionate. and no country so enriched, has yet existed without proportionably encouraging the arts of refinement.

So general had become a taste for Gardening that Men of literature directed their attention to the subject, collected information, and in their writings gave the results of their enquiries for the benefit of others. This is a decisive proof of the interest taken in the art, for no one would have written a book for which he did not expect there would be readers, and it is as certain, those only would be readers who took a delight in its subject; an author could reckon only for readers among those who desired information, no one would read a work on the cultivation of plants for the sake of amusement

In the reign of Edward the III. the first work written in this country on the cultivation of the soil is supposed to have been composed. The author was Walter de Henly; it is entitled, "De Yconomia, sive Housbrandia". Bishop Tanner says the subject is treated of well, according to the usage of the time.* Nicholas Bollar, an Oxonian of skill in Natural Philosophy, wrote three books " De Arborum plantatione ;" and another work in two books " De generatione Arborum et modo generandi et plantandi" and some other tracts still in M. S.†

A fondness for Plants as an object of study, was now awakened, and is an earnest that the attention to their cultivation proportionably increased, for although Plants were sought after cheifly with a view to ascertain their medicinal qualities, yet the spirit of true Botanical Science was awakening, many MSS. existing that were written at this period, devoted entirely to a tracing of the characteristics of Plants, their Synonyms &c. The first Royal Professor of Botany may be said to have been appointed in this age, in the person of John Bray, by Richard the II, (1377—1399.) who allowed him an annual pension for his knowledge and skill in Botany and Physic.‡

The following authors also flourished during the period of which we are treating.

HENRY CALCOENSIS, a prior of the Benedictine Order. His love of Science and Literature induced him to travel into France, Germany and Italy, solely to enjoy an intercourse with the learned. He wrote in one book a "Synopsis Herbaria," and translated Palladius "De Re Rustica" into the Gaelic, about A. D. 1493.

WILLIAM HORMAN, a native of Salisbury, was educated

* Pultney's Sketches of Botany. v. i. p. 23.   † Ibid. p. 24.
‡ Ibid. p. 22.

at Winchester School, and proceeding thence to New College, Oxford, became there a perpetual fellow in 1477. In 1485 he was elected Schoolmaster and Fellow of Eton, and finally became its Vice-Provost. After several years of retirement, he died in 1835, and was buried in the College Chapel. He was a man of extensive and various erudition. Among his numerous works are "Herbarum Synonyma", and Indexes to Cato, Varro, Columella, and Palladius "De Re Rustica."*

1500. A BOKE of Husbandry. London, 4to. This little work, is very rare, being one of the productions from the press of Wynkin de Worde. It consists of but twelve leaves, and is without date, but certainly was not of a later year than 1500. The following extracts explain its nature. " Here begyneth a Treatyse of Husbandry which Mayster Groshede somtyme Bysshop of Lyncoln made and translated it out of Frensshe into Englyshe, whiche techeth all maner of men to gouerne theyr Londes Tenementes, and Demenes ordinately."

"Here endeth the Boke of Husbandry, and of Plantynge, and Graffynge of Trees and Vynes."

1521. ARNOLDE'S CHRONICLE. The Customs of London. Folio.

This curious book contains a chapter on "The Crafte of graffynge and plantynge and alterynge of Frutys. as well in colours as in taste" and another how to raise a sallad in an hour; ("Percely to grow in an our space.")

1523. Here Begynneth a new tracte or treatyse most profytable for all Husbandemen: and very frutefull for all

* Pultney's sketches of Botany, v. i. 24 & 25.

other persons to rede. Imprinted by Rycharde Pynson, &c. 4to. (1523)

1523. Here Begynneth a right frutefull mater, and hath to name The Boke of Surveying and Improvements. Imprinted by Rycharde Pynson. The yere of our lorde god. MDXXIII. the XV day of July. 4to.

Although the last of these works bears the name of Pynson as Printer, there is little doubt that he was employed by Berthelet another Printer to execute the work for him, for Berthelet was in the habit of employing the Presses of others even at Paris (Johnson's Typographia p. 504.), and to this work is attached an address from "Thomas Berthelet to the reders of this lytell boke." These two works are very rare; I have never seen either of them. I am inclined to consider them as the first editions of Fitzherbert's Book of Husbandry, though there is some reason for doubting this.

SIR ANTHONY FITZHERBERT, was born at Norbury, in Derbyshire.—After studying at Oxford, he removed thence to one of the Inns of Court, and was called to be a Serjeant-at-Law in 1511. He was created a Knight in 1516, and seven years subsequently he was raised to the dignity of a Justice of the Court of Common Pleas. He followed Husbandry as a recreation for forty years. He was a great opponent to the influence of Cardinal Wolsey, and lived to see the disgrace of that ambitious Churchman, not dieing until 1538. He was buried at Norbury. His Law Works are numerous, of which his "Grand Abridgement" is the most noted.[*] The works for which he deserves notice here, are

1. The book of Husbandry, very profitable and necessary

---

[*] Biographia Britannica.

for all persons, London 1532. 8vo. Editions of it also appeared in 1534, 1546, 1548, (by Thomas Marsh,) 1559 (by John Awdeley,) and 1562, all in 8vo. Many other editions appeared without dates. There was a reprint of this and the following in 1767, in 8vo. with a Treatise of Xenophon's.

2. Surveying; and book of Husbandry. London. 1547. 8vo. Again in 1562, 8vo. and in 1598, 4to.

For the above dates of Editions, I am chiefly indebted to Dr. Watts's Bibliotheca Britannica. There are some differerences of opinion respecting the first appearance of the works but after a careful survey of the various authorities I think the above will be found correct. Johnson's Typographia has been of much use to me on this subject.

THOMAS TUSSER, was a writer of Poetry on Agricultural affairs. He was born at Rivenhall, a village on the high road between the towns of Witham and Kelvedon, in Essex, about the year 1515, of a family afterwards allied by marriage to the higher ranks of Society. He was, against his inclination, educated for a chorister, and became one at a very early age, at the Collegiate Chapel of Wallingford. His voice was fine and he was pressed, as the despotic custom then permitted, for the choir of St. Paul's Cathedral. From thence he proceeded to Eton and became a student there under Udall, about 1534, whose severity of discipline he has recorded. He then proceeded to Trinity Hall, Cambridge, but leaving it on account of ill-health, was dissuaded from returning by William Lord Paget, who kept him about the Court, probably as a chorister, as one of his retainers for ten years, but which he then left without any improvement in his fortune. He retired to Katwade, (Catiwade) in Suffolk, and commenced farmer. It was here he composed his work on Husbandry. The ill-state of his Wife's health induced him after some years to leave his farm and live at Ipswich where she died. He then married a second time to a Miss Moon, and settled at East Dereham, but the temper of his youthful wife, and the harshness of his Landlord, again induced him to move to Norwich, where under the patronage of Dean Salisbury he appears once more to have become a chorister. Ill-health induced him again to remove, and he took a farm, the Glebe land, at Fairstead, in Essex, near his native village. Fearing the death of the Clergyman he moved to London, but hastened thence in 1574 to Trinity College, Cambridge, that he might be beyond the influence of the plague. He however returned to the Metropolis and died there about 1580,* certainly before 1585, as is demonstrated by the Title Page of the edition of his work published that year.

He was buried in the Church of St. Mildred, in the Poultry, according to Stowe, with this Epitaph.

>Here Thomas Tusser clad in earth, doth lie,
> That sometime made the pointes of Husbandrie:
>By him then learn thou maist; here learn we must,
> When all is done, we sleepe, and turn to dust:
>And yet through Christ, to heaven, we hope to goe;
> Who reades his bookes, shall find his faith was so.

This is an outline of nearly all that is known of this extraordinary man. In whatever capacity he at various times lived he acted with ability, yet never so as to benefit his fortune. That he excelled as a Singer is certain, for none but those of more than ordinary powers were admitted into the Royal Choir. As a courtier he was unfrowned upon until the disgrace of his patron. As a farmer it is evident he had correct knowledge from his work upon the subject. As an author and poet the same testifies he was far above mediocrity. Morant, quoting from Fuller, Stowe, and Strype, says, that Tusser at one time was a Schoolmaster. The true reason of his ill-success in life is to be found perhaps in the verses of a Poet, almost his contemporary. Peacham in his "Minerva," a book of Emblems, published in 1612, has a device of a Whetstone and Scythe, with this beneath.

>They tell me, Tusser, when thou wert alive,
> And hadst for profit turned every stone,
>Where'er thou camest, thou couldst never thrive,
> Though hereto, best could'st council every one,
>   As it may in thy *Husbandry* appear,
>   Wherein afresh thou liv'st among us here.
>So, like thyself, a number more are wont,
> To sharpen others with advice of wit,
>When they themselves are like the Whetstone blunt.

His work appeared first in 1557, entitled,

1. "A hundreth good pointes of Husbandry
   Maintaineth good household, with huswifery.
   Housekeeping and husbandry, if it be good:
   Must love one another like cousinnes in blood.

* Phillips's Theatrum Poetarum.

"The wife to, must husband as well as the man,
Or farewell thy husbandry do what thou can."

Editions of this appeared in 1561, 1562 and another "newly corrected and amplified" 1570—1571 (Watts.) To these succeeded an enlarged edition bearing the following title, "Five hundreth pointes of good husbandry united to as many of good huswifery, first devised and now lately augmented, with diverse approved lessons, concerning hopps and gardening and other needful matters, together with an abstract before every moneth &c." 1573. Reprints appeared successively in 1577, 1580 (the first complete edition,) 1585, 1586, 1590, 1593, 1597, 1599, 1600, (Watts) 1604, 1610, 1614, 1620, 1630, (Watts,) 1638, 1672, 1692, all in 4to, and black letter, except that of 1600, which is stated to be in folio. Martyn mentions another edition in 1651. One, entitled "Tusser redivivus" was edited by a Mr. Hilman in 1710, 8vo, and with further notes in 1744. An edition was edited by Dr. W. Mavor in 1812, 4to. and 8vo. with many notes and additions. To this I am indebted for nearly the whole of the preceding imformation concerning the editions of Tusser.

The above work is written in Stanzas of four verses each, and is a series of a kind of proverbs relating to Agricultural affairs. Weston says, the following work is often joined to it. "The Booke of Regarde; containing the castle of delight, the garden of unthriftinesse, the arbour of virtue, and the orchard of repentance".

2. Tractatus de Agricultura, versibus Anglicis. London. 1638 and 1672. This work is ascribed by Haller to the pen of Tusser.* These works are extremely rare.

These are the chief of the authors from whom we are enabled to learn the actual state of Horticulture at this period. In contemporary Historians and Chroniclers, of course there are many incidental notices. Among these is Dr. Bulleyn, who deserves the veneration of every lover of Gardening, for his strenuous advocating its cause, at a time when it had become a fashion to depreciate the products of our English Gardens.

WILLIAM BULLEYN, was born in the Isle of Ely, early in the reign of Henry VIII.† He studied first at Cambridge, and subsequently at Oxford. He travelled in Germany, Scot-

* Watt's Bibliotheca Britannic. † Watts in his Bibliotheca Britannic, says he was born in 1.00.

land, and his native country, studying their natural productions with a zeal and success, that marks him very prominently as a man of Science in that age, so benighted as it was in every thing that appertains to Natural History. In early life he was much in the neighbourhood of Norwich. It was in the East of England it would appear that his relatives resided. His nearest connections had their abode at Blaxhall, in Suffolk, to the Rectory of which place he was appointed, in June, 1550. It is not improbable, that he united the practice of a Physician with that of a Divine, a union of professions which was not thought incompatible even as late as the commencement of the present Century.* It is certain, that being opposed to the doctrine of Transubstantiation, he resigned his Church preferment the year after Mary succeeded to the throne in 1553. When he took his degree in Physic is not known. Soon after his resignation of the living of Blaxhall, he settled in practice as a Physician, in the City of Durham, and became a proprietor with Sir Thomas Hilton, in the Salt Works near Tinmouth Castle. On the death of Sir T. Hilton, Dr. Bulleyn removed to London, and became known as a skilful Physician, and a man of learning. He was elected a member of the College of Physicians about the year 1560. A series of misfortunes now pursued him, but were met by him with that firmness which was to be expected from a man of his strength of mind, and true piety. He lost a great part of his library, with his MS. work on "Healthful Medicines," by shipwreck; and he was malevolently, and unjustly accused by a brother of Sir T. Hilton, with having murdered that gentleman, though, as was fully proved, he had died of a malignant fever. His enemy however would not be foiled completely, but succeeded in throwing him into prison for debt. Whilst in goal he wrote a great part of his medical works. His death occurred Jan. 7th 1576.†

The following portraits of him exist.

William Bulleyn, Physician; a wood print; profile; with a

* Dr. Gower of Chelmsford practiced as a Physician, and performed the Clerical duties of Chignall near that town as late as 1760.

† Biographia Britannica.

long beard. Prefixed to his "Government of Health," 1648; 8vo. with his initials.

William Bulleyn; a copy by W. Richardson.

There is a whole length of him cut in wood, with four verses in English. It belongs to his works in Folio.

Wilhelmus Bulleyn; M. D. &c. F. Wil. Stukely. 1722, floruit 1570; small.* This engraving was executed at the expense of Dr. Stukely, who was one of his descendants.

His works were published collectively and are entitled, "A Bulwarke of defence against all Sicknes, Sorenes, and Wounds, that doe daily assaulte mankind; which Bulwarke is kept with Hillarius the Gardener; Health the Physician, with their Chirurgion, to help the wounded Soldiers, &c. with his Boke of Simples. London. 1562. folio: Another edition bears date, 1579. Folio.

REMBERT DODOENS or DODONŒUS,—although a foreign Botanist, deserves mention, if it was only on account of his works being the foundation, upon which our own Botanist and Gardener, Gerarde, founded his " Herbal," as Lyte had done his before; but besides this he was an encourager of Horticulture himself. This Physician and Botanist was born near Mechlin in Flanders in 1517. He studied at Louvaine: became conspicuous for his learning whilst young; travelled into Italy; and on his return was appointed Physician to the Emperor Maximilian the II.—as he was afterwards to Rodolph the II.—The importunity of his friends procured his dismission from the Emperor's service. He then practised at Antwerp; and was afterwards appointed professor of Physic at Leyden, where he died in 1585—6. He wrote on subjects connected

* Grainger.

with Astronomy, Geography and Physic, but is chiefly noted for his productions on Botany. He commenced publishing in 1552. He wrote "Frugum Historia," 8vo.—"Herbarium Belgicum, 8vo.—But his chief work appeared in 1583 in which he included all his other Botanical writings under the title of "Sterpium Historiæ Pemptades," in folio—Each Pemptade is divided into five books. The first Pemptade, contains numerous dissimilar plants in alphabetical order; the second, Florist's Flowers and the umbelliferous Plants; the third, Medicinal Roots—Purgative Plants—Climbing and Poisonous Plants—with most of the cryptogami he was aware of;—the fourth, Grain; Pulses; Grasses; Water, and marsh Plants; the fifth, edible Plants—Gourds—esculent Roots—oleraceous and spinous Plants;—and the sixth, Shrubs and Trees—The appendix is compiled chiefly from Dioscorides, Cato and Pliny, relating to the progress of Botany and Agriculture, among the Romans: as well as being in commendation, of Gardens, with rules for laying them out, and advantageously managing them.*

We have seen in the preceding chapter that the Gardens of the age were extensive, and from the slight mention we have of some of their inhabitants, it is pretty certain they were well stocked. We however have no particular list of them until the time of Tusser. That his Catalogue would be a correct one of our horticultural products at a much earlier period, is certain. In the reign of Edward the III, Cucumbers were cultivated, it is a mistake however to consider that Melons were likewise, for the Melons of those, and of later writers, were the Pompions of our times.† It is certain however from concurrent testimonies that the cultivation of edible vegetables and fruits was exceedingly neglected. A bushel of Onions in the reign of Richard the II, usually cost about twelve shillings, estimating

* Pultney's Sketches of Botany—Haller's Bibliotheca Botanica.
† See this in Lytes Herbal, A. D. 1619.

the charge according to the value of our present currency. In the reign of Henry the VII, (1485—1509,) it appears in a MS. signed by the Monarch himself, preserved in the Remembrance Office, that Apples were from one to two shillings each, a red one fetching the highest price.* Yet it was not because the varieties of our Garden products were few. Tusser enumerates of "Seedes and herbes for the kychen, herbes and rootes for sallets and sawse, herbes and rootes to boyle or to butter, strewing herbes of all sortes, herbes, branches, and flowers for windowes and pots, herbes to still in summer, necessarie herbes to grow in the garden for physik, not reherst before," above one hundred and fifty species. Of fruits, he mentions many kinds of Apples; Apricoches; Bar-berries; Bollese, black and white; Cherries, red and black; Chesnuts; Cornet-Plums, (Cornelian Cherry?); Damisens, white and black; Filberts, red and white; Gooseberries; Grapes, white and red; Grene or Grass Plums; Hurtil-berries, (Vaccinium vitis-idœa;) Medlers or Merles; Mulberries; Peaches, white red and yellow fleshed; Peres of many kinds; Peer Plums, black and yellow; Quinces; Raspes; Reisons (Currants?); Hazel-Nuts; Strawberries, red and white; Services; Wardens white and red; Walnuts; and Wheat Plums.

The Almond was introduced in this reign. Some Authors also affirm that the Cherry having been lost during the turmoils of the Saxon dynasty, was introduced again during this reign by Rich. Haines, the Kings Fruiterer; but this is an error, for Warton gives a quotation from Lidgate, a Poet who lived about 1415, which proves that Cherries were then so common as to be hawked about the streets. Although the Lemon was not cultivated in this country until the reign of James I., it is upon record that the Leatherseller's Company gave six silver pennies for one, which was served up at a Civic feast given to Henry

* Pearmain Apples are as old as the days of King John, (1199—1216.) Rot. Fin. 6. John. m. 13. Blount's Ant. Tenures. p. 69.

VIII., and Anne Bulleyn, in honour of the coronation of the latter. Thus, as Apicius, the Roman epicure and glutton, first taught his countrymen the use of this fruit, so Henry, his peer in sensuality, first partook of it in this country.

To these may be added the Fig, which we have seen was cultivated here as early as 278 (p. 35.) and makes up a list of Fruits as complete as that which comprises those now cultivated by us, without the aid of Glass and artificial Heat. Yet notwithstanding this, culinary vegetables were as scarce in the concluding years, of the reign of Henry VIII. (1509—1546) as good Apples were in that of his father. Sugar was the sauce usually eaten with every kind of flesh meat. Neither was it because vegetables were little estimated, for Catherine, his last Queen, was accustomed to send a messenger to Holland, or Flanders, when she required a Sallad;* and the Cherries of an Orchard in Kent, sold in 1540, for one thousand pounds.† To what is that deficiency in the produce of our Gardens then to be attributed? There seems to be but one answer; the unskilfulness of our Gardeners. The want of encouragement which they met with was the just result of their own want of desert. Dr. Bulleyn says we had excellent Apples, Pears, Plums, Cherries, &c. of our own growth before those Garden products were imported from Holland and France, and the only rational conclusion is, that the similar growth of our country would not bear comparison with them. The fruits and culinary vegetables of our neighbours, were therefore luxuries; wealth knew no obstacle in the way of indulging in them; it became a fashion to have them upon Table; and the spirit of commerce was now too much alive to allow the fashion to fade away from a want of the means of indulgence. The Gardeners of London and Kent, were regular importers of these edibles. In excuse for this inferiority of our Garden

* Humes Hist. of England, anno 1547. † Philip's Hist. of Fruits, p. 79.

produce, it was a conclusive assumption to assert, that our climate and soil were unfavourable to their growth. Against this unfounded opinion, Dr. Bulleyn stood forward, the patriotic, and we may add the successful opponent: for although the error would naturally have a tendency to correct itself, it is too much to consider that the opinion of a man of his estimation would be delivered without effect. From this period our practical Horticulture was more attended to, and with its improvement the embassies to Holland for a Sallad ceased.

The evil would have a tendency to correct itself. When the Market Gardeners witnessed the high prices which were so extensively paid for the objects properly of their own cultivation, they would be tempted to raise them themselves of equal goodness, that their profit might be the greater. Gentlemen would excite their private Gardeners to similar efforts, that they might enjoy such luxuries without such a consequent expense. Henry VIII., sent his Gardener, who was a French Priest, named Woolf, to travel on the continent, for the express purpose of acquiring a better knowledge of his Art. He is said to have introduced various Sallad and Pot-herbs, varieties of the Apricot, Musk Melons, the Kentish Cherry, &c. to that Monarch's Garden at the palace of Nonsuch, in Surrey, about the year 1524.* The learned Linacre, who died in 1524, first introduced the Damask Rose from Italy; Thomas, Lord Cromwell, about the same period, or rather, at the close of the reign of Henry VII., added three Plums to our list of Fruits, among them the Perdrigon from Italy, and Bishop Grindal, one of the earliest encouragers of Botany, first introduced the Tamarisk from Switzerland, and during his residence brought the Gardens at Fulham palace, into great repute. They were celebrated for their Grapes, which he brought to great perfection.

* Goughs British. Topog. v. i. p. 133.

It was not until the close of the period which we are considering, that we find either the size of the pleasure Garden, or the style of laying it out at all improved. The effects of the Feudal System were not yet sufficiently passed away to allow of any general alteration, or even improvement in the style of Architecture. Our nobility still dwelt in Castles, and these retained the usual defences of Moats, Drawbridges, &c. This was especially the case, the nearer they approached to the Scotch or Welch borders; in the vicinity of London, Villas and Palaces had long since sprung up. Those which retained all the customary fortifications, had Gardens within the moat, as well as without, for the Orchard mentioned by Leland in 1540, as existing at Wreshill Castle near Howden in Yorkshire, evidently partook of the nature of pleasure grounds. "The Gardens within the mote, and the Orchards without, were exceeding fair. And yn the Orchárdes, were mountes, opere topioriō, writhen about with degrees like the turnings in cokil shelles, to come to the top without payn."*
King James I. of Scotland, who was confined for some years as prisoner in Windsor Castle, early in the 15th Century, gives us in a poetical effusion a description of its Garden, which similarly intimates to us that it was of contracted space and formal adornments,

> Now was there maide fast by the touris wall
>   A Garden faire, and in the corneris set
> An herbere grene, with wandis long and small
>   Railit about, and so with treeis set
>   Was all the place, and hawthorn hedges knet,
> That lyfe was now, walkyng there for bye
> That myght within scarce any wight espye.
>   So thick the bewis and the leves grene
>   Beschudit all, the alleyes all that there were,

---

* Lelands Itinerary. p. 60.

And myddis every herbere might be sene
The scharpe grecn swete jenepere,
Growing so fair with branches here and there,
That as it semyt to a lyfe without,
The bewis spred the herbere all abont."*

The contracted size of our pleasure grounds by degrees ceased to be their reproach, although their style retained the formal features which continued characteristics of them until late in the 18th century. In the the eighteenth year of the reign of Henry the VIII. (1509—1546,) the gardens of his palace of Nonsuch, were formed. This palace and its grounds were one of the prides of our country in that age, or as Leland says;

Unrivall'd in design the Briton's tell
The won'drous praises of this nonpareil.
This which no equal has in art or fame,
Britons deservedly do Nonsuch name.

"The palace, says Hentzner in 1598, is encompassed with parks full of deer, delicious gardens, groves ornamented with trellis work, cabinets of verdure, (Summer houses or seats cut in yew?) and walks so embowered by trees, that it seems to be a place pitched upon by pleasure herself to dwell in along with health. In the pleasure and artificial Gardens are many columns and pyramids of marble: two fountains that spout water, one round the other like a pyramid, upon which are perched small birds, that stream water out of their bills. In the grove of Diana, is a very agreeable fountain, with Actæon turned into a stag, as he was sprinkled by the goddess and her nymphs, with inscriptions. Here is, besides, another pyramid of marble full of concealed pipes, which spirt upon all who come within their reach."† From an account taken of this Garden during the usurpation, in 1650, it appears to have

* The Quair by James I., Edited by Lord Woodhouselee. † Travels in England during the reign of queen Elizabeth. pp. 58—59. Ed. 1797.

been cut and divided into several alleys and compartments set round with thorn hedges. On the North side was a Kitchen Garden very commodious, containing 72 Fruit Trees, and encompassed by a wall fourteen feet high. On the West was a wilderness covering ten acres, severed from the little Park by a hedge. In the privy Gardens were pyramids, fountains, and basins of marble, one of which is "set round with six Lilac Trees; which Trees bear no fruit, but only a very pleasant smell;" also 144 Fruit Trees, two Yews, and one Juniper. Before the Palace was a bowling Green, surrounded by a balustrade of Freestone. The whole was surrounded by two Parks, which were also enclosed by Henry VIII., the one containing 911 Acres, the other 671 Acres.

In the Gardens of Lord Burleigh at Theobald's, which were encompassed by a broad ditch of Water, were a great profusion of Trees and Plants, Obelisks, Pyramids, a Jet D'eau, Labyrinths, circular Porticoes, a summer House, Baths of lead, full of fish, &c. These Gardens were large. The chief Garden covered a space of seven acres; besides which were the pleasure Gardens, privy Gardens, and laundry Garden. In the first were nine knots artificially and "*exquisitely*" made, one of which was set forth in likeness of the King's arms. "One might walk twoe myle in the walks before he came to the end.*"

At Hampton Court, which was laid out about the middle of this reign by Cardinal Wolsey, there was a labyrinth, which still exists, covering only, the quarter of an Acre of ground, yet its walks extending by their volutions over nearly half a mile. The walls also were covered with Rosemary, a fashion then very generally adopted.† It was also long celebrated for its trees cut into grotesque forms, which Dr. Plot admired and dignified with the name of *Topiary Works*.‡

* Lyson's Environs of London. Hentzner's Travel's p. 38. Peck's Desiderata Curiosa. † Ibid. p. 58. ‡ History of Oxfordshire, p. 380.

We have thus traced the progress of Gardening in its several departments in this country from the accession of our third Edward, to the conclusion of the reign of Henry the VIII., a period of more than two Centuries, the first one hundred and fifty years of which, were characterized by a still lingering taste for hunting, chivalry, and War; by Crusades to the Holy Land, and as wild expeditions to the continent; and above all by the civil horrors induced by the contest between the houses of York and Lancaster. Notwithstanding these circumstances so hostile to domestic improvement, and the cultivation of the social Arts, we have seen that the art of Gardening in its various departments had continued to advance, and in the concluding years of the period had improved most distinguishably. So true is the observation that good is often the offspring of evil; for our foreign wars introduced us to the Horticulture of France, who excelled us in the practical parts of the Art; to the disposition of the Pleasure Grounds of the Easterns, which were magnificent ; and to numerous new plants of which previously we had been ignorant. Our navigation was improved by the voyages made on these expeditions, and thus led to other and more distant climes, which in their turn afforded to us their vegetable riches. To these favourable circumstances may be added the increase of our commerce, and the invention of Printing, which above all others tended to foster the progress of every Art and Science, by enlarging the sphere of intercourse, and rendering the experience and knowledge of every man of learning, the property of his age.

ON THE STATE OF

GARDENING IN ENGLAND,

From the accession of Queen Elizabeth, to the accession of George the First.

A. D. 1558.——A. D. 1714.

Previous to the reign of Elizabeth, (1558—1602.) Horticulture was considered, as little more than a mechanical Art; but brighter days were now arrived to it. Botany, previous to this period, was almost unknown as a *Science*, and it must be acknowledged that Botany, is a chief part of the only foundation, upon which an enlightened practice of Horticulture can be raised. In this reign, England was enriched with the first regular establishment for the scientific cultivation of Plants in the Physic Garden of Gerarde, (1567.) It was not however in England alone, that the study and cultivation of plants became more popular, there were many tributary streams to this branch of the river of Science; our ancestors were only followers of an example that was set by many continental powers, and which seems to have risen from a desire for the improvement of a knowledge of Plants, and their culture, which pervaded Europe simultaneously at this period. Padua took the lead by establishing a public Botanic Garden, whilst under the Venetians, in 1533. Lucas Ghinus at Bologna, who was the first public professor of Botany in Europe, was a strenuous advocate of such Institutions, By his influence a similar Garden was established at Bologna in 1547, where Dr. Turner, whom we shall presently notice, first imbibed much of that knowledge, which rendered him eminent in this country. Among the earliest private Gardens of the same kind was that of Enricus Cordus, at Bremen, who died in 1538; and of Mordecius at Cassel, who flourished about the same time. Gesner constructed the first Botanic Garden in Switzerland at Zurich, in 1560; one was established at Paris, in 1570; at Leyden, in 1577; Leipsic, 1580; Montpelier, 1598; Jena, 1628; Oxford, 1632. This last owes its foundation to the munificence of Henry Danvers, Earl of Danby, who for the purpose gave five Acres of ground on the banks of the Charwel, to the South of St. Mary Magdalenes. He built Greenhouses and Stoves, enclosed it with Stone Walls fourteen feet high, erected a house for the Gardener, and endowed the establishment. Sir Jacob and Sir Andrew Balfour endowed one at Edinburgh, in 1680; and the Apothecaries company founded that at Chelsea, in 1673. This last named expensive establishment was commenced at a time when the Company was without any disposable funds; and when to enter upon the undertaking, as well as to re-erect their Hall, burnt down in the Great Fire, they were obliged to have recourse to the private resources of the members.—Conduct which redounds to their honour, for the outlay was without any prospect of pecuniary advantage, but merely from a desire to promote the objects of Science.

The advantage to Horticulture, by this establishment of Botanic Gardens was of the first importance. No Plant can be cultivated with success. unless its native climate, soil, and habits are attended to. This and still more is acquired in a Botanic Garden, where Plants and their congeners are associated in cultivation. National establishments of this kind have the power both by a command of foreign intercoure, and liberal funds to collect specimens of new Plants from other countries. Here the man of Science can pursue his studies under favourable circumstances otherwise unattainable in ascertaining the relationship of individuals, comparing dubious species, witnessing their state at different periods of growth, the soils they most delight in, &c. Facts which however more belonging to the research of the Botanist, throw most beneficial light upon Horticulture. Dr. Turner, who died in 1568, was undoubtedly the earliest in this country that discovered any considerable knowledge of Plants; contemporary with him was Dr. Bulleyn, already mentioned; and the same age gave birth to Penny, Lobel, and Gerarde, men devoted to the cultivation and collection of Plants. Their writings and example were most favourably met and followed by persons of fortune. Private Gardens performed no trivial part in encouraging the spirit of discovering new Plants, and improving their culture. Dr. Turner whilst at Cologn had a Garden for "rare plants." In England, the Duke of Somerset had one at Sion House, and at a later period, Dr. Turner had two, one at Wells, and another at Kew.* Mrs. Gape at Westminster had a small one, which furnished the first specimens for the Chelsea Garden. We shall have occasion to mention many others in the course of this chapter. It must not be supposed that Botany, as a systematic Science yet existed. Generic and Specific characters were little regarded.—Systematic arrangement beyond that of the Alphabet was scarcely thought of. Every Herbalist was a Florist, and in both capacities the chief object with them seemed to be, to discover new Plants, for they did not then distinguish between a species and a variety. Parkinson, Clusius, Gerarde, &c. were all raisers of Florists flowers. They appeared to strive to increase their acquaintance with individuals, and thus left a mass of detached subjects, which the genius of

* Pultney's Sketches. v. i. p. 63.

Ray, Tournefort, Linnœus, &c. afterwards arranged and illustrated by their systems.

It was not in Botany alone, that the knowledge of the age was rapidly improving, but in the whole circle of the Arts and Sciences. The Reformation was not confined to religion. By delivering the human mind from servile thraldom, and teaching Man instead of bowing blindly to custom, merely on account of its antiquity, to have a self-dependence; to search all things, and retain only that which is good; it gave an impetus to improvement, which no tyrant opposition could check. Such men as Bacon, Peiresc, and Evelyn arose, and whilst the first traced the path which Men of Science should tread, the two latter lent their talents and wealth to sustain them whilst pursuing it. Bacon, it has been well observed, was the first who taught that Man was but the servant and interpreter of nature; capable of discovering truth in no other way than by observing and imitating her operations; that facts were to be collected, and not speculations formed; and that the materials for the foundations of true systems of knowledge, were to be discover- not in the books of the ancients, not in metaphysical theories, not in the fancies of men, but by experiment and observation in the external world. Peiresc was a munificent Man of Letters, his house, his advice, his purse were opened to the votaries of every Art and every Science. His library was stored with the literature of every age and nation; his Garden was stored with the most rare exotics, and thence he delighted to spread them over Europe. Evelyn trod in the same steps. When we cast our eyes over a list of the men of science and literature of all denominations that adorned this age, especially in Botany and Chemistry, the two Sciences of all others the most important to Horticulture, we shall not be surprized to find how rapidly it was rising from being a mere art of Empiricism. And when we note how the thirst for foreign researches was prevalent, we shall easily percieve by what means new plants were gained to every department of our Art. Cavendish, but especially Raleigh, by their visits for profit as well as fame, to the Spanish Settlements of America in 1580—88, led the way, and were followed by Raymond and Lancaster in 1591, who laid the foundation of that anomalous co-partnership of commercial monarchs, the East India Company. Annual Fleets now returned from the East, laden with curiosities of both the Animal and Vegetable kingdoms. Though the views of men were not yet liberal enough to prompt them to voyages of discovery, with an unmixed desire of extending the field of Science, or an enlarged wish of benefit to mankind, yet new Plants in common with other hitherto strange natural products attracted attention, and being imported as novelties, became by degrees to be desired, and sought for as necessaries and luxuries. The Potatoe, Tobacco, and Tea need alone be instanced.

The following list of Authors, and of their works are the sources from which I have been chiefly enabled to extract information on the state of Gardening, during the period we are considering.

DIDYMUS MOUNTAIN.

1. The Gardener's Labyrinth, containing a discourse of the Gardener's life, in the yearly travails to be bestowed on his plot of earth for the use of a Garden; with instructions for the choice of seeds, apt times for sowing, setting, planting, and watering; and the vessels, and instruments serving to that use and purpose; wherein are set forth divers herbes, knottes, and mazes, cunningly handled for the beautifying of Gardens; also the physike of eche herbe, &c. Gathered out of the best approved writers of Gardening, Husbandrie, and Physike, &c. 1571, 4to. Black Letter.

2. The second part of the Gardener's Labyrinth; uttering suche skilful experiences and worthy secretes, about the parti-

cular sowing and removing of the moste Kitchen herbes; with the wittie ordering of other daintie herbes, delectable Floures, pleasant Fruites, and fine Rootes, as the like hath not heretofore been uttered of any; beside the Physicke benefits of each Herbe annexed, with the commoditie of Waters distilled out of them, right necessary to be knowen, 1577. 4to. Again, 1578. Again, in 1608, 4to. and in 1652, folio.

1576. A Perfite Plateforme of a Hoppe-Garden, and necessarie Instructions for the making and mayntenance thereof, &c. By REYNOLDE SCOT, London, 4to. Black Letter, with wood cuts. A previous edition bears the date of 1574, and a subsequent one that of 1578. Wood in his Athenæ Oxoniensis, says, that Mr. Scot, was the younger son of Sir John Scot, of Scots' Hall, near Smeeth in Kent. He was educated at Oxford, and was known for his knowledge of the works of obscure authors. He was very fond of Husbandry and Gardening, and his work is more original than his contemporaries usually produced.

1580. A Posie of Gillie Flowers. By Humphry Gifford. London. 4to. Of this work I know nothing but the name. It is probably only a collection of Poetry.

1586. Gardener's Labyrinthe. By H. Dethycke. 4to. Black Letter. Again in 1594. These are only editions of Didymus Mountain's work above mentioned. Mountain it appears was just dead, and Dethycke, who was his friend had promised him to edit the work. "Its instructions and rare secrets," we are told in the dedication are partly translated from the Greek and Latin writers of antiquity; and partly were afforded by living practitioners. The catalogue of " tender herbes and pleasant flowers," contains Marjorum, Savoury, Herb Fluellin, Bugloss, Blessed Thistle, Angelica, Valerian, Balme, Annis, Dill, Fennell, Organy, Mintes, Rue or Herb Grace, Sperage, Arache, Spinache, Beetes, Endive, Borage, Rochet, Taragon, Parsley, Sorrell, Strawberry, Lettuce, Artichoke, Marigold, Rose Campions. Flower Armoure, Flower Petilius, Columbines, Sweet Johns, Pinks, Heart's Ease, Pionie, Red Lilie, Herb Sticas, or Lavender-Gentle, Batchelor's Button, Gilliflowers, and Carnations.

1588. The Good Housewife's Hande-mayde. Anon. 8vo.

THOMAS HILL, Hyll or Hyle, appears to have been a hacknied compiler of books. It appears he resided in London and published numerous works on Dreams, Physiognomy, Mysteries, Astronomy, Arithmetic, an Almanac, &c. He died early in the seventeenth Century. He wrote also, The profitable Arte of Gardening; to which is added much necessarie matter, and a number of secrets, with the Physicke helps belonging to each hearbe, and that easily prepared. To this is annexed two proper treatises, the one entituled the marvailous government, propertie, and benefit of Bees, with the rare secretes of the Honnie and Waxe, And the other, the yerely conjectures mete for Husbandmen. To these is likewise added a Treatise of the Arte of Graffing and planting of Trees. Gathered by Thomas Hyll, citizen of London—London. 1563, 16mo. The same, London, 1568, 12mo. 1574 and 1579, 4to. Again, in 1586 without the author's name, again in 1593, All in Black Letter. Again in 1608, 4to. 1594, 16mo.

1591. Short Instructions for Gardening and Grafting, with diverse Plotts and Knotts for Gardeners. London. 4to. Anon.

LEONARD MASCHAL, was a gentleman residing at Plumstead, in Sussex.

1. On the Government of Cattle. 4to., with his Portrait, 1596.

2. A Book of the Art and manner how to graff and Plant all sortes of Trees, how to set Stones and sow Pepins, to make wild Trees to graffe on, as also remedies and medecines, with other new practices, by one of the Abbey of the St. Vincent, in France, with the addition of certain Dutch practices: set forth and Englished by L. M. London, 1572, 4to. and 12mo. 1578, 4to. 1580. Black Letter. 1580, 1582, 1590, 1592, 1652, 1656, all in 4to.

3. The Countryman's Jewel, in three books, 1680, 8vo.

SIR HUGH PLATT or Platte, Knt. is stated by Mr. Weston in his Catalogue of English Authors, to have been "the most ingenious husbandman of the age he lived in." From the same author, and from Sir Hugh's own works we learn, that he spent part of his time at Copt Hall, in Essex, then possessed by Sir Thomas Henneage, near which he had a country seat. In 1594, he lived at Bishop's Hall, in Middlesex, and had an estate near St. Albans. In the title page of his works he is stiled " of Lincoln's Inn, gentleman," and therefore, although he does not inform us of what profession he was, further than that it was widely differing from cultivating the earth, we are justified in concluding that he was in the law. He had a very extensive correspondence with the lovers of Gardening, &c. He probably lived in St. Martins Lane, where he had a garden. He was living in 1606. The following are his works.

1. Dyvers Soyles for manuring pasture and arable land, 1594, 4to.

2. The Jewel House of Art and Nature, containing divers rare and profitable inventions, together with sundry new experiments in the Art of Husbandry, Distillation and Moulding. Faithfully and familiarly set down according to the author's own experience.' 4to. 1594. Again in 1653, edited by Dr. Beati.

3. The Paradise of Flora, 1600.

4. The Garden of Eden, or an accurate description of all Flowers and Fruits now growing in England, with particular rules how to advance their nature and growth, as well in seeds and hearbes, as the secret ordering of Trees and Plants. small 8vo. 1660, 5th Edit.—A posthumous publication.

5. The second part of the Garden of Eden, &c. Never before printed, 1660.

" The Garden of Eden," is the same as " the Paradise of Flora," with the mere alteration of the title, by a Mr. Charles Bellingham, a kinsman of Sir Hugh's. The second part of the " Garden of Eden," is entirely an original composition of Bellingham's.

1592. A short Instruction very profitable and necessary, for all those that delight in Gardening, to know the time and season when it is good to sow and replant all manner of seeds. Whereunto is annexed, divers plots both for planting and graffing for the better ease of the Gardener. Translated from the French. London, Black Letter 4to, with wood cuts.

CONRAD HERESBACH was born in 1508. He became counseller to the Duke of Cleve, and died in 1570. He wrote several theological works as well as " Rei Rusticœ libri quatuor," which was published in 1570, and "Legum rusticarum et operarum per singulos menses digesta," in 1595. He would not command our attention in this work if his "Rei Rusticœ," had not been translated by Barnaby Googe. Googe was a Poet, born in Lincolnshire, educated at Christ's College, Cambridge, studied at Staples Inn, London, and through the influence of his relative Sir William Cecil, became Gentlemen pensioner to the Queen. In 1563, appeared his "Eglogs, Epitaphs, and Sonnets," which is a very rare book. In 1565, he translated and published "the Zodiake of Life," from the Italian, by Palingenius. His translation of Heresbach was printed in 1578, though the preface is dated 1557, it is entitled "Foure Bookes of Husbandrie, containing the whole art and trade of Husbandrie, Gardening, Graffeing and Planting with the antiquitie and commendation thereof." It was reprinted in 1614, by Gervase Markham, with additions.

The work is in dialogue—The first book relates to husbandry or farming, and gives a lively sketch of the buildings, practice, and manners of the country gentlemen of the age; and that it applied to those of this country appears evident from the few interpolations which may be detected as inserted by Googe. Book the second, is a dialogue between Thrasybulus and Marius, of Gardens, Orchards and Woods, opening with a declaration of the antiquity of Horticulture—proceeds with a very just description of the best situation of a Garden, the necessity for a good supply of Water, and the time for applying it, of enclosing a Garden by Walls, &c. but with especial directions how to form a quickset hedge.—He then insists upon always digging the ground some months before inserting the crops, "that which you mean to sow in the end of Summer, may be digged in the spring, &c"—" the beds are to be made 12 feet long, and 6 broad, that they may be easier weeded."—Of dungs he prefers that of the Ass. He then gives a list, of garden herbs with their times of sowing. Coleworts, Raddish, (one sort) Rape, Fennel, Annise, Garden Poppy, and Turnip, Beets, (red and white) Lettuce, Sorrel, Mustard, Coriander, Horse Radish, Mallows, Bugloss, Dill, Garden Cress, Saffron; Sage, Mint, Prinperuel, Nigella, Orace, Cucumbers, Gourds, Hyssop, Spinach, Basil, Purslane, Savory, Chervill, Rue, Marjorum, Onions, (2 sorts) Garlick, Hops, Lupines, Peas, Leeks, (2 sorts) Pennyroyal, Rocket, Naven (Cole?) Parsley, Smallage, Endive, Carrots, Parsnips, Asparagus. The observations about the age of various seeds, and the time which elapses before the seedlings appear, after the seed is sown, are just and demonstrate an attention to facts not usual to the age. Then follow directions about the most favourable age of the moon, during which to sow. The best as all suppose is " the moon being aloft and not set"—Of Asparagus he gives directions to cultivate judicious and nearly as followed at present, with directions to cook them, " as my friend William Pratt very skillful in these matters telleth me." " If you breake to powder the horne of a Ram and sowe it watrying it well, it is thought it will come to be good Sperage,' (Asparagus.)—The absurdities about Rue are curious " being stolen it prospereth the better; it is sowed with cursing as Cummin, &c. and cannot abide the presence of an unclean woman."—Lettuces 3 sorts—the modes of blanching are curious—the absurdity of imparting various tarts to it and other herbs, is characteristick of the age.—Endive was bleached in various ways. " That by " tieing the leaves together and covering them with some little earthen vessel" seems to have anticipated our mode of blanching Sea Kale, &c. Coleworts and Cabbages 6—Strawberries he only mentions as brought from the woods and grown in the Gardens—Raspberries, Liquorice, Gooseberries (one sort) little attended to, Gourds, Pompions and Cucumbers, he appears well aware of, but there is much confusion of names, it is evident that his Melons were only some variety of Pompions. The Artichoke he says, is so called from the French Artichault, which is a corruption of Alticocalum compounded of the Arabick article, Al, and Cocalos, a Pine apple. Saffron was grown in large breadths—Rosemary was very much cultivated in the pleasure Garden, being "sette by women for their pleasure, to grow in sundry proportions as in the fashion of a Cart, a Peacock or such like things as they fancie".

The edifices Heresbach alludes to when he mentions " hotte houses," were nothing like our present structures fitted up with glass. They were sheds to which occasional warmth was imparted by Stoves, &c.

Basil "used to bee set in the middest of knottes and in windowes, for the excellent savour that it hath"—the same remark is made of Marjoram. Having thus gone through the inhabitants of the Kitchen Garden, he commences treating of such plants as are grown for pleasure, with Lavender, Flowergentle, otherwise Amaranthus, Lavender Cotton, Gillyflowers three sorts. Of Roses he mentions several sorts; his directions for making them grow double, varying the colour &c. are a tissue of errors—That the soil, or manure in which flowers are grown has influence on the colour of Plants is certain. A very remarkable fact is afforded me by a friend, that he has repeatedly bloomed the common Primrose of a red colour by growing it in soot,—Lillies—Violets several sorts.—He then proceeds to the Physic Garden. Hellebore or Bear's-foot—Angelica—Elecampane (Helecompany) Wormwood, and Savine, form the whole list—He then proceeds to direct how vermin may be destroyed—Of planting an Orchard he treats slightly yet judiciously—the ground to be dug extensively round the place where each tree is to be placed, &c.—Upon the association of plants he also insists. "Because there is a natural friendship and love between certain trees, you must set them the nearer together, as the Vine and the Olive, the Pomegranate and the Myrtle"—some have a natural hatred " as the Vine with the Filbert and the Bay" &c. The Advocate of Vegetable sensation will account for these phenomena on principles, which are assigned for the congregation, and association of Zoophytes; the Chemist will point out the exhalation of certain gasses, the secretion of certain constituents and aromas which are mutually salutary, &c. The fact is incontestable that Plants do affect certain associations. The Corn Flower (Cyanus) is found only in fields where grain is grown, &c.—Of grafting he is pleased to give what is now considered a tissue of fables—as that the Medlar may be grafted upon the Pine—the Pomegranate upon the Ash—the Damson on the Apple—the Cherry upon the Fir, &c. The directions for grafting and inoculating are slight but for the most part correct.

He then proceeds to the nursery, in which there are very few directions given, but among them the very erroneous one of planting deep.

Heresbach then proceeds to dwell upon the cultivation of the Vine, which he does in a manner so full and satisfactory as would not discredit a writer of the present day.—Then of the Olive, and then of the Apple, of which there were many, but the "cheefe in price" were the Pippin, the Romet, the Pomeroyal, and the Marligold.—On its cultivation he is very meagre—on the keeping of the Fruit he is more full and correct.—The Pear he says, he has himself grafted with success when in bloom.—They had evidently no keeping varieties—though of Apples he had seen some that had been preserved three years.—Quinces, Medlars 2.—Service—Pomegranate—Orange and Lemon—showing how to shelter them with Straw, &c. in winter.—Mulberry—Cornel—Ziziphus.—Pistachio Nuts—Bay—Almonds, bitter and sweet—Walnut—Hasel and Filbert—Chesnut—Cherry—Plumbs seven kinds "whereof the Damson is the principal," which demonstrates that of this fruit, they were very deficient.—Peach, of this they must have had but poor varieties, since he says, the Apricot was much preferred, being "used as a great dainty among noblemen." Some short, general, and for the most part judicious observations on the shelter, pruning, &c. of Trees and the cultivation of Timber conclude the book.—Book the third is "Of feeding, breeding, and curing Cattle"—the fourth "Of Poultry, Fowl, Fish and Bees"—Upon the whole, the work is certainly, as he makes one of the characters say in the dialogue, on a subject "not thoroughly entreated of by others"—and therefore by implication more perfectly by himself—It is a book repleat with just observations, and though short and imperfect still superior to any work that had preceded it, and in fact is superior in the details of cultivation to Parkinson's Paradisus, that appeared more than half a Century subsequently. Too much however is taken from Greek and Latin Authors, rather than from contemporary practitioners. Theophrastus, Cato, Columella, Pliny, &c. are continually quoted as authorities, and, in unison with them, absurd practices, and superstitions the most gross, are given with all the earnestness of truth.

JOHN GERARDE, was born at Nantwich in Cheshire, 1545; was educated a Surgeon, and practised in London, where he attained considerable eminence in his profession. He was favoured by the College of Physicians, highly extolled by Lobel, by Drs. Bulleyn and Browne, and chosen master of the company of Surgeons. He was patronized by the great Lord Burleigh, who was a great admirer of Plants, having a better collection at the time than any nobleman in the kingdom. Gerarde was superintendant of his Lordship's Garden, for twenty years He lived in Holborn, where he had a Physic Garden of his own, probably exceeding, in the number and varieties of its products, any then in England. He seems to have travelled when young, up the Baltic. His Garden contained nearly eleven hundred sorts of Plants, exotic and indigenous. In his Catalogue he describes 1033 species. This Catalogue was his first publication, and appeared in 1506; ca-

titled, " Catalogus Arborum, Fruticum, ac Plantarum, &c. in horto Johannis Gerardi," 4to. Another edition was published in 1599. In 1597, was published his " Herbal, or General History of Plants," fol. and another edition seems to have appeared in 1599. This was founded on the works of Dodoëns, though even the originality of translation is denied him, and given to Dr. Priest and Lobel. Gerarde, divides the work into three books,—1st. Grasses, Grain, Rushes, Reeds, Flags, and bulbous rooted Plants.—2nd. Herbs used for food, medicine, or ornament. 3rd. Trees, Shrubs, Fruit bearing Plants, Rosins, Gums, Roses, Heaths, Mosses, Mushrooms, and sea Plants.— The whole divided into 800 chapters. In each chapter the several species are described, then follow the habitat, time of flowering, names and qualities. From various causes, but especially from being in English, and obtaining so learned an editor, in 1636, as Johnson, it remained the standard Botannical work, for more than a Century. Gerarde, was certainly as good a practical Botanist as the age afforded. Gerarde died in 1607. Of his "Catalogue" scarcely a copy remains, except one in the British Museum, and another in the Bodleian Library.

The portraits of Gerarde, mentioned by Grainger, are, John Gerarde; engraved by William Rogers, for the first edition of his " Herbal."

John Gerarde ; engraved by Payne, for Johnson's edition of the same work.

WILLIAM LAWSON, an author who professed to write entirely from experience, published the following works,

1. A new Orchard and Garden ; or the best way for planting, graffing, and to make any ground good for a rich Orchard : particularly in the North, and generally for the

whole commonwealth; with the country Housewife's Garden, for herbs of common use; their Virtues, Seasons, Profits, Ornaments: variety of knotts, models for Trees, and plots for the best ordering of grounds and walks. As also the husbandry of Bees, with their several uses and annoyances: all being the experience of forty and eight years labour, and now the third time, corrected and much enlarged. Whereunto is newly added the art of propagating Plants, with the true ordering of all manner of Fruits, in their gathering, carrying home, and preservation.—Followed by a most profitable new treatise from approved experience of the Art of propagating plants. By Simon Harwood—London 4to. 1597—1615—18—23—26—48—49. Again much enlarged in 1665 and 76. It was printed along with Markham's Way to get Wealth, 1648 and 1660.

2. Tractatus de Agricultura—London 4to. 1656 and 1657.

1599. Gardener's Kitchen Garden. This Work is mentioned in Platt's Garden of Eden.

A new book of Good Husbandry. By G. CHURCHY, of Lyons Inn. A translation of Dubravius on Fish, &c. is added.

1600. In this year was published, Approved experiments touching Fish and Fruit to be regarded by the lovers of Angling. By JOHN TAVERNER. 4to.*

1604. The Fruiterer's Secrets. 4to. Black Letter. Without the author's name. It contains some curious directions for preserving Fruits, &c.†

* Hawkin's Life of Isaac Walton. † London's Encyclopædia of Gardening. p. 1099. Edit. 5th.

1608. Flora's Paradise beautified. Anonymous.

1609. A Treatise on Mulberries, by W. S.

1612. An old thrift newly revived. Of planting and preserving of Timber and Fuel, by R. C. In four parts, 4to.

1613. New directions of experience authorized by the King's most excellent Majesty, as may appear, for the planting of Timber and Fire wood, &c. And how wood may be raised from hedges, as may plentifully maintain the kingdom for all purposes without loss of ground: so as within thirty years all spring woods may be converted to tillage and pasture. By ARTHUR STANDISH, London, 4to. Again in 1614. Standish, two years previously, had written, "The Commons Complaint of the waste of Wood, and dearth of victuals, &c." and this appears as an answer to it.

1615. Draughts for Gardeners, Glaziers, and Plaisterers. By WALTER GIDDE or Gedde, London.

1622. In "a Treatise on the Art of making silk," by JOHN BONFEIL, 4to. there is a chapter containing, "Instructions how to plant and dress Vines, and to make Wine, and how to dry Raisins, Lemons, Pomegranates, Almonds, and many other Fruits," pp. 36—88.

GERVASE (Gervas, or Jarvise) MARKHAM, was born at Gotham in Nottinghamshire, the younger and portionless son of Robert Markham Esq. about the middle of the 16th Century, as we are assured by the circumstance of his being when in the prime of life, champion and gallant of the Countess of Shrewsbury, in 1591, and in whose cause he was dangerously wounded in a duel by Sir John Holles.* He served as a Captain in the Royal Army during the Civil Wars. The period of his death is uncertain. He was a very voluminous writer, and appears to have been the first Englishman who, depending upon the produce of his Pen for subsistence, became a hackney author.† His works which deserve notice here are contained in the following list, besides which he wrote many on horsemanship, the diseases of cattle, &c.

1. The English Husbandman. 2 parts, London, 1613, 4to. The same enlarged, 1635.

2. Maison Rustique, or the country Farmer, translated from the French; and the Husbandrie of France, Italie, and Spaine, reconciled and made to agree with ours here in England, London 1616, folio.

3. Farewell to Husbandry; or the enrichment of all sorts of barren grounds. London. 1620—21—25—31—49. all in 4:o.

4. Enrichment of the Weold of Kent; or a direction to the husbandman, for the true ordering, manuring, and enriching of all the grounds within the Weolds of Kent and Sussex; and may generally servé for all the grounds in England of that nature. London. 1631—1649, 1675—4to.

5. The Country Housewife's Garden. 1623—1648. 4to.

6. The Way to get Wealth, in six parts. 1648—Editions in 1660, and 64. are said in the Title pages to be the tenth and eleventh.

There are two portraits of him extant.

* Collins's Historical collections of the families of Cavendish, Holles, &c.
† Harte's Essays on Husbandry, v. ii. p. 32.

1. Mr. Gervase Markham. A small oval, in the title of his "Perfect Horseman." 8vo.

2. Mr. Gervase Markham. Enlarged from the above. B. Reading. Sc. 8vo. T. Rodd. exc.

1633. In this year, Dr. Thomas Johnson, edited a new edition of Gerarde's Herbal, Folio, of which edition Haller, says, "Dignum opus, et totius rei herbariæ eo ævo notæ, compendium."

Sir HENRY WOTTON, was born at Bocton Hall, Kent, in 1568.—From a Tutor at home he was sent early to Winchester School. At a fit age he became a Commoner of New College, Oxford, where he continued until his eighteenth year, and was then transplanted to Queen's College, and the same year wrote his Tragedy of *Tancred*. At twenty he proceeded. M. A—at which time he gained much distinction for his three Latin Lectures *de Oculo*. At the age of twenty four he commenced his travels, which he continued nearly nine years, in France, Germany, and Italy.—He returned to England when about thirty— was in exile as a partizan of the Earl of Essex—returned in the reign of James the I. and was three times Ambassador at the Court of Venice,—and several times to various of the German Princes. In 1624 he was appointed Provost of Eton College, of which office he died in the possession, December, 1639.—

He chiefly deserves notice here on account of his casual remarks upon Gardening, in his Essay on the Elements of Architecture. He is most unaccountably superficial and slighting in his animadversions upon a proper scite for building a house upon—for after giving the warning opinions of several predecessors he adds " But such Notes as these wheresoever we find them in grave or slight authors, are to my conceit rather wishes than precepts, and in that quality I will pass them over. Yet I must withal say that in the seating of ourselves (which is a kind of marriage to a place) builders should be as circumspect as wooers, lest when all is done, that doom befal us, which our master (Vitruvius) doth lay upon Myteline " a Town in truth, saith he, finely built, but foolishly planted."*

Of the style to be admired in Gardening he is as concise; the little he says however is just, and evinces that correct taste which dictates, that though the grounds at large, by degrees as we proceed from the mansion, should become irregular and imitations of picturesque nature, yet in the immediate neighbourhood of the house, Art should be more manifest. "I must note a certain contrariety between building and gardening, for as fabricks should be regular, gardens should be irregular, or at least cast into a very wild regularity. To exemplify my conceit, I have seen a Garden, for the manner perchance incomparable, into which the first access was a high walk like a Terrace, from whence might be taken a general view of the whole Plot below, but rather in delightful confusion, than with any plain distinction of the species. From this the beholder descending many steps was afterwards conveyed again by several mountings and valings, to various entertainments of his scent and sight, which I shall not need to describe for that were poetical, let me only note this, that every one of these diversities, was as if he had been magically transported into a new garden. But though other countrys have more benefit of Sun than we, and thereby more properly tied to contemplate this delight, yet have I seen in our own, a delicate and diligent curiosity, surely without parellel among foreign nations, namely, in the Garden of Sir Henry Fenshaw, at his seat in Ware Park, where I well remember, he did so precisely examine the tinctures and seasons of his flowers, that in their

* Reliquiæ Wottonianæ, edited by Isaac Walton. 3rd Edit. p. 9.

settings, the inwardest of which that were to come up at the same time, should be always a little darker than the outmost, and to serve them for a kind of gentle shadow, like a piece, not of Nature, but of Art. Of figured fountains I will describe a matchless pattern done by the hand of Michael Angelo de Buonaroti, in the figure of a sturdy woman washing and winding of linen clothes, in which act, she wrings out the water that made the fountain; which was a graceful and natural conceit—the Artificer, implying this rule; that all designs of this kind should be proper."*

JOHN PARKINSON, was born in 1567. according to the date on his portrait prefixed to his " Paradisus."—He, was by profession an Apothecary, and so eminent as to act in that capacity to James the I.—He was also a distinguished Horticulturist and Botanist, his " Theatre of Plants" obtaining for him, from Charles the I. the title of " Botanicus Regius Primarius."—He spent nearly forty years in travelling. (Paradisus p. 63) He was proprietor of a garden well stocked with scarce plants. The time of his death is not ascertained, but it occured between 1640, and 1656. His first publication was " Paradisi in sole Paradisus terrestris, or a garden of all sorts of pleasant flowers which our English ayre will permitt to be noursed up, with a kitchen garden of all manner of herbes, rootes, and fruites for meate or sause, used with us, and an orchard of all sorte of fruit bearing trees and shrubbes fit for our land; together with the right orderinge, planting, and preserving of them, and their uses and vertues. 1629." folio, with an engraved title page representing the garden of Eden, a portrait of the author, and 109 wood cuts of fruits and flowers. The dedication to the Queen. A second edition appeared corrected and enlarged, after his death, in 1656. In 1640 appeared his " Theatrum Botannicum or Theatre of Plants, or an Herbal of large extent, &c."—The most extensive Botannical work then extant.

* Reliquiæ Wottonianæ. p. 64—5.

His " Paradisus," we learn from the dedication, was written long before it was published.—" Some through an evil disposition" charged him as having obtained the work from some other person—a charge we may believe to be without foundation, as we have no mention of it but in his own preface.

In the first Chapter he considers, " The situation of a Garden of pleasure, (i. e. a Flower Garden,) with the nature of soyles, and how to mend the defects, &c." Sheltered from the North; and not on the East, or on the West side of the house, not on moorish ground, or near any manufactory, that may taint the air with smoke, " especially of Sea Coals which of all others is the worst, as our City of London can give proof sufficient, wherein neither herb nor tree will long prosper, nor hath done ever since the use of Sea Coals began to be frequent therein."—Black mould the best soil, stiff clay the worst.—In the directions for manuring and mixing soils, he is concise and judicious.—Chap. 2. " The frame or forme of a Garden of delight or pleasure."—The plans he gives are the very quintessence of regularity and formality.—One remark is judicious, and is confirmed by modern approbation," the fairer and larger your allies and walks be, the more grace your Garden shall have"—his plans however are in strange opposition to this rule for to have as many as are represented in them, they must be small and mean.—Chap. 3. Of the Herbes, &c, of which the borders of the beds may be formed.—Germander used before his time to be used for this purpose, as Thrift was chiefly then, Germander was still more in use, because " the cuttings are much used as a strawing herbe for houses." —Hyssop, Marjory, Savory, and Thyme, were employed for the purpose, but Lavender Cotton was in greater request " of late daies" being rare, novel, and for the most part but in the gardens of great persons"—Juniper and Yew were also used, but he recommends above all the Box, though it was " only received into the Gardens of the curious."—Of dead materials for edgings, sheet lead, oak boards, shank bones of sheep, tiles, round whitish pebbles, are severally admired, but especially the last " for durability, beauty of the sight, handsomeness in the work, and ease in the working and charge,"—but Jaw Bones " used in the Low Countries, are too gross and base,"—For the Hedge; Privet, Sweet Briar, White Thorn, and Roses, alone or mingled, were employed. Lavender, Rosemary, Sage, Southernwood, Lavender Cotton, the Cornell Tree, and and Pyracantha were used by some persons.—Chap. 4. Of the nature and names of divers out-landish flowers, &c. In which he mentions of Daffodils " almost an hundred sorts," including our Narcissus, Jonquil, &c. of Fritillaria, "half a score,"—Hyacinths above 50—of the Crocus 20, Spring and Autumn flowering, &c. Meadow Saffron many varieties. Lillies 20, including Crown Imperials, and Martagons. Of Tulips " which are the pride of delight almost infinite," he had 160 in his own possession, yet he doubted not there were ten times as many. So generally was this flower admired, that he says scarce any Lady of worth but was a delighter in them. Anemonies (Lobel, gives a list of 38 varieties,) Bear's Ears or French Cowslips, Flower-de-luces, Hepaticas, Cyclamen, Leucoium, Musk Grape flower, Star flowers, Spiderwort, Wolf's Bane, Christmas flower, Bell flower, Yellow Lark spur, Flower-gentle, Flower of the Sun, Marvel of Peru, Double Marsh, and French Marigold, double Red Ranunculus, Jasmines, double Honeysuckles, Ladies Bower, Roses, Bay Cherry, Oleander, Syringas, Pyracantha, Lacerustinus, and Mezereon, conclude his list of flowers, &c. " to be planted in Gardens of pleasure for delight."—Chap. 5. Of such flowers as being cultivated in this country for a great length of period were considered as English flowers.' These consists of Primroses and Cowslips, yellow and green, both double and single—Single Rose Campions, white, red, and blush—double red Rose Campion—Nonsuch white, blush orange, and double orange—Batchelor's Buttons, white and red—Wallflowers double and single—Stock

Gilliflowers—the single " in every woman's Garden"—the double possesed by few.—Queen or Winter Gilliflowers—Violets—Snapdragon—Columbines many varieties single and double—" Larkes *heeles*, or spurres, or toes"—many single and double, " the double rare"— Pansies— Double Poppies—Double Daisies, many varieties—Double and French Marigolds.—Carnations and Gillyflowers many, they being " the queen of delights and of flowers"—Pinks—Sweet Williams—Sweet Johns many—Pæonies, single and double—Hollihocks many, single and double—Roses many " the white, the red and the damaske are the most ancient standards in England"—Chap. 6. The order and manner to plant and replant out-landish flowers, &c.—of which " our English Gardeners are all or the most part of them utterly ignorant"—" all bulbous roots should be planted in July, August or September; and not in the Spring"—a form of practice which shews Parkinson to have been as ignorant of this branch of Floriculture as needs be — His directions for planting such flowers as bloom nearly at the same time together are judicious and demonstrations of correct taste, as, are his arrangements in knots, the creeping flowers near the edge, and the highest in the middle. His directions about planting bulbs deep are egregiously wrong, and indeed the only reason he assigns, is because they are thence protected from hard frosts, which they could only be injured by if planted as he directs in Autumn. His directions about arranging fibrous roots when planting might be attended to with advantage by modern Horticulturists. The Sun-flower, &c. he says required to be raised early in a hot-bed, or they never perfected their seed but in very hot Summers—Either these plants have changed their habit, or our climate is much ameliorated.— His observation upon giving little water to bulbs, and not employing any Water that is just drawn from a well or pump, are confirmed as true by modern practice. Chap. 7. The months of the year in which the scarcer flowers bloom—not differing from the periods now.—Chap. 8. Informs us " that because Carnations and Gillyflowers be the chiefest flowers of account in all our English Gardens" he treats more largely here of the "true manner and order to increase and preserve them."—Propagating them by layers he says is "of later invention"—To protect the Carnations from Earwigs some persons placed them in cups with a rim full of Water round—a totally inefficient remedy, as these vermin are gifted with wings.—The whole chapter contains as judicious directions for the culture of this flower as any that modern times have produced—the only point on which he does not afford instruction being the nature of the Soil best suited to them. Modern ingenuity has improved the arrangement, and conveniences of shelter for them—but Parkinson's mode of culture is little altered to this day.—His statement that Snow is injurious to them is erroneous.—Chap. 9. "That there is not any art whereby any flower may be made to grow double, that was naturally single, nor of any other scent or colour than it first had by nature; nor that the sowing or planting of herbes one deeper than other, will cause them to be in flower one after another, every moneth in the yeare." Against these opinions he argues acutely and philosophically much above his age, though he does "thinke some constellations, and peradventure changes of the moone, &c. were appointed by the God of nature, as conducing and helping to the making of those flowers double, that nature had so produced."

Then commences his description of individual species—Crown Imperial & Frittilaries, thirteen varieties. Persian Lily—Martagon 18—Lilies 8—Tulips various, early and late flowering, 137. and refers to many others which he does not describe. He talks of sowing a peck of Tulip seed, an evidence how largely they were cultivated.—Of the cultivation of this flower he is tolerably copious and correct, addressing his remarks here as upon other occasions to "Gentlewomen for their delights," floriculture then, as now, finding its best patrons among the fair sex. Narcissus, and Daffodils 95—Bulbous rooted Violet 5—Hyacinths 50—Star of Bethlehem 11—Moly 16—Asphodels 8—Spiderwort 5—Meadow Saffron 19—Crocus 31—Irises 73—Gladiolus 6—Orchises 6, and says there were many more. Dog's Tooth Violet 3—Cyclomens 10.—Of Anemones 67 are specified, but there were innumerable others to distinguish which "would gravell the best experienced this day in Europe." Yet the art of raising varieties from seed was not familiarly known here in his time, he says, but practised extensively in the Low Countries, some of their varieties bearing such a high price that no Englishman would buy them.—His directions for cultivation are slight but in conformity with modern practice—Aconites 4—Ranunculuses 23—Marsh Marigold—Hepaticas 10—Cranes Bill 9—Sanicle 3—Navelwort 4—Moonwort—Auriculas 22, and notes that there are many others. Primroses and Cowslips 21—Lungwort 3—Borage 3—Bugloss 3—Lychnis 11—Wallflowers 7—Stock Gillyflowers 10—Honesty, or Satin flower 2—Linaria 6—Antirrhinum 4—Willow flower--Columbines 5—Thalictrum 2—Hollow Root 3. Lark Spurs 6, and some varieties—Balsam Apple—Nasturtium, it was not then a kitchen herb—Violets 5 including Pansies—Barrenwort—Poppies 4, and some others not specified.—Nigella 3—Pellitory 2—Featherfew—Chamomile 2—Adonis—Oxe Eye, 3—Sun flowers—Marigolds 2—Star wort 2—Golden Mouse ear.—Scorzonera 2—Goat's Beard 2—French Marigold 8. Carnations and Gilliflowers 52, and some varieties besides. Pinks, 20—Sweet Johns and Williams 8—Daisy 8—Scabious 3, Blue Bottles 3—Spanish Knapweed—Bastard Saffron—Acanthus 2—Thistles 6—Fraxinella 4—Lupines 4—Everlasting Sweet Peas &c. 4—Medica 5—Caterpillars 2—Red Satin Flower—Peony 6—Black Hellebore 2—White Hellebore 2—Ladies Slipper 3—Lily of the Valley 2—Gentian 6—Rose Plantain—Campanulas 9—Convolvolus 5—Stramonium 4—Tabacco 2—Marvel of Peru 6—Hollihocks 8—Amaranthus 4 Goldilocks 3—Love Everlasting 2—India Reed—Mandrakes.—Love Apples 3—Foxglove 7—Mullein 10—Valerian 3—Cuckoo

Flowers 2—Candy Tuft 3—Periwinkle 3—Clematis 6—Passion Flower, then called Moracoc or Virginia Creeper—Spurge Olive 3—Laurustinus—Oleander—Portugal Laurel—Double blossomed Cherry—Double blossomed Apple—Double blossomed Peach—Honey-suckles 8—Jasmine 3—Lilacs 5—Gelder Rose—Roses 24, and others not specified. Cistus 7—Rosemary 4—Myrtle 3—Pomegranate 3—Winter Cherry—India Fig—Arbor Vitœ—Judas Tree—Laburnum Tree—Trefoil 2—Bastard Senna 3—Spanish Broom—Virginian Silk—Privet—Variegated Sage—Marjoram 3—Lavender 3—Lavender Cotton—Basil 3—Thyme 4—Hyssop 5—Variegated Grass 3.

At page 461 commences "The Ordering of the Kitchen Garden"—In the first Chap. " on the situation" there is little else in addition to that given in the chapter on a similar subject for the Pleasure Garden, and of that little the chief part is erroneus.—Chap. 2. On the form of the Garden, contains nothing relating to that subject, but serves to demonstrate that the practice of this department, was not so much attended to, by stating that Radishes, Lettuces, Onions, Parsnips and Carrots may be sown promiscuously together, and drawn from each other as wanted, and that Cabbages were usually planted round the beds containing other crops.—Chap. 3. is chiefly on the growing of Seeds, of which he says "our chiefest and greatest Gardeners" provided themselves every year of many kinds, but not all from their own ground. English seed of the following kinds was esteemed more than any that was imported, viz. Radish, Lettuce, Carrots, Parsnips, Turnips, Cabbages, and Leeks, yet to raise Cabbage seed was very difficult in our climate, the stocks being spoiled by the severe winters, to obviate which " they bring them into the house, and there wrap them either in cloths, or other things to defend them from the cold, and hang them up in a dry place until the beginning of the March following, &c."—But little Onion seed was grown by

Gardeners here, and that "for their own, or their private friends spending."—Chap. 4. "How to order Artichokes, Melons, Cucumbers, and Pompions" but it is chiefly occupied with the second—It demonstrates the ignorance which existed as to forcing; for though he directs the seed to be sown in a hot bed, it was not to be done until April, and the plants were to be moved out into very rich soil without bottom heat, and to "cover them with straw, (some do use great hollow glasses like unto bell heads) or some such other things to defend them from cold evenings or days, and the heat of the sun while they are young and new planted"—The Melon he says was eaten with Pepper, Salt and Wine.—Chap. 5. " The ordering of divers sorts of herbes, &c." enumerates Rosemary, Thyme, Savoury, (Winter and Summer) Mints 3, Clary, Nep, Costmary, Pot Marjoram, Pennyroyal, Allisander, Parsley. Fennel, Borage, (red, white, green and yellow) Bugloss, Marigolds, Langedebeefe?—Orach, Beets, Blites, Bloodwort, Patience, French Mallows, Olives and Garlic.—Chap. 6. Of Sallet Herbs. Commences with Asparagus " a principal and delectable Sallet herbe" which was boiled and eaten with Butter and Vinegar—Of its cultivation he is cursory and nothing near so correct as Cato in his " De Re Rustica"—Lettuces, (eleven sorts) Cabbage and " open Lettuces" that were to be tied together that the inner leaves may become whitish."—Lamb's Lettuce, Purslane, Spinach " a Sallet that hath little or no taste, and therefore Cooks know how to make many a good dish of meat with it, by putting Sugar and Spice thereto," Cabbages and Coleworts 11, almost confined to the poorer sort of people, yet some might be dressed so as " to delight a curious palate." The mid-ribs of the leaves were boiled and eaten cold with vinegar and oil. Cauliflowers " are to be had in this country but very seldom, for that it is hard to meet with good seed." Endive plain, and curled. His mode of bleaching in sand, is the best that can be practised. Succory, Red Beet, " seed obtained from abroad," Sorrel. Chervill, Sweet Chervil, or Cis, Ram-

pion—Cress—Rocket—Tarragon—Mustard—Horse Radish—
"the root thereof ground like mustard," and eaten generally
with fish. Tansey—Burnet—Skirrets—Clove—Gillyflowers,
mixed with Sugar and Vinegar "make a sallet now-a-days in
the highest esteem with Gentles and Ladies of the greatest
note."—Goat's Beard. Chap. 7. Of divers Physical herbs.
Angelica " so good a herb that there is no part thereof but is
of much use"— Rue—Dragons—Valerian—Asarabacca—Masterwort—Balm—Chamomile—Featherfew—Costmary—Maudlin—Cassidonie—Smallage—Blessed Thistle—Winter Cherry,
Celandine—Tobacco—Spurge—Bear'sfoot—Soloman's Seal—
Liquorice. At page 474, he commences a more distinct account
of Herbs &c. accompanied by cuts. Of those not mentioned
before are Sage, large and small leaved; Rhubarb (Rhea raponticum) which was introduced by Parkinson, being sent to him
"from beyond Sea" by "Mr. Dr. Matth. Lister," Dill—
Parsnips 2—Carrots 4—Turnips 5—Radishes 4—Onions 5—
Leeks 5—Scallions—Garlic—Caraway—Spanish Potatoes—
Virginia Potatoes, our common Canada Potatoes (Jerusalem
Artichoke) Artichokes 8—but of these "our English red Artichoke is in our country the most delicate meat of any of the
other, therefore divers thinking it to be a several kind, have
sent them into Italy, France, and the Low Countries" where
they always degenerated in two years. The Chardon "we
cannot find the true manner of dressing, that our country may
take a delight therein,"—Beans 2, much grown; Kidney
Beans "almost infinite sorts and colours" "more oftentimes at
rich men's tables than at the poore." Pease 9—Cucumbers 6
—Melons 3. The best seed from Spain, formerly "only eaten
by great personages," " but now divers others that have skill
and convenience of ground for them, do plant them and make
them more common". Pompions and Gourds; Strawberries
were evidently of inferior sorts, and not properly cultivated;
he mentions 7 kinds—

At page 535 commences "The ordering of the Orchard," Chap. 1. treats of the situation and soil of the Orchard concisely, but judiciously. His reprobation of the practice of digging and manuring a hole merely, where each Tree is to be placed, instead of trenching and ameliorating the whole scite, might be repeated with justice to many planters of the present day. Chap. 2. Of the form of an Orchard, contains this judicious direction, that the tallest standards, as Pears, Cherries, should be placed to the north, and so gradually those of the smaller altitude, that the most shelter may be afforded, and the least sun prevented to them. Quinces were grown against the North and West Walls. Chap. 3. Of Grafting, is generally correct and in accordance with our present practice. He especially insists upon budding, in preference to grafting for all Stone fruit: That the White Thorn is the best stock for the Medlar to be grafted upon; a fact which Botany justifies, Smith having demonstrated them to be of the same Genus.—Upon raising varieties from seed, he observes, that instead of waiting twelve or more years, to ascertain if they are worth preserving, the fact may be ascertained in a fourth the time by grafting from them, a judicious practice which has been lately brought forward to the Horticultural World, and the additional interest of novelty claimed for it. Chap. 4. Is directions for the various modes of grafting. Of budding he says, " though sufficiently known in many places of this land, yet as I understand, good Gardeners in the North parts, and likewise in some other places, can scarce tell what it meaneth." Chap. 5. Is of propagating Roses by budding and by seed. Chap. 6. Is some general directions about grafting and moving trees. Chap. 7. Of pruning is very superficial and general. Chap. 8. Of the enemies and diseases of Fruit, he is in general correct, often judicious. He recommends Vinegar to be applied to the canker of Trees, a practice Chemistry supports, since Vauquelin has demonstrated the disease arises from the alkalescent state of the Sap. —His plan of preventing Ants ascending Trees by tarring the stems, and of preventing the attacks of Hares and Rabbits by smearing the trunks with a mixture of Cow dung, and Urine, are practices still in use. Chap. 9. Is of the transplanting of Evergreens. Chap. 10. Is of the ordering of Vines, a Fruit Tree he says formerly grown in abundance in Vineyards, especially by the Monks, the Wine of which supplied them year by year; " but they have long since been destroyed, and the knowledge how to order a Vineyard is also utterly perished with them." He mentions many gentlemen having tried to have them, bringing Frenchmen over to attend them, but the produce was uniformly "small and heartless;" and the Vine in his time was scarcely attended to, even when grown against a Wall. Chap. 11. Is of preserving Grapes through the Winter in sand, &c. At page, 557, commences his list and descriptions of the Fruits " proper for our climate." Raspberry red, white, and thornless—Currants red 2, white and black.—Goosberries or Fleaberries 5.—Barberry—Filberts 3—Grapes 23—Figs 3—Service 2—Medlars 3—Lote 3—Cornell 2—Cherries 36—Plumbs 61—Apricots 6—Peaches 21, and others without names. Nectarines ("have been with us not many years") 6. —Almonds, bitter, and sweet—Oranges, which he says were grown in large boxes, to be pulled into the house, or under a wall covered with a sear cloth, and " some comfort in the colder times" was given them by a stove. This is the first rude attempt that we have notice of by an English writer, approaching to the idea of a hot-house, or conservatory, but with the notice we have before of Bell-glasses, was evidently leading to their construction; no tent or mean provision, he continues, will preserve them. Apples 78. and many others, or perhaps merely names for others already specified. Quinces 6—Pears 64—many others, and the varieties increasing yearly. Walnut—Sweet Chesnut, just come from Turkey, and but little known—he confounds it with the Horse Chesnut—Mulberries 3. His Corollary to the Orchard, commences at page 598, and contains the Bay, Pine, Fir, Evergreen Oak, Cypress, Arbutus, Evergreen Privet, Pyracantha,

Yew, Box 3, Savine, Christ's Thorn, Larch, Lime (properly Line or Linden Tree) Tamarisk 2, Sycamore—Bladder Nut, —Sumach 2, and Virginia Vine or Ivy.

Thus concludes this work, which though containing not so much on the cultivation of the plants, as we deem necessary in a work of general Horticulture, may be the more excused, as that what he wrote was original, the result of his own practice and enquiries.

There are three portraits of Parkinson known.

1. Johannis Parkinsoni, pharmacopœi Londinensis effigies. LXII. œtatis annum agentis, a nato Christo, 1629. Before his Paradisus Terrestris. Wood Cut by Christopher Switzer.

2. John Parkinson. A small oval, in the title of his "Theatre of Plants." By W. Marshall.

3. John Parkinson. An Oval by W. Richardson.

1631. Observations on Sir Francis Bacon's Natural History, so far as it concerns Fruit Trees. By FRANCIS AUSTEN. 4to. Again in 1657.

GABRIEL PLATTES was of humble origin, but of his lineage, place of nativity &c. I have discovered nothing. His works however demonstrate that he was a practical man of clear intellect, and observing mind. Being a needy man, he at times was dependant upon the bounty of others for subsistence, amongst those who chiefly administered to his relief was S. Hartlib, to whom he bequeathed his papers, few of which were published. He died miserably in the streets, almost in a state of nudity. That he was justly estimated by his contemporaries is evident. Harte says of him, that "he had a bold adventurous cast of mind"—Weston in his Catalogue of English Authors says, he was an original genius in husbandry and an ingenious writer. Another author stiles him " a singular honest man,"—a fourth says "he had as excellent a genius in agriculture as any man that ever lived in this nation before him."—Yet this man was permitted to live in poverty, and to die ultimately of want, affording another testimony that those who benefit by the efforts of another's genius, but seldom feel grateful for, or appreciate the benefits they receive, but whilst they are enjoying them, as Frederick of Prussia said in discarding Voltaire " Having extracted all the juice, I merely neglect the rind." He was the author of,

1. A Treatise of Husbandry. 4to. 1638. and 1674.

2. Practical Husbandry improved, a discourse of infinite treasure, hidden since the World's beginning, in the way of husbandry. 4to. 1639—1653—1656.

3. Recreatio Agricolæ. London. 1640. 4to.

4. The Profitable Intelligencer. London. 1644. 4to.

5. Observations and Improvements in Husbandry, with twenty experiments. London. 1653. 4to. He also wrote, " Art's Mistress," containing his own experiments for fifty years, which however was not published, (Weston's Catalogue, p. 15.)

1640. The Countryman's Recreation, or the Art of Planting, Graffeing, and Gardening, In three Books. With a perfect platforme of a Hop Garden. Without the author's name. 4to. London.

The Expert Gardener, collected out of Dutch and French Author's. Without an author's name. Another Edition with plates appeared in 1654. Dr. Watts in his Bibliotheca Britannica, mentions as bearing the date 1640, "The Expert Gardener, or a Treatise concerning Gardening and Grafting. London. 4to. By C. DE SERCY. Whether these are the same works I cannot determine.

SIR RICHARD WESTON of Sutton in Surrey, was ambassador from the court of James the I. in 1619 to Frederick V. Elector Palatine, and King of Bohemia. He deserves a record here from his having written a work on the Agriculture of Flanders, which, as it has been remarked (Philosophic Transactions) has profited England to the amount of many millions by rendering us acquainted with the practice of that country. It is entitled,

1. A discourse of husbandrie used in Brabant and Flanders, shewing the wonderful improvement of land there: and serving as a pattern for our practice in this commonwealth 4to. 1645. The second edition enlarged, was edited by Hartlib in 1652.

2. Brief discoveries of ways and means for manuring and improving land, 1646.

3. He was present at the battle of Prague, of which he has left a curious account still preserved in MS.

The "Discourse of Husbandrie" was dedicated to Samuel Hartlib, who published it without knowing at the time who was the author. In another edition (Weston thinks in 1655) Hartlib annexed Dr. Beati's annotations to it. It has always been estimated as an excellent work.

1645. An essay on Timber Trees. By JOSEPH HALL, of Shedley in Yorkshire.

WALTER BLYTHE, was an officer in the army of Oliver Cromwell. Dr. Beale calls him, "Honest Captain Blythe." He was instrumental in introducing many improvements into Ireland and Scotland. He wrote,

1. The English Improver improved; or the survey of Husbandry surveyed, discovering the improvableness of all lands. 4to. with plates. 1649. 3rd edit. 1653. Professor Martyn in Miller's Dictionary, terms it "an original, and incomparable work for the time.".

2. Survey of Husbandry, discovering the best methods of improving all sorts of lands. 1649. folio.

SAMUEL HARTLIB, came to England about 1630, though Warton places his arrival ten years later; which is certainly an error, as he is known to have been intimate with Archbishop Usher and Joseph Mede, long previous to that year. He was the Son of a Poland Merchant, settled at Elbing in Prussia. —He carried on an extensive agency business, was an active supporter of Drury's scheme of uniting the Protestant churches; and assisted in establishing the embryo of the Royal Society. He wrote several Theological Tracts; was intimate with Milton, who dedicated to him his "Tractate on Education," on which topic likewise Sir William Petty corresponded with him. Towards the close of his days he became poor, and applied to the parliament for relief. Cromwell allowed him an annuity of one hundred pounds. The time of his death is not recorded. He was the esteemed associate of the talented men of his time. He deserves our attention from being a great promoter of the Art of cultivating the earth. He wrote,

1. A legacy, or an enlargement of the Discourse of Husbandry used in Brabant and Flanders, 1650.—1651, and 1655 4to. He also edited a work, the MS. of which was given to him by the Hon. Colonel John Barkstead, Lieutenant of the Tower, the author of which was an old clergyman, at Loving-land, near Yarmouth; it is entitled,

2. A designe for Plentie, by an universall planting of Fruit Trees; tendered by some wel-wishers to the Public, 4to. no date.

3. Concerning the defects and remedies of English Husbandry, in a letter to Dr. Beati. London. 1651. 4to. An Edition in 1659, is entitled " The compleat Husbandman, or a discourse of the whole Art of Husbandry, "&c.

" The famous work, says Weston, attributed to Hartlib," and called " the Legacy," was only drawn up at his request, being corrected and revised by him. It consists of one general answer to the query.—What are the actual defects and omissions, as also the possible improvements in English Husbandry?"—The real author was R. Child; and it contains the contributions of most of the persons eminent for agricultural skill at that period.*

1651. The Reformed Husbandman, By ADAM SPEED, Gent. 4to. He also wrote, " Adam out of Eden." 1659. 12mo.

1653. A Treatise of Fruit Trees. Showing the manner of Grafting, Setting, Pruning, and ordering of them in all respects, according to divers new and easy rules of experience, gathered in the space of twenty years. Whereby the value of lands may be much improved

* Weston's Catalogue of English Author's. p. 27.)

in a short time, by small cost and little labour. Also discovering some dangerous errors both in the Theory and Practice of the Art of planting Fruit Trees. With the alimental and physical use of Fruits. Together with the spiritual use of an Orchard. Held forth in divers similitudes between natural and spiritual Fruit Trees, according to Scripture and experience. By RALPH AUSTEN, Practiser in the Art of Planting. Oxford, 4to. Again in 1662, and 1667.

1654. The Blood of the Grapes. By—WHITAKER. 8vo:

The Countryman's Recreation, or the Art of Planting, Graffeing and Gardening. In three books. London. 8vo.

JOHN TRADESCANT, was born in Holland. Parkinson mentions his having travelled several years into various parts of Europe. He was in Russia, and accompanied the fleet sent against the Algerines in 1620, and collected on that occasion plants in Barbary, and the isles in the Mediterranean. His name is frequently mentioned by Johnson and Parkinson, Pultney conjectures that he was unknown to Gerarde, or was not in England at that time. He was Gardener in succession to Robert, Earl of Salisbury (Lord Treasurer of England,) Lord Wotton, at Canterbury, and the Duke of Buckingham.* He was also Gardener to Queen Elizabeth, as his father was before him.† He settled in England, and founded his Garden at Lambeth. About 1629, he was appointed Gardener to Charles the I.—He died about 1652,—His son John, who followed the same trade as his father, made a voyage in pursuit of Plants to Virginia, and brought many new ones back with him. He

* Parkinson's Paradisi in Sole, p. 152. † Walton's complete Angler by Hawkins. 5th Edit. p. 24.

died in 1662. They introduced many new species into England, and among Gardeners; "Tradescant's Spiderwort," "Tradescant's Aster," &c. are still recognized. They were the first who made any considerable collection of natural curiosities in this country, which their delight in the pursuit enabled them to do, aided as they were by the liberality of contemporary men of wealth. Their Museum, called "Tradescant's Ark," was an object of general curiosity, and was the constant resort of the great and learned. A description of it was published in 1656, entitled "Museum Tradescantianum, or a collection of varieties preserved at South Lambeth near London. By John Tradescant," 12mo. After a list of natural and artificial curiosities, follows one in English and Latin, of the Plants in his Garden, and another of his benefactors and contributors, among which are the names of the King, Queen, and many of the highest nobility. Prefixed is a print of both the Tradescants, engraved by Hollar, whose engravings being in request among collectors, most copies of the book which are to be found are deprived of this. The work is arranged under the following heads. 1. Birds with their Eggs. 2. Four-footed Beasts. 3. Fish. 4. Shells. 5. Insects. 6. Minerals. 7. Fruits, Drugs, &c. 8. Artificial Curiosities. 9. Miscellaneous Curiosities. 10. Warlike Instruments. 11. Habits. 12. Utensils and Household Stuff. 13. Coins. 14. Medals.

The Son bequeathed the Museum by a deed of gift to Mr. Ashmole, who lodged with his wife, in his house for a summer, and the name of Tradescant, as Pultney observes, "was unjustly, sunk in that of Ashmole," It being now known as the Ashmolean Museum. Ashmole left it to the university of Oxford. The wreck of their Garden, as it existed in 1749, is described by Sir W. Watson in the 46th volume of the Philosophical Transactions.—Hawkins says, that Ashmole agreed to purchase Tradescant's collection, and that Tradescant and his wife made a conveyance of it to him, which upon Tradescant's death soon afterwards, he was obliged to enforce by a suit in Chancery, upon his succeeding in which, Mrs. Tradescant drowned herself. A monument to the three Naturalists is in Lambeth Church Yard. It was repaired in 1773, and the following epitaph engraved upon it, as had been intended at its erection,

> Know, stranger, e'er thou pass, beneath this stone
> Lie John Tradescant, grandsire, father, son.
> The last died in his Spring; the other two
> Liv'd, till they had travelled art and nature thro',
> As by their choice collections may appear,
> Of what is rare in land, in seas, in air:
> Whilst they (as Homer's Iliad in a nut)
> A world of wonders in one closet shut.
> These famous Antiquarians that had been
> Both gardeners to the rose and lily Queen,
> Transplanted now themselves, sleep here; and when
> Angels shall with their trumpets waken men,
> And fire shall purge the world, these hence shall rise
> And change their gardens for a Paradise.*

Grainger mentions the following portraits of the Tradescants.

Johannes Tradescantus, pater, rerum selectarum iusignem supellectilem, in reconditorio Lambethiano prope Londinum, etiamnum visendam, primus institutit ac locupletavit. Hollar fecit. 12mo.

John Tradescant, with his Son, and their monument. J. T. Smith, 1793.

Johannes Tradescantus, filius, genii ingeniique paterni verus hæres, relictum sibi rerum undique congestarum Thesaurum,

---

* Walton's complete Angler by Hawkin's. Edit. 5th. p. 25.

ipse plurimum adauxit, et in museo Lambethiano, amicis visendum exhibet. Hollar fecit. 12mo.—The original paintings of the above are in the Ashmolean Museum.

DR. JOHN BEALE, was a most ardent promoter of Horticulture, especially of Orcharding. He was a native of Herefordshire, which country he greatly benefited, as Gough in his Topography records. His family, which had long flourished in Herefordshire, seemed to inherit a zeal for the plantation of Orchards, and the individual of whom we are now sketching the biography, was fully gifted with the family hereditament. He so raised and extended the reputation of the Orchards of his County, and their produce, that in a few years it gained some hundred thousands of pounds by the increased reputation.* His enthusiastic love of the agricolan arts is manifested in every one of his writings. He was a man of talent, and the companion of the men of genius contemporary with him. Many of his letters are preserved in Boyle's works. That philosopher thus speaks of him, "There is not in life, a man in this whole island, nor on the continents beyond the seas, that could be made more universally useful to do good to all." He was in the church. He was born in 1603—and died in 1683. He wrote,

1. A Treatise on Fruit Trees, shewing their manner of grafting, pruning, and ordering: Of Cyder and Perry: Of Vineyards in England, &c. Oxford. 1653 and 1657. 4to and 1665. 12mo.

2. The Hereford Orchards; a pattern for the whole of England. By J. B. London. 1657. 12mo. and 1724. 8vo.

This is dedicated to Samuel Hartlib, and is the most cele-

* Gough's Antiquities, p. 193.

brated of his works, as it deserves to be, being a most excellent little work whether viewed as a practical directory, or as a literary production.

3. Observations on some parts of Bacon's Natural History, as it concerns Fruit Trees, Fruits and Flowers. Oxford. 1658. 4to.—Printed again with his Treatise on Fruit Trees in 1665. 12mo.

4. General Advertisement concerning Cider, appears in Evelyn's Sylva.

5. Letters about the Improvement of Nurseries, Orchards &c· London 1677. 4to.

6. Experiments and Observations on Vegetation and the running of the Sap.

7. The connection of certain parts of the Tree with those of the Fruit. These two last appeared in the Philosophical Transactions for 1669.

8. Remarks on the Vinetum Britannicum, &c. Several Papers by him on the Mineral Springs of Somersetshire, Worcestershire, &c. were inserted in the Philosophical Transactions. Some writers have made two persons authors of the above works. From 6 downwards, being by Dr. John Beale, and those preceding by Mr. John Beale.

1658. The Gardens of Cyrus, or the Quincunxial Lozenge, or net work plantations of the ancients, artificially, naturally and mystically considered. This was published at the end of a work upon some Urns discovered in Norfolk, entitled "Hydriotaphia." London. 8vo.

Certain Miscellany Tracts in Scripture, of Gardens. This was a posthumous publication, forming part of the author's "Miscellany Tracts" edited by Dr. Tenison. London. 8vo. 1684.

The above were the works of Sir THOMAS BROWNE, the celebrated Physician and Antiquary; born in London 1605, and died at Norwich 1682. He is best known as an author by his "Religio Medici" and "Enquiries into vulgar and common Errors."

1659. Proceedings concerning the improvement of all manner of land, &c. By THOMAS DUCKETT.

1660. The right manner of ordering Fruit Trees, By— GENDRE. 8vo.

1664. ENGLAND'S happiness increased, or a remedy against all succeeding dear years, by a plantation of Potatoes. 4to. Without the author's name.

JOHN EVELYN, "like another Virgil, says Switzer, was appointed for the retrieving the calamities of England, and re-animating the spirit of his countrymen for their planting and sowing of Woods,—to him it is owing that Gardening can speak proper English." This distinguished individual was born at Wotton in Surry, the mansion of Richard Evelyn Esq. his father, on the 31st of October, 1620. He commenced his education at Lewes, in Sussex, and completed it at Baliol College, Oxford. In 1640 he entered as a student of the middle Temple, but proceeded in 1644 on the grand tour of Europe, to Italy. In 1647 he was united to the daughter of Sir Richard Browne, and thence became possessed of Saye's court in Kent. Having exerted himself in promoting the restoration of Charles the II. he was appointed a commissioner for the sick and wounded during the Dutch War. He was one of the first

Fellows, and of the Council of the Royal Society on its establishment in 1662. It was by his persuasion that Lord Henry Howard in 1667. presented the Arundelian Marbles to the university of Oxford, for which he received its thanks, and the degree of Doctor of Laws. He was also appointed one of the Commissioners for rebuilding St. Paul's Cathedral; had a place at the Board of Trade; and was one of the Council for the management of the Plantations. After the accession of James the II. he became one of the Commissioners for executing the office of Lord Privy Seal, and in 1695 Treasurer of Greenwich Hospital, by his many preferments forming an exception to the observation, which too often is correct, that the Stuarts usually neglected or deserted their friends.

When Peter the Great of Russia, was in England, he resided at Saye's Court, where he was long remembered for the great damage committed by himself and attendants, especially in the Gardens, where he repaid his landlord's kindness, by being frequently wheeled through the ornamental hedges, and over the borders in a Wheelbarrow.

Evelyn died at Wotton, February 27th 1705---6, and was interred in the family vault there, after a life of unweared utility, sincerely regretted by every man of Science, and every patriot. His writings and examples were of the greatest service in promoting the Arts of cultivation.*

His family delighted in the same pursuits as he did himself. There is, says D'Israeli, what may be termed a *family genius*, in the home of a man of genius he diffuses an Electrical atmosphere, his own preeminence strikes out talents in all. Evelyn in his beautiful retreat at Saye's Court, had inspired his family with that variety of tastes which he himself was spreading throughout the nation. His son translated "Rapin's Gardens,"

* Diary and Correspondence of J. Evelyn.

which poem the father proudly preserved in his "Sylva;" his lady ever busied in his study, excelled in the arts her husband loved, and designed the frontispiece to his "Lucretius;" she was also the cultivator of their celebrated garden, which served as an example of his great work on "Forest Trees."*

It was in consequence of a recommendation of Evelyn's in his Fumifugium, that fragrant plants should be grown in nurseries, &c. in the low grounds near London, that the Lime Trees were planted in St. James's Park.

His Horticultural and other Literary Works are as follows,

1. The French Gardener; instructing how to cultivate all sorts of Fruit Trees and Herbs for the Garden; together with directions to dry and conserve them in their natural state. By Philocepos. London. 1658, 1672, 1675, and 1691. 12mo.—This translation has passed through many editions. to most of which are appended "the English Vineyard" by John Rose. The third edition, which bears date 1672, is the only one I have seen, it is illustrated by several plates.

2. An Essay on the first book of Lucretius, in English verse. 8vo.

3. Fumifugium, on the inconveniences of the air and smoke of London dissipated. London, 1661. 4to.

4. Sculpture. or the History and Art of Chalcography, and engraving on copper. 8vo.

5. Sylva, or a discourse of Forest Trees, and the propagation of Timber in his Majesty's dominions. To which is

---

* D'Israeli's Literary character illustrated. p. 235.

annexed Pomona, or an appendix concerning Fruit Trees. In relation to Cider, the making and several ways of ordering it. London. 1664, 1669, 1679; with great additions and improvements in 1705; and 1729 all in folio. Dr. Hunter of York, edited an elegant edition with copious notes, and beautiful engravings in 1776. 2 vols. 4to. a second edition, to which the "Terra" is added, appeared in 1786. It has passed through two other editions. The one of 1812, in 2 vols. 4to. received Dr. Hunter's last corrections. Evelyn published his Sylva and Pomona at the request of the Royal Society.

6. A parallel of the Ancient Architecture with the modern. folio.

7. Kalendarium Hortense, or the Gardener's Almanack, directing what he is to do monthly throughout the year, and what Fruits and Flowers are in their prime. London, 1664, 8vo. This work was afterwards printed in folio with his "Sylva" and Pomona; and the same including his "Terra." London. 1676 and 1691, both in 8vo. It was published with the addition of his discourse on Sallads, in 1706, 8vo. previous to which there had been nine editions.

8. Public Employment, and an active Life preferred to Solitude. 8vo.

9. An idea of the perfection of Painting. 8vo.

10. A discourse on the History of Trade and Navigation.

11. Terra, a philosophical discourse of Earth, relating to the culture and improvement of it for vegetation and the propagation of Plants, as it was presented to the Royal So-

ciety, April the 29th, 1675—London, 1675. folio. The same including his "Pomona" and "Acetaria" London, 1676, and 1678. 12mo, and 1706, folio. Dr. Hunter, as before stated, published it with notes and illustrations with the "Sylva," in 1786, previous to which he had published it seperately in 1778. 8vo. as he did in 1786. 4to.

12. Pomona &c. was published seperately. London 1679. folio.

13. Numismata, or a discourse of Medals. folio.

14. M. de la Quintinye's Treatise of Orange Trees, with the raising of Melons, omitted in the French editions, made into English by J. E. London. 1693. folio. With Engravings.

15. Acetaria, or a discourse of Sallets. London 1699, 12mo.

16. Letter concerning the damage done to his Gardens in the preceding Winter. This is in the Philosophical Transactions. iii, p. 28. 1684.

In 1660 appeared "The right manner of ordering Fruit Trees, &c, translated from the French of Le Gendre. London". 8vo. This translation has been ascribed to Evelyn. If there is some doubt of this, there is still more respecting the real Author. Le Gendre being only an assumed name. The most probable opinion seems to be that it was written by Robert Arnaud d'Andilly, a clergyman born at Paris in 1589, and who died in 1674. The original was published at Paris in 1652 entitled "De la manière de cultiver les Arbres Fruitiers". Evelyn contributed largely to Mr. Houghton's "Husbandry and Trade improved," he also wrote the plan of a Royal Garden, and an illustration of the Horticulture of the Gorgics, never published.

1670. England's improvement, revived in a Treatise of Husbandry and Trade. By JOHN SMITH. London. 4to. Again in 1673.

JOHN DE LA QUINTINIE, was born at Poictiers in 1626—under the Jesuits of that City he finished his course of Philosophy, and commenced the study of the Law, proceeding then to Paris to be called to the bar as an Advocate, but the cultivation of Plants being his favorite study, M. Tambonneau prevailed upon him to accompany his son into Italy, and thus to render himself acquainted with the best modern practice of the Art, as he already was with that of the ancient—Upon his return M. Tambonneau gave to him the sole planning and direction of his Gardens—Having now the opportunity, he instituted numerous experiments, and refuted many of the old tenets of Botanists and Gardeners—amongst others he demonstrated, that the Sap of Plants does not retire and accumulate in the roots during Winter—and that transplanted Vegetables do not acquire nourishment from the soil by means of the old fibrous roots, nor at all until fresh fibres are produced.—He published the results of his practice and study in his "Compleat Gardener," which was translated entire by Mr. Evelyn, and in an abridged form by Messrs. London and Wise, the best part of this work is on the management of fruit trees—the whole however is disfigured by repletion of language and of style—Lewis the XIV. the great Condé, and other men of genius, were fond of conversing with him on the various pursuits of his Art. Charles the II. of England made him an offer of a considerable Pension if he would engage in his service—He visited England twice during that monarch's reign and received many marks of his favour, as also from the nobility, with some of whom he corresponded until the time of his death—His letters, according to Perrault, were published in London, which Switzer observes he never saw. Evelyn during Quintinie's stay with him, prevailed on him to impart his mode of cultivating Melons, for which he was distinguished.--Louis made him Director General of his Fruit and Kitchen Gardens, and by his directions those of Versailles were much enlarged, and their produce improved—He formed there the Potagery " which, says Switzer, appears so very surprising to all Strangers"—" he was, continues the same Author, the person that refined the business, and pleasure of Kitchen, and Fruit Gardens to a pitch beyond what was ever until that time seen, and more than was ever thought possible for one man to be able ever to do; and (till the succession of two eminent persons (London and Wise) in these kingdoms, who have very much outstript him) has not had his fellow in any Century that History gives us account of." He died about the year 1700, lamented by the lovers of the Arts, and Louis expressed his own sorrow to Madame Quintinie by saying, " I am as great a sufferer by his loss as you, and I despair of ever repairing the loss of him by any other person."*

The following is a list of his works, the first of which only is known to have been printed during his life

1. Traité des Jardins Fruitiers et Potagers. Amsterdam. 1690. With plates. 4to.

2. Instructions sur les Jardins Fruitiers et Potagers, avec un Traité des Orangers, et des Réflexions sur l'Agriculture. 4to.

The above have passed through many editions in France. The English Translations have before been mentioned.

* Perrault's Hist. of illustrious Men of the Age of Louis 14th. Switzer's Icnographia Rustica, v. 1. p. 43, &c. and Nouveau Dict. Historique.

ROBERT SHARROCK, was born at Adstock in Buckinghamshire. He commenced his education at Winchester School, and seems to have gained the presentation to New College, Oxford, where he took his degree of Doctor of Laws. He became prebend, and archdeacon of Winchester, and Rector of Bishop's Waltham and of Harewood in Hants. He died in 1684.* He wrote,

1. The history of the propagation and improvement of Vegetables by the concurrence of Art and Nature. Written according to the observations made from experience and practice. Oxford, 1660, without his name. 8vo. Again, Oxford. 1666, and 1672. 8vo. with the author's name.

2. Improvements to the Art of Gardening; or an exact Treatise of Plants. London, 1694. folio.

3. De Officiis secundum Humanæ Rationis dictatæ, &c.

4. Judicia de variis Incontinentiæ Speciebus.

5. De finibus virtutis Christianæ.

1664. The complete Gardener's Practice. By STEPHEN BLAKE. London. 4to

1670. The complete Vineyard, or an excellent way for the planting of Vines, and ordering of Wines and Wine Presses, according to the German and French manner. London. 8vo.

The American Physician, or a Treatise of the Roots, Trees, &c. growing in the English Plantations. With a discourse of the Cocoa Tree, and the ways of making Chocolate. London. 12mo. 1672.

* Wood's Athenæ Oxoniensis.

The Flower Garden, or how most flowers are ordered, increased, &c. London. 1672, and 1734. 12mo. United with "The complete Vineyard" it was published in 1683. 12mo.

The above three works were from the pen of a WILLIAM HUGHES.

1665. Flora, Ceres and Pomona, or a complete Florilege furnished with all requisites belonging to a Florist. By JOHN REA. London. Folio. With Engravings. Again in 1676.

From this work we learn that the Author was a professional Gardener, and at the time he wrote, far advanced in years and retired from business. He was patronised by Lord and Lady Gerarde, to whom he dedicates his work. He lived at Kinlet, near Bewdley in Worcestershire. His works contain ample Catalogues of Flowers, Shrubs, &c. amongst them may be noticed 300 Tulips, (184 in the first Edition;) 360 good Carnations; Fruits proportionably numerous; and yet the size of his gardens is ludicrously small "Fourscore yards square for the Fruit, and thirty for the flower Garden, will be enough for a nobleman." He mentions the Horse Chesnut as rarely producing Fruit here; and of the Larch being seldom seen.

Although he is designated "gent," yet from the style of his dedications I should consider him to have been none of the higher class. He evidently was skilled in Gardening, having given designs, lists of Plants, &c. for Lord Gerard's Garden, in Staffordshire. I am inclined to think he was a nurseryman, for he says he had been forty years a Planter, and which had occupied more time, than could have been spared for "diversion." He had a very extensive collection of Plants. He was evidently a Royalist.

JOHN ROSE, was considered the best Gardener of his time, he acted in that capacity successively to the Earl of Essex, at Essex House, in the Strand, (where he was in 1665,) to the Duchess of Cleveland, to the Duchess of Somerset, and Charles the II. at St. James's. He appears to have been a man of general talent being admitted to the society of the virtuosi of the age. Mr, London, was a favourite pupil of his. Rose went to study the style of the Gardens of Versailles, at the expense of the Earl of Essex. There is a portrait of Rose in oils, at Kensington Palace, representing him giving the first Pine-apple cultivated in England to Charles the II. whilst that monarch was on a visit to Rose's, mistress the Duchess of Cleveland, at Downey Court, Buckinghamshire.* He was dead at the time Switzer wrote his Icnographia in 1718.† He wrote,

1. The English Vineyard vindicated, and the way of making Wine in France. 1675—1676—and 1690. 8vo. This first appeared at the end of Evelyn's French Gardener in 1672. 12mo.

2. A Treatise upon Fruit Trees. This is mentioned by Switzer, but is a work I have never seen.

The English Vineyard is dedicated to the King, to whom he was then (1672) Gardener. The preface is by Mr. Evelyn and informs us of the origin of the work. Talking with Rose about Vines "he reasoned so pertinently upon that subject, as indeed he does upon all things which concern his hortulan profession" that he persuaded the latter to allow him to give his opinions a literary dress. Chap. 1. Is of the Vines best suited to the climate of England, and consist of, The Black Cluster. White Muscadine. Parsley leaved Grape. White Muscadella. White and Red Frontiniac, and a White Grape not named but with

* There is a copy of this in Water Colours, in the Library of the London Horticultural Society. † Switzer's Icnographia Rustica, v. 1. p. 68, &c.

red wood, and a dark Green leaf, Chap 2. Of the Soil for a Vineyard. Chap. 3. How to prepare the ground for planting. Chap. 4. How to plant. Chap. 5. How to dress, prune, &c. Chap. 6. How to cultivate after the first four years, until it needs renewing. Chap. 7. On manuring the Vineyard. It concludes with the Art of making Wine by Mr. Evelyn.

I have never seen an Essay. " On the admirable virtues of Coral," said to be by this author.

JOHN WORLIDGE, (sometimes even in his own title pages, spelt Woolridge.) Of this author I have been able to gather no further information than is afforded by his works, namely, that he was a gentleman, and a great lover of Gardening and Rural Affairs. He was author of the following Works.

1. Systema Agriculturæ; the mystery of Husbandry discovered. By J. W. gent. London. 1669—1677—1681 and 1687, folio. 1697—1716. 8vo.

There is a good deal concerning Gardening in this work.

2. Treatise of Husbandry. London. 1675. folio

3. Systema Horticulturæ, or the Art of Gardening, &c. Plates. By J.W. gent. London. 1677. The third Edition 1688. 1700. 2 vols. 8vo.

4. Vinetum Britannicum. London. 1678. 1691. 8vo.

5. The most easy way of making Cyder. London. 1678—1691. 8vo, and in 1687. 4to.

6. Apiarium. London. 1691. 12mo.

The third in the above list most deserves our notice as most relating to the art whose History we are tracing. It is entitled "Systema Horticulturæ, or the Art of Gardening. In three Books. The I. treateth of the excellency, situation, soil, form, walks, arbours, springs, fountains, water-works, grottos, statues, and other magnificent ornaments of Gardens, with many necessary rules, precepts and directions concerning the same. The II. treateth of all sorts of trees planted for ornament or shade, winter-greens, flower-trees, and flowers, that are usually propagated or preserved in the gardens of the best Florists, and the best ways and methods of raising, planting, and improving them. The III. treateth of the Kitchen Garden, and of the great variety of Plants propagated for food or for any culinary uses: together with many general and particular rules, precepts, observations, and instructions for making hot-beds, altering and enriching any sort of garden ground, watering, cleansing, and adopting all sorts of earth to the various plants that are usually planted therein; to the great improvement of every sort of land, as well for use and profit as for ornament and delight. Illustrated with Sculptures, representing the form of Gardens according to the newest models."

The title page as above, promises by far too much, for the work is slight and superficial. By endeavouring to say something upon every subject relating to the art, he has not been able to treat sufficiently in detail of any one. He has divided the work into forty seven sections, of which the 45th. on Watering, and the 47th. containing Miscellaneous Experiments and Observations, are the best. The last, which is by much the longest in the book contains many excellent recommendations and notices.

1669. De cultu Hortorum, Carmen. By RICHARD RICHARDSON. London. 4to.

———— Observations and Advice œconomical. 12mo. Anonymous.

———The epitome of Husbandry. By S. B. 12mo. This is a complete plagiary, the first 181 pages being copied from Fitzherbert and the remainder from Mascall, Blythe, &c. The plagiarist was Samuel Blagrave, or, as some say Billingsly.*

1670. The Compleat Vineyard. By—ILIFFE. 12mo.

1672. A short and sure guide in the practice of raising and ordering of Fruit Trees, Oxford, 12mo. dedicated to Lord Windham.

This is a posthumous publication of FRANCIS DROPE, B. D. being edited by his brother, a Physician at Cumner, in Berkshire, where our Author was born, and of which place his father was vicar. Wood informs us that Francis was very fond of Gardening. He died at Oxford.

CHARLES COTTON, though well known as the editor of Walton's Angler, and as a Poet, is only one of the Scriptores minores of Horticulture. He was born at Beresford in Hertfordshire, the seat of his father, on the 28th of April, 1630.— He finished his education at Cambridge; Travelled for some years, and then married in 1656. He commenced publishing in 1663, and twelve years afterwards appeared the only work of his requiring notice here, viz. " The Planter's Manual, being instructions for Raising, Planting, and Cultivating all sorts of Fruit Trees." 12mo. 1675. He was fond of Literary pursuits, and his chief amusement otherwise was Angling. He died, under considerable pecuniary embarrassment, in the Parish of St. James's Westminster, September, 1687.†

MOSES COOKE, was the son of a farmer on the sea coast

---

* Weston's Catalogue of English Authors, 41. † Walton's complete Angler, edited by Sir J. Hawkins, edit, 5.

of Lincolnshire, and brought up to the trade of a Gardener, of which we have his own authority that he was very careful to improve. "I always took notes of what I did set or sow, the time, and on what ground, &c. and when it proved well, I noted it so; but when ill, I did endeavour as much as I could to know the reason, which when once found I noted it well: I also always was very wary of taking things upon trust"—By such attention he became a proficient. Evelyn in his Diary mentions him as skilful in the mechanical parts of Gardening, not ignorant of mathemactics, and somewhat of *an adept in Astrology*. He was gardener to the Earl of Essex, at Cashiobury, from about 1660 to 1681, in which last named year, in conjunction with Messrs. Lucre, London and Field, he founded the Brompton Park Nursery. The time of his death, like that of his birth, is unascertained. He was probably dead in 1694, at which period none of the original firm remained in the Brompton Nursery, but Mr. London. He wrote,

1. The manner of raising, ordering and improving Forest and Fruit Trees; also how to plant, make and keep Woods, Walks, Avenues, Lawns, Hedges, &c. with several figures in Copper plates proper for the same. With Arithmetical and Geometrical tables, for measuring and dividing Land, Timber, &c. To which is now added, A discovery of subterranean Treasure or how to discover and prepare various minerals by Mr. GABRIEL PLATTES. London. 1679. 4to. Plates. In 1700. 8vo. Again in 1717 and 1724.

2. The art of making Cider. This was published in Evelyn's Works.

The first mentioned work, after due allowance for quaintness, is demonstrative of a thinking mind, and is upon most Points a work of authority.

1677.—Nurseries, Orchards, Profitable Gardens, and Vineyards encouraged. By ANTHONY LAWRANCE. London. 1677. 4to.

1679—The complete Gardener. Anonymous. 4to.

1680. 1. The Practical Planter of Fruit Trees. London. 8vo. A second edition, revised and enlarged in many places; together with an addition of two entire Chapters of Greens, and Greenhouses. London. 1680.—1683, 1695, and 1696. 8vo. Plates.

   2. Systema Agriculturæ, being the mystery of Husbandry discovered. London. 1681. folio.

   3. Plain and full instructions to raise all sorts of Fruit Trees that prosper in England, with directions for making liquors of several sorts of Fruit. London. 1681—1690—1696—1699 all in 8vo.*

These three works are by T. LANGFORD.

Of the last mentioned, Evelyn says "As I know nothing extant that exceeds it, so nor do I of any thing which needs be added to it."

   A collection of Husbandry. By—HOUGHTON. 2 vols. 4to. 1681. In folio 1697. These appeared periodically but were revised and published collectively by Bradley in four volumes, 8vo. in 1727. Evelyn was one of the contributors to this work.

1683. 1. The English Gardener, or a sure guide to young

* Watt's Bibliotheca Britannica.

Planters and Gardeners. With engravings. London. 1683, 1688 and 1699, 4to.

2. The new art of Gardening, with the Gardener's Almanack, containing the true art of Gardening, in all its particulars. 1. Site of a proper plat of Ground, for planting Fruit Trees; with the manner of planting, grafting, imbuding, inoculating, and ordering all sorts of Fruit Trees, and fruits in all seasons. The art of making Cyder, Perry, and Wines of divers sorts of Fruits. 2. Of the Kitchen Garden, and, what things are proper to be done in it, as to herbs, plants, roots, berries, Fruits, &c. 3. Of the flower garden, how to order it, and rear choice flowers, slips, layers, sow seeds, make off-sets, and plant them in their proper earths, seasons, and due waterings, with the names and descriptions of the most material ones. 4. Of greens, how to order and preserve them with rules for the conservatory, and green house.—To each head is added an Almanack, showing what is to be done every month in the year, London.—No date, (1713,) 12mo.—It originally appeared in 1697. 8vo.

This little work of 160 pp. is evidently as stated in the preface, the result of " long experience."—The author's directions for avoiding the injuries of frosts and manuring trees are good, his descriptions of the various fruits slight. He classes the Apricot as a Peach. His general directions are usually correct, those for individuals are generally wanting. In his Gardener's Almanack or Kalender, he gives correct directions and a list of such Apples, and Pears, &c. as are in season each month.—In the Kitchen Garden he is still more scanty, giving but few general directions, and a list of Kitchen Garden Plants. His idea of a Hot bed, extends to little more than a sheltered, thickly manured border, and when he does dwell upon additional heat, he recommends Hog's dung to be employed; and straw whelmed over, supported from the plants by forked sticks. He is judicious on the subject of watering. He recommends pigeons', sheep's dung, &c. to be infused in the water.— Of the flower Garden he says little, but in the Almanack he gives good lists of flowers blooming in the several months. Flowers that will bear extreme cold, those that are less hardy, and those most tender.—Of the Plants for the Green House or Conservatory, and work to be done, he says but little. In describing the house however, he has some judicious remarks, such as the benefit of having double doors, that in entering or coming out, one may be shut before the other is opened.—Throughout he recommends an attention to astrology, as sowing when the moon is in Taurus, and pruning when it is in Cancer, &c.—He mentions, having himself grafted the Pear when in full blossom; and supports the idea of grafting upon stocks of a different genus. He terms Cyder, " a curious drink."

3. The Mystery of Husbandry. London. 1697 or 1699, 12mo.

These three works were written by LEONARD MEAGER.

1683. The Florist's Vade-Mecum. London. 12mo.

The Gardener's Almanack. London. 12mo.

The author of these little works was SAMUEL GILBERT, All that I have learnt of him is that he married a daughter of John Rea, whom we have just mentioned; and that he was author of "Fons sanitatis, or the healing Spring at Willowbridge Wells, in Somersetshire." His portrait engraved by R. White, appears in his "Vade-Mecum." It is entitled

"Samuel Gilbert, Florist." A third edition of this work, Grainger states was printed in the reign of Queen Anne (1702—1714;) Weston gives the date, 1702. In his Gardener's Almanack is a very accurate and full description of the varieties of Roses cultivated in our gardens at the time it was written.* He stiles himself in the Title Page of his "Vade-Mecum"—Philerimus.

1683.—The Scot's Gardener, whereunto is annexed the Gardener's Kalendar. Edinburgh. 4to.

The Author of this book was JOHN REID, Gardener to Sir George Mackenzie of Rosehaugh in Aberdeenshire. He was one of the earliest Scotch writers on Horticulture.

1683. On the management of Orange Trees 12mo. Anonymous. From the Dutch by Commelyn.

SIR WILLIAM TEMPLE, was the son of Sir John Temple, and born in 1628, at London, or according to Switzer at Sheen. He commenced his education under his maternal Uncle the learned Dr. Hammond, continued his studies at Bishop Stortford School, and concluded them under Dr. Cudworth at Emmanuel College, Cambridge—From the University he proceeded abroad, and at the Restoration was chosen a member of the Irish Parliament. In 1665 he went on a secret mission to Munster—was employed afterwards in forming the triple alliance between Sweden, Holland, and this country, and became resident minister at the Hague, in which capacity he promoted the union between the Prince of Orange and Princess Mary. In 1679 he became Secretary of State, but in the following year retired from office to his country seat, Sheen in Surrey, where he was repeatedly visited by his Sovereigns, Charles the II. James the II. and William the III. He died

* Loudon's Encyclop. Gardening, p. 1101.

in 1700. His works have been published in 2 Vols. folio, and 4 vols. 8vo. In the first volume of them is contained his Essay entitled " the Garden of Epicurus; or of Gardening in the year 1685," which entitles him to notice in this place.—This Essay is devoted chiefly to inculcate that taste for formal design in Gardening, which was the prevailing one of his time. When we compare it with the plan given by Lord Bacon, in a preceding age, for a similar construction, we find but this difference, that if both plans were reduced to practise Sir William's would be rather the most mathematical and undeviatingly formal.— Moor Park was his model of perfection. When he descends to more practical speculations he is seldom in error, among which we may specify his observations upon planting Peaches in the north of Britain, which experience has demonstrated to be correct; although Switzer seems to doubt the possibility above 100 miles from London. Sir William acquired his taste and knowledge of Gardening during his stay at the Hague. He introduced several new fruits, especially of Grapes. His name still attaches to a variety of the Nectarine. He had a garden at his seat at Sheen in Surrey, to the good cultivation of which Evelyn bears testimony. Nothing can demonstrate more fully the delight he took in Gardening than the direction left in his will, that his heart should be buried beneath the Sun Dial of his Garden, at Moor Park, near Farnham, in Surrey. In accordance with which it was deposited there in a Silver Box. Affording another instance of the ruling passion unweakened even in death. Nor was this an unphilosophical clinging to that which it was impossible to retain; but rather that grateful feeling common to our nature, of desiring finally to repose where in life we have been happy. In his Garden Sir William Temple had spent the calmest hours of a well spent life, and where his heart had been most peaceful he wished its dust to mingle, and thus at the same time offering his last testimony to the sentiment, that in a Garden,

His secura quies; et nescia fallere vita.

1685. The complete Planter and Ciderist 8vo. Without the author's name.

1688. Essays on Husbandry. By—COWLEY. folio.

1691. In the Archeologia Britannica (v. xii. p. 181.) is an account by J. GIBSON of several Gardens near London, existing at this period.

1694. A new invented Stove, for preserving Plants in the Green House in Winter. By SIR DUDLEY CULLUM. In the Philosophical Transactions for 1694. In the Abridgement of them, v. iii. p. 659.

1697. Husbandry anatomized. By—DONALDSON

NICHOLAS FACIO DUILHIER, was born in Switzerland in 1664. He studied at Geneva, and particularly devoted himself to Mathematics. He settled at Utrecht as a Tutor, but being suspected of Spinosism, he came over to England in 1687. He here taught Mathematics, obtained a patent for Jewel Watches, was elected Fellow of the Royal Society, and was appointed Tutor to the Marquis of Tavistock. When the French Prophets appeared, he joined in all their absurdities, and as a punishment was subjected to the Pillory in 1707. His death occurred at Worcester in 1753. Some of his MS. are preserved in the British Museum. He deserves notice here for his work entitled,

Fruit Walls improved, by inclining them to the Horizon; or a way to build walls for Fruit Trees whereby they may receive more sunshine and heat than ordinary. By N. F. D. a Fellow of the Royal Society. Plates by Gribelin. London. 1699. 4to.

To the writing of this work he was led by his mathematical

studies, for upon such principles and the laws of Optics, he demonstrates the advantage of receiving rays of Heat and Light at a right angle.

GEORGE LONDON died about Christmas 1717. Switzer glosses over his birth and education—That industry and strong talent which afterwards obtained for him the patronage of the nobility, and others in after life, were early discerned by his master Mr. Rose, who took particular pains in instructing him and bringing him into notice. After being with Mr. Rose four or five years, Switzer was informed, that, that gentleman sent him into France for improvement, Soon after his return he entered the service of Bishop Compton—A few years afterwards he entered into the speculation of Brompton Park Nursery, before mentioned.—This was in 1681, and his partners were Messrs. Cook, Lucre, and Field. In 1694, the two last named partners having died, and the first retired, Mr. London remained sole proprietor. He took Mr. Henry Wise, into the concern. At that time the Garden covered more than one hundred Acres of ground. Bowack, who wrote an account of Kensington in 1705, says that some affirmed that if the Stock of these grounds was valued at one penny per plant, the amount would exceed £40,000.[*] London at the time of entering into this speculation was gardener to Bishop Compton, as Mr. Cook was to the Earl of Essex; Mr. Lucre held a similar situation under the Queen Dowager at Somerset House; and Mr. Field held a like situation at Bedford House in the Strand, belonging to the Duke of Bedford. Brompton Nursery, says Evelyn, "was the greatest work of the kind ever seen, or heard of, either in Books or Travels." Switzer agrees in considering the stock of the grounds as worth nearly £40,000.[†] After the Revolution London was made superintendant of all the Royal Gardens, with a Salary of £200, per

[*] London's Encyclop. Gardening. p. 1068. [†] Icnographia, Rustica, i. p. 78.

annum, and a Page of the Back Stairs to Queen Mary. He had the care of conveying Princess Anne, to Nottingham from the fury of the Papists previous to the Revolution being completed—He was in conjunction with Mr. Wise, Director of nearly all the Gardens and Parks of note in the Kingdom. Soon after the Peace of Ryswick, he accompanied the Earl of Portland, Ambassador Extraordinary to King William, into France—At this time (April 1698) he made the Observations on the Fruit Gardens of Versailles, which are in the Preface to the Abridgement of M. Quintinie's Work, which he, in conjunction with Mr. Wise, translated. On the death of King William, Mr. Wise being appointed to the care of the Royal Gardens by Queen Anne, Mr. London chiefly devoted himself, to his country business, visiting once or twice a year most of the considerable Gardens in England—He was accustomed to ride 50 or 60 miles a day—His northern circuit he performed in five or six Weeks—his western in about the same period—in the Southern and Eastern districts he was occupied but three or four days. Switzer intimates that his knowledge of Botany was slight, his industry great, but the cultivation of Fruit his peculiar excellence, though in that of all kind of Flowers and Shrubs he was as skilful as any man in his time. Switzer is not much of authority when speaking of his excellence in designing, which he considers to have been not great.* The Gardens of Wanstead House were began by him for Sir Richard Child, in 1706, and were nearly his last undertaking; he died before completing the Gardens of the Earl of Caenarvon, at Edger in Herts†.—His activity and continued exertion on horseback brought on a fever which caused his death after an illness of a fortnight's duration.

MR. HENRY WISE was, like London, a pupil of Mr. Rose. But little is known of him more than I have already mentioned;

* Icnograph. Rust. v. i, p. 79—82.   † Ibid. p, 84.

He survived Mr. London.* He was the designer of the grounds at Blenheim. They published in conjunction the two following translations.

1. The complete Gardener: or directions for cultivating and right ordering of Fruit Gardens and Kitchen Gardens. With the Gardener's Kalender, directing what is to be done every month in the year. By Monsieur de la Quintiney. Now compendiously abridged and made of more use, with very considerable improvements. By George London and Henry Wise. London 8vo. 1st Edit. 1699, 1706, 1710; 1717, 6th edition; 7th edition, 1719. Plates.

2. The Retir'd Gardener. Being a translation from the Sieur Louis Liger. The whole revised with several alterations and additions which render it proper for our English culture, By George London, and Henry Wise, 2 Vols. 1706, 8vo.

Volume the first contains the ordering, and improving a fruit and Kitchen Garden, with one part of the Flower department. The second volume contains the manner of planting and cultivating all sorts of Flowers, Plants, Shrubs, and under Shrubs, necessary for the adorning of Gardens, &c. A second edition revised by Mr. Joseph Carpenter, appeared in one volume, in 1717, 8vo.

To give a regular analysis of these works is impossible, the heads of chapters are so numerous. "The complete Gardener," commences with an original and very excellent dissertation on the benefit of sheltering plantations in the neighbourhood of Fruit Trees. The succeeding forty seven pages are occupied by various remarks upon the situation, soil, manures, &c. most be-

* Lawrence's Clergyman's Recreation —Preface.

neficial for Gardens, the whole of which is meagre, and thrown together without the least order. Then follows a list of 73 Pears, and 35 Peaches, 63 Plumbs. Of Cherries and Apricots little is said. Only 8 Apples, 8 Grapes, and 11 Figs.—The descriptions of the Pears and Peaches are full and satisfactory. At page 96 commences the most judicious portion of the work upon planting and pruning, and perhaps no publication could be mentioned, which contains more full and general information upon the training of Trees than this. At page 158, begins the directions for gathering and preserving fruit, which are tolerably full and judicious. The Kitchen Garden begins to be treated of at p. 189. as slight and unsatisfactory as can be imagined to be contracted within less than 60 pages. To this succeeds a Kitchen Gardener's Kalender; with a detail of such products as each month should afford; and rules for judging whether there is any deficiency. The last chapter of the work is a very useful one, containing an enumeration of the time the various Kitchen Garden crops continue in perfection.

"The Retir'd Gardener" is a more comprehensive, and excellent work. It is much more full upon Floriculture than the other departments of Gardening. The plan of the work is to enumerate each species that is an object of culture, to describe its cultivation, the form, &c. and then its History, this last might have been omitted without any loss, being a mere tissue of mythological absurdities.—The directions for the course of cultivation are in general very excellent; and it would perhaps be difficult to find much better in more modern works, than those for the Orange, (vol. 2. p. 652.—78.) The work concludes with a description and plan of M. Tallard's Garden; besides which are given many plans of Trelliage, Arbours, Parterres, Bowling Greens, &c. all perfectly formal. A Gardener's Kalender is given in the first volume, descriptions, and figures of tools, &c. As a whole we cannot but agree with the Translators in considering the work, as "perhaps better than any thing of this nature that has ever yet appeared (1706) in Public, in one entire treatise."

1700. Nourse's Discourse on the benefit and improvements of Husbandry.

1704.—The Husbandman's Magazine. By—SMITH. 12mo.

A Dictionary of all sorts of Country Affairs, Trading, &c. London, 8vo. Anonymous.

Dictionarum Rusticum; or a Dictionary of Husbandry, Gardening, Trade, and Commerce. With plates. 2 vols. 8vo. Without the Author's name. Again in 1726 and 1728.

1706. The Solitary or Carthusian Gardener, being Dialogues between a Gentleman and a Gardener. London. 8vo. Anonymous. I presume this is the same as "the Gentle Gardener" mentioned by Weston.

WILLIAM FLEETWOOD was born in the Tower of London, where his father had his residence, in 1656. He commenced his education at Eton, was elected thence to King's College at Cambridge; became successively Chaplain to their majesties William and Mary, Vice-Provost of Eton, Fellow of King's College, Canon residentiary of St. Paul's, and Rector of St. Austen's, London. Just previous to the King's demise, he was presented to a canonry of Windsor, when he resigned his London living to reside near Eton. In 1706, he was created Bishop of St. Asaph, and eight years afterwards was translated to Ely, of which he died the diocesan in 1723, and was buried in the cathedral. He was universally considered the best preacher of his time; and his theological writings were generally read and admired, their influence being confirmed by the benevolent heart and mind which produced them, and the exemplary life by which he illustrated them. Some of his writings were not the less perused from having been burnt publicly, by order of the ministry in 1712. These were the preface to his Sermons on the Deaths of Mary, of the Duke of Gloucester, of William, and on the accession of Queen Anne. This mode of censuring an author is, perhaps, of all others the most ill-advised, for as Dr. Johnson has well expressed it "fire is a conclusive but not convincing argument; it will certainly destroy any book, but it refutes none"; and if it is intended by the conflagration to warn persons from perusing it, Goëthe gives his testimony of the contrary tendency. Having seen a book publicly committed to the flames, he says "We never rested until we had procured a copy of it, and we were not the only persons who longed for the forbidden fruit. Had the author tried to discover a good method of promoting the circulation of his work, he could not have lit upon a better expedient."* Fleetwood requires our notice from being the author of,

Curiosities of Nature and Art in Husbandry and Gardening. London. 1707. 8vo.

His works were published in a collected form in one volume, folio. 1737.—

His Sermons on the Relative Duties were published in 1716. With his Portrait. 8vo.

JOHN MORTIMER, was a Merchant on Tower Hill, London, in 1693. He was fond of Agricultural pursuits, and in that year became possessed of an Estate in Essex, Filiols, or, as it is now called, Toppingo Hall. He was descended from a branch, settled in Somersetshire, of the ancient family of Mortimer. He had three wives, and his second Son, Cromwell

* Memoirs, v. i. p. 99.

by his third wife, was a Physician, and Secretary to the Royal Society. Mr. Mortimer was an ingenious man. He much improved Topingho Hall; the beautiful Cedars still flourishing there were planted by him. He was a Fellow of the Royal Society. He wrote several pamphlets on religious education. He is mentioned here on account of his having written,

The whole art of Husbandry, or the way of managing and improving of land, being a full collection of what hath been writ either by ancient or modern authors; with many additions of new experiments and improvements not treated of by others; as also an account of the particular sorts of husbandry used in several counties, with proposals for its further improvement. To which is added, The Countryman's Kalendar. 2 vols. 1707. 8vo. Again in 1709, 1712 and 1714. The fifth edition is dated 1721. The last Edition with improvements was in 1761.

This work was approved of in the age in which it appeared, and was even translated into the Swedish language and published at Stockholm in 1727. The first volume is devoted entirely to Agriculture, and of its merits I shall not hazard an opinion. The second volume is devoted to Planting, Arboriculture, and Gardening. It is terse and superficial throughout; tinctured with vulgar prejudices. He gives no lists of varieties of any of the Kitchen Garden plants. Of Apples he enumerates about 110—Pears 138—Cherries 32—Plumbs 71—Apicots 5—Peaches 47—Nectarines 16—of others few or none, and the directions for cultivation are slight and imperfect. His descriptions of Green Houses are grossly deficient, and would convey the information that Glass was not employed in their construction even at the time of publishing the fifth edition; and even advocates the warming them by open fires in holes sunk in various parts of the floor. He dismisses the cultivation of the Potatoe in ten lines, more than four of which are occupied by the following observations. "The root is very near the nature of the Jerusalem Artichoke, but not so good or wholesome. These are planted either of roots or seeds, and may probably be propagated in great quantities, and prove good food for swine."

1711. The English Herbal or History of Plants, containing 1. Their names Greek, Latin, and English. 2. Species, or various kinds. 3. Descriptions. 4. Places of growth. 5. Times of flowering and seeding. 6. Qualities or properties. 7. Their specifications. 8. Preparations Galenic and Chymic. 9. Virtues and uses. 10. A complete florilegium of all the choice flowers cultivated by our florists interspersed through the work, in their proper places, where you have their culture, choice, increase, and way of management, as well for profit as delectation, adorned with exquisite icons or figures of the most considerable species. By WILLIAM SALMON, M. D. fol. 2 vols. 1711. This compilation is chiefly on the medical qualities of Plants.

Van Oosten's Dutch Gardener, or the complete Florist. London. 8vo. Weston mentions an edition dated 1703.

1712. The Theory and Practice of Gardening, and all that relates to fine Gardens: from the French of M· Le Blond. By—JAMES. London. 4to. With cuts. Mr. James made another translation from the same author in 1728. See that year.

From the very full extracts which I have given from Heresbach, Parkinson, &c. it will be seen that in the Kitchen Garden and Orchard, there are few Plants, now cultivated by us in those departments, which they did not contain in the period of our History now before us; we have it is true many superior varieties, and in the Flower and ornamental Shrub department we much excel them. The Art of Forcing and Preserving Plants in Hot Houses was the offspring of the next age.

An estimate of the greater attention now paid to Gardening for the public supply, may be formed from a knowledge of the cheapness of some articles. Early in Autumn (1594) half a peck of Filberts were to be had for sixpence. In September, (1619) 20 Lettuces were to be bought for fourpence; 16 Artichokes for three shillings and fourpence, but 2 Cauliflowers cost one and sixpence each. In the reign of James the I. (1602—1625.) superior varieties of the Melon, a large pale Gooseberry, the Lemon Tree, several varieties of Sallad Herbs and Cabbages were introduced. Melons appear to have been especial favourites of this monarch. "I have sent, says Sir Henry Wotton, writing from Venice, in 1622, the choicest Melon seeds of all kinds, which his Majesty doth expect, as I had order both from my Lord Holderness and from Mr. Secretary Calvert." And Sir Henry "sent withall a very particular instruction in the culture of that plant." He sent also to the Earl of Holderness "a double yellow Rose of no ordinary nature, for it flowereth every month (unless change of clime do change the property) from May till almost Christmas." He also introduced one of our Amaranths in 1613.*

The Tradescants were ornaments of the reign of Charles the I. (1625—1648) The chief decorations of our Parterres, and many of our finest varieties of Fruits were obtained to us by their researches and Travels. It will be observed however from Parkinson that intertropical Plants had been very sparingly introduced. Real Stove Plants are rarely mentioned. American Plants were more abundant, as might be expected from our freer intercourse with their native country, especially

* Reliquiæ Wottonianæ by J. Walton, Edit. 3rd. pp. 316—424.

with Virginia. By far the greater number of Garden plants mentioned by the above named Author are European and Grecian Exotics, some Asiatic and a few of Northern Africa.

The taste for flowers, we have seen in a previous section, was prevalent in this country at a very early period; a great increase of information as to their cultivation, as well as new varieties, were introduced by the Flemish Worstead Manufacturers, who were driven over to Norwich during the persecutions in their country, by Philip the II. and by the Duke of Alva in 1567. They brought over with them Gilliflowers, Provence Roses, and Carnations. This was in the reign of Elizabeth (1558—1602.) who was herself very fond of flowers. Tulips, and the Damask, and Musk Roses, appear to have been introduced early in her reign. Gerarde says, in 1596, that a principal collector and propagator of Tulips, had been so for twenty years, and had an immense variety. There is mention of a Florists' Feast at Norwich so early as 1637, at which a play, or pageant, termed " Rhodon and Iris," was performed,*

In 1671, Evelyn mentions, Sir T. Brown's Garden there as being a "paradise of rarities," and that the parterres of all the inhabitants were rich in excellent flowers. In short Gerarde and others mention cultivators of flowers almost in every county of the kingdom. The taste pervaded every rank. The Duke of Somerset, the Duchess of Beaufort, Dr. Turner, Mr. Lete, a London Merchant, the Artisans of each manufacturing town, are mentioned as delighting in flowers and flowering shrubs.

This fondness for flowers first manifested itself in Holland, and in that country arose to an extraordinary height, continuing until the middle of the last century, at which time two hundred

---

* Linnœan Transac. ii. 296. Rays Catalogus Cantabrigium.

pounds were given for one Hyacinth Root; and more than six hundred pounds for the *Semper Augustus* Tulip.†

Queen Elizabeth we have seen was a great delighter in flowers. Nor were many of her subjects less so. Johnson in his "Mercurius Botanicus," (1634) gives a list of 117 Exotics cultivated by Mr. Gibbs, of Bath, many of which he had brought himself from Virginia.

Among other eminent patrons of Horticulture and Botany, were Sir Walter Raleigh, Lord Zouch, and Lord Hunsden, who all, during their travels acquired and introduced to this country many new plants. Sir Nicholas Bacon, the Lord Keeper, was a distinguished patron of Gardening in this reign. It was upon the Gardens of his beautiful mansion of Gormanbury, that his chief care and cost were bestowed. Several Apples were introduced in this reign by Mascal. Peas, Fuller states, were chiefly imported from Holland, as " dainties for ladies."

James the I. was an eminent patron of Horticulture. He is especially to be distinguished in the annals of the Art, for having in the third year of his reign formed the Gardeners of London, and those within a circuit of six miles around it, into a corporate body, consisting of a Master, Wardens, Assistants, and Commonality. No one was to practice as a Gardener unless approved of by this Company, within the above limits. They were empowered to examine all, and seize such seeds or other Horticultural products, as they might esteem defective; also to impose fines, and the offenders by the magistrates to be committed to prison until they were paid. This Charter, as stated in its preamble, was granted on account of the great disappointment caused to persons having defective samples supplied to them. It was confirmed in the 14th year of the same reign.

* Beckmann's History of Inventions.

This manifests how widely and generally Gardening was pursued, and that a disappointment in its products was esteemed by the monarch, worthy of the exercise of his prerogative to prevent. I by no means approve of the spirit of monopoly by which it supports, and am as hostile to any thing in the form of legal regulations, for the conducting of private business. If left to themselves, the most honest tradesman, and the best goods will soon find the greatest encouragement, penal enactments generally retard improvement, and if they do otherwise than effect that which it is evident will be brought to pass speedily by public experience, it is worse than useless.

An institution arose in the same reign that requires no such restricted approbation. An academy was formed in Scotland for the improvement of Gardening, which it would appear, was in existence as late as 1724.—It had professors who delivered Lectures.* The same monarch appointed a Royal Botanist in the person of Matthias de Lobel, the first of whom we have mention since the time of Richard the II. (see p. 46.) Lobel was under the patronage of Lord Zouch, and cultivated a garden at Hackney of which his lordship bore the expense. Lobel had a considerable correspondence with Foreign Botanists and by that means was enabled to introduce many new Exotics into England.† He died about 1616, aged 78.

The succeeding Monarch, Charles the I, was particularly fond of Gardening, as we shall see when considering the art of design as practised in his reign. Gardening continued greatly to improve and met with general patronage.

Some persons state that in this reign a proclamation was issued directing all magistrates to assist the company of Gardeners instituted by James, in the execution of their authority.

* Bradley's General Treat. on Husbandry and Gardening, v. i. p. 134.
† Pultney's Sketches of Botany, v. i. p. 98.

It is certain a very favourable one was made.* This monarch created the place of Royal Herbalist, and conferred it on Parkinson. Orangeries were now much in request, the Queen had 42 Trees in hers, at Wimbledon, which were valued at £10 each.

During the Commonwealth, as it is very erroneously termed, (1648—1660) Cromwell was a great improver of Agriculture and the useful branches of Gardening. We have seen that he allowed Hartlib an annuity of one hundred pounds.

Charles the II. (1660—1685) was a great patron of our Art in general. Regular glazed edifices for the preservation of tender plants, appear to have been first erected in this reign. Evelyn mentions Loader's Orangery in 1662, and those of the Duke of Lauderdale and Sir Henry Capel. The last mentioned also had a Myrtilleum. - The Green-house and Hot-house in the Chelsea Garden are mentioned by the same author, as well as by Ray in 1685. "What was very ingenious, says Evelyn, was the subterraneous heat conveyed by means of a stove under the conservatory, all vaulted with brick, so that Watts the Gardener, has the doors and windows open in the hardest frosts, excluding only the snow."† In the hot-house Ray mentions that there was a Tea Shrub.

Dwarf Fruit Trees were brought to great perfection by this monarch's Gardener, Rose, at Hampton Court, Carlton and Marlborough House Gardens, so much so, that London, in the preface to his "Retir'd Gardener," in 1667, challenges all Europe to equal them. M. Quintinnie could not accept the challenge.‡

* Bradley's General Treat. on Husbandry and Gardening, v. i. p. 137.
† Bray's Memoirs of Evelyn, v. i. p. 606. ‡ Switzer's Icnographia Rustica, v. i. p. 53.

For the encouragement of his Gardeners, and to insure their utmost exertions, as not being liable to capricious removal, this monarch gave them Patents of their places.*

The statement of Sir W. Temple would argue for the belief that the varieties of Peaches, Grapes, &c. now in cultivation, are hardier, or that our climate has much changed since the period we are considering, for he says that they cannot be looked for as good to the northward of Northamptonshire; and even as late as the early part of the last Century, those Fruits were not considered as capable of being grown in the north of England, "I own it is with pleasure, says Mr. Lawrence, that I *expect* to hear of good Grapes at York and Durham."† Evelyn in his translation of Arnaud d'Andilly's "Essay on Fruit Trees," perhaps the best practical work of its age, is the first to censure the vicious though then prevalent taste, of clipping them into regular forms.

Arthur Capel, Earl of Essex, was a great patron of Gardening in this reign. He introduced many varieties of Fruit from France. The Gardens at Cashiobury near Watford, Herts, were chiefly founded by him under the care of Moses Cook, "one of the first places, says Switzer, were the ingenious spirit of Gardening made the greatest figure."‡ In this opinion he is supported by Daines Barrington and Evelyn.

Evelyn in his Diary affords much information on the history of Horticulture. He says he saw the first Pine Apple presented to the King in the Banqueting house in 1661, and tasted of it. He speaks most highly of Sir William Temple's Gardens at East Sheen. Sir William introduced some of our best peaches, cherries, grapes, and apricots from Holland.‖

---

* Cook upon Forest and Fruit Trees. p. 62. † Fruit Gardener's Kalender. p. 19. ‡ Ienographia Rustica, v. i. p. 62. ‖ Ibid. and his own works.

In the reign of James the II. (1685—1689) Bishop Compton had enriched the Gardens and Greenhouses of Fulham Palace to such an extent, that they were considered as containing a greater variety of plants than any other in England. This he was enabled to do by the happy coincidences of the increasing commerce of the nation, the more frequent intercourse with Holland, where vast Botanical collections from her colonies had been made, and by a protracted residence of thirty eight years at his See. To his taste for Gardening was united a knowledge of Botany, a scientific attainment, observes Dr. Pultney, not usual among the great of those days. He was a great encourager of Mr. London ; was one of the first to encourage the importation and raising of ornamental exoticks, was very curious in collecting them, as well as in cultivating Kitchen Garden Plants, especially Kidney Beans.* In his Stoves and Gardens, he had above 1000 species of Exotic Plants, a greater number than had been seen in any private English collection. In his Gardens he cultivated a great many plants that had been previously esteemed too tender to be exposed unprotected to our climate. Every thing was done under his own superintendance.†

The above prelate, was one of the few men, arising generally at wide intervals, who seem perfect characters. Whatever part he had to perform, he always acted correctly; always was firm in the performance of his duty uninfluenced by fear, unwarpt by interest. Whoever scrutinizes the character of Bishop Henry Compton, cannot but come to the conclusion that he was one of the best characters that History records. He was born in 1632 and died in 1713. It was in company of this Prelate that Mr. London, as previously mentioned, (p. 124.) attended Princess Anne from London to Nottingham, to prevent her being carried off to France by the Papists.

* Switzer's Practical Kitchen Gardner. p. 237. † Switzer's Icnographia Rustica, v. i. p. 70.

Horticulture was now borne vigorously forward in this country; nor was it here alone that it was fostered, and gathered strength. We had previously received an impulse in this Art from Holland; we had surpassed our teacher, and we now strove for the pre-eminence with France, who certainly had been also in a great measure our Tutor. Louis the XIV. at this time domineered over France. His vanity and ambition however conferred this benefit upon his country, and thence to such nations as had intercourse with it, that in ministering to the gratification of those passions, he became a munificent patron of the Arts and Sciences. Horticulture participated in the general encouragement. His father had commenced on a diminutive plan, the Trianon, but Louis the XIV. ordered the creation of the stupendous and splendid Gardens of Versailles, Marli, and Fontainbleau. Partaking of the spirit of the monarch, the nobles and wealthy members of the community aimed at distinction by the display of Horticultural taste. Among these, the Gardens of St. Cloud, belonging to the Duke of Orleans, were particularly to be distinguished. The best scholars of the country united in lauding the prevailing taste, and the praises of Horticulture resound in the verses of Rapin and Boileau. Quintinie was the prince of French Horticulturists; as Le Notre was of their Garden Designers.

William the III. (1689—1702) we shall see introduced the Dutch style of laying out Gardens. He delighted in blanched Vegetables, and it was by his instrumentality that forcing Asparagus was introduced here, being previously unknown.* Mary his Queen delighted in the practice of Gardening more than he did. She superintended in person all improvements made during her life. She was particularly fond of Exoticks, and allowed Dr. Plukenet two hundred pounds annually for assisting her in collecting and cultivating them. Her fondness for Gardening is mentioned by Dr. Tillotson in her funeral sermon.†

* Switzer's Practical Kitchen Gardener, p. 173. † Icnographia Rustica, v. i. p. 77.

During the reign of Anne, (1702—1714.) the progress of Horticulture was of uninterrupted success, and is memorable in our Hortulan Annals, as being the Era in which a genuine taste for design in Gardening arose.

It cannot fail of being remarked, by those who are acquainted with the Horticultural writers of the period, we have been passing over, that the knowledge they betray of the Art of cultivating Plants, is nothing near commensurate to the pains which were taken to collect them. It is only to be accounted for by the plea, that the Gardeners of the age could not at once become acquainted with the habits of the new plants crowding upon them, and it was the results of their experience, which were to act as beacons to those who succeeded. There is no doubt however that they were grossly ignorant, and that this very great obstacle to the improvement of their Art, was not removed till the 18th Century was somewhat advanced. " The want of some moderate degree of learning, says their contemporary Horticulturist, Switzer, and the unwillingness that naturally is in many Gardeners to look back on authors and books, that relate to their profession, cannot be enough lamented. Books and Herbals that have given an account of the names, properties and virtues of plants, would improve their minds, and implant a much greater love and affection to their employs, than generally is found among them. In short it would not only improve their minds, but their dispositions, I had almost said manners too, and reduce them into such an œconomy, as would make them fit company for men of sense and learning. On the contrary, how often do we see them, in good places too, that never open a book; nor can they either read, spell, or pronounce rightly the very plants and herbs, they every-moment have in view; and then no wonder if many useful kinds of plants are totally neglected and forgotten by them. The SPIRŒA FRUTEX is by some called the FIERY FROSTIVE, and the CHŒROPHYLLUM—CARTFOYLE."*
This ignorance passed away as the succeeding Century advanced.

* Preface to Practical Kitchen Gardener, p. xvi.

We may now proceed to consider the style in which the pleasure Gardens and Grounds of the period we are tracing were disposed. It only differed from the formal taste of preceding periods, in being on a more extensive and expensive scale. The deformities were only enlarged and rendered more splendid. The beau ideal of such structures in that age, is to be found in the writings of Lord Bacon, and Sir W. Temple. Those Gardens which are indeed prince-like, says the former,* should not be less than thirty Acres. This space to be divided into three parts. The first part, consisting of four Acres, should be a lawn without any plot or parterre. It was a custom, which he has the good taste to ridicule, to have many little knots, or beds of different coloured earth near the house. Then was to come the main body of the Garden, a square, divided into regular figures: A main walk extending the whole length, garnished with rows of orbicular-headed Laurels, and terminated by a Summer House. The parterres on each side to be exactly like each other, in the forms of ovals, quincunxes, triangles. &c. Trees or Shrubs were to be planted in similar forms, and similar corresponding monotony;

————————————each alley has its brother,
And one half of the Garden justs reflects the other.

These were to be accompanied by arched walks hung with Bird Cages, and little mirrors " for the sun to play upon;" evergreens cut into Pyramids and Columns; fountains; pigmy streams; and mythological Statues. Such were commonly adopted, and such even this sagacious Philosopher admired; he reprobates however something scarsely of worse taste, namely Canals, Aviaries, and Evergreens cut into the forms of Animals, yet these were pretty generally adopted likewise. He recommends the Garden to conclude with a Heath or Desert, which in some degree resembles the natural style now pursued,

* Lord Bacon Essay's on Gardens.

but this was not adopted in his time. Such is a general outline of the ornamental style of Gardening of that age, and we shall proceed to exemplify it by descriptions and illustrations of one or more of the chief Gardens formed in each reign.

In the reign of Elizabeth, arose Hatfield House, in Hertfordshire, the seat of the Lord Treasurer Burleigh. Heutzner describes the gardens, "as surrounded by a piece of water, with boats rowing through alleys of well-cut trees, and labyrinths made with great labour. There are jets d'eau, and a summer House, with many pleasant and fair fish ponds, and abundant statues," which he enumerates. Knottes and Mazes, and divers herbes, "cunningly handled for the beautifying of Gardens," are given in Mountains "Gardener's Labyrinth," part the first (1571.) There were two Parks at Hatfield House, one respectively for Red, and for Fallow Deer. Also a Vineyard which was in existence when Charles the I. was detained prisoner there. Cashiobury, Knowle Park, and Holland House, were also laid out in this reign.

James the I. either formed, or planted and greatly improved the Gardens of the palaces at Theobald's and Greenwich. The former are thus described by Mandelso, who visited this country in 1640. "The Garden is a large square, having all its walls covered with trellis work, and a beautiful jet d'eau in the centre. The parterre hath many pleasant walks, part of which are planted on the sides with espaliers, and others arched over. Some of the trees are Limes and Elms, and at the end is a small mount, named the mount of Venus, placed in the middle of a labyrinth. It is one of the most beautiful spots in the world."* From Bacon's own writing we may imagine what his Garden was, which Sir Henry Wotton says " was one of the best he had ever seen at home or abroad."

* Voyages de Mandelso, i. 598.

During the reign of Charles the I. and the Protectorship. I am not aware any particular Gardens were laid out, but it is certain there was no alteration of taste. The domestic wars of the period at all events would check its improvement. Comenius in his "Janua Trilinguis" published at Oxford during that period, describes a pleasure Garden as containing a green grass platt set about with choice and rare flowers and plants; pleasant walks and bowers bounded by pleached, i. e. topiary, work; trickling fountains and jets d'eau.

During the residence of Charles the II. at the court of France, he became enamoured of the French style of ornamental Gardening, introduced at that period by Le Notre. I know of no prominent features of this style different from that of previous years, or that are not to be found for the most part in the Gardens of declining Rome, except unlimited expense. The alleys were increased in length—the jets d'eau made of greater power —the most expensive and grateful plants profusely employed— the parterre enlarged—the statues made of costly materials, by the best Sculptors. But still alleys, jets d'eau, mazes, parterres, and statues, clipt trees, and mathematical formed borders are there as in previous ages. Versailles was formed by Le Notre at an expense of 200,000,000 francs. The water works, which are not played off more than eight or ten times a year, cost, it has been calculated, about £200 per hour.*

Charles the II. sent for M. M. Perrault and Le Notre. The latter came and superintended the planting of Greenwich and St. James's Parks; but the other declined the monarch's invitation. Charles had formed a grand design for the grounds at Hampton Court, of which the Semicircle was the commencement, but it was not completed. The Canal in St. James's Park was dug by the orders of the same Monarch. The central walk of the same Park he had paved with Cockle shells, and

* Neil's Horticultural Tour, p 409.

instituted the office of Cockle Strewer. Waller the poet terms it "the polished Mall." Moncony in 1663, describes Spring Gardens or Vauxhall as being " much resorted to; having walks both of Grass and Sand; dividing the ground into squares of twenty or thirty yards, which were enclosed with hedges of Gooseberries, whilst within were Raspberries, Roses, Beans, and Asparagus."*

Chatsworth in Derbyshire, belonging to the Duke of Devonshire, and the most magnificent residence in England, was laid out in this reign. It is believed from a design by Le Notre. Banquetting rooms, and similar expensive Garden buildings, are conjectured by Daines Barrington to have been first erected in this country during the reign of Charles, by Inigo Jones, at Beckett near Farringdon. At Beaconsfield, the Poet Waller about the same period formed his residence. The ground being very irregular he was at great expense to have it reduced to regular slopes and levels. He seems to have had a dawning taste for landscape Gardening, since in the remoter parts of the grounds, which were not extensive, he did not introduce any appearance of Art.

Of Cashiobury, before mentioned, Evelyn remarks, " No man has been more industrious than its noble owner, (Earl of Essex,) in planting about his seat, adorned with walks, ponds, and other rural elegancies. The gardens are very rare. There is an excellent collection of the choicest fruit. *My lord is not illiterate beyond the rate of most noblemen of his age.*" Of Hampton Court the same author remarks. "It was formerly a flat, naked piece of ground, but now planted with sweet rows of Lime Trees, and the Canal now near perfected; as also the Hare-Park. In the garden is a rich and noble fountain, with Syrens, and other statues cast in copper by Fanelli, but there is no plenty of water. The cradle walk of

* Balthasar Moncony's Travels.

hornbeam in the garden is, for the perplexed twining of the trees, very observable. There is a parterre which they call Paradise, in which is a pretty banquetting room, set over a cellar." Of Ham House in Middlesex, the seat of the Duke of Lauderdale, he observes, " the parterres, flower gardens, orangeries, groves, avenues, courts, statues, perspectives, fountains, aviaries, and all this on the bank of the sweetest river in the world, must needs be admirable." He also describes many other seats all laid out in the same style.*

Thus the style of Gardening continued to the reign of William and Mary (1689—1702) when this mathematical order of laying out grounds was in its zenith. It was now rendered still more opposed to nature by the heavy additions of crowded hedges of Box, Yew, &c. which however by rendering the style still more ridiculous perhaps hastened the introduction of the more natural taste which burst forth a few years after. William, Daines Barrington informs us, brought a taste for clipt Yews, and splended gates and rails of Iron into fashion. Such were common in Holland and France. These latter fences were a great improvement, supplanting the stone Walls, previously used as boundaries, and thus allowing a more uninterrupted view, received the name of *Clair-voyées* They were very much employed about Hampton Court, and the next in extent were formed by Switzer at Leeswold in Flintshire, laid out by that Gardener in Bridgeman's first style, a mixture of the natural and formal. William and his royal Consort made Hampton Court, their cheif residence. It was under their direction that the Great Garden, the Privy Garden, the Wilderness, and the Kitchen Garden were rapidly constructed. An Alcove, and arched trellis were formed at the end of one of the Alleys, and four urns placed before the principal parts of the house, which are supposed by Daines Barrington to be the

---

* Bray's Memoirs of Evelyn, v. i. p. 432, &c. Gibson's notes on Gardens in the Archæologia, v. xii.

first so employed in England. For sometime after the death of the Queen, William neglected this palace, but he at length returned to it, and amongst other improvements added to the grounds the Great Terrace next to the Thames, " the noblest work, says Switzer, of that kind in Europe."* Kensington Gardens were commenced by this monarch. They were small, but neatly kept. The approach was under a double row of Elms, from the town of Kensington, through an enclosed field, rendered still more unsightly by a gravel Pit. To remove this disfigurement London and Wise were afterwards employed, to effect which they introduced a mimic fortification, the bastions counterscarps, &c. of which were of clipped Yew and variegated Holly, which was long an object of wonder and admiration, under the name of the " siege of Troy." Such vegetable sculptures, and embroidered parterres, were now in the highest vogue. Sir William Temple's, beau ideal of a Garden, given in his " Essay on the Gardens of Epicurus," is that of a flat, or gently sloping plot of an oblong shape, stretching away from the front of the house, the descent from which to it was from a terrace running the whole length of the house, by means of a flight of steps. Such a Garden he says, existed at Moor Park, in Hertfordshire, formed by the celebrated Lucy, Countess of Bedford, one of the chief wits of her time. It was on the slope of a Hill, with two Terraces, rising one over the other, and united by a magnificent flight of steps. A parterre, wilderness, highly ornamented Fountains, Statues, Alcoves, and Cloisters, were its prominent parts and ornaments.

Queen Anne, was a patroness of Gardening, and manifested at least an acquiescence to a better taste. She allowed the Box to be removed from the Gardens at Kensington, had them remodelled, and added another, says Switzer, " behind the Greenhouse, which is esteemed amongst the most valuable pieces of work, that has been done any where." Several other improve-

* Icnographia Rustica, v. i. p. 76.

ments in these Gardens, were made at Mr. Wise's recommendation. The old Gardens were finished. The gravel pits turned into a shrubbery, through which were winding walks, so much admired by Addison, that he compares Mr. Wise, to an Epic Poet, and this improvement to an episode in the general effect of the Garden. During this reign the parterre before the Great Terrace at Windsor, was covered with turf. The Box Work at Hampton Court was removed, and the Gardens fresh laid out. London and Wise, were the Garden designers of this age. Wise was occupied three years in completing the grounds of Blenheim. Exton Hall, Edger, Wanstead, and in short most of the seats, in the old style, were laid out by these designers. Switzer enumerates many of them, concluding with Castle Howard, the seat of Earl Carlisle, " 'Tis there, he exclaims, that Nature is truly imitated, if not excelled, and from which the ingenious may draw the best of their schemes, in natural and rural Gardening. 'Tis there she is taught even to excel herself in the *Natura linear*, and much more natural and promiscuous disposition of all her beauties."* In making nature more natural our author could go no higher! The alteration and improvement of design in Gardening, was now apparently a national object, and the shades of Charles, William and Mary, might have viewed with regret, if permitted, the devastations which were spreading among all the formalities, and tonsile labours of their days. The rise and progress of Landscape Gardening, however, belongs to the next Chapter.

* Icnographia Rustica, v. i. pp. 83. et infra.

ON THE

PROGRESS OF GARDENING

In England during the 18th Century.

That improvement which so gradually dawned upon Gardening during the period of which we have just concluded, the consideration, burst forth in full splendour during the 18th. Century. Never did circumstances more successfully combine for the improvement of any art, than they did for the promotion of Horticulture in all its branches during the hundred years I am now entering upon.

To be an efficient cultivator of Plants, a knowledge of Botany we have already observed is requisite. Whilst that Science remained the chaos of unarranged facts, and ill-classified individuals, which it was until the master mind of Linnæus reduced its confusion and discord to harmony in 1737, it required for its acquisition the devotion of a life. Such acquisition the new system of classification rendered comparatively easy in a few months. That Gardeners availed themselves of the advantage needs no further instance than Phillip Miller, in whom the perfect Botanist and Horticulturist were combined, and who was a correspondent of the chief men of Science then living.

For the working with full effect of the spirit of the immortal Swede, our own Ray had prepared the arena. Indefagitable, enthusiastick in his pursuits, of clear and comprehensive mind, he gave an impetus to Botany and its correllative Arts, more effectual to their advancement than they had recieved during ages of years preceeding. For fifty years he most successfully laboured to clear the path of the Science and to increase her stores. Nor does he enjoy his fame only among his countrymen, it is afforded to him by all Europe. Haller says, he was the improver and elevator of Botany into a Science, and dates from his life a new era in its History. In little more than twenty years, Ray recorded an increase in the English Flora of 550 Species. His "Catalogus Plantarum Angliœ" in 1670 contains 1050 Species: His Synopsis in 1696 describes more than 1000 Species. A Phalanx of Botanists were then contemporaries which previous ages never equalled, nor succeeding ones surpassed. Ray, Tournefort, Plumier, Plukenet, Commelin, Rivinus, Bobart, Petivir, Sherard, Boccone, Linnæus, may be said to have lived in the same age.

I will not pass unnoticed, as being of this period, Abraham Cowley, the well known Poet, Physician, and Author of "The four Books of Plants. "Considering, says his Biographer and Critic, Botany as necessary to a Physician, he retired into Kent to gather plants, and as the predominance of a favourite study effects all subordinate operations of the intellect, Botany in the mind of Cowley turned into Poetry."* Although he deserves little praise as a Botanist, or as a Gardener, he merits notice as assisting in their advancement by winning to them and encouraging the attention of the literary. Of the influence which Botanists possess over the forwarding the interests of Horticulture, I shall quote but one more instance. Sir Arthur Rawdon was so gratified with the magnificent collection of West Indian Plants possessed by

* Johnson's live's of the Poets.—Cowley,

Sir Hans Sloane, that he dispatched a skilful gardener, James Harlow, to Jamaica: who brought thence a Vessel nearly freighted with vegetating and dried Plants, the first of which Sir Arthur Rawdon cultivated in his own garden at Moira in Ireland, or distributed amongst his friends, and some of the continental Gardens. His taste for Exotick plants was probably much encouraged by his intimacy with Dr. William Sherard, who being one of the most munificent patrons and cultivators of Exotick Botany during that "golden age" of the Science, appeared, as Hasselquist observed, "the regent of the Botanic Garden" at his house at Sedekio near Smyrna, where he was British Consul, for here he cultivated a very rich garden, and collected the most extensive Herbarium that was ever formed by the exertions of an individual. It contained 12,000 species. His younger brother, Dr. James Sherard, cultivated at Eltham in Kent one of the richest Gardens England ever possessed.*

But it was not only in the collecting and arranging of Plants that Botany was adding fresh stores and zest to Gardening. Previous to this period little was known of the structure of Plants and the uses of their several parts. Grew, Malpighi, Linnæus, Hales, Bonnet, Du Hamel, Hedwig, Spallanzani, &c. cleared away in a great measure the ignorance which enveloped Vegetable Physiology. Previous to their days the male bearing plants of Diœcious Plants, as Spinach, and the male flowers of Cucumbers, &c. were recommended to be removed as useless; they taught the importance of checking the return of the sap; the mode of raising varieties; in short all the phenomena of vegetable life which throw so much light upon the practise of the Gardener, were first noted and explained by the labours of these Philosophers. Another class of Philosophers who contributed a gigantic aid to the advance of Horticulture, where those Chemists who especially devoted

* Pultney's sketches of Botany. v. ii, p. 150.

themselves to the Vegetable World. Such men were Ingenhouz, Van Helmont, Priestley, Sennebier, Schraeder, Saussure, &c. To them we are indebted for the most luminous researches into the food of plants, the influence of air, of heat, of light and of soils. Previous to their researches the immense importance of the leaves of Plants was unknown. Cultivators were unaware that by removing one of them they were proportionably removing the means of breathing and of nourishment from the parent plant; and mankind in general were ignorant that it is by the Gas which Plants throw off, that the animal Creation is alone enabled to breathe.

The scientific institutions of previous years, which had merely existed, now were in a state of vigorous exertion. The Botanic Garden of Chelsea, was especially distinguished under its Curator Philip Miller. This Garden, as previously stated, was founded in 1673, though the inscription over the gateway is dated 1686, until which year it was not effectually arranged. It was strengthened and rendered permanent by Sir Hans Sloane, in 1721. He having purchased the manor, gave the scite, which is a freehold of four Acres, to the Company on the conditions that they should pay £5 per annum for it, and that the demonstrator of the Company, in their name, should deliver annually fifty new species of Plants to the Royal Society, until the number amounted to 2,000. This presentation of Plants commenced in 1722, and continued until 1773, at which time they had presented, 2550 species.

If old Botanical institutions improved, so also new ones were formed. The Kew Gardens, were commenced in 1760, by the Princess dowager of Wales, mother of George the III. The exotick department was established chiefly through the influence of the Marquis of Bute, a great patron of Gardening. It was placed under the care of Mr. W. Aiton, and it has since become one of the most celebrated Botanical Institutions in the world.

The Cambridge Botanical Garden was also founded in 1763, by Dr. Walker, vice-master of Trinity College. He gave the scite comprising nearly five Acres, in trust to the Chancellor, Masters, and scholars of the University, for the purpose of establishing the Garden. Thomas Martyn, the titular Professor of Botany, was appointed reader on Plants, and Charles, son of the celebrated Philip Miller (who had aided Dr. Walker in selecting the ground,) was made first Curator.*

Previous to this period, the number of Exoticks cultivated in this country probably did not exceed 1,000 species; during this Century above 5,000 new ones were introduced. Some tolerably correct idea may be formed of the improvement arising to Horticulture, from this spirit of research after plants, by a knowledge that [in the first edition of Miller's Dictionary, in 1724, but 12 evergreens are mentioned. The Christmas flower, and Aconite were rare, and only to be purchased at Mr. Fairchild's nursery at Hoxton. Only seven species of Geranium were then known. In the preface to the eighth edition of the Dictionary, in 1768, the number of plants cultivated in this country, are stated to be more than double those which were known in 1731. The publication of the seventh edition of that work in 1759, was of the greatest benefit to Horticulture. In it was adopted the classical system of Linnæus. It gave a final blow to the invidious line of distinction which had existed between the Gardener and the Botanist, and completed the erection of the Art of the former into a Science, which it had been long customary to esteem as little more than a superior pursuit for a rustic. From being merely practised by servants, it became more extensively the study and the delight of many of the most scientific and noble individuals of this country. Miller improved the cultivation of the Vine and the Fig, and was otherwise distinguished for his improvement of the practice as he had been of the Science of Gardening. Having thus decisively

* Loudon's Encyclopædia of Gardening, pp. 86, & 1071. edit. 5.

gained the attention of men of science, the rapid progress of Horticulture from this era is no longer astonishing. The Botanist applied his researches to the increase of the inhabitants of the Garden; and the better explanation of their habits. The Vegetable Physiologist adapted his discoveries to practical purposes by pointing out the organs and functions which are of primary importance; and the Chemist by his analysis discovered their constituents, and was consequently enabled to point out improvements which Practice could only have stumbled on by chance and perhaps during a lapse of ages.

The general introduction of forcing houses likewise gave to our Science a new feature. Green-houses we have seen were in use in the 17th Century, but no regular structures roofed with Glass, and artificially heated, existed until the early part of the one succeeding. Though a pine apple had been presented by his Gardener to Charles the II. (p. 112.) it is certain that they only were successfully cultivated here about 1723, by Mr. Henry Talende, Gardener to Sir Matthew Decker at Richmond; Mr. Loudon gives the date as 1719. Mr. Bradley says that Mr. Talende having at length succeeded in ripening them, and rendered their culture "easy and intelligible," he hopes Ananas may flourish for the future in many of our English Gardens."†
That forcing was rare, and but of late introduction is further proved by Mr. Lawrence, who in 1718 observes that he had heard that the Duke of Rutland at Belvoir Castle in Lincolnshire, hastened his Grapes by having fires burning from Ladyday to Michaelmas behind his sloped Walls, a report to which he evidently does not give implicit credence, but which " it is easy to concieve."† That such however, was the fact, is confirmed by Switzer, who further adds in 1724, that they were covered with Glass. The walls were erected, he says, at the suggestion of Mr. Facio whom we have before mentioned. (p. 122.)

* Bradley's general Treatise on Husbandry and Gardening.
† Lawrences Fruit, Gardener's Kalender. p. 22.

The Walls failing in their anticipated effect were covered with Glass, and thus led to the first erection of a regular forcing structure of which we have an Account.* Lady Wortley Montague in 1716, mentions having partaken of Pine Apples at the Table of the Elector of Hanover; and speaks of them as being a thing she had never seen before, which, as her Ladyship moved in the highest English Circles, she must, had they been introduced to Table here.

Mr. Fowler, Gardener to Sir N. Gould, at Stoke Newington, was the first to raise Cucumbers in Autumn, for fruiting about Christmas. He presented the King, George the I. with a brace of full grown-ones on New Year's Day 1721.†

Even as late as the commencement of the century we are tracing, every garden vegetable in a greater or less degree, was obtained from Holland. The supplyers of the Royal Family sent thither for Fruits and Pot Herbs; and the seedsmen obtained from thence all their seeds. But in 1727, Switzer boasts of the improvements made in his Art. Cucumbers that twenty five years before were never seen at table until the close of May, were then always ready in the first days of March, or earlier if tried for. Melons were improved both in quality and earliness. "The first owing to the correspondence that our nobility and gentry have abroad, now equalling if not excelling the French and Dutch in their curious collections of seed, but the second is owing to the industry and skill of our Kitchen Gardeners." Melons were now cut at the end of April, which before were rare in the middle of June. The season of the Cauliflower being in perfection was prolonged from three or four, to six or seven months. Kidney Beans were now forced. The season of Pease and Beans was extended to a period from April until

---

* Switzer's Practical Fruit Garden, p. 318.   † Bradley's General Treatise on Husbandry and Gardening, v. 2. p. 6L.

December, which previously only lasted two or three months, &c.*

The early part of this Century witnessed the labours of Professor Bradley, who was one of the first to treat of Gardening and agriculture as Sciences. Although deficient in discoveries, his works are not destitute of information derived from contemporary Gardeners and other writers. He wrote luminously on the buds of trees; on bulbs; and especially on the mode of obtaining variegated plants and double flowers. He must be looked upon as a benefactor of Horticulture, for he at least made himself acquainted with the discoveries of others, and recording them in his widely circulated works, he diffused such increased Knowledge, and he diffused over the whole such philosophical views as the Science of the age afforded, and that such views were needed requires but one proof, namely, that the celebrated Evelyn directs that attention should be paid to the Moon in some of the operations of Gardening. Speaking of Grafting he says " The new Moon, and old Wood is best."

The patrons of Horticulture were now numerous and munificent. The Duke of Chandos; Compton, Speaker of the House of Commons; Compton, Bishop of London; Dubois of Mitcham; Dr. Uvedale of Enfield; Dr. Lloyd of Sheen; Dr. James Sherard, already mentioned; Collison at Mill Hill; the Duke of Argyle; Sir John Hill, then only Dr. Hill; Drs. Pitcairn and Fothergill; Duke of Marlborough; Mr. Salisbury; Duke of Northumberland; le Comte de Vande, &c. had all fine Gardens and collections of Exoticks.

Some of our most celebrated Nurserymen flourished during this Century. Fairchild; Gordon; Lee; and Gray introduced many plants during its first half. Hibbert of Chalfont and

* Preface to Switzer's Practical Fruit Gardener.

Thornton of Clapham deserves particular mention for their encouragement of Exotick Botany. The Garden and Hot Houses of the latter were among the best stocked about London.

A great stimulus to the culture of ornamental plants was given by the publication of the Botanical Magazine, which commenced in 1787; the works of Lee, Lodiges, &c. and this taste was further revived by the publication of Maddocks's Florist's Directory in 1792.* The various works which appeared, and the influence which they had in promoting the interests of our Art may be judged from the biographical and critical sketches which follow.

JOHN LAWRENCE or LAURENCE was admitted B. A. of Clare Hall, Cambridge, in 1688. He was presented to the Rectory of Yelvertoft, in Northamptonshire, in 1703, previous to which he had become M. A. To the cultivation of the Garden of the Rectory House he assiduously applied, and though its soil was shallow, and on the worst description of subsoil, viz. a white clay, in three years he grew in it some of the choicest fruit. In 1721, he moved to the Rectory of Bishop's Wearmouth, in the County of Durham. In 1723, he was a prebendary of Salisbury. He died at his rectory, in 1732. He was a naturalist and very fond of Horticulture, especially that part of it which includes the culture of fruits, priding himself upon the richness of his deserts. Working in his Garden, he tells us was " the best and almost only physick" he took. He is represented as hospitable and generous, but we cannot entertain a very high opinion of his honour, if Lintot the Bookseller adhered to the truth in complaining that in his " New System of Gardening," in different words he had republished what he had previously sold to him (Lintot) in the form of " The Clergyman's and Gentleman's Recreation." He wrote,

* Loudon's Encyclopœdia of Gardening, 86. edit. 5.

1. The Clergyman's Recreation shewing the pleasure and profit of the art of Gardening, London, 8vo. 1714, 1715, 1717. The sixth edition appeared in 1726.

2. The Lady's Recreation in the Art of Gardening, London, 1717, 1718, 8vo. This work I find has a mere assumption of Mr. Lawrence's name, for he states in one of his succeeding publications that he never saw it until after it was printed.

3. The Gentleman's Recreation; or the second part of the art of Gardening improved, containing several new experiments and various observations relating to fruit trees, particularly a new method of building Walls with horizontal shelters. With an appendix to fix a meridian line by the brother of the Author, Edward Laurance. London, 8vo. 1714; 1716. The third edition is dated 1723.

4. The Fruit Garden Kalendar; or a summary of the Art of managing the Fruit Garden, teaching in order of time what is to be done therein every month in the year, containing several new and plain directions more particularly relating to the Vine. With an appendix of the usefulness of the Barometer. London. 8vo. 1718.

5. A new system of Agriculture, being a complete body of Husbandry and Gardening. In five books, 1726, folio.

6. Paradise regained, or the art of Gardening, a Poem, London. 1728. 8vo.

"The Clergyman's Recreation" is concise, but perhaps there is no work that has less of error in its directions. In his directions for pruning, training; and the preparation of an infusion of Wall-Nuts leaves to destroy worms, &c. he has recorded his practical knowledge of various directions which have been in late years recommended as improvements. It is chiefly confined to the cultivation of Wall Fruit. He mentions nothing about Apples; and is much too pragmatical upon the diseases to which Trees are subject.

"The Gentleman's Recreation" as he states in his introduction, is " an Appendix to the former" or Clergyman's Recreation. It is a miscellaneous collection of notes for the most part relating to the cause of barrenness in Fruit Trees; and the superiority or fresh earth to some plants rather than dungs.— The most original observations are upon the benefits of horizontal shelter in preventing the blasting of Wall Fruit. The observation upon permanent nails to which to tie the branches of Wall Trees are equally worthy of the claim of novelty.

" The Fruit Gardener's Kalender" is composed of many excellent observations and directions. He mentions as a common practice ringing the branches of fruit trees to make them bear, which he calls " circumcising" them.

Upon a review of the whole, Mr. Lawrence must be ranked among the great benefactors of Horticulture, and as one of the most excellent of writers upon the Art, inasmuch as that the contents of his works are evidently the results of his own observations, made during the experience of many years practice of this his favourite recreation.

1715. In this year commenced the publication of " Vitruvius Britannicus, or British Architect, containing plans, &c. of buildings aud Gardens, public and private, in Great Britain; 200 Copper plates. London, large folio. 5 vols. A volume appeared respectively in

1715, 17, 25. 67, and 71. It was the united production of C. J, WOLFE, and JAMES GANDON.

The Landed Man's assistant. By G. Clarke, 12mo.

Art's Improvements: or experiments in Building, Agriculture, Gardening, &c. London. 8vo. By T. SNOW, author of *Apopiroscopy*.

STEPHEN SWITZER, was a general Gardener and Seedsman of the reigns of Anne and George the I. He was a native of Hampshire. He acquired his knowledge of the Art under the great masters of the day, London and Wise, having been, as he states in the Title page of his "Icnographia Rustica," for several years their servant. He completed his apprenticeship at the close of the 17th. Century. In 1706, he was employed under London in laying out the grounds of Blenheim. When Mr. Lowder was superintendant of the Royal Gardens at St. James's, Switzer was employed in them in the capacity of Kitchen Gardener. In 1724, he was Gardener to the Earl of Orrery, as appears from the Dedication of his Practical Fruit Gardener. The same Dedication is retained in the edition of 1731. He appears at one time to have been in the same capacity servant to Lord Brooke, to Lord Bathurst and also to Lord W. Russel, who suffered in 1683. Gardeners in his time were accustomed to ply about Westminster Hall and the Royal Exchange offering Trees, Seeds, &c. for sale. In the first named place having commenced business as a Nurseryman and Seedsman, he kept a stand for the sale of his productions, bearing the sign of the Flower Pot, and close by the entrance to the Court of Common Pleas. His Garden was at Milbank. Where he resided I have been unable to determine, he dates his "Disertation on the true Cytisus of the ancients" in 1731, from New Palace Yard, Westminster. Mr. Loudon says he died in 1745, at which time he must have been eighty years of age.

For the foregoing very imperfect sketch of his life I am indebted solely to accidental notices contained in his own works. It is an instance of the partiality of fame, that of this Horticulturist no contemporary authors make mention, whilst of Bradley and others, infinitely his inferiors in every point we have full particulars. This neglect, and even persecution attended him through life. It appears from his own account in 1731, that some "great man some years deceased, charged him with not finishing his work, and embezzling several hundred pounds, the falsity of which is visible and speaks for itself." His brother seedsmen also opposed him with considerable acrimony because he was not bred to that trade, but as a Gardener. Neglect has pursued him beyond the grave, for his works are seldom mentioned or quoted as authorities of the age he lived in. To me he appears to be the best author of his time, and if I was called upon to point out the Classic Authors of Gardening, Switzer should be one of the first on whom I would lay my finger. His works evidence him at once to have been a sound practical Horticulturist, a man well versed in the Botanical Science of the day, in its most enlarged sense; of considerable classical and literary attainments, and above all a religious character; they completely warrant us in receiving as correct the modest notice he takes of himself in the preface to the first volume of his " Icnographia Rustica."

"I hope, he says, I shall not be altogether unfit for this work, by the happiness I have had in an education none of the meanest for one of my profession, and of having a considerable share in all parts of the greatest works of this kingdom, and under the greatest masters; and even that which some may probably reckon otherwise, I mean some small revolutions and meaness of Fortune, as it has sometimes thrown me upon the greatest slavery, so it has at other times amongst the best men and books; by which means, and I hope an allowable industry and ambition and an eager desire of being acquainted with all parts of this nation, as well as the useful parts of Gardening, I have tasted both rough and smooth, as we plainly call it, from the best business and books, to the meanest labours of the Scythe, Spade, and Wheelbarrow." That by misfortunes he had been reduced to a humble station in Gardening, he often glances at. From the above Preface, we also learn, that he had travelled on the continent, especially in France, paying particular attention to the style of design in Ornamental Gardening. This preface is throughout well worthy of perusal; independent of an eloquent, though in places far too florid style, it breathes an appropriate feeling of love for his art, a spirit of candour in warning Gentlemen of those errors both of expense and penury which were alike sure to defeat their object, in the ornamental disposition of their Parks, or " Extensive Gardening" as he appropriately terms it, " a kind, he observes,, not yet much used with us. It is curious among other warnings to find him telling the landed Proprietor, to beware of the Scotch Gardeners, who even in his day appear to have been objects of jealousy, and caused him to forget his accustomed suavity. "These Northern Lads, which whether they have served any time in this Art or not, very few of us know any thing of, yet by the help of a little learning, and a great deal of impudence, they invade these southern provinces, and the natural benignity of this warmer climate has such a wonderful influence on them, that one of them knows, or at least pretends to know, more in one twelvemonth than a laborious, honest south countryman does in seven years." "The three exports of Scotand—Gardeners, Black Cattle, and Doctors," is a toast now often given. The following is a list and analysis of his published works.

1. Icnographia Rustica, or the nobleman, gentleman, and Gardener's Recreation, containing directions for the general distribution of a country seat, into rural and exrenivse Gardens, Parks, Paddocks, &c. and a general system of Agriculture, illustrated with great variety of copper

plates done by the best hands from the author's drawings, London, 1718, 3 vols. 8vo.

An edition of the first volume of this work appeared in 1715, 8vo. entitled " The Nobleman, Gentleman and Gardener's Recreation, or an Introduction to Gardening, Planting, Agriculture, and the other business and pleasures of a country life." Mr. Felton informs me that this, with the exception of about a page and a half of new matter added to the History of Gardening, is verbatim the same as the first volume of the " Icnographia."

The first Chapter is an entertaining though superficial History of Gardening. For that part which treats of the Art during the age in which Switzer lived, I am indebted however for many notices. Of the style in which he details the facts, or the eloquence he displays in praising his favourite Art, I need not dwell. It is much too pompous in many parts. Like the Poets of his age he often bestows a labour upon trifles, which even when moulded to his wish, do not compensate for the exertion. One example shall be sufficient. In proving that Gardening was as old as the Creation, he observes. "It is evident from the latter end of the afore-mentioned Chapter (Genesis ii.) where that operation is recorded of taking the rib from Adam, wherewith the woman was made; yet tho' from this Chirurgery may plead high, yet the very current of the Scriptures determines in favour of Gardening!"

In the 2nd Chap. the soil most suited for Gardens, especially where trees are to be planted, is very slightly considered, but he dwells much upon fresh Earth, compounded of Clay, &c. for light Soils, and of Sand, &c. for tenacious ones, being of more importance than Dungs, which he considers chiefly as "a good ingredient to mix with earth, and other compost." These composts, their turning, and other directions, are much the same as those we find in later authors. Chap. 3. is devoted to the consideration of the use Water is to Plants, and of that which is best for them. He is decidedly opposed to those who consider water the sole food of plants. Rain water he considers best for them. The plan of watering Trees, &c. with water impregnated, with dungs, lately so ably advocated by Mr. Knight, Switzer gives directions for performing without at all considering it a new plan. We have observed it in much older authors. Pigeon, sheep, and horse dungs, he considers best for the purpose. Chap. 4. is consumed in considering the influence of the Sun upon the earth, and relates to any thing but Gardening. Chap. 5. is upon the influence air has over Vegetation. He here seems to have again anticipated Mr. Knight who in the Horticultural Transactions, has some experiments to prove that the motion which the winds impart to Plants assists their growth. Switzer speaking of the benefits of the breezes, enumerates their " blowing open and extending natures offspring." He dwells much upon the dry air of March, bein injurious to new Plantations, and strictly enjoins watering the roots, " more plantations miscarry on account of this neglect than by any cause whatever." Chap. 6. is devoted to the processes of Vegetation, in the course of this he makes an observation, little attended to now, but to which I bear decisive testimony, that standards generally bear sooner and better than dwarfs.—Of different plants regaining different soils, manures, &c. and hence deducting that water, is not their chief nourishment, he argues earnestly, and in a manner rarely found in writers of his age, and on such subjects. Chap. 7. is occupied by a consideration of Forest Trees, their culture &c. Its Section 1. contains the opinions of the ancient and, more modern Poets, concerning the beauties of Groves and Umbrageous situations; if Switzer is not so melodious in his sentences, they serve as vehicles for Rhapsodies, perhaps as full of inspiration, and certainly as fervent as the warmest admirer of Woodland scenes can compel his imagination to soar with;

"I cann't, he exclaims, but think I may, with the universal consent of Mankind, suppose that nothing on this side Heav'n is comparable to it"—What impelling Passion could say more? —When less rapturous he is more eloquent; Jeremy Taylor, would not have blotted such a Passage as this—" Every gentle breeze of air, a virtuous man will readily esteem the immediate breathing of his Maker; and every awful bend of a Tree, the premonitions of his approaching end; every green walk will remind him of the very steps he is taking towards happiness, the whole design of no less than Heaven itself."

After recommending to the Gentlemen of his time the introduction of more Forest Trees into their grounds rather than Evergreens, he proceeds to consider of the propagation of them in imitation of Virgil, into those that are produced spontaneously, those which are raised from seed, those from suckers, those from cuttings, and those from grafts, &c.

It is needless to refute here the opinion to which he accedes, that some plants are produced immediately from the components of the soil, and not from seed previous received, or as Virgil expresses it, " sponte sua veniunt,"—Equivocal generations is one of the errors which the monarch of Botanical knowledge has completely demonstrated.—In the section on raising Forest Trees from seed he is more happy; I have compared his course of cultivation with that given in the best works of the present day, and I have not ascertained any point demonstrative of improvement in the time, that has supervened since he wrote—he advocates a moderately fertile seed bed, for he concludes "if they will do well in an indifferent Soil, they will do better in good"—his directions for sowing are ample and correct, his mode of sheltering the beds judicious;—he recommends with convincing observations that Autumn is the best seed time—He particularly dwells also upon the importance of stirring the ground among the Trees, a recommendation which in 1828 the Society of Arts gave one of their Medals to Mr. Withers of Holt, for advocating.—Sec. 4th. on raising Trees from Suckers, contains little else but an anecdote in support of Salmasius's declaration that the Elm can be raised from Chips of its own trunk—Sec. 5. of raising Sallows, &c. by slips or Truncheons is equally unimportant—Sec. 6. of Layers—contains directions for the common method of pegging down shoots that proceed from stubs or stools.—Sect. 7. On Cuttings, grafts, &c. is insignificant, and containing little to the purpose—Sec. 8. is a bare recapitulation—Sec. 9. comprises the treatment necessary in the Nursery to which the plants are conveyed from the seed beds.—He here insists upon the benefit of removing them with speed from the one to the other, carefully shading their roots; even recommending a kind of close barrow for moving them in—so important he was aware it was to prevent their fibres becoming dry—Yet this practice we have lately seen treated of, as if it was a new illumination.—Sec. 10. Treats of pruning and dressing the Trees in the Nursery.—In this section he is uniformly judicious—he directs an annual autumn pruning of the side shoots to keep the tree streight and handsome, specifying that they should be " close cut off" a particularity of direction which might be attended to with no inconsiderable advantage by most timber growers of our times.—If ever Timber Trees are pruned at all it is usually by some ruthless Hedger with his Bill, needless wounds are inflicted which check the growth, and stumps of branches are left, which decaying, gradually carry infection into the heart of the Tree.—He directs manuring and stirring the surface with restrictions accurate and methodical—though one of his axioms that Timber trees cannot shoot too fast (p. 236) if durability is to be considered, may be successfully disputed.—As also the practice of cutting their roots round to keep them together conveniently for moving, which is very erroneous—as indeed is the practice of shifting, &c. which he pursued, it is better to sow where the tree is to remain, or at most to move but once. In Sect. 11. He comes to consider their final removal, and in this he is more at variance with our present practice than in any of his others, inasmuch as that for some varieties he recommends a pruning of the Roots and all to be planted deep " at least two feet". Although he justly argues against the idea of always planting any side of the tree to the same point of the compass yet still he does not seem to be altogether faithless in Pliny's notions regarding the Winds which should prevail, and the age of the moon, at the time of planting (p. 248.) He expresses himself more regardless of them afterwards (p. 261.) Sect. 12—is on the several sorts of Soil on which Trees thrive best—for poor, gravelly, dry ground he recommends the Abeal and Witch Elm —for dry, sandy, deep soils, the Beech, Hornbeam, &c.— Here it may be remarked that the great benefit of raising the plants from seed on the spot where they are to continue is for such soils most strenuously supported by him; a practice which cannot be too generally adopted for however at first there may appear a gain by planting three or more years old Trees, yet in the course of a few years the seedlings will generally surpass their competitors. For moorish, boggy land he recommends Alders, Willows, &c. and a Tree which in Lincolnshire they call " Eller" (p. 253) In springy wet gravels—Abeals, Poplars, Alders, and Elm—on stiff, rank, cold Clay—by being trenched, &c. Oak, Ash, &c. may be grown, without any such care, the Abeal, Poplar and all '• the Vimineous kinds"— On moderately fertile soil, as pasture land any tree will flourish —and the Ash but more especially the Abeal will grow in any ground (p. 263—4) Sect. 13.—contains a compilation from Evelyn's Sylva and other works shewing the opinions of their authors upon the above subject—i. e. the soils best suited to the various kinds of Trees—Sect. 14. contains a summing up from the preceding, or 11 Aphorisms deduced from the preceding dissertations—Chap. 8. Is directions for raising Coppices —he directs the stirring of the ground, insists upon its being trenched; and very justly reprobates the raising of Corn, &c.' among the young plantations—For sowing he merely directs Acorns, Beech Mast, &c. " to be sown promiscuously, at a discretionary thickness, not too thick or thin"—the Drill and Dibble fortunately are now so generally adopted in this practice, that we need not reprobate this absurd mode of broadcast sowing.—When the seed is covered in he recommends on light soils a thin covering of well rotted compost—and on heavy soils a top dressing of slacked Lime—He here also mentions as the proper mode of planting that which, in very late days has been considered an ingenious and certainly rational discovery " the sets should have hills about them like Hop hills that the Roots may be well covered without planting too deep"—his directions about hoeing, &c. are too cursory.—The Addenda which concludes his consideration of Woods and Coppices, commences with an eulogium upon them as superior to trees planted in rows, tortured into Espaliers, &c.—He then proceeds to recommend in the making of Hedges White Thorn, Holly, &c. to be employed when grown to the height, even of 5 or 6 feet in preference to planting small seedlings--It is certain such practice is most desirable and may, where there is opportunity to employ proper care, he successfully followed—but Nurserymen will not allow plantations of Quick to attain such growth that consequently requires so much room in their spaces, and unless the Plants be had from such situations, where the Roots by frequent transplantings have been kept together, the trouble and consequent expence is great and the success uncertain. He concludes by an appeal to country gentlemen in favour of planting, shewing by conclusive arguments the pleasure and profit it affords to themselves and their posterity;—as well as its importance to the country; pleas which must influence all mankind as including the selfish, the parents of families, and the patriot —Chap. 9 Contains a consideration of Springs, and Water Works, commencing with a consideration of the origin of Springs, crude and unphilosophical, and the rest consumed in directions for conducting Water and forming reservoirs in which there is nothing worthy of notice.—Chap. 10. "Of Statues." Of those incongruous Horticultural introductions he appears to have been a great admirer, and is almost pathetic in lamenting that the Roman and French Gardens "abound so much in them, that in that point they are still likely to out-doe us."—He then proceeds to point the appropriate situations for Jupiter, Mars, Neptune, &c; to recommend an Academy of Statuary under Royal patronage for the instruction of young men, who when sufficiently adepts might be taken into the service of noblemen and gentlemen who allowing them wages, &c. would soon "furnish themselves with Statues"—In continuation and equal bad taste, he recommends "all Lodges, Granges, and other buildings that Gentlemen are obliged to build for conveniency, in the form of some antiquated Place!"—although in the next and almost concluding sentence he confesses that our building exceed those of all other nations in "plainness, strength and good architecture."—Chap. 11. Ot Grass and Gravel "natural ornaments of our country seats by which we much excel all other nations"—In lieing Turf he justly reprobates doing so on rich land it being on that account more subject to Worm-casts and over luxuriance. He proceeds to give directions for making a proper soil in case it is too rich. For he remarks it is well known as finest from Commons and sheep walks, though that from the coarsest pastures by continued rolling, &c. may be brought to be equally fine, and not so apt to become mossy and weedy; this last assertion is certainly apocryphal if not positively wrong. For cutting the turfs, he describes the mode of marking it out into parrellograms, 1 foot wide, an inch thick, and 3 feet long, which are the most convenient size for moving about. He concludes by stating the mode of raising a Turf from seeds, and dissuading from the practice. He gives directions for making, if necessary, a binding gravel for Walks, the depth which it ought to be laid, from 6 to 12 inches, not skreened but merely the largest stones raked out, and not laid too rounding it making them seem narrow, and being inconvenient. A walk 20 feet wide, should be 4 inches higher in the middle, than at the sides (p. 334.) In his Conclusion to the volume, he gives some additional directions about forest Trees, and here most erroneously recommends Oaks planted from the seed Bed, being first cut close down, to within a bud or two of the ground, and this for poor soils even to be repeated, "twice or thrice after the first years planting"—Oaks and Beech should always be grown in Coppices, and never singly, otherwise they become crooked and have wide spreading heads—The Elm is "one of the most hospitable Plants of all, since whatever grows under it will prosper, which Ash, Yew, and several other Trees will not suffer"—He justly reprobates the practice too common even now, of planting Ash in the Hedge Rows, it causes them to become "thin and there is nothing but gaps." As for planting out of the Hedge Rows about the fields, it is a practice which needs no comment, since no Agriculturist ever did, or will follow it.—His other observations upon Trees, Planting, and Designing, are a mere summary of what he had stated before, and the ending like the commencement of the volume, is in the strains of various Poets laudatory of the pleasures of the country.

Vol. 2. The first one hundred and thirty four pages are occupied with geometrical definitions, and arithmetical rules necessary to be known by Surveyors and Designers of Grounds. To this is appended numerous figures, some of which are very curious as representations of the extremes to which the topiary art was pursued. To this follows, on the formation of Court Yards; and of Terrace Walks. These last he directs to be very large and the surface in chequer work of Gravel, Grass, Pavement, and Cockle Shells!—Chap. 6. is of the Parterre.—Chap. 7. of Woods and Groves.—Chap. 8. of Espaliers and Hedges.—Chap. 9. of Fruit Gardens, Planting, Pruning, &c.—Chap. 10. Of Orchards and Vineyards.

Vol. 3. commences with an Introduction to Rural and extensive Gardening, beginning with a praise of its object, the mode of weaving the " utile harmoniously with the dulce" and the method by which it may be rendered profitable instead of expensive. In doing this he objects to needless expense in extensive walls; espaliers of Forest Trees; variety of exotics; levelling and inexperiencing of designers.—To the justness of the second, fourth and fifth objections all must subscribe, but unless our grounds are to become mere Kitchen grounds; and be deficient in the majority of our vegetable beauties, who will retrench his Walls, or thin the ranks of his exotics?—But here we must not mistake the object of our author, he was endeavouring most correctly to shew that many delighters in Horticulture, might do so, might improve nature in her arrangements even to profit; and that many who aimed at profit need not lose sight of beauty in their compositions.—Chap. 1. Sect. 1. Is on "design in general, and the necessary qualifications of a good designer."—Design is to be founded on variety, a principal most correct, but which he illustrates by a quotation from the Spectator, the charms of variety are in this well insisted on, but the illustration of Jets d'eau, in which is a formality of motion, is at once incongruous and unvarying—" A little regularity is allow'd near the main building" to the justness of which I think no person of true taste can object. Sudden transitions surprise, a gradual procession from finished Art to wild Nature is pleasing and soothing--the mind expands by degrees without exertion.—Nothing to me appears more destitute of taste than a mansion rising as it were out of the sward of a Park which touches its very Walls—I would almost rather have it surrounded by monsters in evergreens. There certainly should be a girding of parterres, expanding through Lawns, and Plantations, into the Park and its Wooded scites. —A Designer he contends must be a student of Nature—acquainted with the Poets, a tolerable Mathematician, Historian, and Architect; active, vigorous, and ready—qualifications which if not all necessary will ever be found useful.—Sect. 2. "On the choice of situations."—He very justly prefers a low situation, that is not feny, to one that is high, if not well wooded and a good soil; for in the first " though the owner may want prospect, he can want nothing else, that the nature of his happy situation can furnish him with," (p. 13.)—but the circumstances which are essential, and must determine every scite are the concurrence of wood, water, and proper soil.—Chap. 3. Sect. 3. Is " Of the proper choice of soils, &c. for a country seat."—It is a chapter which contains as much as is necessary to say upon a subject of so much importance, and yet to which so few general rules will apply.—The sum of the whole is that the best soil for general purposes is either a sandy loam, or a black pasture mould, one or two feet deep, on a substratum of gravel, chalk, or shelly rock.--He describes symptoms, the growth of various weeds, &c. by which the richness of soils may be estimated, but before any situation is rejected, otherwise desirable, on account of the superficial soil, he recommends a hole to be dug to ascertain the substrata, for a poor sand may have a boggy marle within its bosom which mixed with it would render it fertile, and he observes, " I dare affirm that there is no superficies of earth, how poor soever it may be, but has in its own bowels something or other for its own improvement." A maxim, which however indisputable in a literal sense, yet too general to be true in a practical view, for the remedy in many lies too deep to be available, but still it is so far founded upon fact, as to deserve the attention of every cultivator. He enters very minutely into particulars, without however being tedious, and the whole chapter may be advantageously perused for instruction.

Chap. 4. Sect. 4. Is devoted to an amplification of his ideas on " Rural and extensive Gardening," as briefly alluded to in the previous ones, or his mode of combining profit with pleasure. He then proceeds to give directions for staking out the ground, levelling, &c. laying turf, and making walks.—To enter into particulars is needless, the prominent feature of his designs is the introduction of an immensity of woods, and even to the very walls of the house he approximates Trees to the exclusion of the Flowers and Shrubs; he deprecates all borders, and makes Turf usurp their place.—The Elm and the Grasses are all in all. So far he aimed at a beneficial revolution of taste, his mode radically removes clipt evergreens, and flower borders worked in patterns, but though " in medio tutissimus," how seldom does any one avoid extremes, Switzer certainly does not. Let any one examine his plan which faces p. 44, and he will find it nearly one mass of Trees, had it been entirely so it would have been better, for the little enclosures sprinkled through it, if producing moderate pasturage, would certainly be very unproductive under tillage. With regard to the form and disposition of his plots, there is little to admire, they are a mere trifle better than in the most formal style of Gardening which he deprecates, he still conducts us to the mansion over three terraces in regular succession; every pond, every plantation, is in a regular geometrical figure; the walks are broken lines, or formal curves, ships are floating upon pigmy pools of Water; Statues of Heathen deities are scattered about. which as they can be little attractive for their execution, are ridiculous as being misplaced. The description of these and observations on the engraved plans, accompanying them, occupy the 5th, 6th, and 7th chapters; the 8th contains a particular description of "Mr. Blathwayt's Gardens at Durham, near the Bath in Gloucestershire," which is only a varied arrangement of the formalities above described. At p. 129 commences his " management and improvement, of land," in treating of which he purposes not merely to state what practices are proper, but by plain arguments, " to demonstrate why it is so."—Sect. 2. commences " of Summer Fallowing, &c." his theory of benefit by which, being a mere chaos of words, needs no comment ; he insists upon its being advantageous, and in conclusion very convincingly recommends dung only to be carried on just immediately before it is turned in with the plough, though we may observe now as he did then, "farmers in many countries spread it, or at least lay it in small heaps on their fields, perhaps five or ten weeks before they plough it in."—Sect. 3. is " of Winter Fallowing" which he observes kills weeds and reduces the soil into mould. The earth should be turned as often as you can, &c. but as for his theoretical reasons of benefit, he certainly could not have understood them himself.

In Section 4. he treats of " Earths and their improvements," dwelling first upon the qualities of soils as indicated by their colours, then of the smell which they emit as being similarly indicative, next of their feel to the touch or handling. The sum of which is that the best soils, are of a lively chesnut or hazel colour, cut like butter, stick not obstinately, but are short, tolerably light, breaking into small clods, sweet, will be tempered without crusting, or chapping in dry weather, or turning to mortar in wet. In the conclusion of these observations among some remarks upon the nutritive parts of soils, which he justly considers to be those which are soluble, he lays too much stress upon its saline particles, which however valuable they certainly are, must only be considered as secondary to their soluble vegetable, and animal constituents.—He next insists upon the great influence the substratum has upon a soil, upon the cropping and management of various soils, fallowing, &c.—He justly reprobates burning land, for however quickly it will bring a Clay Soil into Tillage, yet " by honest, painful husbandmen, and those who have a regard to posterity, or the real benefit of their landlords, is not reckoned a good way, neither will it hold so long, or carry so many crops, it enervates and destroys very much of those juices which are the proper aliment and spirit of vegetation."—He then proceeds to consider Chalking as highly beneficial, especially to

" all sour, surly lands."—Chemistry rationally explains, the time and mode of applying it.—He next dwells upon the ploughing in green Crops for manure, the best of which he says are Buck Wheat and Tares, in which our present Agriculturists agree.

Sect. 5. Is dedicated to manures, and first of horse or stable manure, which he considers as best for cold, clayey soils, as that of horned Cattle is for hot ground—he recommends small quantities to be applied at a time and often repeated, in compost rather than simply varying them with the soil.

Section. 6. On Sheep and Hog's dung, and Night soil, is short and superficial, though he strongly recommends them, yet he does not seem to dwell enough on what are certainly the richest of all manures.—Sect. 7 and 15 are on the dungs of Pigeons and Poultry, in which there is nothing worth notice, than the error that they ought to be left exposed to the air some time before being used, which he recommends.

Sect. 8. Is chiefly devoted to Marle, the discrimination of the varieties of which are as vague as usual, where chemical characters are unknown or unnoticed. He classes them according to their colour; his practical observations are good, except in the proportions he mentions as being applied, varying from 60 to 400 loads per Acre, the smaller number being in most cases too large.

Chap. 3. Sect 1. is on " the superficial dressings of land, after they are sown" which he mentions as a practice, " within these few years discovered." Among these he reckons folding sheep upon wheat during the winter months. Sect. 2. Is on the dressing land with coal ashes,—3. with wood ashes, —4. with kiln ashes.—5. with saw dust.—6. with turf ashes, 7. with lime,—8. with malt dust,—9. with sea sand, in the course of which there is an observation worthy of the attention of all those employing saline manures, and all manures are more or less composed of salts, viz. that being soluble, they are all apt to sink deep, and out of the reach of the crops growing on the lands treated with them, consequently it is better to apply small quantities often on the surface; than a larger quantity, or to plough it in.—Sect. 10. is on the superficial application of pulverized earths,—11. of turf ashes,—12. of burning vegetable refuse,—13. of soap ashes, soot, &c.—14. of animal exuviæ, &c.—15. of pigeon's dung, &c.—16. of sea shells,—17. of paring and burning, which he terms burn-bating and devonshiring, as being first practised in the county of Devon. It should only be adopted he observes on land, " of inconsiderable value," inasmuch as that it gives heavy crops for a few years, and then it is worse than before. It is the most false of all possible Husbandry, never to be practised but upon heavy clays, that the ashes which result when incorporated, may render them more open and pulverulent. It is by much the most reasonable plan to pare off the surface, and lay it in a heap with a mixture of Chalk and salt, which being frequently turned and incorporated, will bring the stubborn Vegetable matters into a decomposing state, in not so short a time but much more œconomically; more than one half the carbonaceous matter is dispelled by burning; nearly the whole is retained, and taken advantage of by the other slow process of decomposition. Sect. 18. On burning grass lands,—19—on burning heath and fen,—20, on claying land, afford little, but a repetition of what might be gathered from preceding ones.

Sect. 21. Is of Enclosures, Fences, &c. one of the best written in the work—replete with truth and information. We shall only dwell upon one statement,—" a country enclosed maintains at least triple the number of inhabitants as a champion country, so great are the profits attending this husbandry. It is always found that a farm divided into many enclosures

yields a greater rent than if the same were in but few." These
are facts which experience confirms and which admit of easy
explication ; they are facts, which every farmer, every landlord, should be convinced of, and no where do they stand more
in need of the conviction than in many parts of Suffolk and
Norfolk. Chap. 4.—Sect. 1. is occupied with a description of
the various parts of a plough, the different species of this im-
plement, [the qualifications necessary for a good ploughman,
and the times and modes of ploughing suited to different soils.
Sect. 2. Of sowing contains plain directions for the practice
as performed in Agriculture, which I shall not stop to notice.—His admonition frequently to obtain seed from another
soil, if possible from one poorer, and of a more northern latitude, is now a trite recommendation,—that it is beneficial it
is certain, and the explication easy. The greatest suscepti-
bility of germination is of course desirable; the quicker a
seed vegetates, the sooner it is out of the reach of accidental
injury or destruction ; and it may be taken as an axiom in the
general accurate, that under natural circumstances, the plant
from the latest vegetating seed of a given species is the weak-
est;—now seed raised in a cold climate germinates much more
rapidly in a warmer one, than when again sown in a soil of the
same latitude; Adanson states that seed raised at Paris, has
its period of germination accelerated from one to three days
in different individuals (Familles des Plantes, v. i. p. 84.)
Again plants growing in a poor medium, acquire a habit of enlarging their roots for the sake of increasing their surfaces of
introsusception; plants from seed raised from plants growing on
a poor soil, I have observed to possess much more abundant roots, than similar ones from seed raised in richer
soils. From these causes arise the benefit of obtaining seed
from a northern poor soil—and we would make one observation, which has often arisen to us when reflecting on the aptitude which plants have of acquiring habits, that it is an argument for their being endowed with sensation, which we could

never find satisfactorily answered.—A habit, an aptitude to repeat certain acts acquired by a frequent repetition of them, could never occur to any arrangement of parts destitute of sensation, much less could such an insentient form impart such aptitude to its progeny, yet Plants do both.

Chap. 5. Is a very superficial sketch of draining Feny Lands.—Chap. 6. concluding the work, is on the culture of Hops, correct in its statements, but meagre in its details.

2. *The Practical Kitchen Gardener, or a new and entire system of directions for his employment in the Melonry, Kitchen Garden, and Potagery in the several seasons of the year. Being chiefly the observations of a Person train'd up in the Neat Houses or Kitchen Gardens about London. Illustrated with Plans and Descriptions proper for the situation and disposition of these Gardens—And in a supplement the method of raising Cucumbers, and Melons, Mushrooms, Borcole, Brocoli, Potatoes, and other curious and useful Plants, as practised in France, Italy, Holland, and Ireland.—And also an account of the labour and profits of a Kitchen Garden, and what every Gentleman may reasonably expect therefrom in every month of the year. The whole Methodized and improved by Stephen Switzer.*—1727. 8vo.

The dedication is to Lord Bathurst—The preface is chiefly of the qualification of a Gardener, and the plan of the work of which we are about to give the anatomy. Chap. 2.—Is of the general choice of a situation and soil proper for a Kitchen Garden. Chap. 3. Of the soil particular to all kinds of kitchen vegetables, its improvements &c. Chap. 4. Of the different culture proper for kitchen herbs and plants. Chap. 5. Of Water, its uses in a Garden—Chap. 6. Of Melons, Cucumbers, Pumpkins, Gourds, &c.—Chap. 7. Of the situation proper for a Melonry, of the hot-beds, glasses, &c. The varieties of this fruit it appears were innumerable "being almost in any Garden of account now in England—the fruit being so very common"— Chap. 8. Melon seed, its age manner of sowing, &c. He reproves De la Quintynie for depending for his supply of seed on such Melons as are cut for table—one or two of those which are first ripened ought to be allowed to grow until thoroughly decaying from over ripeness. —Chap. 9. Of the time and method of sowing Melon seeds, after culture, &c.—He justly opposes Bradley's recommendation of sowing in October—those sown in February or March coming just as early.—Chap. 10. Of the culture in the Nursery Bed—He is the first who insists upon the necessity of transplanting into a second Hot Bed, previous to planting out finally, which he says is better for their fruiting by the check it gives them, than growing and moving them without disturbance in Pots.—Chap. 11. Of cultivation in the Fruiting Bed.—Chap. 12. Of the properties of good Melons, &c.- As a whole I do not hesitate to declare that these directions are as copious and correct as any that are afforded by modern writers—The only improvements that Science has since afforded in this difficult branch of cultivation, is more certainty as to temperature by introducing Thermometers in place of trying Sticks, and more to insist upon the importance of impregnating the fertile blossom. To which may be added a better discrimination and estimate of varieties. They were as early in obtaining fruit as now.—Chap. 13. Of Cucumbers. He says there were formerly only three varieties, but in his time eight.—Chap. 14. Of making hot-beds, in which nothing is added to what he details on the same subject for Melons.— Chap. 15. Of Cucumber seed, &c. He is friendly to steeping seed in Water wherein Saltpetre, &c. has been dissolved. —Chap. 16. Of the time of sowing.—Chap. 17. Of ridging out Cucumbers—The same remarks apply to the Cucumber which I have made, as to the Melon culture—the slight superiority we now possess is owing to the same causes.

The uncertainty which prevailed as to the sexuality of Plants is thus manifested in Switzer "I do not find by any observation I have ever made that the leaving on of false blossoms be for the advantage or disadvantage of the Vines, and setting of the fruit, or whether they are the male kind so necessary as it is supposed for the impregnation and forwarding the fruit in the others"—Chap. 18, 19, 20. Of the Gourds, Pompions, &c.—Chap. 21. Introductory.—Chap. 22. Of the Cauliflower, Cabbage, Borecole, Brocoli, &c. " our English Herbals" Switzer says heretofore mention but 6 kinds as cultivated in gardens which were the Common Colewort, White Loaf Cabbage— Red Cabbage— Cauliflower— Savoy— and Parsley Colewort—but lately were introduced the Sugar loaf, Battersea, and Russia, Borecole (3 kinds) and Brocoli "the seed for which we have transported to us every year from Naples or Venice"—Chap. 23. Of Cabbages.—Chap. 24. Of Savoys. Chap. 25. Of Borecole, Brocoli, 3 kinds. Chap. 26. Of the Beet (4 kinds)—27. Spinach round and prickly seeded—28. Garden Mallows—29. Garden Sorrel—30. Artichoke 3 kinds the large red English or Roman, the Crown, and the large Green. " the last but in few hands as yet"—31. Spanish Chardon—32. Asparagus, several varieties as Battersea, Gravesend, Canterbury, &c.—33. Of forcing Asparagus—34. Of bulbous and other Roots—35. Of the Parsnip, Carrot, &c. Of the first only one variety, and of the latter but two—36. Of the Radish. 2 kinds with fusiform roots, 2 turnip-rooted. The latter " not very plentiful in England"—According with an old erroneous Practice he treats of Horse Radish conjointly with the Raphanus—37. Of Scorzonera and Salsafy—38. Of the turnip 4 varieties—39. Of the Onion and other Alliums—40. Of the Skirret—41. Of the Potatoe—42. Of Legumes, Peas, Beans, &c.—43. The Bean, many kinds as the Hotspur, Gosport or Spanish, Sandwich, Broad Windsor, &c.--44. Of Garden Peas 19 varieties.--45. Of the Kidney Bean "there are more diversity of species than of any other Garden Plant we have from foreign parts"—The white were preferred as in the time of Parkinson.

It would seem that Switzer first introduced the Scarlet Runner from Holland from the mention he makes of it (p. 241) 46 and 47 are of Sallet herbs that are eaten undressed containing— Cellery, Alisanders, Fennel, Succory, Endive, Lettuces, Mint, Tarragon, Sage, Chives, Onions, Cibouls, Burnet, Rocket, Sorrel, Cresses, Rampion, Corn Sallet, Turnip, Hartshorn, Mustard, Chervil, Spinach, Lap-Lettuce, Purslane, Nasturtium, and Cucumbers--48. Of Sallet Herbs that are blanched but chiefly of Celery, which was but lately introduced from Italy where it was not long known. It is not mentioned in Parkinson's Paradisus—49. Succory, Endive, broad leaved and curled—50. Lettuces 16 kinds—51. Of Mint and perenial Sallet Herbs— 52. Of small Salleting--53. Of the season for different Sallets; quantity to be used, &c.—54. Of gathering and preparing Sallets—55. Of Sweet Herbs for the kitchen or distilling—56. Pot herbs, Thyme 8 kinds—Marjoram 7 varieties—Parsley 3 varieties—Savory 2 varieties—Hyssop. 7 varieties—Marigold 4 varieties—57. Sorrel, Beet, Borage, 4 varieties, Bugloss 3— Orach, Blite, Herb Mastick, Sage 8 varieties—Mint 9 varieties besides Pepper Mint which was then rare and lately introduced (p. 304)—Basil 2—Tansey 4—Coastmary—58 Carduus Benedictus, &c.—Angelica—Balm 3—Fenugreek, Dill, Poppy, Caraway, Anise, Coriander, Wormwood 3—Elecampane, Rhubarb, Lavender, Stœchas, Scurvey grass, Rue 2 —Chamomile 3--59. Of the Mushroom—60. Of the method of raising Mushrooms—61. Of the Truffle, then little known—62. A catalogue of all the Plants mentioned in the foregoing Chapters—63. Of Kitchen Garden seeds—64 to 76 inclusive, mostly directions of work to be done in the Kitchen Garden— 77.—Describes an annexed plan for a garden—78. On raising early Melons, Cucumbers, Mushrooms, &c. as practised in France and other countries—79. Of several incidental works being an Appendix to the Kalender given in the preceeding chapter—The 80th. or last Chapter contains an account of what produce may be *expected from the* kitchen garden in each month.

3. The Practical Fruit Gardener, being the newest and best method of raising, planting, and pruning all sorts of Fruit Trees agreeably to the experience and practice of the most eminent Gardeners and nurserymen, revised and recommended by the Rev. Mr. Lawrence, and Mr. Bradley. 2nd Edition with three new plans, and other large additions, 1731. 8vo. The first edition appeared in 1724.

It is dedicated to the Earl of Orrery. Chap. 1. Of the excellency of Fruit. 2. Of planting Fruit Trees. 3. Of the situation for a Kitchen and Fruit Garden. This union of the two for consideration is most proper, for both esculents and Fruit Trees must be kept in view in a walled enclosure necessarily containing both. 4. Of Draining. 5. Plan of a Fruit Garden. 6. Raising Fruit Trees and proper Stocks. 7. Management of Fruit Stocks in the nursery. Times of budding, &c. 8. Reasons and manner of inoculating, grafting, &c. He decidedly declares that the stock influences the flavour of the grafted Fruit. 9. Methods of Grafting. He here particularizes as being a continental custom to propagate apples, pears, &c. by passing a branch through the hole of a flower pot, filled with earth and cut it off as soon as rooted. 10. Choosing Fruit Trees and pruning them for planting. 11. Proper season for planting. He controverts the reasons of those who advocate planting in spring, and agrees with the old English proverb, quoted by Dr. Beal. "Plant at All-Hallows, tide and *command* them to prosper. Plant after Candlemas and *entreat* them to grow."—He mentions the successful practice of planting large trees in summer as a new improvement. 12. Of pruning the Roots. 13. Of Peaches and Nectarines. 14. Of Peaches. 15. List of Peaches and Nectarines,—about 20 of the first and 7 of the latter. 16. Of the Apricot 2 or 3. 17. Of Plumbs 34 kinds. 18. Of Pears 70 kinds, and alludes to others. 19. Of Apples 26. 20. Of Cherries 6. 21. Of Vines. 22. Against planting in too rich a soil. 23. Of Vines proper for the climate of Great Britain 10—24. Of Fig Trees, 4 kinds. 25. Of pruning Vines, &c. 26. Of the best methods of perfecting Fruits in England, by improving the soil. 27. Of Ticketing Fruit Trees. 28. Of the Quince 4 kinds, Medlars 3, Service and Mulberry 3 sorts, 29. Of the Walnut, Filbert, Hazelnut, &c. 30. Of Gooseberries 6, Currants 4, Raspberries 3, Berberries 3 & Strawberries 4. 31. On Dressing, Borders of Fruit Trees. 32. A Proemial discourse on pruning 33. Of Winter Pruning. 34. 35. 36. Of Pruning Peach, Apricot and Plum Trees. 37. Of strengthening weak Trees and correcting over-luxuriance. 38. Of guarding against Blights. In this (p. 287.) he anticipates Mr. Harrison, Gardener to Lord Wharncliffe's remedy for blossoms exposed to frost. viz. sprinkling them with water before sun-rise. 39 Of ripening Fruit against Paling, Reed Hedges, &c. 40. Of gathering and preserving Fruit. 41. Of the positions or aspects of Walls, in which he prefers a south-east exposure and opposes the use of sloping Walls. 42. References to a plan showing the best disposition of Walls. 43 of Forcing Grapes, &c. In which occurs the first mention of an approach to a glazed Hot-house, and which was erected at Belvoir Castle, belonging to the Duke of Rutland. 44, and 45. a plan for expeditiously watering Gardens. 46. On the disposition of Walls and distance between trees. 47. Of an early fruit Garden. 48. Of ordering or managing forcing Walls, annexed to which are some plans including Hot-houses, &c. As a whole the work is superior to the age in which it appeared and well supports Switzer in the claim I have always been ready to allow, that of being the best Horticulturist of his time.

4. Compendious method of raising Italian Brocoli, Spanish Cardoon, Celeriac, Finochi, and other foreign Kitchen Vegetables. As also an account of the La Lucerne, St. Foyne, Clover, and other Grass seeds. With the method of burning Clay for the improvement of land, lately com-

municated to the Author by a person of worth and honour of North Britain. London. 1728. The fifth edition is dated 1731.

Besides the vegetables mentioned in the Title page, he treats in this work of the Mushroom, Chervil, Alisander, Borecole, Murcian Kale, Peas, Beans, Cabbage, Lettuces, Radishes and Trefoyle.

5. An introduction to a general system of Hydrostatics and Hydraulics. London. 1729. 2 vols. 4to.

6. A disertation on the true Cytisus of the Ancients. London. 1731. 8vo.

To this dissertation are appended some further improvements of Lucerne, burning of Clay, an account of seeds with the consequences which attend the good or bad management of them, and a Catalogue of Seeds, Trees, Flowers, &c. which he sold.

7. Universal System of Water and Water-Works, Philosophical, and Practical, with plates. London. 1730. 2 vols. 4to. The third edition made very complete, especially that part which relates to the burning of Clay.

This last mentioned work, I have never seen, from their similarity of subject. size, &c. it would appear to be only an edition of No. 5.

8. Country Gentleman's Companion, or ancient Husbandry restored, and modern Husbandry improved. 1732 8vo.

RICHARD BRADLEY, deserves a pre-eminent notice here, as being one of the first writers on Horticulture, who concentrated in any considerable degree, the light of other sciences for its improvement. His first writings were in the Philosophical Transactions for 1713, " On the motion of the Sap in vegetables and microscopical observations on vegetation and on the quick growth of mouldiness on Melons," (vol. xxix. p. 486. and p. 490.) He was elected F. R. S. and afterwards Nov. 10th, 1724, Professor of Botany at Cambridge. This last honour he obtained in a clandestine and dishonourable manner, besides which he neglected to perform the duties of his professorship. The University, perhaps too leniently, allowed him to remain nominally their professor, but Dr. Martyn was appointed to deliver the lectures as Reader on Plants. At the close of his life, his conduct was so dissipated, that it was in contemplation to deprive him of his honorary title, and steps were taken to carry this into execution, when death in 1732, snatched him from the disgrace which his talents, and his unwearied applications had long sheltered him from. The means which he used to obtain the Professorship was a false recommendation from Dr. Sherard to Dr. Bentley; and boasted assurances that by his own interest and pecuniary resources he could obtain a Botanic Garden for the University. It was soon discovered these promises were baseless, and that he was ill-qualified for his appointment, by being totally ignorant of the learned languages. This is true, although his name is appended as the translator of Xenophon's Œconomicks, he being paid by the publisher to allow the authority of his name.*

The following is a list of his works,

1. Historia Plantarum Succulentarum, complectens hasce insequentes Plantas, Aloen scilicet, Ficoiden, Cereos, Melocardium, aliasque ejus generis quæ in Horto sicco coli non possunt, secundum Prototypum puta naturam in tabellis œeneis insculptas, carumdem descriptiones huc accedunt et

* Preface to Dr. Martyn's dissertation on the Æneis. Plunket's Sketches of Botany, &c.

cultura" 4to. This commenced publishing in 1716, in Decades, of which five only appeared. The second Decade appeared in 1717, the third in 1725, and the two last in 1727. They were re-published with a new title in 1734.

This is a work of merit, and is still valued on account of the plates, as being referred to by Linnœus, and as containing Plants which are not figured elsewhere.

2. New Improvements of Planting and Gardening, both Philosophical and Practical, London, 1717. 8vo. This passed through several editions, viz. 1718, 1719, 1724, and the 6th in 1731, all in 8vo.

3. A new Improvement of Planting and Gardening, both Philosophical and Practical, explaining the motion of the Sap and generation of Plants; with other discoveries never before made public, for the improvement of Forest Trees, Flower Gardens, or Parterres; with a new invention whereby more designs of Garden Plats may be made in one hour, than can be found in all the books now extant. Likewise several rare secrets for the improvement of Fruit Trees, Kitchen Gardens and Green House Plants. To which is now added the Gentleman's and Gardeners' Calendar. The whole illustrated with Copper-plates.— 1720. 8vo.

The new Invention here mentioned for designing Garden Plats was the Kaleidscope revived by Dr. Brewster a few years since.

4. A Philosophical account of the works of Nature, endeavouring to set forth the several gradations remarkable in the mineral, vegetable and animal parts of the creation,

tending to the composition of a scale of life. To which is added an account of the state of Gardening, as it is now in Great Britain and other parts of Europe, together with several new experiments relating to the improvement of barren ground, and the propagating of Fruit Trees, Timber Trees, &c. With many curious cuts—1721 4to. A second Edition was published in 8vo. as appears from an Advertisement in Ellis's Farmer's Instructor.

5. A Treatise on Husbandry and Gardening. 1721 8vo.

6. The Monthly Register of new experiments and observations in Husbandry and Gardening; made for the months of April and May, 1722; wherein is explained 1. The method of bringing Herbs, Flowers, and Fruits to perfection in the winter; with an account of a new-invented Wall to forward the ripening of Fruit, &c. 2. An Account of transplanting Forest Trees and Fruit Trees of any bigness in the Summer season ; so that gentlemen may make complete Plantations in a few days as effectually as if they had been growing for many years. Also a new method for the improvement of Tulips. To which is added, 3. An answer to some objections lately made against the circulation of the Sap, mentioned in the chapter of the improvement of Tulips—2nd. Edition. 1723. 8vo.

7. A general Treatise of Husbandry and Gardening, containing such observations and experiments as are new and useful for the improvement of land; with an account of such extraordinary inventions and natural productions as may help the ingenious in their studies, and promote universal learning. With a variety of curious cuts. 1723. 8vo.

8. A philosophical Treatise of Agriculture ; or a new method

of cultivating and increasing all sorts of Trees, Shrubs, and Flowers; being a very curious work, enriched with useful secrets in Nature for helping the vegetation of all sorts of Trees and Plants; and for fertilizing the most stubborn soils. By G. A. Agricola. M. D. and Dr. of Philosophy at Ratisborne. Translated from the German with remarks. Adorned with cuts. The whole revised and compared with the original; together with a Preface confirming this new method. 1723.

9. Family Dictionary, containing the most approved methods for improving estates and gardens, 1726—2 vols. folio.

10. Practical Discourses concerning the four Elements as they relate to the growth of Plants, viz. 1. Of the improvement of land in general. 2. Of the principles of water, and the necessity of it for vegetation. 3. Various methods relating to the draining of lands. 4. Of the several Parts of Plants and their respective offices. 5. Of the anatomy and motion of juices in Plants. 6. Of the different ways of propagating plants. 7. How to make plantations either for pleasure or profit. 8. Rules for pruning, &c. 9. Of a Kitchen Garden and the particular management of Vines and Figs. 10. Of a Flower Garden; with some new observations relating to flowers and exotick plants. With a collection of new discoveries for the improvement of land either in the farm or garden. 2nd edition. 1733. 8vo. The first edition appeared in 1727. 8vo.

11. Dictionarium Botanicum, or a Botanical Dictionary for the use of the curious in Husbandry and Gardening. 1728. 2 vols. 8vo. Plunket considers this the first Botanical Dictionary that appeared in England.

12. The Vineyard, being a treatise shewing, 1. The nature and method of planting, manuring, cultivating, and directing of Vines; 2. Proper directions for drawing, pressing, making, keeping, fining and curing all defects in the Wine; 3. An easy and familiar method of planting and raising Vines to the greatest perfection; illustrated with several useful examples. 1728. 8vo.

13. The Gentleman and Gardener's Kalendar directing what is necessary to be done in every month in the year in the Kitchen Garden, Fruit Garden, and Nursery; Management of Forest Trees, Green Houses, and Flower Garden, with directions for the making and ordering Hop grounds. London. 1718. The 3rd. edition 1720. 8vo. This was an enlarged reprint of the fourth book of his "New Improvement of Planting, &c.

14. A general treatise of Husbandry and Gardening; containing a new system of vegetation; illustrated with many observations and experiments, formerly published monthly and now methodized and digested under proper heads with additions and alterations. In four parts. London. 1726. 2 vols. 8vo.—A compressed edition of this appeared with Notes in 1757. 1 vol. 8vo.

15. Calendarium Universale. London. 1718, and 1726. 12mo.

16. A Catalogue of the Seed Plants mentioned in Townsend's Tract, and to be found in a Seedsman's Shop. London. 1720.

17. The Country Gentleman, and Farmer's Monthly Director London. 1721, 1727, 1729 and 1732. 8vo.

18. New Experiments relative to the generation of Plants. London. 1724, 1734. 8vo.

19. Treatise on Fallowing Ground, raising Grass, Seeds, &c. London. 1724. 4to.

20. A Survey of ancient Husbandry and Gardening collected from the Greeks & Romans. 4 plates. London. 1725. 8vo.

21. Experimental Husbandman and Gardener. London. 1726. folio.

22. Discourses concerning the growth of Plants. Westminster. 1727. 8vo.

23. A complete body of Husbandry. London. 1727. 8vo.

24. The Weekly Miscellany for the improvement of Husbandry, Arts and Sciences. Twenty-one Numbers 1727. 8vo.

25. The Science of good Husbandry; or the Æconomicks of Xenophon, translated from the Greek. London. 1727. 8vo. It is merely an old translation modernized in language, &c.

26. An account of Mr. Cowell's Aloe in blossom. London. 1729. 8vo.

27. Proposals for the improvement of waste Lands. 8vo. 1723.

28. British Housewife and Gardener's Companion. 1726. 2 vols. 8vo. With engravings.

29. The Riches of a Hop Garden explained. 1729.

To analize the above numerous works which bear the name of Bradley, would be a useless task, since if we except some experiments which he instituted to prove the circulation of the Sap, and the sexuality of Plants, they contain nothing which is not contained in previous or contemporary authors. His works however may be read with pleasure as abounding in information collected from books, and men of learning, with whom he maintained a very enlarged correspondence. Little as he was of an original author he must be regarded as one of the best friends of Horticulture; the theoretical and scientific views that he had of Vegetation and the several practices of Gardening, which he laboured to illustrate with experiments and practical knowledge procured from others, contributed greatly to direct the attention of amateurs as well as practitioners into the true mode of acquiring a correct knowledge of the Art.

His works had a very wide circulation, being upheld by the appended Title of his professorship, and by coinciding most opportunely with the increasing love of Gardening, and consequently rapidly increasing introduction of exotics which was one of the characteristics of his age. Bradley laboured indefatigably and successfully to promote the improvement of Horticulture, and however we may despise the man, we should respect the benefactor. It must be remarked that, the "General Treatise of Husbandry and Gardening" (14) was intended by him as a summary of what he had previously written on the subject. In his "New Improvement of Planting and Gardening," he has introduced the whole of Dr. Beales's scarce and valuable Tract on the "Herefordshire Orchards".

1716. The Young Gardener's Director. London. 12mo. With a plate representing knots of Flowers; and a frontispiece being a view of an old Garden.

The Gentleman Gardener instructed. London. 12mo. The 8th. edition is dated 1769.

The two above mentioned works were by the Rev. Henry STEVENSON, of East Retford, Nottinghamshire.

1717. Paradise Retreived; demonstrating the most beneficial method of managing Fruit Trees, with a Treatise on Melons and Cucumbers. London. 8vo. By SAMUEL COLLINS, Esqr. of Archerton in Northamptonshire.

————The Lady's Recreation; or the third and last part of the Art of Gardening improved. London. 8vo. By CHARLES EVELYN, Esqr. son of the author of "Sylva" &c.

————The Retir'd Gardener. By—CARPENTER. 8vo. with engravings.

————The Country Gentleman's Vade-Mecum. By —JACOB. 12mo

1718. Rapin of Gardens. A Latin Poem in four books. Englished by Mr. Gardiner. London. 8vo. The third Edition is dated 1728.

JAMES GARDINER, author of the above work, was born in 1679. His father was the Bishop of Lincoln. Our author was a Fellow of Jesus College, Cambridge. He was M. A. in 1704, and at the time he died, March 24th. 1732, was Sub-Dean of Lincoln. He wrote several fugitive pieces of Poetry, but I am not aware of any other seperate publication by him than the above.

His portrait by Vertue after J. Verelst, is prefixed to his translation of Rapin,

THOMAS FAIRCHILD, was one of the few Gardeners of his time who united a love of Science with the practice of his art. He is mentioned throughout Bradley's works as a man of general information and fond of scientific research, and in them are given many of his experiments to demonstrate the sexuality of plants and their possesion of a circulatory system. He was a commercial Gardener at Hoxton, carrying on one of the largest trades as a nuseryman and florist that were then established. He was one of the latest English cultivators of a Vineyard of which he had one at Hoxton as late as 1722. He died in 1729, leaving funds for insuring the delivery of a sermon annually in the Church of St. Leonard's, Shoreditch, on Whit-Tuesday, "On the wonderful works of God in the Creation; or On the certainty of the resurrection of the dead, proved by the certain changes of the animal and vegetable parts of the creation."

Besides several letters published in Bradley's Works and a paper "On the different and sometimes contrary motion of the sap in plants" in the Philosophical Transactions for 1724 (xxxiii. p. 127) he published,

The City Gardener; containing the most experienced method of cultivating and ordering such Evergreens, Fruit Trees, Flowering shrubs, Flowers, Exotick Plants, &c. as will be ornamental, and thrive best in the London Gardens. London. 1722. A small octavo pamphlet.

1724. A Treatise on the manner of Fallowing ground, raising of grass, seeds, and training Lint and Hemp. Anonymous. 12mo.

PHILLIP MILLER, was born in 1691. His father as is stated by Professor Martyn, Dr. Plunket, &c. was Gardener to the Apothecaries' Company at their Garden at Chelsea, and the subject of this notice succeeded him in that employment in 1722. Miller was precisely the man of which Horticulture at the period in which he lived was in need. Exotics were pouring in from every clime under the patronage of a general taste for their acquisition, and the scientific researches and directions of Sloane, Sherard, Catesby, &c; Hot-Houses and Conservatories were multiplying, and their inhabitants accumulating to a hitherto unheard of extent, and to manage these constructions, and their sensitive inhabitants, required judgment and science which but few Gardeners then possesed. Practical skill and Botanical science were united in Miller, and some of his contemporaries, as Fairchild, Gordon, Knowlton, and others, but as he exceeded them in knowledge, so did he in the benefit he conferred upon Gardening by the suffusion of his acquirements through the Horticultural community in his publications. Mr Loudon, on the authority of Watts, a nurseryman at Acton, who worked under Miller, asserts that his father was a Market Gardener near Deptford or Greenwich, and that Miller himself, had a small Florist's Garden somewhere about the spot covered by the King's Bench Prison, Southwark. Being considered an ingenious Florist, when Sir H. Sloane gave the scite of their Garden to the Apothecaries' Company, they appointed him Gardener. It would seem there is no evidence but the assertion of Professor Martyn, to support the statement that Miller's father was his predecessor in the office*

Miller was attached by long habit to the Botanic arrangements of Ray and Tournfort, and it was not until the seventh edition of his Dictionary appeared, that, overcome by the ar-

* Field's Hist. of Chelsea Gardens,—Encyclopedia of Gardening, p. 1103.

guments of Sir W. Watson and Mr. Hudson, he adopted the Linnæan System. His works rendered him the world's acquaintance — By foreigners he was termed emphatically "Hortulanorum princeps". He was elected member of the Botanical Academy of Florence and of the Royal Society of London, to whose council he was likewise occasionally chosen. --He was much consulted on the subject of laying out grounds &c. especially by the Dukes of Bedford, Northumberland and Richmond. He had many pupils, among other distinguished ones the late Mr. Forsyth and Mr. W. Aiton. As old age crept on, it would seem the self sufficiency and querulousness of an Octagenarian caused a disagreement with his employers, which induced him to resign his office in 1769. The Company accepted his resignation but they continued to him his Salary He was succeeded by the late Mr. W. Forsyth. He fixed his residence adjoining that part of Chelsea Church Yard where he lies interred. He died Decr. 18th, 1771. The Horticultural Society erected an obelisk over his grave in 1810.

Switzer and other contemporaries give evidence of his open, generous character; and Professor Martyn observes, "He was of a disposition too generous, and careless of money, to become rich, and in all his transactions observed more attention to integrity, and honest fame than to any pecuniary advantages." There is a portrait of Miller, engraved by Maillet, prefixed to a French translation of his Dictionary, published at Paris in 1785.

The following is a list of his writings.

1. The Gardener's and Florist's Dictionary, or a complete system of Horticulture. 1724. 2 vols. 8vo.

This appears to have been the production of a Society of Gardeners of which Miller was the Secretary; this work however he greatly improved and enlarged, and in 1731 appeared what is always considered the first edition of "The Gardener's Dictionary containing the methods of cultivating and improving the Kitchen, Fruit and Flower Gardens. As also the Physic Garden, Wilderness, Conservatory, and Vineyard according to the practice of the most experienced Gardeners of the present age. Interspersed with the History of the Plants, the character of each genus, and the names of all the particular species in Latin and English, and an explanation of all the terms used in Botany and Gardening. Together with accounts of the nature and use of Barometers, Thermometers, and Hygrometers proper for Gardeners; and of the origin, causes and nature of the Meteors, and the particular influence of Air, Earth, Fire and Water upon Vegetation, according to the best natural Philosophers. Adorned with Copper Plates." 1 vol. folio. The 2nd, Edition. 1733. 1 vol. fol. 3rd, 1737 —4th. 1743—5th. 1748—6th. 1752—The seventh edition distinguished as embracing the Linnæan arrangement appeared in 1759. It is entitled "The Gardener's Dictionary; containing the best and newest methods of cultivating and improving, the Kitchen, Fruit, Flower Garden and Nursery. As also for performing the practical part of Agriculture; including the management of Vineyards, with the methods of making and preserving the Wine, according to the present practice of the most skilful Vignerons in the several Wine countries of Europe. Together with directions for propagating and improving, from real practice and experience, all sorts of Timber Trees.—The 8th edition was published in 1768. In 1792 appeared the ninth edition, edited by Professor Martyn of Cambridge—In this the lists of species are completed in every genus with which Botanists were then acquainted, with the exception of the minuter Cryptogamic plants of which only the generic characters are noted, and such species as are employed for food, or in the arts—The Botanical and Historical parts respecting each species is given first, and lastly the necessary cultivation of the genus with any difference that may be required for some of the species. This prevents much of the confusion and tautology which occurred in the previous editions.

Miller published an abridgement of his Dictionary in 1735, 2 vols, 8vo. A second edition in 3 vols, 1741. A third in 1748. A fourth in 1754. A fifth Edition in 1 vol. 4to, in 1763, and a sixth of similar size in 1770. It was published in Dutch in 1746, and in German in 1750. In French in 1785.

Thus has this great record of our Art progressively improved, and will ever remain a monument of its author's acquirements, and a standard for reference. The practical contents are ample and correct; and for forming an opinion of the scientific part we need only quote the observation of Linnæus, who said of it "Non est Lexicon Hortulanorum sed Botanicorum."

2. A method of raising some Exotic seeds which have been judged almost impossible to be raised in England—This appeared in the Philosophical Transactions vol. xxxv. p. 485. No. 403.—By germinating them in a bark bed, and transplanting them into earth.—1728.

3. An Account of Bulbous Roots flowering in bottles filled with Water. vol. xxxvii. p. 81. No. 418. This practice was then lately discovered.

4. A Catalogue of Trees, Shrubs and Flowers, which are hardy enough to bear the cold of our climate and the open air and are propagated in the gardens near London. 1730. fol.—Plates coloured. Arrangement Alphabetical. Without his name.

5. Catalogus Plantarum Officinalium quæ in Horto Botanico Chelseiano aliuntur—1730. 8vo.

6. The Gardener's Kalendar.—8vo. 1731.—This has been a popular work and passed through many editions. To an edition in 1761, was prefixed a "short introduction to the knowledge of the Science of Botany," which was afterwards printed as a separate work. The fourteenth edition is dated, 1765.

7. Figures of Plants to illustrate his Dictionary. These commenced in folio numbers in 1755, and were completed in 300 Tables, forming 2 vols. in 1760.

8. The method of cultivating Madder, as it is practised by the Dutch in Zealand. 1758. 4to.

9. A Letter to Mr. Watson relating to a mistake of Professor Gmelin, concerning the Spondylium vulgare hirsutum, in the Philosophical Transactions. vol xlviii. p. 153.

10. Elements of Agriculture, from the French of Duhamel. 1764. 2 vols. 8vo.

11. A Letter to the Rev. Thomas Birch, D. D. Secretary to the Royal Society. Phil. Transact. vol xlix. p. 161.

12. Remarks upon the Letter of Mr. John Ellis, F. R. S. to P. C. Webb, Esq. Ditto vol. l. p. 430.

These relate to some disputed point respecting the staining qualities of some American Sumachs.

1726. The Gentleman Farmer, or certain observations on the Husbandry of Flanders, compared with that of England. Anon. 12mo.

———The Gardener's Universal Calendar. London. 8vo. by BENEDICT WHITMILL.

1727. The Vineyard: a Treatise shewing the nature and method of planting, manuring, cultivating, and dressing Vines in foreign parts. 2. Proper directions for drawing, pressing, making, keeping, fining, and curing all defects in the Wine. 3. An easy and familiar method of planting and raising Vines in England, to the greatest perfection; illustrated by several useful examples. 4. New experiments in grafting, budding, or inoculating, whereby all sorts of fruit may be much more improved than at present; particularly the Peach, Apricot, Nectarine, Plumb, &c. 5. The best manner of raising several sorts of compound fruit, which have not yet been attempted in England. Being observations made by a Gentleman, (S. J.) in his travels. London. 1727. 8vo. A second edition appeared in 1732.

From the Title Page it would appear to be the same work as that mentioned in the list of Bradley's works (12.) "The Vineyard" of that author I have never seen, having inserted it among the number of his publications on the authority of Mr. Loudon.*

1728. The Villas of the ancients. Illustrated with plates. London. fol. By ROBERT CASTEL, a London Architect and Antiquarian.

———— Le Blond's Theory and Practice of Gardening; and of Orange Trees. 4to. Plates. It is the same as James's work bearing the same name and date.

BATTY LANGLEY, was an Architect and Garden designer. He was born in 1696 at Twickenham, where he continued to reside.

He published the following works.

* Encyclopædia of Gardening. p. 1102. Ed. 5.

1. Practical Geometry, applied to the arts of Building, Surveying, Gardening and Mensuration. London. 1726.

2. The sure method of improving an Estate by Plantations of Oak, Elm, Ash, Birch, and other Timber Trees. London 1728. 4to. 1 Plate.

3. Pomona, or the Fruit Garden illustrated: being the sure method of preserving the best kinds of Fruit, with directions for Pruning, Nailing, &c. With 79 plates. London. 1729. fol.

4. New principles of Gardening; or the laying out of Pastures, Groves, Wildernesses, Labyrinths, Avenues, Parks, &c. 4to. 1728. With engravings.

JOHN COWELL, was a Nursery man at Hoxton of whom frequent mention is made in the works of Bradley and other Horticultural writers of the same period. He appears to have died about 1730, for Switzer speaks of him as "late of Hoxton" in the following year.

Cowell was author of the following works,

1. Account of the Aloe in Blossom, Torch Thistle, and Glastonbury Thorn. London. 1729. 8vo.

2. The Curious and Profitable Gardener, containing the newest method for improving Land by Grain or Seed, also a description of the Great Aloe, and other Exotics, with the manner of preserving them in Winter. London. 8vo. 1730. The edition of 1732 is the same as this with a new Title.

1729 A Dissertation on Cyder and Cyder Fruit. By H. S. Esq. of Pynes in Devonshire. The author of this was Mr. Hugh Stafford. Again in 1753 much enlarged.

1730 Observations on Agriculture. By G. RYE. Dublin 8vo.

1730 Catalogus Arborum, Fruticumque, tum Exoticarum tum Domesticarum, &c. or, The Gardener's Catalogue of Trees and Shrubs, both Exotic and Domestick which are hardy enough to endure the cold of our climate in the open Air, ranged in an alphabetical order according to their most approved Latin Names; with an Index of the English Names referring to the Latin. To which is added the character of each genus in English, and a short account of the growths of each tree or shrub, illustrated with 21 Copperplates, in which there are above 50 beautiful Plants which were designed by the famous Mynheer Van Huysum, and are represented in their proper colours. Done by a Society of Gardeners. folio. London.

This work was the joint production of a Society of some of the most eminent Florists and Nurserymen of that period as Fairchild, Furber, Smith, Driver, James, Low, the Grays, Whitmill, and Hunt. Miller was their Secretary; and this work it is conjectured both by Weston and Martyn, gave rise to the folio edition of his Dictionary, which appeared in the following year. This Society are also said by Weston to have assisted Miller in the writing of his Dictionary in octavo which appeared in 1724. Only one part of this "Catalogue" was published. In the preface it is stated, that the trade finding great inconvenience from the vague nomenclature of Plants which then existed, resolved upon this work for the publick benefit. They probably found a more difficult task than they at first imagined.[*]

[*] Weston's Tracts on practical Agriculture and Gardening. Martyn's preface to Miller's Dictionary

1732. An Essay concerning the best methods of pruning Fruit Trees, also the method of pruning Timber Trees, and also a discourse concerning the improvement of the Potatoe. London. 8vo. Anonymous.

———The nature and method of planting, manuring, and dieting a Vineyard. Anonymous. 8vo.

———The great Improvement of Commons that are enclosed for the advantage of Lords of the Manor, the Poor, and the Public, with methods of enriching all Soils and raising Timber. To ripen fruit at all times of the year; an improvement in raising Mushrooms, Cucumbers, &c. Anonymous.

ROBERT FURBER, was the founder of the Kensington Nursery, now held by Messrs. Malcom. He was distinguished as a Nurseryman, especially in the raising of Fruit Trees. He published the following works,

1. Fruits for every month in the year. 12 Plates fol. 1732. These are prints of the best kind of fruits grown in this country.

2. An Introduction to Gardening, or a guide to Gentlemen and Ladies in furnishing their Gardens, being several useful Catalogues of Fruits and Flowers. London. 1733. 8vo.

1732   1. A Flower Garden for Gentlemen and Ladies, or the Art of raising Flowers to blow in the depth of Winter; also the method of raising Salleting, Cucumbers, &c. at any time of the year. London. 8vo. by SIR THOMAS MOORE.

The same Gentleman also wrote,

2. The Flower Garden displayed, containing above four hundred representations of the most beautiful Flowers coloured to the life, with the art of raising Flowers in the depth of Winter. With 12 engravings of the seasons. 1732 4to. Again in 1734, with the addition of the "Flower Garden for Gentlemen, &c."

————The nature and method of planting, manuring, and dieting a Vineyard. 1732. 8vo. By SIR ALEXANDER MURRAY, of Stanhope, Author of some Scotch political works.

1735. Merlin: a Poem; humbly inscribed to her Majesty. To which is added the Royal Hermitage. With several curious representations both of the Cave and Hermitage. By a Lady. London. 8vo.

————The Rarities of Richmond; being exact descriptions of the Hermitage and Merlin's Cave in the Gardens there. London. 1735. 8vo. Anonymous. Again in 1736 with Merlin's life and prophecies.

WILLIAM ELLIS, a farmer of Little Gaddesden near Hemel Hempstead in Hertfordshire. He evidently was a man of intelligence. He had travelled much, both in this country and on the continent. He wrote the following works.

1. The Timber Tree improved; or the best practical methods of improving different lands with proper Timber. London, 1738. 8vo.

2. Complete Modern Husbandry, containing the practice of Farming; Chiltern and Vale Farming: Improvements on Fruit and Timber Trees, &c. 1744. 8 vols. 8vo. Again in 1750 and 1752.

He also edited " The Farmer's Instructor, or the Husbandman's and Gardener's useful and necessary Companion" which was originally written by Samuel Trowell, Gent. This was published in 1747. 8vo. He also mentions another work he was about publishing entitled " Ellis's Country Housewife."

Mr. Trowell, Ellis says, was a very ingenious gentleman, and celebrated Garden Artist, and mentions his "writings on Gardening" which I have never seen. He was Steward of the Estates belonging to the Benchers of the Inner Temple. He was dead in 1747. He published a new Treatise of Husbandry and Gardening. London. 8vo. 1739. which was translated into German in 1750.

1738.—The complete Seedsman's Monthly Calendar, shewing the most easy method of raising and cultivating every sort of Seed belonging to a Kitchen and Flower Garden: with necessary Instructions for sowing of Berries, Mast, and Seeds, of Evergreens, Forest Trees, and such as are proper for the improving of land. Written at the command of a person of honour. London. 8vo. Anonymous.

1739. An Essay upon Harmony, as it relates chiefly to situation and building. London. 8vo. Anonymous.

1740. A Catalogue of Trees and Shrubs which are prepared for sale. By CHRISTOPHER GRAY, Nurseryman of Fulham.

Gray was the founder of the Fulham Nursery, now held by Messrs. Whitley and Co. It had many rare plants contributed to it by Catesby, Collison, Miller, Dr. Gordon, and others, The greater part of Bishop Compton's collection was added to it by purchase of his successor. The first Magnolia grandiflora introduced to this country, was planted in Gray's Garden.

1744. Adam's Luxury and Eve's Cookery, or the Kitchen Garden displayed. London. 8vo. Anonymous

———Curious Experiments in Gardening; modes of propagation, &c. Illustrated with Wood Cuts. 1730. 12mo.

1744. A Treatise concerning the Husbandry and Natural History of England. 8vo. This purports to be a production of Sir Richard Weston (see p. 95.) but is only a bad abridgement of Hartlib's Legacy.

1745. A plan of Mr. Pope's Garden and Grotto, with a character of his writings.

SIR WILLIAM WATSON, deserves our notice more as the friend of Horticulture, than as ranking among the Authors of works on that Art. He was the son of a respectable Tradesman, in St. John's Street, Smithfield, and born in 1715. He was educated at Merchant Tailor's School; and from thence removed to be apprenticed to an Apothecary. He was early distinguished for his love of Botany. In 1738 he married and commenced business for himself. In 1741 the Royal Society elected him a member. To its "Transactions" he contributed many papers in almost every branch of Natural History. Sir Hans Sloane the founder of the British Museum nominated him one of its Trustees. He was an early and very assiduous experimenter in Electricity, for his discoveries in which he received in 1745, the Copley Medal from the Royal Society. He took the degree of M. D. in 1757, previous to which he had been elected a Member of the Royal Academy of Madrid; and Doctor of Physic by the Universities of Halle and Wittembergh. He became a Licentiate of the College of Physicians in 1759; one of the Physicians of the Foundling Hospital in 1762; one of the vice-Presidents of the Royal Society; Fellow of the College of Physicians, and one of the Elects in 1784. He was knighted in 1786. In the course of that year he began to decline in health and his death occurred May 10th, 1787.

There is an engraving of him an oval, by Ryder, 1791, after a painting by L. Abbot.

His chief writings relating to Horticulture are,

1. Critical Remarks on the Rev. Mr. Pickering's Paper concerning the Seeds of Mushrooms. This appeared in the Philosophical Transactions. v. xlii. p. 599. and v. xliii p. 51.

2. Account of the remains of the Garden formerly belonging to the Tradescants at Lambeth. Phil. Trans. xlvi 160.

3. Account of the Garden at Fulham formerly belonging to Dr. Henry Compton, Bishop of London. Phil Trans. xlvii. 241.

1746. The Gentleman's Gardener's Director of Plants, Flowers, and Trees; with a garden Kalender. London. 8vo. The fifth Edition is an enlarged one bearing date 1765. By DAVID STEPHENSON, M. A. author of "a new Mechanical Practice of Physic".

Miller and Weston mention "the Gentleman Gardener instructed" 12mo. by this Author, 1746. 8th. Edition, 1769. Are these different works?

1747. The Complete Florist. London 8vo. Anonymous. It consists of 100 engravings of Flowers, coloured and plain.

1748. A Dialogue upon the Gardens of Lord Viscount Cobham at Stowe in Bucks. London. 8vo. Anonymous.

1749. Catologue of Hot-House, Green-House, Hardy, and Herbaceous Plants, Flowering and Evergreen Shrubs Fruit and Fruit Trees. Edinburgh. 8vo. By DICKSON, JAMES, and Co. Nurserymen and Seedsmen, Edinburgh. An enlarged edition appeared in 1796, enumerating alphabetically all the plants described in the Hortus Kewensis.

————Directions for cultivating Vines in America. By AARON HILL.

1750. The Beauties of Stowe, with engravings. 8vo. By GEORGE BICKMAN.

1752. An Account of the Emperor of China's Gardens at Pekin. London. 8vo. Anonymous.

1753. The Kitchen, and Flower Gardens compleat, in four sheets.

————A Catalogue of Seeds and Roots under their proper heads. By W. WEBB. Seedsman.

FRANCIS COVENTRY, was a native of Cambridgeshire, He took his degree of Master of Arts, at Magdalen College Cambridge, in 1752, and entered into Orders, but died prematurely in 1759 immediately after being presented to the donative of Edgeware. He is well known as the Author of the satirical Novel "Pompey the little." He wrote "Penshurst" a Poem in Dodley's Collection; and "a Poetical Epistle to the Hon. Wilmot Vaughan;" but deserves particular notice here from being the Author of an admirable Essay in "The World" No. XV. Apl. 12. 1753, entitled "Strictures on the absurd novelties introduced in Gardening, and a humorous description of Squire Mushroom's Villa."

1753. A Treatise on the Hyacinth; containing the manner of cultivating that flower, on the experience lately made by the most eminent Florists in Holland. Translated from the Dutch by BARTHOLEMEW ROCQUE. London. 8vo.

Rocque was a florist at Walham Green. He wrote several Agricultural Works, as on Lucerne, &c. He was a great cultivator of Grasses.

JAMES JUSTICE, was one of the principal Clerks of Session in Scotland, and a Fellow of the Royal Society. His father was a Merchant, who importing bulbous roots from Holland, is said first to have given the son a taste for their culture which increased to a passion for Gardening in general that was uncontroulable. He had a Villa and Garden at Crichton near Dalkeith, upon which he expended his fortune, and was ultimately obliged to sell it, after devoting himself in its retirement, to the practice, of Gardening for thirty years. To acquire information on the culture of bulbous rooted flowers, he twice visited Holland and travelled once into Italy for further improvement in his skill and taste. He was unsparing of expense in procuring Exotics and new varieties. He was the first to introduce the Pine Apple into Scotland, and had as he states the largest collection of Auriculæ in Europe. He died in 1762 or 3. He was the Author of the following work,

The Scot's Gardener's Director, Edinburgh, 1754, 8vo.—Another Edition appeared in 1764, after his decease, entitled "The British Gardener's Director, chiefly adapted to the climate of the Northern Counties, directing the necessary work in the Kitchen, Fruit, and Pleasure Gardens, and in the Nursery, Green-House and Stove." Edinburgh 8vo. Another edition dated the same year, arranged as a monthly Kalendar is very different from the others. There was another Edition in 1767. Professor Martyn says " It is an original and truly valuable work, founded upon reflection and experience".

SIR JOHN HILL, was the son of a clergyman, and born about 1716. He was apprenticed to an Apothecary at Westminster, and there being led to the study of Botany, obtained from his proficiency in that Science the patronage of the Duke of Richmond and Lord Petre, who employed him in their Gardens. He became a writer almost upon the whole cycle of the Sciences, and by the labour of his pen, for it mattered to him but little what his subject was, he often acquired fifteen hundred pounds per annum. So that emolument was to be gained he apparently was not very scrupulous in what schemes he engaged. That he was a man of talents cannot be denied to him but that he prostituted them is demonstrated by the contempt in which he was generally held. In 1746 he translated Theophrastus "On Gems." "A general Natural History" in 3 vols. folio; "a supplement to Chambers' Cyclopædia" and a periodical named " the Inspector" rapidly followed each other. He obtained a Doctor's Degree at St. Andrews, and then endeavoured in vain to be elected a Fellow of the Royal Society. He vented his disappointment in a Pamphlet and a quarto volume, which in however bad spirit they were dictated are acutely written. He profited much by being a proprietor of quack Medecines. Having obtained the patronage of the Earl of Bute, he published under his auspices " a System of Botany" in 26 volumes folio; for which pompous work he was created a knight of the Order of Vasa, by the King of Sweden. He wrote several novels and farces. He died Nov. 22nd. 1775. He had a dispute with Garrick, having published a pamphlet in

1759 entitled "To David Garrick Esq. the Petition of I, in behalf of herself and sister," in which he charged that actor with pronouncing many words spelt with I as if the vowel U was made use of. The pamphlet is sunk into oblivion, but the Epigram with which Garrick replied to him is one of the best in the English language.

> If 'tis true, as you say, that I've injured a letter,
> I'll change my notes soon, and I hope for the better;
> May the just rights of letters, as well as of men,
> Hereafter be fixed by the tongue and the pen!
> Most devoutly I wish that they both have their due,
> And that I may never be mistaken for 'U.

Hill also became embroiled in a contest with Woodward the Comedian, who answered him in a pamphlet with this motto.

"I do remember an Apothecary, culling of simples," alluding to a story that Hill was forbidden the entrance to some nobleman's gardens, for having purloined several valuable plants.

There is a portrait of him after a painting by F. Cotes, 1757, engraved by R. Houston. An oval, with a solitaire.

The following are his chief works relating to Gardening.

1. A method of raising Trees from the leaves. Under the assumed name of Thomas Barnes, London, 1758, 8vo.

2. Eden; or a complete body of Gardening, 60 coloured plates, London. folio.

3. Complete body of Husbandry, with plates, folio.

4. The Gardener's new Kalender, with plates, London.

5. An idea of a Botanical Garden in England, 1758.

6. Account of a stone which upon being watered produces mushrooms, plates 2, London, 1758, 8vo.

7. Method of producing double flowers from single by a regular course of culture, illustrated with 7 plates, London 1758.

8. The origin and production of proliferous flowers, with the culture at large for raising double from single, and proliferous from double, 7 plates, London, 1759, 8vo.

9. The practice of Gardening by T. Perfect, a pupil of Dr. Hill, London, 1759. 8vo.

10. Botanical Tracts, London, 1762. A collection of previously published Pamphlets.

11. The construction of Timber explained by means of the Microscope. London, 1770. 8vo.

12. The Vegetable System, or Experiments on the structure and life of Plants, 1759.

1754. The Gardener's Pocket Book, or Country Gentleman's Recreation; being the Kitchen, Fruit, and Flower Garden displayed in alphabetical order, by R. S. Gent.

THOMAS HITT, appears to have been a native of Aberdeenshire. He served his apprenticeship under the gardener of John, the 3rd. Duke of Rutland, at Belvoir Castle, in Lincolnshire, who was like his father a great delighter in Gardening, especially the culture of Fruit Trees. Hitt lived sixteen years with Lord Robert Sutton at Kelham House, in Nottinghamshire. During almost all the period he was a serving Gardener, he lived with one branch or other of the Rutland Family. In 1755, he lived with Lord Robert Manners at Bloxholm in Lincolnshire. He eventually became a nurseryman, a designer of Gardens &c. in Kent. He died about 1710. He wrote upon Husbandry in general, and upon the improvement of waste land in Aberdeenshire, but his chief work is

1. A Treatise of Fruit Trees, London, 1755. A second edition appeared in 1757. Third Edition, Dublin, 1758. Miller mentions a third Edition 1768, London:

It is the result of long experience, and is decidedly one of our best practical works upon the art of training trees. The characteristic of his plan is to check the rise of the sap by making the stem take a tortuous course.

At his death his MSS came into the possession of James Meader, then gardener to the Duke of Northumberland, from which he published " The Modern Gardener."

2. A Treatise of Husbandry, London, 8vo. 1760.

1756, On the Heat and Cold of Hot houses, London, 8vo. anonymous.

——————— Observations on Husbandry, published from the original MSS of the late Edward Lisle, Esq., of Crux-Easton, Hants, with Notes and observations by his son T. Lisle. D. D. 4to.

Mr. E. Lisle settled at Crux-Easton in 1793—4, being then about 27 years of age. He died in 1722. His son resided at

Beauclere in Hants. There was another edition of his works in 2 vols. 8vo. There is an engraved portrait of Mr. E. Lisle, by S. F. Ravenet prefixed to his "Observations."

SIR WILLIAM CHAMBERS, of Scottish parentage, was born in Sweden in 1726, but came to England when only two years old, and was placed at Ripon School. On arriving at manhood he became Supercargo of a Swedish East India ship, and made one voyage in that capacity to China. On his return he commenced the study of Architecture, under the patronage of Lord Bute, by whose interest he was appointed Drawing Master to the Prince of Wales, afterwards George the III.—His first architectural erection was a villa for the Earl of Besborough at Roehampton. He was afterwards employed in laying out the Royal Gardens at Kew, where he introduced the Chinese ornaments. In 1771 he was invested with the Swedish Order of the Polar Star. He became a Fellow of the Royal and Antiquarian Societies. In 1775 he was appointed to conduct the erection of Somerset House, being Architect to the King, Surveyor General to the Board of Works, and Treasurer of the Royal Academy. In 1758 his style of design, &c. was severely attacked in two satires termed "An heroic Epistle" and "An heroic Postscript to Sir W. Chambers" which came from the pen of Mason the Poet. Sir W. Chambers died in 1796.

There are two engravings of him after a portrait by Sir J. Reynolds, one by J. Collyer, 1785, the other by V. Green 1780. 3. An engraving by Houston, 1772, after a painting by F. Cotes. 4. A profile by D. Pariset, after a drawing by P. Falconet.

The following are his published works.

1. Designs for Chinese Buildings, Furniture, Dresses, Ma-

chines, and Utensils, engraved from the originals drawn in China; to which is annexed a description of their Temples, Houses, Gardens, &c. London. 1757. Large fol.

2. A treatise on Civil Architecture. London. folio. This reached a third Edition

3. Plans, Elevations, Sections, and perspective views of the Gardens and Buildings at Kew. London. 1763, and 1765. Folio.

4. Dissertations on Oriental Gardening. London. 1744. 4to.

As an Architect Sir William Chambers stands high; the portico of Lord Besborough's Villa is particularly correct and elegant; the Grecian Mansion of the Marquis of Abercorn at Duddingtone near Edinburgh; and the Gothic one of Milton Abbey in Dorsetshire, are monuments of his taste. Somerset House was a failure. His Chinese Gardening was puerile in the extreem.

JOSEPH SPENCE, D. D. was born in 1698. He was educated at Winchester School, and proceeded thence to New College, Oxford, of which he became a Fellow. He acquired the friendship of Pope from an "Essay" published in 1727, on that poet's Odyssey, on the following year he was elected Professor of Poetry at Oxford and held that appointment until 1738. In 1731 he published an Account of the Stephen Duck, and procured for him the living of Byfleet. About the same period he travelled with the Earl of Lincoln, and on his return was presented with the lixing of Great Horwood in Buckinghamshire; and soon afterwards was appointed Professor of Modern History. In 1747 he published " Polymetis, or Enquiry into the agreement between the works of the Roman Poets, and the remains of ancient Artists." In 1754 he received a prebendal Stall in Durham Cathedral. In that year he directed the public attention to Blacklock, the blind Poet; as he afterwards did to Robert Hill the learned Taylor. His last publication was "Remarks and Dissertations on Virgil, with some other Classical observations, by the late Mr. Houldsworth. Published with Notes and additional Remarks by Mr. Spence." Several minor pieces of our authors are in Dodsley's and other collections. He was accidentally drowned in a canal of his own Garden at Byfleet in Surrey, August 20th. 1768. There is a portrait of him in Nichols's " Poets", T. Cook, sc. Another prefixed to his "Polymetis" by G. Virtue, after the original by Isaac Whood. Since his death have been published "Spence's. Anecdotes concerning eminent Literary Characters." He was a friend of Lord Walpole who esteemed him a man of taste and judgment in Gardening. The work which entitles him to our notice is,

Some account of the Emperor of China's Gardens, &c. &c. By Sir Harry Beaumont. London 1757 8vo.

1757. The practical Husbandman. By R. MAXWELL, Esq. of Arkland,

1. The distinguishing properties of a fine Auricula. Newcastle 8vo.

2. The Dutch Florist. Newcastle 12mo. 1758.

These two works were by JAMES THOMPSON, a florist at Newcastle.

1757.—An heroic Epistle to Sir W. Chambers—London. 4to.

1758—An heroic Postscript. London, 4to.

These severe and spirited Satires, have been erroneously

attributed to John Baynes by Nichols in his "Literary Anecdotes." They are now known to have proceeded from Mason the Poet, of whom we shall have occasion to make farther mention, at least when charged with being their author he did not deny that he was so. Warton thought they were the joint offspring of Walpole and Mason, or as he expressed it "They may have been written by Walpole, and buckram'd by Mason."

REV. WILLIAM HANBURY, rector of Church Langton Leicestershire, He died in 1778. He was exceedingly fond of Planting. He planted fifty Acres of Nursery Ground, the produce of which he dedicated to the improvement of the Church and Parish. It was instituted however in the first instance for the encouragement and improvement of the Art of Planting. There is a portrait of him, a private plate, engraved by R. Earlom, 1775, after the original by W. Penny. He was author of the three following works,

1. An Essay on Planting and a scheme to make it conducive to the glory of God, and the advantage of Society. London. 1758. An 8vo. pamphlet.

2. The Gardener's new Calender. London. 1758. 8vo.

3. A complete body of planting and gardening, containing the Natural history, Culture, and Management of deciduous and evergreen Forest Trees, with practical directions for raising and improving Woods. As well as a general system of the present practice of the flower, fruit, and kitchen Gardens.

This work commenced publishing in December 1769, and was completed in 150 sixpenny weekly numbers, in 1773, forming two volumes, folio.

The five following papers by ROBERT MARSHAM, Esq. of Stratton in Norfolk appeared in the Philosophical Transactions.

1. Observations on the growth of Trees. (Phil. Trans. Abrev. xi. 320. In the year 1758.)

2. On the usefulness of washing and rubbing the stems of Trees to promote their annual increase. (xiv. 124. 1776—xv. 138—1781)

3. Indications of Spring (xvi. 561—1789)

4. On the measures of Trees. (xviii. 100.—1797)

1759.—A Treatise on Grasses, and the Norfolk Willow. London. 8vo.

  The Gardener's Catalogue of Hardy Trees, Shrubs, Flowers, Seeds, &c. London. 8vo.

The above are by—NORTH, a Nurseryman, who formerly occupied the Gardens at Lambeth, now held by John Hay.

JOHN MILLS, Esq. F. R. S. was author of the following works, not one of which are worthy of more particular notice.

1. Practical Treatise on Husbandry, from the French of Duhamel. 1759. 4to. With additions, Plates, &c.

2. A new and complete System of Practical Husbandry 1762. 5 vols. 8vo. This was published in weekly numbers and compleated in 1763. It was twice translated into German in 1764.

3. The natural and chemical Elements of Agriculture from the German of Gyllenborg. 12mo. 1770.

4. Essays on Agriculture. 8vo. 1772.

1760. The London Gardener. London. 8vo. Anonymous.

THOMAS HAMILTON, EARL of HADDINGTON was born in 1734, and died May 19th. 1794. This nobleman was a great encourager of improvements in the arts of cultivation, The fine plantations which are about the family mansion at Tynningham near Dunbar, are monuments of his fondness for arboriculture. He was the author of

A Treatise on Forest Trees. Edinburgh. 1760. 8vo.

JAMES LEE, a native of Scotland, was one of the best Gardeners of his time. He was for some time under Philip Miller at the Chelsea Garden; and afterwards Gardener to the Duke of Argyle at Whitton, Middlesex, who was a great importer of Exotick Trees, and for that reason only, invidiously nick-named by Walpole "A Tree-Monger". In conjunction with Kennedy, then Gardener to Lord Bolton at Chiswick, Lee commenced the business of a Nurseryman, at the Vineyard Hammersmith. He was patronized by a great many of the nobility and gentry, to whom he became known by his extensive knowledge of Natural History; and his Garden became particularly rich in plants from the extensive correspondence he kept up with Linnæus and other contemporary Botanists.—He died in 1797. He was author of,

1. An Introduction to Botany; containing an explanation of the Theory of the Science, and an interpretation of its technical terms, extracted from the works of Linnæus, &c. 12 Plates. 1760. 8vo. A work which Pultney speaks fa-

vourably of, as having tended to a general diffusion of a knowledge of the Linnæan System.

2. Catalogue of Plants and Seeds sold by Kennedy and Lee.

1760. Observations towards a method of preserving the seeds of Plants in a state of Vegetation during long voyages London. 8vo. By SAMUEL PULLEIN, M. A. This Gentleman was also author of several publications upon the Mulberry, Cotton Plant, and Silkworm.

1760. Adam armed; or an Essay endeavouring to prove the advantages and improvements the Kingdom may receive, and the inconveniences and impediments it may avoid and remedy by the means of a well ordered and duly rectified Charter for incorporating and regulating the Professor of the Art of Gardening; humbly offered and presented by the Master and Company of the same. London. fol. No author's name, or date, but published about this year.

1763. The Botanist's and Gardener's new Dictionary; containing the Names, Classes, Orders, Generic Characters, and Specific distinctions of the several Plants cultivated in England, according to the System of Linnæus. To which is prefixed an Introduction to the Linnæan System of Botany. London. 8vo. By JAMES WHEELER, nurseryman at Gloucester.

——— An Essay on the Theory of Agriculture, intended as an introduction to a Rational System of the Art— Anon. 12mo.

1764. The Dutch Florist, or a true method of managing all sorts of Flowers with bulbous roots. Translated from the Dutch of Van Campen. 4to.

1764. **Museum Rusticum et Commerciale**: or select Papers, on Agriculture, Commerce, Arts, and Manufactures. Drawn from experience, and communicated by gentlemen engaged in these pursuits. Revised and digested by several Members of the Society for the encouragement of Arts, Manufactures, and Commerce. 6 vols. London. 8vo.

This was succeeded by a similar work entitled " De Re Rustica" which commenced in 1768 and was completed, two vols, 8vo, in 1770.

——————The complete Farmer, or Dictionary of Husbandry. 4to. Anonymous. 2nd. Edition, 1768.

WALTER HARTE, was born at Kentbury in Buckinghamshire about 1697. He was educated at Malborough School and at St. Mary's Hall, Oxford, where, in 1720, he took his Master's degree, he became Vice-principal of the Hall, and a Canon of Windsor through the interest of Lord Chesterfield. He was also Vicar of St. Austle and St. Blaze, Cornwall. At one period of his life he was tutor in the family of Earl Peterborough. He died in 1768. He published " A history of Gustavus Adolphus," several Poems, &c. but is recorded here as being Author of,

Essays on Husbandry, and a Treatise on Lucerne. By W. H. Canon of Windsor. Plates. 1764. and 1770.

Every reader must agree with Dr. Johnson (what species of literature has this giant of learning not criticized!) in considering these Essays "good". It would appear that Dr. Harte was a very vain man. On the day his " Gustavus Adolphus" was published he left London to avoid the influx of praise he was sure would attend it; and was ashamed to return as it was a complete failure.

WILLIAM SHENSTONE, was born in November 1714, at his paternal seat, the Leasowes in Hales-Owen. After passing with applause through two Schools he proceeded in 1732 to Pembroke College, Oxford. He here published a small volume of Poems in 1737. In 1742 he produced his "Schoolmistress" having two years previously published "The Judgment of Hercules. In 1745 he took the Estate of the Leasowes, much against his will, under his own management, and during the remainder of his life made it his study to ornament and improve the beauty of his ground. It is certain he was the envy of wealthier and less tasteful neighbours. Their envy, and the praise which fed his vanity, rendered him ever desirous of excelling, and he squandered on the decorations of his grounds, sums that should have obtained him necessaries and comfort. Though his grounds were beautiful, his house was mean and delapidated; he was annoyed by creditors, or as his biographer Dr. Johnson expresses it "his groves were haunted by beings very different from fauns and fairies." He died of a putrid fever, Feb. 11th. 1763. With his Poems we have here no concern, but we shall have occasion to speak of the Leasowes hereafter, and must now record that in his works collected after his death, and published in 3 vols. 8vo. in 1764, are "Unconnected Thoughts on Landscape Gardening."

There are three engraved portraits of him. 1. By Prancker, prefixed to his "Works," 1764, 8vo. 2. By Hall in 1780, after the original by T. Ross, painted in 1738. 8vo. 3. By T. Cook in Bell's edition of the "Poets."

JOHN ABERCROMBIE, was born at Edinburgh in 1726, near which City his father conducted a considerable Market Garden. From his infancy he was employed to assist in this undertaking which was one particularly suited to his taste, and to improve and simplify his Art through after life, engrossed his attention—At fourteen he became an apprentice of his father. His education was plain and superficial, but possessing sound sense, and a habit of reasoning upon just principles, he was an agreeable Companion—He was thoroughly grounded in his profession, the practice of years being retained and concentrated by a habit of committing to paper all the observations he made in its pursuit from a very early age—Soon after his appenticeship expired, being about eighteen, upon some domestic misunderstanding, he came to London, where he obtained employment in some of the Royal Gardens at Kew and at Leicester House. Afterwards he became Gardener to Dr. Munro and other gentle- men. He was present at the Battle of Preston Pans, which was fought under his father's Garden Wall. He was a loyalist, or as he termed himself " a king's man." About 1751—2 he became Gardener to Sir James Douglas, during his continuance in whose service he married. Fearing his family might become troublesome he left his situation in 1759, and returned to Scotland with the intention of becoming Kitchen and Market Gardener, but came again to England after an absence of only ten months. He was engaged in the service of several noblemen and gentlemen until 1770, when he engaged a Kitchen Garden and small Nursery Ground between Mile End Road and Hackney, attending Spitalfields Market with the products until 1771—2—at this period he became a publican in Dog-Row, Mile End, his house was afterwards converted into the Artichoke Tea Gardens. By the importunity of his wife he left this, and entered into the Seed and Nursery business at Newington and Tottenham Court, carrying on at the same time an extensive trade as a Kitchen Gardener and Florist. About 1778 he prepared his " Every Man his own Gardener," which has passed through many Editions. He actually paid Mr. Thomas Mawe, Gardener to the Duke of Leeds, twenty pounds to allow his name to be attached to this work by whose name it of course has been generally known. Afterwards becoming more confident he published his " Gardener's Pocket Journal, or Daily Assistant", which obtained a very extensive sale and has since passed through an edition of 2000 Copies annually—Besides these he compiled The Universal Dictionary of Gardening and Botany, 4to.—The Gardener's Dictionary—The Gardener's Vade-Mecum—The Kitchen Gardener and Hot-bed Forcer—The Hot-house Gardener—The Wall Tree Pruner—The Gardener's best Companion &c.—He died from an accident on the 2nd. of May, 1806—He at one period after the publication of his "Every man his own Gardener," had actually embarked to superintend the Gardens of the Empress of Russia, but the sight of the Ocean inspired him with terrors which he could not overcome.* Abercrombie was induced to become author by a visit which he received in 1770 from Mr. Davis, a London Bookseller, and the celebrated Dr. Goldsmith, who made overtures to him for an original work, the latter promising to revise the language, which he afterwards neglected to do.

After the publication of the second Edition of his "Every Man his own Gardener" he accepted an invitation from Mr. Mawe whose name he had borrowed for the Title page; but when introduced to him having never before seen him he was so powdered and dressed that Abercrombie mistook him for his master the Duke of Leeds. They were however mutually pleased with each other, and subsequently continued to correspond.

From 1796 to the time of his decease he continued to reside in Charlton St, Somers Town, excepting when visiting or professionally employed. He was occasionally employed to plan Gardens and Pleasure Grounds for which he was sometimes handsomely remunerated. When unemployed he was a constant pursuer of knowledge and information at the various Nursery Grounds and Gardens near the Metropolis.†

---

* Memoir prefixed to his Gardener's Pocket Journal—Gentleman's Mag and Monthly Mag. for 1806. † Loudon's Encyclopædia of Gardening p. 1106; Ed. 5.

The following is a list of his Horticultural works in the order in which they were published,

1. Every Man his own Gardener, being a new Gardener's Calendar, with complete lists of Forest Trees, Flowering Shrubs, Fruit Trees, Evergreens, annual, biennial, and perennial Flowers; Hot-house, Green-house, and Kitchen Garden Plants, with the varieties of each sort cultivated in the English Gardens. London. 1774—

This work has passed through upwards of twenty Editions, and is now one of our standard works. In later editions Abercrombie's own name has appeared in the title page together with that of Thomas Mawe which it originally bore alone, though he had nothing to do with its composition.

2. The Universal Gardener and Botanist; or a general Dicenary of Gardening and Botany, exhibiting in Botanical arrangement, according to the Linnæan System, every Tree, Shrub, and Herbaceous Plant that merits culture. London. 1778. 4to. Mr. Weston says the first Edition appeared in 1770.

3. The Garden Mushroom, its nature and cultivation, exhibiting full and plain directions for producing this desirable plant in perfection and plenty. London. 1779. 8vo.

4. The British Fruit Garden, and Art of Pruning; comprising the most approved method of planting and raising every useful Fruit tree, and Fruit bearing shrub. London. 1779 8vo.

5. The Garden Mushroom its nature and cultivation. London. 1779. 8vo.—1802. 12mo.

6. The complete forcing Gardener, for the thorough practi-

cal management of the Kitchen Garden, raising all early crops in hot-beds, forcing early fruit, &c. London. 1781. 12mo.

7. The complete Wall Tree pruner, &c. London. 1783. 12mo.

8. The propagation and botanical arrangement of Plants and Trees useful and ornamental. London, 1785. 2 vols. 12mo.

9. The Gardener's Pocket Dictionary, or a systematical arrangement of Trees, Herbs, Flowers and Fruit, agreeable to the Linnæan method, with their Latin and English names their uses, propagation, culture, &c. London. 1786. 3 vols. 12mo.

10. The Daily Assistant in the modern practice of English Gardening for every month in the year, on an entire new plan. London. 1789. 12mo.

11. The Universal Gardener's Kalendar, and system of practical Gardening. London 1789. 12mo.—1808. 8vo.

12. The complete Kitchen Gardener, and Hot bed forcer, with the thorough practical management of Hot-houses, Fire Walls, &c. London 1789. 12mo.

13. The Gardener's Vade-Mecum, or companion of general Gardening; a descriptive display of the Plants, Flowers, Shrubs, Trees, Fruits, and general culture. London. 1789. 8vo.

14. The Hot-house Gardener, or the general culture of the Pine Apple, and the methods of forcing early Grapes, Peaches, Nectarines and other choice Fruits in Hot-houses, Vineries, Fruit houses, and Hot-Walls, with directions for raising Melons and early Strawberries, &c. Plates, London. 1789. 8vo.

15. The Gardener's Pocket Journal and annual Register, in a concise monthly display of all practical works of general Gardening throughout the year. London. 1791. 12mo.

Of these works there needs little comment. They are the sound results of lengthened experience. " Every Man his own Gardener" was re-edited in 1816 by Mr. Mean. But the editions and numbers that have been sold, have never been equalled by any other Horticultural Work, except Abercrombie's own " Pocket Journal", of which cheap, and useful work, about two thousand are annually sold. The fourteenth edition is dated 1815, and I know not how many have appeared since, but there is usually a fresh one every year.

For the last twenty years of his life he lived in a great degree upon Tea, taking it three times a day, seldom or never eating meat. He frequently declared that Tea and Tobacco were the great promoters of his health. His pipe was his first companion in the morning and the last at night. He often smoked for six hours without interruption. He never remembered taking Physic until after the occurrence of the accident which caused his death ; nor of having a day's illness before his last, but one about twenty three years previously.

The best portrait of Abercrombie is prefixed to Debrett's edition, 2 vols. 8vo. He is also represented at full length when seventy-two in the 16th Edition printed in 1800.*

1766. The Gentleman and Farmer's Architecture, being plans for Parsonage and Farm Houses, with Pineries, Greenhouses, &c. on 25 plates. folio. By J. LIGHTOLER, a London Architect.

JOHN LOCKE, one of the greatest of Philosophers, belongs

* Felton, On the portraits of English Authors of Gardening. p. 26.

to the list of English Authors on Horticulture. He was born at Wrington in Somersetshire, where his father was an attorney, Aug. 29th, 1632. He commenced his education at Westminster School, and concluded it at Christ-church, Oxford, to a studentship of which College, he was elected in 1652. He obtained his degree of M. A. in 1658. He then applied to the study of Physic, and graduated in 1674. He did not practice regularly as a Physician, but was much consulted, especially by the Earl of Shaftsbury, to whose son he became tutor. In 1675 he visited France, and during his stay at Montpelier paid much attention to the cultivation of the Vine, and the rearing of Silk Worms. When Lord Shaftesbury became an exile in Holland, Mr. Locke followed him, for which he lost his studentship by order of the King. He returned to England in the same fleet with King William. He then went to reside at Oates in Essex, the seat of Sir Francis Masham, whose Lady, a daughter of Dr. Cudworth, was his great friend. About 1696 he was appointed one of the Commissioners of Trade and the plantations, which place he resigned in 1700. He died at Oates, Oct. 28th, 1704. Of his numerous Philosophical works we shall make no detail. His dissertation on "The human mind" and "On Education" will render him famous throughout Time. The publication for which he here requires notice is entitled,

Observations upon the growth and culture of Vines and Olives, the production of Silk, and the preservation of Fruits; printed from the original MS. in the possession of the Earl of Shaftesbury. London. 1766. 8vo.

This posthumous publication was written at the suggestion of the Earl of Shaftesbury and is dedicated to him.

Of engraved Portraits of this Philosopher, Bromley enumerates fifteen.

1. Prefixed to his "Human Understanding," by Vander Banc, after S. Brownover. Folio. 2. By La Cave after G. Kneller. Folio. 3. Prefixed to his "Letters on Toleration," 1765, by Cipriani. 4. A bust by J. Faber. 5. In "Hist des Philos. Mod," 1762. by J. C. Francois. 6. After a painting by Greenhill; Printseller, Gunst. Folio. 7. In Birch's "Lives" by J. Houbraken. 8. By J. Nutting, after Brownover. 8vo. 9. By B. Picart after Kneller. 12mo. 10. By J. Smith. 11. By P. Tanjé. These two are after Kneller's picture in 1704. 12. By G. Virtue, 1713, after Kneller's picture in 1697. 13. By G. Virtue in 1738, after the same. He is also in a plate with Bishop Burnet, Prideaux, and Clarke; and in another with Sir I. Newton, &c.

1767—The rise and progress of the present Taste in planting Parks, Pleasure Grounds, Gardens, &c. from the time of Henry the VIII. to King George the III. In a poetic Epistle to the Right Honourable Charles, Lord Viscount Irvin. London. 4to. Anonymous.

Of this work Mr. Loudon observes, that it is very scarce. He never observed but one copy and that in Mr. Forsyth's Library.* Martyn mentions it in 8vo.

JOHN GILES, born in 1725. He was at one time Gardener to Lady Boyd at Lewisham in Kent. In 1777, he was foreman to Messrs. Russell at their Nursery in that village. He died in 1797. He wrote,

———— Ananas: or a Treatise on the Pine Apple, in which the whole culture, management, and perfecting this most excellent plant is laid down in a clear and explicit manner To which is added the true method of raising the finest Melons with the greatest success, &c. London. 1767. 1 Plate, 8vo.

* Encyclopædia of Gardening. 1107. Ed. 5.

Weston mentions another work on the Pine Apple, published this year, anonymously.

1767. Modern Eden; or the Gardener's universal Guide, containing plain instructions for performing every branch of Gardening whether of ornament or utility; in which are laid down the best methods for raising all the products of the kitchen and Flower Gardens, and the training, pruning, and entire management of Fruit Trees, &c. By JAMES RUTTER, (Gardener at Wandsworth,) and DANIEL CARTER, (Gardener at Battersea,) London, 8vo.

———— The Practical Farmer, or Herefordshire Husbandman. Anon. 12mo.

1768. The Fruit Gardener, containing the method of raising Stocks for multiplying Fruit Trees, with directions for laying out and managing Fruit Gardens. By JOHN GIBSON, M. D. 8vo.

Gibson had been a navy Surgeon, and afterwards graduated. He was author of several medical works. The preface to the above publication contains an account of the Fruit Gardens of the Ancients.

1768—An Essay on Design in Gardening. Anonymous. 8vo. By a Mr. Mason.

WILLIAM GILPIN, one of the Reformers of the old style of ornamental Gardening, was a native of Carlisle. He pursued his University studies at Queen's College, Oxford, where he took his degree of Master of Arts in 1748. He was for many years a Schoolmaster at Cheam in Surrey. Subsequently he obtained the vicarage of Boldre in Hampshire, and a prebendary of Salisbury. He died in 1804 at the advanced age of eighty. He bequeathed the profits of his numerous publications for the endowment of a School at Boldre. His religious works are many, and that on the Church Catechism particularly excellent, but we shall here confine our attention to those relating to the Art of Garden Designing. The scope of his observations will be given in another part of this work.

1. Observations on the River Wye, and several parts of South Wales, &c. relative chiefly to Picturesque Beauty, made in the Summer of 1770. London. 1783, 8vo.

2. Observations relative chiefly to Picturesque Beauty, made in the year 1772 on several parts of England; particularly the mountains and lakes of Cumberland and Westmorland. London. 1787. 2 vols: 8vo.

3. Observations chiefly relative to Picturesque Beauty, made in the year 1776 in several parts of great Britain, particularly the Highlands of Scotland. London. 1788. 2 vols. 8vo.

4. Remarks on Forest Scenery, and other Woodland views, relative chiefly to Picturesque Beauty. Illustrated by Scenes in the New Forest, Hants. In 3 books. London. 1791. 2 vols, 8vo.

5. Three Essays. On Picturesque Beauty. On Picturesque Travel. On Sketching Landscape. To which is added a Poem on Landscape Painting. London. 1792. 8vo.

6. Observations on the Western Parts of England relative cheifly to Picturesque Beauty. To which are added a few remarks on the Picturesque Beauties of the Isle of Wight, 18 Plates. London. 1798. 8vo.

7. Observations on the coasts of Hampshire, Sussex, and Kent, relative chiefly to Picturesque Beauty, made in the Summer of 1774. London. 1804, 8vo.

8. Observations on several parts of the Counties of Cambridge, Norfolk, Sussex and Essex; also several parts of North Wales relative chiefly to Picturesque Beauty. Made in two Tours, the former in the year 1769, and the latter in 1773. London. 1809, 8vo.

It may be observed here that his powers of describing Scenery were most peculiar and effective; or as Dallaway expresses it "he had the happy faculty to paint with words." No one though reading for mere amusement can fail of being delighted with his elegant descriptions, and tasteful observations.

GEORGE MASON, was a classical Scholar, and Critic of eminence, though somewhat dogmatical. He was a Bachelor, and being connected with the Sun Fire Office, resided generally in London. I know nothing more of his private history. His only publication connected with our Art is,

An Essay on Design in Gardening. London. 8vo. 1768.

This was greatly enlarged and re-published in 1795. Two Appendixes to it were published in 1798. This is chiefly an historical and critical work.

1768. A Treatise on the culture of Peach Trees, to which is added a Treatise on the management of Bees. By —WILDMAN. Dublin, 12mo.

1769. A new Gardener's Dictionary, or the whole Art of Gardening fully and accurately displayed; containing the most approved methods of cultivating all kinds of Trees, Plants, and Flowers. London, folio.

This commenced publishing in 1769, and was completed in 60 numbers in 1771. It was by JOHN DICKS, Gardener to the Duke of Kingston at Knightsbridge.

1769. The Practical Gardener and Gentleman's Directory for every month in the year; with proper directions for raising Mushrooms. To which is prefixed an Essay on vegetation, soil, manure, and the nature and form of Stoves, Hot-beds, &c. With a Copperplate exhibiting at one view the several aspects for planting a fruit Garden; By JAMES GARTON, London, 12mo.

——— The Royal Gardener; or complete Calendar of Gardening for every month in the year, digested in regular order, and so contrived as to exhibit in a clear and comprehensive manner the business to be done in the Flower, Fruit and Kitchen Garden at all Seasons. Likewise directions, founded on experience, for sowing, planting, pruning, transplanting, engrafting, and every other particular necessary to be known by such as desire to aim at a perfect knowledge of this most ancient, healthy, and agreeable Science. By ANTHONY POWELL, Gardener to George the II. This gentleman also translated from the French "The Garden or the Art of laying out Grounds. By James De Lille." London. 1789. 12mo. The original appeared in Paris, in 1782, 12mo.

1769. A Treatise on the Anana; or Pine-Apple containing plain and easy directions for raising this most excellent Fruit without Fire, and in much higher perfection than from the Stove. To which are added full directions for raising Melons. By ADAM TAYLOR, Devizes, 8vo. A plate.

Taylor was Gardener to J. Sutton, Esq. New York, near Devizes.

1770. The Rational Farmer, or a Treatise on Agriculture and Tillage. By M. P. (Matthew Peters) Member of the Dublin Society. 8vo.

I do not know whether this gentleman resided in the Isle of Wight. If he did there is a portrait of him engraved by J. Murphy, 1773, after a painting by—Peters.

RICHARD WESTON was a man of literature of whom Agriculture and Gardening, "had been the principal study and amusement for many years". He resided at Kensington-Gore near London. I know nothing further of his history, but that he was author of the following works.

1. Tracts on practical Agriculture and Gardening, in which the advantage of imitating the Garden culture in the field is fully proved by a seven years course of experiments. To which is added a complete Chronological Catalogue of English Authors on Agriculture, Gardening, &c. London. 1769. 8vo. Anonymous. An enlarged edition appeared in 1773 with the author's name.

2. The Universal Botanist and Nurseryman, containing descriptions of the species and varieties of all the Trees, Shrubs, Herbs, Flowers, and Fruits, Natives and Exotics, at present cultivated in the European Nurseries, Greenhouses, and Stoves, as described by modern Botanists; arranged according to the Linnæan System, and their names in English. To which are added a copious Botanical Glossary, several useful Catalogues and Indexes. Plates. London. 1770,—74. 4 vols. 8vo.

3. The Gardener and Planter's Calendar; containing the

method of raising Timber Trees, Fruit Trees, and Quick for hedges; with directions for forming and managing a Garden every month in the year. Also many new improvements in the Art of Gardening. London. 1773, 8vo.

4. A Catalogue of Green-house and Stove plants on 5 sheets, 1775.

5. Tracts on Alabaster or Gypsum, describing its powerful effects as a very cheap manure, &c. London, 1791, 8vo.

6. A Catalogue of Trees, Shrubs, Plants and Fruits. 1775, and a supplement, in 1780, 8vo.

COLIN MILNE, L. L. D. was born at Aberdeen, and educated at Marischal College in that town under Dr. Campbell his uncle. He removed to Edinburgh, but on becoming tutor to Lord Algernon Percy, he took orders in the Church of England. He became the Rector of North Chapel, Essex, and Lecturer at Deptford. He received his Doctor's degree at Aberdeen. He died in 1815. He was a good naturalist and published several Botanical works of which we shall only notice his "Botanical Dictionary" 1770, 8vo. Again in 1778, and 1806. It contains many discussions interesting to Gardeners.

1770. Martyn gives a list in this year of the following Anonymous works, all in 12mo.

The Gardener and Planter's Calendar.

——Gardener's Pocket Calendar.

——Gardener's Alphabetical Calendar.

——Pocket Kitchen Gardener.

——Pocket Flower Gardener.

THOMAS WHATELY (some write it Wheatley) Esq. of Nonsuch Park near Epsom in Surrey, was I presume the son of the Rev. Joseph Whately, who became possessed of that residence by the will of his Uncle, Joseph Thompson Esq. who though a Dissenter left it to him on condition that he should take Priest's Orders, which he did and resided there until he died. In 1770—1, he published his work on Gardening, but soon after becoming secretary to the Earl of Suffolk, a member of Parliament, and Secretary of the Treasury, he had little time unemployed for literary pursuits. He had two brothers one of them a Clergyman. He died in 1772.* I have seen him mentioned as *Sir* Thomas Whately. After his death appeared some remarks upon Shakespeare, which are only part of a larger work which he had in contemplation. The work which deserves our particular notice is entitled,

Observations on Modern Gardening illustrated by descriptions. London. 8vo. 1770. Martyn says an Edition in his possession is the 3rd, dated the next year. Another Edition in 4to. appeared in 1798, with Walpole's History of Gardening inserted in the form of Notes; and an Appendix containing an Essay on the different natural situations of Gardens which had some years previously been published without an author's name, by Dodsley (See 1775.) It was translated very speedily into French by Latapie and afterwards by Masson de Blamont; and was praised though not above its merits by all the continental Reviews. Ensor pronounced its style inimitable. Loudon pronounces it " the grand fundamental, and standard work on English Gardening." Of the principles of Taste which it advocates I shall not mention anything here. It treats first of the materials the Landscape Gardener has to work with; secondly of the scenes producible with them; and lastly the subjects of Gardening. He illustrates his principles by descriptions of Blenheim, Claremont, Esher, Hagley, Ilam, Leasowes, Painshill, Peirsfield, and Stowe.

* Preface to the 2nd Ed. of his Remarks on Shakespeare.

JAMES MEADER, Gardener to the Duke of Northumberland at Sion House, and afterwards to the Empress Catherine at Peterhoff, near Petersburgh. He was a writer of satirical verses.* He published the following works,

1. The modern Gardener, or Universal Calendar, containing monthly directions for all the operations of Gardening, to be done either in the Kitchen, Fruit, Flower or Pleasure Gardens, as likewise in the Green-house and Stove; with the method of performing the different works, according to the best practice of the most eminent Gardeners. Also an Appendix giving full instructions, for forcing Vines, Peach, Nectarine Trees &c. in a new manner: never before published: selected from the diary MSS. of the late Mr. Hitt. Revised, corrected, and improved by J. M. London. 1771. 12mo.

2. The Planter's Guide, or Pleasure Gardener's Companion; giving plain directions, with observations for the proper disposition and management of the various Trees and Shrubs, for a Pleasure Garden Plantation. To which is added a list of hardy Trees and Shrubs for ornamenting such Gardens. Embellished with Copperplates. London. 1779. royal 8vo.

1772. A Treatise on Forest Trees; containing not only the best methods of their culture hitherto practiced, but a variety of new and useful discoveries, the result of many repeated Experiments. To which are added directions for the disposition, planting, and culture of hedges. By WILLIAM BOUTCHER a nurseryman at Comely Garden, near Edinburgh. London. 4to— Again in 1775. Edinburgh?—

WILLIAM MASON, was born on the 23rd of February, 1725, at Hull, where his father resided as Vicar of one

* Encyclop. of Gardening. p. 1108. 5. Ed:

of its Churches, St. Trinity. In 1742 he was admitted of St. John's College, Cambridge, between which year and 1745, when he became B. A. he wrote several minor poems. He afterwards removed to Pembroke Hall of which he was unexpectedly nominated Fellow in 1747. He continued writing poetry and in 1751 published his Tragedy of "Elfrida" after the model of the old Greek writers. In 1754 he entered the church, becoming Rector of Aston in Yorkshire, and one of the king's chaplains, for both of which appointments he was indebted to Lord Holderness. In 1759 he published another Tragedy "Caractacus" on the same plan as his first, but both are more fitted for the Library than for the stage. He continued to write Poetry, and occasionally to preach before the King, but both his Verses and Sermons had too much of Whiggism in them. In 1765 he married Mary, daughter of W. Sherman Esq. of Kingston upon Hull, but she died in two years after their union. He continued to write until within a very short period of his death, which was occasioned by a hurt on his shin, which rapidly mortified and caused his dissolution on the 7th of April, 1797, at Aston.

There are two portraits of him. One, an etching by C. Carter, after a painting in 1771 by L. Vaslet, 4to. The other a half length by W. Doughty, 1779, after a painting by Sir J. Reynold's.

In 1772 appeared the first Book of his "English Garden," and the other three followed seperately in 1777, 1779, and 1782. London. 4to. Another edition was published in 1785. London. 8vo. with Notes and a Commentary by W. Burgh, L. L. D.

The blank verse of this poem we need not here particularly criticize, it is harmonious, but its delicacy verges often to weakness: The three first books were received with great applause for they certainly convey much instruction in an elegant form. The fourth book which contains the pisode of Nerina is misplaced because too long, it is rather a poem of itself, neither are its merits sufficiently manifest to make us not feel the intrusion.

1772.—The Art of planting and cultivating the Vine, &c. according to the most approved methods in France. By LOUIS de St. PIERRE, a Planter and native of South Carolina. London. 12mo.

1775. An Essay on the different natural Situations of Gardens. London. 4to. This date is on the authority of Dr. Watt, &c. Mr. Loudon states 1774. I have never seen the work.

1776. The Gardener's Pocket Calendar. By THOMAS ELLIS, Gardener to the Bishop of Lincoln. London. 12mo.

1776—A Treatise on Planting and Gardening. By—KENNEDY. York. 8vo.

JAMES ANDERSON, was born at Herdmanston, or Hermiston, near Edinburgh in 1739, on a farm long in the possesion of his ancestors. His education was the fruit of his own exertions. At fifteen the care of the farm devolved upon him by the death of his parents, and it could not have fallen into abler hands, as was demonstrated by his skilful management. He studied Chemistry under Dr. Cullen, and thus improved and guided his experience by the lights of Science. He soon left Herdmanston and took an uncultivated farm of 1300 acres in Aberdeenshire, which he managed most beneficially for twenty years, and then let, enjoying an annuity from it during the remainder of his life. He wrote, "Thoughts on Planting" in the Edinburgh Weekly Magazine, subscribing himself Agricola;

these were revised and published at Edinburgh in a seperate form in 1777. 8vo. This acquired him much reputation and the University of Aberdeen conferred on him the degree of Doctor of Laws in 1780. In 1783 he gave up his farm and removed to Edinburgh where he projected the North British fisheries, and was employed by government to survey the coast of Scotland. He then commenced a periodical termed "the Bee," which was ably supported, but the Doctor suffered from some political papers appearing in it, of which he was entirely ignorant. About 1797 he removed to the neighbourhood of London, fixing his abode at Isleworth where he wrote "Recreations in Agriculture" &c. He continued to lead a very domestic, happy life, being excessively fond of the cultivation of his Garden, until 1808, in which year he died leaving a widow and six surviving children of a family of thirteen. He wrote many works, reviews, essays, &c. we shall only mention as relating to our Art, besides that already noticed.

A description of a Patent Hot-house, which operates chiefly by the heat of the Sun, and other subjects; without the aid of Flues, Tan-Bark, or Steam for the purpose of heating it, &c. London. 1804. 12mo.

1777—1. Letters on the Beauties of Hagley, Envil, and the Leasowes; with critical observations on the modern Taste of Gardening. London. 2 vols. 12mo.

————2, Description of Hagley Park. London. 8vo.

These two works were written by JOSEPH HEELEY, ESQ.

1777—A Treatise on the forcing of early Fruits, and the management of Hot-Walls. By WILLIAM WILSON. London. 12mo.

Wilson, was a Scotchman; he worked for some time under

Miller, who recommended him to Sir James Cockburn, Bart. at Petersham. He was afterwards with the Earl of Glasgow, near Paisley.

1778—The Practical Gardener, directing in the most plain and easy manner, what is necessary to be done in the Kitchen, Fruit, and Flower Garden, the Green-house and Wilderness. London. 8vo. No author's name.

———The Beauties of Flora displayed, or Gentleman and Lady's Pocket Companion to the Flower and Kitchen Garden. London 8vo. By N. SWINDEN, Gardener and Seedsman at Brendford End, Middlesex.

1779. A Catalogue of the Plants in the Garden of John Blackbourne, Esq. alphabetically arranged according to the Linnæan System. London. 8vo. By ADAM NEALE, gardener to the above gentleman near Warrington, Lancashire.

WILLIAM SPEECHLEY, was the son of a respectable farmer, and was born at a village, near Peterburgh, in Northamptonshire. A strong genius, and great industry, which displayed itself very early in his sketches of fruit, flowers, designs, &c. and engraving them on Copper Plates, was assisted by a good education. He began his noviciate as a Gardener at Milton Abbey, now Earl Fitzwilliam's; from thence he proceeded to Earl Carlisle's at Castle Howard. He became head Gardener to Sir W. St. Quintin, and in 1767 removed to the same situation at the Duke of Portland's at Welbeck in Nottinghamshire. The Duke sent him in 1771 on a tour to the chief Gardens of Holland. Soon after the Stoves at Welbeck, which became so justly celebrated, were erected from Speechley's designs and under his inspection. About 1796 he was engaged by Sir John Sinclair to write some papers on Domestic Œcnomy which however never were published in the Tranactions of the Board of Agriculture, for which they were designed. He then began writing " A General Treatise on Gardening", but the death of a younger Son who was established in an extensive farm at Woodborough Hall, induced Mr. Speechley to leave Welbeck and settle at that farm, where he continued some years. He tried a course of Agricultural Experiments, and wrote Essays for which he received the Honorary Medal of the Board of Agriculture. After this he left his farm and retired to King's Newton Hall, near which the only surviving branch of his family lived, and whose removal into Oxfordshire caused Mr. Speechley to remove into that Country, where he died, at Gt. Milton, on the 1st of October, 1819, in the 86th year of his age, having survived his wife two years.*

Speechley was not at all a man of Science, but being a man of acute observation and long experience, he perhaps surpassed every practical Gardener of his age. It is certain that he contributed more than any one to improve the cultivation of the Pine Apple and Vine, before the appearance of his two works there being little on record that afforded any material information to their cultivators. He was author of the following works.

1. A Treatise on the cultivation of the Pine-Apple, and the management of the Hot-house; together with a description of every species of Insect that infects Hot-Houses with effectual methods of destroying them. York. 1779. 8vo. 2nd Edition. 1796.

2. A Treatise on the culture of the Vine, exhibiting new and advantageous methods of propagating, cultivating, and training that plant, so as to render it abundantly fruitful. With new hints on the formation of Vineyards in England. York. 4to. 1790. Afterwards in 8vo.

* Gardener's Magazine. v. 3. p. 384.

3. Practical hints on domestic and rural Œconomy relating partly to the utility, formation and management of Fruit, Kitchen, and Cottage Gardens and Orchards, &c. London, 1820, 8vo.

HORACE WALPOLE, EARL of ORFORD, the youngest son of Sir Robert Walpole, Prime Minister of George the 1st, was born in 1718. He was educated at Eton, and King's College, Cambridge. In 1738 he entered upon public life as Inspector General of Exports and Imports, which office he exchanged for Usher of the Exchequer. He was also appointed Comptroller of the Pipe, and Clerk of the Extracts. In 1739 he travelled into France and Italy with Mr. Gray, the Poet, who had been his fellow Student at Eton, but at Florence they quarrelled and parted; they were however reconciled a few years afterwards. In 1741 he was the representative in Parliament of Callington in Cornwall; in 1747 he was elected for Castle Rising, and in the two succeeding Parliaments for Lynn. In 1768, he retired from public business to his seat at Strawberry Hill, near Twickenham. In 1791, he became Earl of Orford, on the death of his nephew, but never appeared in his seat as a Peer of Parliament. He died March the 2nd, 1797.

The following portraits have been engraved of him. 1. A three-quarter length, when a Commoner, by M'Ardell, 1757, after Sir J. Reynold's. 2. By Pariset after Falconet. 3. By B. Reading after Reynolds.

That the Earl of Orford was a man of taste, and an encourager of the men of genius of his age is the best light in which as a public character we can look upon him; that he was gifted with a strong genius though often asserted is very doubtful that his researches were frequently superficial his writings testify, and this is further supported by the fact that he was a Sceptic. He very powerfully contributed to abolish the mathematical style of Gardening, being one of the most strenuous advocates of Landscape Gardening, as is manifested in his only literary production that we shall mention, being an Essay "On Modern Gardening," written in 1770, forming the concluding Chapter of his "Anecdotes of Painting in England" which though printed in 1771, did not appear to the public until 1780.

In this Essay, being determined to demonstrate that rural Gardening was the true and new taste, to establish the opinion, Historians both sacred and profane which appeared to militate against his doctrines, are passed over with indifference and contempt. To his sketch of the improvements introduced by Bridgeman and Kent, and those Garden Artists their immediate successors, we may afford the best praise, he appears to be a faithful, and is an eloquent annalist.

ERASMUS DARWIN, was born at Elston, near Newark in Nottinghamshire, on the 12th of December, 1731. He was educated at Chesterfield Grammar School, and St. John's College, Cambridge. He proceeded Bachelor of Medicine at the latter place, and then proceeded to Edinburgh, which he left as soon as he had acquired the degree of M. D. He commenced practicing at Nottingham, but removed soon after, in 1756, to Litchfield. In the following year he married, but he lost his wife in 1770. In 1781 he married a second wife, and by her persuasion removed to Derby. In 1781 appeared the first part of his "Botanic Garden or Loves of the Plants"; the second part appeared in 1789. In 1793 he published Zoonomia, and demonstrated himself in this instance to be either a fool or a hypocrite, openly avowing himself an Atheist. He died very suddenly, April 18th 1802, previous to which had appeared the only other of his works which it is necessary for me to mention.

Phytologia, or the Philosophy of Agriculture and Gardening with the Theory of Draining Morasses, and with an improved construction of the Drill Plough. London. 1800. 4to.

1781. **The Young Gardener's best Companion for the Kitchen and Fruit Garden.** London. 12mo. By SAMUEL FULMER.

JOHN COAKLEY LETTSOM, was born in 1744, of Irish, Quaker parents, on the little Island of Vandyke, near Tortola, where his father was a planter. Being sent to England, and placed under the care of Samuel Fothergill, a celebrated preacher of the Society of Friends, he was sent by this gentleman to a School at Warrington. He thence passed to an apprenticeship with an Apothecary at Settle in Yorkshire; and finished his Surgical studies at St. Thomas's Hospital. The death of his elder brother tempted him to visit his property at the West Indies, which finding chiefly comprised of Slaves, he emancipated, and settled himself at Tortola. He soon returned to Europe, and graduated at Leyden. He finally settled in London, and there by the friendly interest of Dr. Fothergill, soon acquired a most extensive practice. He was a zealous Philantrophist; member of most of the European and American literary and scientific institutions; and is well known as an author. He died Nov. the 1st. 1815, many years previous to which, he had ceased to be a member of the Society of Friends.

There is an engraved portrait of him by T. Holloway, ad vivum.

The works for which he deserves our notice are,

1. Hortus Uptonensis; or a catalogue of Stove and Greenhouse Plants in Dr. Fothergill's Garden, at his death. London, 1781. 8vo.

2. Grovehill; a rural and horticultural sketch. London. 1804. 4to.

3. On the Beta Cicla, (Mangolt Wurtzel) or Root of Scarcity In the Caledonian Horticultural Trans. i. 420.

1783. Some Thoughts on building and planting, addressed to Sir James Lowther. Bart. This, which is anonymous, appeared in Dodsley's collection of Poems for this year.

——————An Essay on Landscape. From the French of Ermenonville. 12mo. Anonymous, but known to be by Mr. Malthus.

1. Flora Diœtetica, or the history of esculent Plants both domestic and foreign, in which they are accurately described and reduced to their Linnæan, generic, and specific names, with their English names annexed. London. 1783. 8vo.

2. A Dictionary of the ornamental Trees, Shrubs, and Plants, most commonly cultivated in the Plantations, Gardens, and Stoves of Gt. Britain; arranged according to their Linnæan generic names, and containing full and accurate descriptions of the genera and species, with their names properly accented. Norwich. 1790. 8vo.

These two works were by CHARLES BRYANT of Norwich.

1783. On Gardening. Translated from the French of l'Abbe de Lisle. 4to.

WILLIAM FALCONER, M. D. F. R. S. and physician to the Bath General Hospital. There is a portrait of him engraved by J. Fittler, after a painting by Daniel of Bath, 1791, prefixed to his "Influence of the Passions upon Disorders". He was author of the three following works relating to our A

1. An historical view of the taste for Gardening and laying out Grounds among the nations of Antiquity. 1783. 8vo.

This appeared, for the most part, originally in the Literary and Philosophical Memoirs of the Manchester Society.

2. An Essay on the preservation of the health of persons employed in Agriculture; and on the cure of diseases incident to that way of life. London. 1789. 8vo.

3. Miscellaneous Tracts and Collections relating to Natural History; selected from the principal writers of Antiquity on that subject. London. 1793, 4to.

1734. Elements of Modern Gardening; or the Art of laying out Pleasure Grounds, ornamenting Farms, and embellishing the views about our Houses. London. 8vo.

WILLIAM CURTIS, F. L. S. was born at Alton in Hampshire, in 1746. He was apprenticed to his grandfather, then an Apothecary in his native town, and whilst in his noviciate distinguished himself for his eager pursuit of Botany. At the age of twenty he entered the service of Mr. Talwin in Gracechurch St. London, and who he eventually succeeded in business. His love of Botany was however predominant, and disposing of his trade he commenced Lecturer and Demonstrator in his favourite Science. He first had a Garden at Bermondsey, then a larger one at Lambeth, which he left for a third at Brompton. In 1771 he published "Instructions for collecting and preserving Insects" and in the following year a translation of the Fundamenta Entomologiæ of Linnæus with the title of " An Introduction to the knowledge of Insects"—In 1773 he was appointed Lecturer of the Chelsea Garden. He died in 1779 and was buried at Battersea. The following are brief notices of his writings which claim our particular notice.

1. Flora Londinensis. London. 1777—1798 2 vols. folio. Containing six fasciculi of seventy-two plates each.

2. Botanical Magazine. 1787. London. In monthly numbers. 8vo. Still continued, and will be noticed in the next section.

3. Practical Observations on the British Grasses. London. 1782. 8vo. 2nd Edition 1790.

4. A history of the Brown-tailed Moth. 1782. London. 8vo.

5. A Catalogue of British Medical, Culinary, and Agricultural Plants, cultivated in the London Botanical Garden. London. 1784. 12mo.

6. Directions for the culture of the Crambe Maritima or Sea Kale, for the use of the Table. 8vo. with a Plate. There is a new Edition with late improvements.

Besides the above he wrote several Papers in the Transactions of the Linnæan Society; on Aphides, &c. His botanical Lectures were published after his death, with coloured Plates.

1785. 1. Miscellanies on Ancient and Modern Gardening, and on the scenery of Nature. London. 8vo. Without the Author's name. By S. FELTON.

He has since published with his name

2. On the Portraits of English Author_ - ' dem.- ing. London. 1828. 8vo.

3. Gleanings on Gardens, chiefly respecting those of the Ancient style in England. London. 1822. 8vo.

With the author of these works I have not the pleasure of a personal acquaintance, but whoever reads the above works, and his " Life of Sir Joshua Reynolds," will agree with Mr. Loudon in acknowledging, that he has "a mind richly stored with almost every description of literary knowledge," It is a melancholy prospect of human nature taken by some persons, that the mind becomes contracted as age advances, and that especially the literary sexagenarian becomes soured in temper and circumscribed in his views. Many are proofs in support of a contrary opinion, and as living examples I will quote the President of the Horticultural Society and Mr. Felton.

1785. Planting and Gardening, a practical Treatise. 8vo.

———— A Treatise on the management of Peach and Nectarine Trees, either in forcing houses, or on hot and common Walls—Edinburgh—8vo. By THOMAS KYLE, Gardener to the Hon. Baron Steward of Moredun, near Edinburgh. Kyle was one of the best Gardeners in Scotland of his time.[*] The second Edition of the above, Edinburgh. 1787.

WILLIAM MARSHALL, Esq. was a native of Yorkshire He began life as a commercialist, and was a Planter for some years in the West Indies, but returned to England about 1775 and took a farm in Surrey. In 1780 he resided at Gunton in Norfolk as Agent of the Estates of Sir Harbord Harbord, which situation he resigned in 1784, and settled at Stratfold, where he remained two years, occupied in printing some of his writings, and in collecting materials for his " Œconomical Sur-

[*] Encyclopædia of Gardening. p. 1109. Ed. 3.

veys," which he pursued without deviation until his death, having formed a plan to collect the Agricultural practices of each English County, for the composition of two great works "On Landed Property" and "A System of Agriculture," the first of which he published but the latter he did not live to complete. From 1786 to about 1808 he resided at Clement's Inn, London, during the winters, but was travelling in various parts of the country during the summers. He finally purchased a large estate in the Vale of Cleveland of his native County, in 1808, in which retirement he lived eleven years, dieing at a very advanced age in 1819.

Mr. Marshall without the benefit of an enlarged education, became known as an acute observer, and writer of authority. He was often consulted and in many instances planned the disposition of estates, not only as regarded their economical arrangement but their ornamental parts. He was also the projector of a Rural Institute which, in another form, arose as the Board of Agriculture. He was author in addition to the works I have mentioned, and many County Surveys, of the following,

1. On Planting and Rural ornament. London. 1785. 8vo. A second Edition in 2 vols, in 1796. without his name.

2. A review of "The Landsape," a didactic poem; also an Essay on the Picturesque; together with practical remarks on Rural Ornament. London. 1796. 8vo.

1786. 1. A description of certain methods of Planting, training, and managing all kinds of Fruit Trees, Vines, &c. London. 8vo.

2. A sketch of a plan for making the Tract of land called the New Forest, a real Forest, and for various

other purposes of the first national importance. 1793. 8vo.

The above two works were written by the REV. PHILIP le BROCQ, M. A. and Chaplain to the Duke of Gloucester. At the time he published his work on training Fruit Trees he took out a Patent for this improved method of so managing them which he states was first suggested by Lord Bacon, and practiced by Francis X. Vispre, at Wimbledon and Chelsea, who is noticed in the next chronological notice.

1786. A Dissertation on the growth of Wine in England. Bath. 8vo. By FRANCIS XAVIER VISPRE.

———— A method to preserve Peach and Nectarine Trees from the effect of Mildew, and for the destroying the Red Spider in Melon frames, and other insects which infests plants in Stoves and Trees, Shrubs, &c. in the open Garden. London. 12mo. By ROBERT BROWNE, Gardener to Sir H. Harbord at Gunton in Norfolk.

1789. The culture of Forests; with an Appendix in which the state of the Royal Forests is considered and a system proposed for their improvement. London. 8vo. By Lieutenant Col. A. EMMERICH, deputy Surveyor of the Woods and Forests.

JOHN GRÆFFER, a native of Germany, came to this country in the middle of the last Century, and being for some time, a pupil of Philip Miller, became the Gardener of James Vere, Esq. of Kensington-Gore.

He afterwards established a Nursery at Mile End, in partnership with Thompson and Gordon. Soon after the death of Gordon, Græffer recieved the appointment of Gardener to the

King of Naples at Caserta, through the interest of Sir J. Banks. At that place he laid out and well stocked a Garden after the English mode. Lord Nelson appointed him to superintend his estate at Bronte, and many noblemen employed him as a Garden Designer. He continued Gardener at Caserta during the usurpation of Murat, but was murdered near his own house in 1816.* He published

A Descriptive Catalogue of upwards of 1100 species and varieties of Herbaceous or Perennial Plants, divided into six columns, exhibiting at one view, their names, magnitude, height, and situation; time of flowering, colour of their flowers, and the native country of each species. With a list of hardy Ferns for the decoration of the Northern Borders, and the most ornamental Annuals. London, 1789. 8vo.

JAMES SOWERBY, F. L. S. &c. was by profession a portrait painter; but will be ever distinguished as a Botanical Draftsman and Engraver. He was first brought into notice by having made some sketches of Plants from Nature to introduce in the foregrounds of some Landscapes, which being shown to some Botanical friend, they suggested the publication of the "English Botany" which with the powerful assistance of the late Sir J. E. Smith was completed; the only descriptions that were not written by the latter where from the pen of the late Dr. Shaw. Sowerby brought up a numerous family, all of whom share in their father's talent. He was an indefatigable collector of Botanical and Mineralogical specimens, of which he formed an extensive Museum. He died in 1822. He wrote in some of the Scientific Periodicals, and the produce of his pencil are to be seen in most of the illustrations of our later Botanical works &c. He deserves our notice here from being the author of the following works.

* Encyclop. of Gardening. p. 1110. 5. Edt

1. The Florist's Delight, containing six coloured figures, with Botanical Descriptions. London. 1791. Folio.

2. Figures of English Fungi, or Mushrooms. This appeared in parts from 1797 to 1803, when it was completed, forming 3 vols. folio.

1790. Hints for the management of Hot-beds, and directions for the culture of early Cucumbers and Melons. To which are added brief instructions for pruning Wall and Espalier Trees. Bath 8vo. By—BRULLES.

WILLIAM FORSYTH, F. A. S, &c. was born at Old Meldrum, Aberdeenshire, in 1737. He came to England in 1763 and was for some time a pupil of Philip Miller at Chelsea Garden. He became Gardener to the Duke of Northumberland at Sion House, but gave up that situation on being appointed in 1769 to succeed his old master as Curator of the Botanic Garden at Chelsea. Forsyth retained this situation until 1784 when he was appointed Royal Gardener at Kensington and St. James's in the place of T, Robinson Esq. just deceased. For his improvements in the cultivation of Fruit Trees, for his mode of renovating those which are decayed, and for the composition he applied to their wounds, he received a pecuniary grant from Parliament, who considered it a national improvement. That such grant was judicious I am not inclined to deny, it encouraged an attention to Horticulture, but it does not require much research to discover that Forsyth's modes of treatment were known and published by antecedent practitioners. He died in 1804. His published writings are,

1. Observations on the Diseases, Defects, and Injuries in all kinds of Fruit and Forest Trees; with an account of a particular method of cure invented and practiced by the Author. London. 1791. 8vo.

2. A Treatise on the culture and management of Fruit Trees in which a new method of training and pruning is fully described. Plates London. 1802, 4to. The fourth Edition is dated 1806, 8vo. The 7th, in 8vo. 1824.

1791. The Linnæan Transactions were first published in this year.

1792. The Florist's Directory, and complete Treatise on the culture and management of Flowers with a supplementary Essay on Soils, Manures, &c. Plates. London. 8vo. By JAMES MADDOCK, florist at Walworth.

Maddock died about 1806. He was a Quaker, and came originally from Warrington in Lancashire. A new Edition of his Directory with improvements was edited by Mr. S. Curtis in 1822. London, 8vo.

1793. An Essay on Gardening; containing a Catalogue of Exotic Plants, for Stoves and Greenhouses of British Gardens; the best method of planting the Hot-house Vine, &c. with the history of Gardening, and a contrast of the ancient with the modern taste. Cuts. York. 4to. By RICHARD STEELE, gardener, Thirsk, Yorkshire.

JOHN TRUSLER, L. L. D. was born in London in 1735, He was apprenticed to a petty Apothecary, but contrived to desert the Pestle for the Pulpit, and officiated for some time as a Curate. In 1771 he began to publish compilations which, however contemptible, answered their author's object by obtaining for him, in conjunction with the business of a Bookseller which he established, a large fortune. He purchased an Estate at Englefield Green, where he died in 1820. Among his other compilations are

1, The Art of Gardening. London. 1793. 8vo.

2. The Lady's Gardener's Companion. London. 1816. 18mo.

1794. Observations on the Genus Mesembryanthemum; in two parts; containing scientific descriptions of above 130 species, about 50 of which are new: directions for their management, new arrangement of the species, reference to authors, and a great variety of critical, philosophical, and explanatory remarks. London. 8vo. By ADRIAN HARDY HAWORTH, Esq. of Cottenham, near Beverly, in Yorkshire.

Mr. Haworth who is an Amateur Naturalist of no mean acquirements, is author of several papers in the Transactions of the Linnæan and Horticultural Societies, of both which Societies he is a Fellow. He has written upon Entomology, as also the following work.

Synopsis Plantarum Succulentarum, cum descriptionibus, Synonymis, Locis, Observationibus, Anglicanis Culturaque. London. 1812. 8vo.

1794. A practical Treatise on planting. Dublin. 8vo. By SAMUEL HAYES, Esq. M. R. L. A. &c. It had only the author's initials.

——— Plans, elevations, sections, observations, and explanations of Forcing houses in Gardening. By JAMES SHAW. Whitby, folio.

1795. The Landscape, a didactic Poem. Two plates. London. 4to. By RICHARD PAYNE KNIGHT, Esq.

This Gentleman was brother to the President of the London Horticultural Society. He built Downton Hall, near Ludlow, from his own designs, but after residing there some years, he resigned possesion of it to his brother, and dwelt during the rest of his life chiefly in London.

Mr. Knight was born at Wormsley Grange, in Herefordshire, in 1750 and died in 1824.

Whoever has seen the Estate of Downton Hall and read "The Landscape" will need no criticism of mine to point out the taste of their author. Of the latter I shall have occasion presently to speak more fully.

JAMES M'PHAIL, Gardener for more than twenty years to the last Earl of Liverpool, at Addiscombe Place near Croydon. He is author of some Essays on Agriculture and the Poor Laws. Mr. Loudon says he is a skilful cultivator of Pines and Melons. He is Author of the two following Horticultural publications.

1. A Treatise on the culture of the Cucumber; shewing a new and advantageous method of cultivating that Plant, with full directions for the management thereof, and the degree of Heat it requires on every day of the year, &c. To which are added Hints and Observations on the improvement of Agriculture. London. 1794. 8vo.

He raised Cucumbers throughout the year from the same plants.

2. The Gardener's Remembrancer throughout the year, exhibiting the surest and most approved methods of manuring, digging, sowing, &c. The nature of Earth, Water, Heat, Air, and Climate, best adapted for the culture of

Plants and the production of Fruits, Flowers, and esculent Vegetables, in the forcing way; the causes and symptoms of disease and barrenness in Trees of every kind, with means of prevention and cure. To which is Prefixed a a view of Mr. Forsyth's Treatise on Trees. London. 8vo.

SIR UVEDALE PRICE, of Foxley, near Hereford, is the classical author of the following publications.

1. An Essay on the Picturesque, as compared with the sublime and the beautiful, and on the use of studying Pictures for the purpose of improving Real Landscape. London. 1794. 8vo. Again in 1796. In 2 vols. with additions 1797—8.

2. A Letter to H. Repton, Esq. on the application of the practice, as well as the principles of Landscape Painting, to Landscape Gardening, intended as a supplement to the Essay on the Picturesque; to which is prefixed Mr. Repton's Letter to Mr. Price. London. 1795. 8vo.

3. Two Appendixes to an Essay on Design in Gardening by G. Mason, London. 1798. 8vo.

4. A Dialogue on the distinct Characters of the Picturesque and the Beautiful, in answer to the objections of Mr. Knight. London. 1801. 8vo.

HUMPHRY REPTON was born at Bury St. Edmund's in Suffolk in 1752. He went to Ireland with Mr. Wyndham in 1783, and held a lucrative office in the Castle at Dublin until his friend's return in 1788, when Mr. Repton also resigned his situation. He then directed his attention to drawing and architecture but especially ornamental Gardening, in which employ until about fifteen years since, when the taste for the Art seemed to decline, he had an extensive practice. He was a beautiful draftsman, and gave, when consulted upon the laying out of grounds, besides plans and views, his written opinion, combining the whole in a manuscript volume, which he termed the *Red Book* of the Place.* He never undertook the carrying his own plans into effect. He died at Hare Street near Romford, Essex, in 1818, leaving several sons, one of whom married a daughter of the Earl of Eldon. He published the following works.

1. A Letter to Uvedale Price, Esq, on Landscape Gardening. London. 1794. 4to.

2. Sketches and Hints on Landscape Gardening; collected from designs and observations now in the possession of the different noblemen and gentlemen for whose use they were originally made; the whole tending to establish fixed principles in the Art of laying out grounds. 16 coloured plates. London. 1795. folio.

3. Observations on the Theory and Practice of Landscape Gardening, including some remarks on Grecian and Gothic Architecture, collected from various MSS. in the possession of different noblemen and gentlemen; the whole tending to establish fixed principles in the respective Arts. Many Plates. London. 1803. 4to.

4. Observations on the changes in Landscape Gardening. 1806. 8vo.

5. On the introduction of Indian Architecture and Gardening. 1808. folio.

* Encyclopæd. of Garden. p. 80. Ed. 4.

6. On the supposed effects of Ivy on Trees. In the eleventh volume of the Trans. of the Linn. Society. p. 27—1810—

7. Fragments on the Theory and Practice of Landscape Gardening. London. 1817. Folio—In this work his son assisted him.

1796. A Sketch from " The Landscape" a Poem by R. P. Knight. Esq. London. 4to. Without the Author's name but it is believed to have been written by W. Mason the author of " The English Garden."

The plan of an Orchard, exhibiting at one view a select quantity of Trees, sufficient for planting an acre and a half of land, properly arranged according to their usual size of growth, and hardiness of bearing, &c. London. A folio sheet. By GEORGE LINDLEY, nurseryman at Catton, near Norwich. He has written some papers in the London Horticultural Society's Transactions.

An Introduction to the knowledge and practice of Gardening; with hints on Fish ponds. London 12mo. Again in 1798, 1802 and 1805. By the REV. CHARLES MARSHALL vicar of Brixton, Northamptonshire.

An account of the Culture of Potatoes in Ireland. 8vo.

1797. 1. A few minutes advice to gentlemen of landed Property and the admirers of Forest Scenery; with directions for sowing, raising, planting, and the management of Forest Trees. To which is added a catalogue of Forest Trees, Fruit Trees, and Flowering Shrubs, with their usual prices, as sold by the Nurserymen and Seedsmen. Chester, 12mo.

2. Hints to Planters, collected from various Authors of esteemed authority, Manchester, 1807, 8vo.

The above are by FRANCIS DUCKENFIELD ASTLEY, Esq. of Duckenfield Hall, near Aston, in Lancashire.

1797, The Orchardist, or a system of close pruning and medication for establishing the Science of Orcharding, &c. Extracted from the 11, 12, 13 and 14th vols. of the Society's Transactions for the encouragement of Arts, &c. with additions. London. 8vo. By THOMAS SKIP DYOT BUCKNAL, Esq.

——— The Gardens, a Poem from the French of l'Abbe de Lisle. By Mrs. Montolieu. 4to.

1798. Miscellaneous Observations on the effect of Oxygen on the Animal and Vegetable Systems; and an attempt to prove why some Plants are Evergreens and others Deciduous, Part I. Bath. 8vo. By CLEMENT ARCHER, Esq. M. R. I. A.

——— Forms of Stoves for Forcing Houses. London. Royal 8vo. By—ROBINSON, a London Architect.

This Century was the era of a total change in the style of ornamental Gardening. The cause of this revulsion has been the cause of much learned contention, and each writer on the subject seems to have created a Theory of his own. To me it appears to have been the natural result, arising from a general advance of every Science, an improvement of taste but commensurate with that which had occured in every other quality of the Human mind.

When mankind began to domicile, and left the Caves and Bowers which Nature unassisted afforded, for dwellings constructed with Art, and of materials too ponderous for transportation, Gardening must have attended this commencement of property. The value of various herbs being known, each family thus settled, must soon have learned the convenience of having them vegetating near their dwelling rather than to have to seek them, chance directed, as necessity rendered them requisite. Herbs and Fruits would thus be gradually collected round each dwelling and fix its inhabitants more firmly to the spot as abounding more with such necessaries than any other they could hope to discover. To mark individual property, and to exclude Cattle, a fence would naturally be constructed. As the family of the Tenant, and as the number of naturalized plants increased, so in proportion would the inclosure extend. As wealth accumulated, as the Hut rose into the Palace, as comforts were required as well as necessaries, and luxuries were not denied where there was power to acquire them, Walls supplied the place of hedges, and marked the superiority of that Land-owner, whose dwelling was of Stone and not of Mud-plastered wicker-work. Within such enclosure, pomp and the desire of pleasure combined to require something that might enliven its insipidity. Earths of various colours were arranged in beds of mathematical forms, thrown into Terraces, divided by Balustrades, and mounted by flights of stone steps. Water was collected in marble Basins, confined in parallel sided straight Canals, poured over stone steps, or tossed into the air. Plants were arranged in geometrical order; and their foliage clipt into shapes equally regular, or formed into figures monstrous and grotesque. Such novelties where pleasing, and man could do no more in this style, when he increased the size of his Gardens, than vary the arrangement of the repetition; he might turn the kaleidescope at will; but the same materials, the same ideas appeared only in a different succession. Invention was at a stand still, confined to a square plot of wall-girted ground she could do no more. The Trees and Flowers employed were of the rarest kinds; the Basins and Temples of the costliest materials; Vases and Statues of the finest workmanship were scattered through the ground; and then what remained? Nothing but to demolish the Walls, and let in the view of the surrounding country, to teach mankind the beauties of which, under certain combinations, they required no masters. To admire Natural Scenery composed of well blended Woods, Water, and Ground of varied surface, is an innate gift of the human mind; no savage is there so brutal who would not say he had more pleasure in seeing such, rather than a bare, monotonous plain, the writings of no describer of Scenery has escaped to us that does not dwell upon such as being beautiful. This has been demonstrated in each preceeding Chapter of this work, it wanted only some bold innovator to set the example and the natural taste of man would vindicate and adopt the fashion. Who was the first innovator I shall now proceed to enquire.

Tasso and Milton have been considered as the Heralds of this improvement; in the Garden of Armida of the one, and in the Paradise of the other, some of the beautiful combinations of Nature are described; but it really appears to me extravagant to imagine that either of them had an idea that he was giving a design for Garden Designers to copy; and if not they only admired what others had admired before them; they only described what others had previously described. Witness Cicero's description of his Villa at Arpinum; or that of the Villa of Lucullus on the height of Misenum. Witness the grounds which Nero laid out, and Tacitus describes. These in some degree anticipated Addison, Pope, Bridgeman and Kent, who we consider the originators of Landscape Gardening in modern Europe, inasmuch as that they not only admired and described Picturesque Scenery, but they *imitated* it.

There seems to have been almost a spontaneous effort,

reformation in the style of Gardening in France and England. If to either, the palm for priority, I am constrained to think, must be yielded to the former. Dufresnoy succeeded to Le Notre in 1700, as director of the French Monarch's Gardens. He constructed several Gardens in which natural beauties were imitated, but his example was only admired by his countrymen and not followed. Dufresnoy was a man of Taste and a Poet of merit, and that his designs, or similar ones, were executed before such constructions appeared in England, I am more inclined to believe, because Addison, in one of his excellent papers on Imagination in the Spectator, (No 414) says, " English Gardens are not so entertaining to the Fancy as those in France and Italy, where we see a large extent of ground covered over with an agreeable mixture of Garden and Forest, which represent every where an artificial rudeness, much more charming than that neatness and elegancy which we meet with in those of our own country." Now Addison in the same Essay was advocating Landscape Gardening and attempted to exemplify it at his seat, Bilton near Rugby. He had travelled in France but a few years previously; he was a contemporary of Dufresnoy; and therefore is one of the best of authorities.

The Essay of Addison above quoted, is dated June, 1712, and is the first that ever appeared in which an imitation of Nature is advocated as the basis of ornamental Gardening. This was followed by another in the same work (No 477) To this succeeded an Essay by Pope, dated September 1713, in the Guardian (No 173) in which he most successfully ridicules the practice of cutting Shrubs into monstrous forms. In two years after he purchased his villa at Twickenham, and laid out the garden in the style which he admired. In 1732 he published his "Epistle to Richard Boyle, Earl of Burlington", the first work in which any precise rules for Landscape Gardening are laid down, though it is probable he learnt them from Bridgeman, the Garden Designer, and the nobleman to whom the epistle is addressed, he being distinguished for excellence in the art of Design, The rules, from the shortness of the composition, are of course compendious, but they contain the fundamental principles of the Art. Four and twenty lines include the whole.

> To build, to plant, whatever you intend,
> To rear the column, or the arch to bend,
> To swell the terrace, or to sink the grot;
> In all, let nature never be forgot.
> But treat the Goddess like a modest fair,
> Nor over-dress, nor leave her wholly bare;
> Let not each beauty ev'ry where be spy'd,
> Where half the skill is decently to hide.
> He gains all points, who pleasingly confounds,
> Surprises, varies, and conceals the bounds.
>
> Consult the genius of the place in all;
> That tells the waters or to rise, or fall;
> Or helps th' ambitious hill the heav'ns to scale,
> Or scoops in circling theatres the vale;
> Calls in the country, catches op'ning glades,
> Joins willing woods, and varies shades from shades;
> Now breaks, or now directs th' intending lines;
> Paints as you plant, and, as you work, designs.
>
> Still follow Sense, of ev'ry art the soul,
> Parts answ'ring parts shall slide into a whole,
> Spontaneous beauties all around advance,
> Start ev'n from difficulty, strike from chance;
> Nature shall join you; time shall make it grow,
> A work to wonder at—perhaps a STOW.

BRIDGEMAN came into notice about 1720, as a Garden Designer. Of his History nothing remains; the periods of his birth and death are alike unknown. Walpole is the chief of his remembrancers. After London and Wise, he observes, " Bridgeman was the next fashionable designer of Gardens and was far more chaste, he banished verdant sculpture, and did not even revert to the square precision of the foregoing age. He enlarged his plans, disdained to make every division tally to its opposite, and though he still adhered much to strait walks with high clipt hedges, they were only his great lines; the rest he diversified by wilderness, and with loose groves of oak, though still within surrounding hedges. I have observed in the Gardens at Gubbins in Hertfordshire, the seat of the late Sir Jeremy Sambrooke, many detached thoughts, that strongly indicate the dawn of modern taste. As his reformation gained footing, he ventured farther, and in the Royal Garden at Richmond, dared to introduce cultivated fields, and even morsels of a forest appearance. But this was not till other innovators had broke loose too from rigid symmetry." But above all the sunk fence was now introduced as a boundary instead of Walls and other opaque partitions, this Walpole also attributes to Bridgeman, and was as he justly observes the leading step to still wider extending improvements, for the contiguous ground without the fence, must be made to harmonize with the garden it was made to extend from. One of the first gardens laid out in this style was that of the father of Mr. Walpole, at Houghton. It contained three-and-twenty acres and was from the designs of a Mr. Eyre, an imitator of Bridgeman. To these succeeded Kent, who painter enough to appreciate the charms of Landscape, bold and opinionative enough to dare and to dictate, had genius sufficient to strike out a great system-from the twilight of imperfect essays. Mahomet imagined an Elisium, but Kent created many.*

WILLIAM KENT was born in Yorkshire in 1685. He was apprenticed to a Coach Painter, but aspiring to a higher

* Walpole's Anecdotes of Painting, &c.

path he repaired to London, and thence, aided by some gentlemen of his own country, proceeded with Mr. Talwin to Rome where he studied under the Chevalier Luti, and gained the second prize of the second class in the Academy. His first resources failing, he found a patron in Sir W. Wentworth; and finally in Lord Burlington, with this nobleman he returned to England in 1719, and resided at his house. As a painter, however, notwithstanding the influence of his patron, the estimation in which he was held soon sunk to below mediocrity. As an architect and designer of furniture he succeeded better and was much employed. He designed the Temple of Venus in Stowe Gardens. By the patronage of the Queen, and through the interest of many noblemen he was appointed Master Carpenter, Architect, Keeper of the Pictures, and finally chief Painter to the Crown, the emoluments of which produced about £600 per annum. From 1743 to 1748 he was troubled with various inflammatory attacks which terminated his life on the 12th of April in the last named year. He was buried at the Earl of Burlington's vault at Chiswick. It is said that Kent frequently declared that he caught his taste in Gardening from the perusal of Spencer's picturesque descriptions. Walpole, Mason the Poet, and G. Mason highly panegyrize him, and indeed by general consent he is estimated as the first general practiser of Landscape Gardening. For the following outline of his style of design I am entirely indebted to Mr. Walpole, his contemporary. "The great principles on which he worked were perspective, and light and shade. Groupes of trees broke too uniform or too extensive a lawn; evergreens and woods were opposed to the glare of the champain, and where the view was less fortunate, or so much exposed as to be beheld at once, he blotted out some parts by thick shades, to divide it into variety, or to make the richest scene more enchanting by reserving it to a farther advance of the spectator. Where objects were wanting he introduced temples, &c. but he especially excelled in the management of Water. The gentle stream was taught to serpentine seemingly at its pleasure, and where discontinued by different levels, its course appeared to be concealed by thickets properly interspersed, and glittered again at a distance where it might be supposed naturally to arrive, Its sides were smoothed, but preserved their meanderings. A few trees scattered here and there on its hedges, and when it disappeared among the hills, shades descending from the heights leaned towards its vanishing point. He followed nature even in her faults. In Kensington Gardens he planted dead trees, but was soon laughed out of the excess. His ruling principle was that Nature abhors a strait line."

The principal grounds in which the above principles were carried into effect were Stow near Buckingham, then the residence of Lord Cobham. His Lordship was an amateur designer, but employed Bridgeman to assist him. Bridgeman's plans are still in existance. These improvements began in 1714, and were continued with intermissions until about 1755, when Kent was employed to complete and alter the designs. Lord Cobham appears to have been considered by his friends the first demonstrator of Landscape Gardening in this country from the concluding line of an epitaph which is placed to his memory in the garden.

"Elegantiori Hortorum cultu his primum in agris illustrato Patriam ornavit, 1747."

For a full description of this magnificent domain I must refer my readers to an anonymous publication in 1769, entitled "Stowe; a description of the magnificent House and Gardens, &c." 8vo. with plates—"The Beauties of Stowe," by G. Bickman, 1750—Whately's Observations on Modern Gardening—and a later description of Stowe, by Mr. Seely—Hagley, near Bromsgrove, in Worcestershire, still remains in some parts, as it was first laid out by Lord Lyttleton. It is described by

Whately, and in several Poems. Pain's Hill near Cobham in Surrey exists as it was formed by Mr. Hamilton, ninth son of the sixth Earl of Abercorn. Esher and Clermont were both created by Kent, the latter is still kept up in tolerable style, but the first is extinct. Woburn Farm near Chetsey in Surrey, also arose at the period we are considering, being formed by P. Southcote Esq, as a specimen of the Ferme ornèe, which he invented. It is described by Whately and G. Mason, but no longer exists.

Sir W. Chamber's Dissertations on Oriental Gardening appeared in 1774; the English Garden by Mason in 1772; Shenstone's Unconnected thoughts on Landscape Gardening in 1764; G. Mason's Essay on Design in Gardening in 1768; Walpole's Dissertation on modern Gardening in 1770; and the same year gave birth to Whately's Observations on Modern Gardening

These publications, which all advocate the imitation of the scenes of Nature which delight the spectator by their grandeur or their beauty, contributed much to strengthen and extend the new taste for design. Whately's is decidedly the best, and is the first Prose work which lays down rules and directions for Landscape Gardening; Pope had led the way in Poetry; and Mason in blank verse.

The chief Garden Designers who flourished about the period in which these publications appeared were Wright, Brown, Holland and Eames.

Of Wright I know nothing more than is stated of him by G. Mason, which is, that his birth and education were above plebeian that he was a good draftsman; and never contracted to execute his designs. He planned Lord Barrington's seat at Becket near Farringdon; Stoke near Bristol; the Terrace and River at Oatlands, &c.

LANCELOT BROWN was born at Kirkharle in Northumberland in 1715. His first employment was as kitchen Gardener, to a gentleman near Woodstock, and though he moved afterwards to Stowe, and continued there until 1750, Lord Cobham confined his exertions to that department. That nobleman however recommended him to the Duke of Grafton who appointed him his chief Gardener, at Wakefield Lodge, Northamptonshire, where his judicious formation of a Lake first brought him into notice as a designer. Lord Cobham still continued his patron and obtained for him the Royal Gardenership at Hampton Court and Windsor. He was now consulted by all the nobility and gentry, amongst other places he was employed at Blenheim, where by his easy completion in a week of one of the finest artificial lakes in the world, and other improvements, he rose to the acmè of popularity, and the fashion of employing him continued until the period of his death which occurred in 1783. He had filled the office of High Sheriff for the counties of Huntingdon and Cambridge in 1770, having amassed a very large fortune, and become a leading man in his county. He never went out of England, neither did he ever contract to execute his plans. He employed assistants to draw his designs, which were applied for not only in this country but in Scotland, Ireland and even Russia. Repton has given a list of his principal creations, of which Croome Court, in Worcestershire, and Fisherwick in Warwickshire, now destroyed, were the largest. The places he only altered it is impossible to ascertain. Improvement, says Loudon, was the passion of the day; and there was scarcely a country gentleman who did not on some occasion consult him.*

The leading outlines of his plans were easily copied, and imitators innumerable arose to supply the demand for designs; the spade and axe were at work in every estate, and so rapidly did the face of the country alter that in 1772 Sir W. Chambers de-

* Encyclopæd. of Gardening. p. 76. Ed. 5.

clared that if the mania was not checked, in a few years more, three trees would not be found in a strait line from the Land's-end to the Tweed.* Whenever consulted upon the alterations to be made in grounds, he so invariably observed that there were great "capabilities" about it, that he was generally known by the nick-name of "Capability Brown".

That Brown possessed taste to comprehend that which is pleasing, and genius sufficient to obtain such effect in some of his designs, it is impossible for an unbiassed Critic to deny; but on the other hand his greatest admirers cannot pretend that he even approached in any of the branches of design to his predecessor Kent. By his opponents however he has been too much decried, as by his followers he has been too lavishly extolled. His management of the Water at Blenheim can never be excelled; in this material of Landscape it was that he was most excellent. In the management of the ground and the woodland he was less happy, inasmuch as that he seldom varied in his plan. His declivities were all softened into gentle slopes; Plantations belted the Estate; while clumps and single trees were sprinkled over its area. That these were planted without any consideration or object, which taste pointed out as desirable, it is unjust to assert, in many instances still extant a happiness of effect is produced which he must indeed have been a fortunate man to have obtained by chance. The view which he procured of Cheney Church to Latimers, a seat of Lord Cavendish demonstrates that he could create beauties, and renders any contrary supposition gratuitous. That he was not always successful, is most certain, and may be allowed of any man without compromising his claims to the possession of a genius; but of Brown it must also be allowed that he undertook more than he could perform, for one mind, however fertile its inventive powers, could never have furnished fresh designs for the thousands of places which he was required to lay out. Unfortunately

*Ibid. 77.

his numerous imitators were without even a particle of his mental endowments; the art became most monotonous, and, as Mr. Loudon says, the professor required no farther examination of the ground than to take the levels for forming a piece of water, which water uniformly assumed one shape and character, and differed no more in different situations, than did the Belt and the Clump.

Shenstone and Mason at the above period demonstrated that they could succeed in the practice as well as in writing of Ornamental Gardening. The Leasowes when it came into the hands of the former was merely a grazing farm, but he left it a perfect fairy-land. Every thing that a classical taste could point out as decorative; or picturesque in scenery, were secured to it. It was a Bijou, and when Repton blamed him for not being more extensive in his lawn, &c. he neither comprehended the design of Shenstone, or the genius of the place. Whately and Gilpin have both described it very fully. Mason left monuments of his powers at his Rectory at Aston, and in Lord Harcourt's flower Garden at Nuneham in Oxfordshire. Unfortunately there were no professors of talent sufficient to profit by their example, and the more easy mode which Brown and his corrupt imitators adopted was so palpably and ignorantly unvarying that it soon roused the satire of better judges and insured its own reformation.

Brown was evidently aimed at under the name of Layout, in a novel entitled "Village Memoirs," published in 1775, in which he is represented as a general undertaker of Gardens, who introduces the same objects at the same distances in all. The excellent translation in 1783 of Girardin's "De la composition des Paysages," and the admirable preface attached to it written by Daniel Malthus Esq. likewise pointed out distinctly the correct, and true taste in designing. The Picturesque Tours of Mr. Gilpin published between the years 1783 and 1809; the

Essays on the Picturesque by Mr. Price in 1794, and "The Landscape" by Mr. Payne Knight, in the same year, completed the expulsion of the Brunonian system of design.

Gilpin's Tours are full of excellent and many original observations; he has little of hypothesis or theory, he was a judicious observer of Picturesque beauties, and selecting in his descriptions such as are successful in pleasing, whether natural or acquired, he very rationally draws the conclusion that such are the best to imitate. To do this, Taste in the imitator is the chief requisite, for he very justly remarks that the comparative virtue of taste and expense is remarkable; the former with very little of the latter will always produce something pleasing, while the utmost efforts of the latter unaided by the former are ineffectual. All his observations are illustrated by examples, and independant of the native English scenery which he draws from for the purpose, he describes the following demesnes for a similar purpose, Blenheim, Burleigh, Castlehill, Enville, Fonthill, Hafod, Hagley, Ilam, Kiddleston, Leasowes, Mount Edgecumbe Nuneham, Norbury, Persfield, Roch Abbey, Shuckborow, Strawberry Hill, Studley, Trentham, Twickenham, and Wilton. His writings are in a most agreeable style and were generally read. If it is too much to say that they formed the national taste, they served most effectually to correct it.

The Essays of Price, advocate the study of the principles of Painting by those who wish to excel in Landscape Gardening "not to the exclusion of Nature, but as an assistant in the study of her works." What those principles are as relates to the creation of a beautiful Landscape he then proceeds to consider, and which he concludes may be effected in two modes, the characteristics of one are boldness, abruptness, depth and sudden contrasts of shade, &c. such as Salvator Rosa might delight to represent; the other by gentle undulations, with soft blendings of light and shade such as Claude usually represents in his Landscapes.

Knight in his Landscape advocates the same cause; and both in a most masterly manner enforce their principles. These principles were attacked by Repton, Wyndham, Marshall, &c. and defended by Loudon and others.

After studying the writings of the several partizans I have been able to draw but one conclusion, which is, that the principles of Knight and Price are correct if impartially considered, and have been acted upon by the general consent of modern designers; nor can there be a greater proof of this position than that in his maturer practice, Repton acted upon them himself. They differed in no one point of importance, that I have been able to discover, as to what constitutes beautiful points in a Landscape: of course they agreed that such should be imitated; and I have read not one passage in any of their writings which will warrant the conclusion that if assembled together, there would have been a dissentient voice to the observation of Price, that regular Beauty and Utility must not be neglected in the pursuit of the picturesque, for that would be opposed to the dictates of common sense. It could not fail but that the writings of men gifted with so much taste; and the examples which they gave of their respective opinions, for Repton was, and Loudon is a professional designer, should secure the adoption of a chastened style; such was actually the case, and we are now profiting by their labours.

ON

ENGLISH GARDENING

From the close of the 18th Century to the present time.

We have seen under what favourable auspices and with what great improvements Gardening was on the advance at the close of the 18th Century; but the present Century was ushered in with even greater promise of success, for the light of Science was still more powerfully concentrated upon its practices for their benefit, and the illumination which from the same source had first been afforded to it towards the close of the previous Century, began now to be felt and appreciated. This especially applies to the labours of the Chemist and Physiologist. Such combination of Horticultural Art and Science was especially promoted by the institution of the Horticultural Societies of London and Edinburgh. The first of these societies began to be formed in 1804, the latter in 1809. Nothing can more conspicuously display the high estimation in which Gardening is held; nothing can afford a greater guarrantee for its improvement, than the lists of the Fellows of the above societies. In them are enrolled the names of the most talented, the most noble, and the most wealthy individuals of the United Kingdom.

I shall first proceed to trace the Horticultural literature of the period we are now considering, leaving the survey of Gardening in its various branches as now existing to form my concluding remarks.

THOMAS ANDREW KNIGHT, President of the Horticultural Society of London, F. R. S. &c. &c. If the questions were put to me who is the most scientific Horticulturist now living?—Who unites to a knowledge of the Practices of Gardening, the most perfect knowledge of the sciences that ass'st it? Which of living Horticulturists has conferred the greatest benefits upon our art? I should quote Mr. Knight in reply to them all. Whether we follow him in his researches as a Physiologist, in his luminous observations and discoveries respecting the Sap of Plants; as a general Cultivator in the numerous Papers on every branch of Horticulture in the Transactions of the Society of which he is President; and especially in the raising of improved varieties of Fruits and Culinary esculents, we find in all the most ample justification of our opinion that he is the first Horticulturist of our times. Nor is he eminent only in the higher walks of Horticulture, for at Downton Hall he demonstrates that he is capable of securing the correct performance of every detail of Gardening.

Mr Knight was born at Wormeley Grange in Herefordshire, in 1759. "My father, says Mr. Knight in a late communication to me, was a man of much learning and acquirements. Having great power of mind, and living in an extremely quiet and sequestered spot, he was supposed by his ignorant neighbours, in their language, "to know every thing." He died at an advanced age when Mr. Knight was an infant, and as evidence of the respect his knowledge obtained him, whenever in childhood his son sought for information upon any unusual subject, he was told " that his father would have answered him, but that nobody now could." Being born in the midst of Orchards "I was early led, continues this distinguished Physiologist, to ask whence the varieties of fruit I saw came, and how they were produced; I could obtain no satisfactory answer, and was thence first led to commence experiments, in which through a long life of scarcely interrupted health, I have persevered and probably shall persevere as long as I possess the power."

Mr. Knight is author of the following works, besides the numerous papers in the Horticultural Transactions which will be mentioned in their appropriate places.

1. A Treatise on the culture of the Apple and Pear, and on the manufacture of Cyder and Perry. London. 1797. 12mo. The 3rd edition in 1808.

2. Some doubts relative to the efficacy of Mr. Forsyth's Plaister, in renovating Trees. London. 1802. 4to.

3. Report of a Committee of the Horticultural Society of London. London. 1805. 4to.

4. Pomona Herefordiensis, or a descriptive account of the old Cyder and Perry Fruits of Herefordshire. London. 1809. 4to.

5. A Letter on the origin of Blight, and on Raising late Crops of Peas. This is appended to Sir J. Banks's Essay on the Mildew. London. 1806. 8vo. 2nd edition.

His discoveries in vegetable Physiology are recorded in several papers in the Philosophical Transactions.

WILLIAM SALISBURY, of the Botanic Garden, Brompton, is author of the following publications.

1. Hortus Paddingtonensis, or a Catalogue of Plants cultivated in the Garden of J. Symmonds Esq. Paddington House, London. 1797. 8vo.

2. The Botanist's Companion, or an Introduction to the knowledge of Practical Botany, and the uses of Plants, either growing wild in Gt. Britain, or cultivated for the

purposes of Agriculture, Medicine, Rural Economy, or the Arts. London. 1816. 2 vols. 12mo.

3. Hints to the Proprietors of Orchards. 1817. 12mo.

4. The Cottager's Companion, or a complete system of Cottage Gardening, intended to instruct the industrious Poor of the United Kingdom. To which is added a descriptive list of Plants growing wild, which are useful for culinary purposes. 1818. 12mo.

He also wrote an Essay on packing Plants for exportation in Nicholson's Journal. vol. xxx. 339.

HENRY ANDREWS, a Botanical Painter and Engraver residing in London, is author or editor of the following works.

1. Engravings of Ericas or Heaths, with Botanical descriptions. London. 1796. Folio.

2. The Botanist's Repository, with coloured figures of such Plants as have not appeared in any similar publication. Published in numbers between 1797 and 1799, forming 2 vols. 4to. London.

3. A Review of Plants hitherto figured in the Botanist's Repository. London. 1801. 4to.

4. The Heathery, or Monograph of the Genus Erica. published in monthly numbers. In 6 vols. between 1804 and 1814.

WALTER NICOL, was the son of the Gardener who planned and executed the grounds of Raith, near Kircaldy in Fifeshire, and the Kitchen Garden of Wemyss Castle in the same County, both of which are excellent performances. Walter began the study of his art at Raith, but removed to England, and obtained the place of head Gardener to the Marquis of Townsend at Rainham Hall, in Suffolk, the Gardens of which however are no records of his skill. He returned to Scotland and he obtained a similar situation at Wemyss Castle. He finally settled at Edinburgh about 1797 as a Horticultural Designer and Author. in 1810 he undertook an extensive tour through England, for the purpose of visiting our principal seats and plantations, to obtain materials for his " Planters Calendar". This work was scarcely commenced when he died suddenly in March, 1811.

His works are of first authority, and rank as the equals of those of Abercrombie, being the result of long practice during an enlightened era of our Art. He was author of the following works.

1. The Scotch Forcing Gardener; together with instructions on the management of the Green-house, Hot-walls, &c. Illustrated with plates. Edinburgh. 1798. 8vo.

2. The Practical Planter ; or a Treatise on Forest Planting: comprehending the culture and management of planted and natural Timber ; also the management of Hedges, Fences, and the construction of Stone Walls, &c. Edinburgh 1799. 8vo.

3. The Villa Garden Directory: or monthly Index of Work to be done in the Town and Villa Gardens, Shrubberies, Parterres, &c. Edinburgh. 1809. 8vo.

4. The Gardener's Kalendar; or monthly directory of operations in every branch of Horticulture. Edinburgh. 1810. 8vo.

5. The Planter's Kalendar ; or the Nurseryman and Forester's

Guide in the operations of the Nursery, the F(
the Grove. Edinburgh. 1812. 8vo.

This posthumous publication was completed by M

WILLIAM PONTEY, ornamental Gardener, r
Huddersfield. He is planter and forest pruner to
of Bedford.

1. The profitable Planter; a treatise on the cultiva
   Larch and the Scotch Fir Timber, shewing tha
   cellent quality, especially that of the former, v
   them so essentially useful, as greatly to promote t
   of the Country. Huddersfield. 1800. 8vo. 4t
   London. 1814.

2. The Forest Pruner, or Timber owners assistan
   treatise on the training or management of Briti
   Trees, whether intended for use, ornament, o
   including an explanation of the causes of the
   diseases and defects, with means of prevention,
   dies where practicable. Also on examinati
   properties of English Fir Timber, with remarks
   fects of the old, and the outlines of a new syste
   management of Oak Woods. With eight e
   plates. London. 1805. 8vo. 3rd Edition Lon

3. The Rural Improver. Huddersfield. 1823. 4to.

1802. Rural Recreation, or the Gardener's Instru
       hibiting in a clear and perspicuous mann
       operations necessary in the Kitchen, Flower,
       Gardens, &c, for every month in the year.
       Treatise on the management of Bees; Ca
       Plants, &c, By a Society of Practical (
       London. 8vo.

THOMAS MARTYN, F. R. S, &c. was elected Professor of Botany at Cambridge, as his father's successor, in 1761. He took his degree of Batchelor of Arts, while of Emmanuel College in 1756. He afterwards was elected a Fellow of Sidney Sussex College, subsequent to which he took his degree of Master of Arts in 1759; and that of Batchelor of Divinity in 1766. He died the 3rd of June, 1825 in the 90th year of his age.

There is a portrait of him in Thornton's Botany.

The following are a portion of his literary works.

1. An edition of Philip Miller's Gardener's Dictionary, corrected and newly arranged. This appeared between the years 1803—7 in four volumes. folio.

The preface which gives a history of Miller's work; the life of Miller; and the list of Authors, and slight notices of their works, are all valuable; but the body of the work itself, is a code of valuable practical information as regards the cultivation of the Earth, as well as being replete with information for the Botanist. It needs no comment. It is a standard practical work, never to be superseded.

2. Flora Rustica; a description of Plants in common cultivation, pointing out such as are useful or injurious in Husbandry, &c. With coloured plates, from drawings by Nodder. London. 8vo. In 4 vols. commenced publishing in 1792, completed in 1794.

JOHN CLAUDIUS LOUDON, Landscape Gardener. Born in Lanarkshire in 1782; began to practice in 1803; to farm extensively in Oxfordshire in 1809, and in Middelsex in

1810. Travelling on the continent in 1813—14—15; again in 1819; and again in 1828 –29. Now residing at Brayswater.

He is author of the following works.

1. Observations on laying out the Public Squares of London. (Literary Journal. 1803.)

2. Observations on the formation and management of useful and ornamental Plantations; on the Theory and Practice of Landscape Gardening; and on gaining and on banking land from Rivers or the Sea. Edinburgh. 1804. 8vo.

3. A short Treatise on some improvements lately made in Hot-houses. Edinburgh. 1805. 8vo.

4. A Treatise on forming, improving, and managing Country Residences, and on the choice of situations appropriate to every class of Purchasers. With an Appendix, containing an enquiry into the utility and merits of Mr. Repton's mode of shewing effects by slides and sketches; and strictures on his opinions and practice in Landscape Gardening. Illustrated by descriptions of Scenery and Buildings by references to Country Seats, and Passages of Country in most parts of Great Britain, and by 32 engravings. London, 1806. 2 vols. 4to.

5. Hints on the formation of Gardens and Pleasure Grounds, &c. 1812. Plates. 4to.

6. Remarks on the construction of Hot-houses; pointing out the most advantageous forms, materials, and contrivances to be used in their construction; with a Review of the various methods of building them in foreign countries, as well as in England; with 10 plates, from etchings on Stone 1817. 4to.

7. Sketches of Curvilinear Hot-houses; with a description of various purposes in Horticultural and general Architecture to which a solid Iron Sash Bar, lately invented is applicable. 1818.

8, A comparative view of the Curvilinear and common mode of Roofing Hot-houses. London. 1818. folio.

9. The Encyclopædia of Gardening. London. 1818. 8vo. The fifth edition is dated 1827.

10. The different modes of cultivating the Pine Apple from its first introduction to Europe to the improvements of T. A. Knight Esq. in 1823. London. 8vo. 1824.*

He is also Editor of the Magazines of Gardening and Natural History, of the first of which we shall speak hereafter.

Whoever wishes for a complete view of English Gardening as at present practiced, will find no works better calculated for his satisfaction than those of Mr. Loudon. Mr. Loudon being a Landscape Gardener by profession, might be excused if in his publications on that branch of our Art, the abilities of a master were chiefly apparent; that in such he is correct, that he possesses taste to discriminate the beauties, and to reprobate the incongruities of his predecessors; that he has taste to select, and ability to execute; is saying all that can be said of any Landscape Gardener who may succeed to Kent, Mason, Whately, Knight, Price and Repton. It may be said without any reservation of Mr. Loudon.

Of his works on the more general branches of Horticulture I shall confine my remarks to his Encyclopœdia of Gardening.

* Encyclop. of Gardening. p. 1113.

When this work first met my notice I objected to the title as conveying an absurdity, for I conceived that a work confined to Gardening could not be an Encyclopædia, which by its very name professes to embrace the whole circle of the Arts, but when I came to peruse the work, I was inclined to excuse this application of the term, because I found that with the exception of Chemistry, every art and science at all illustrative of Gardening, are made to contribute their assistance.

The introduction contains a History of Ancient and Modern Gardening; and to that part of it which relates to the Horticulture of Greece, Rome, and England I am much indebted. In the Second Part is contained a luminous detail of the facts of Vegetable Physiology, or as Mr. Loudon terms it. "Organology," a word compounded of Latin and Greek which I cannot but object to. This is chiefly compiled from Mr, Keith's valuable work on Physiological Botany; and the chief objection which I always had to the original is continued to this, viz. its system is unnecessarily intricate.

The sole use of arrangement is to assist the memory by a connection of facts, and thus at the same time to facilitate reference. We conceive that if the facts of Keith's System had been arranged under the heads of 1. root, 2. stems, 3. branches 4. leaves, 5. flowers, 6. seeds with the appendages and anomalies of each, and a second part containing the anatomy of Plants and the phenomena of Vegetable life as regularly and connectedly developed, it would be a much more complete System; there would be a much greater unity and regular subordination of parts than is at present obtained by Divisions and Subdivisions for the Conservative Organs, and Reproductive Organs, Conservative Appendages and Reproductive Appendages; Decomposite Organs, Composite Organs, and Elementary Organs.

On the nomenclature, description and classification of Plants according to the Linnæan and the Jussieuæan Systems; Vegetable Geography; On Earths, Soils, the influence of heat, and other contingencies, on vegetation follow, and without having much claim to originality are replete with information; though I cannot but regret that more stress is not laid upon the assistance which Mr. Loudon admits is to be derived by Horticulture from the researches of Chemists. Book 3. is devoted to the implements and edifices usually found in Gardens; and here again I have to regret that the immense variety of information given is so unnecessarily split into sub-sections. Book the 4th is on the operations of Gardening, which completes the second part. Part the third which contains the detail of culture necessary for each Garden Plant, Landscape Gardening, &c. and Part the fourth on the present state of Gardening in Gt. Britain are as satisfactory, as replete with information, and as well arranged as can be. A most useful Kalendarial Index; and a copious alphabetical one complete the work.

Taken as a whole it is the most complete book of Gardening ever published, for errors in dates are mere casualities and I should have no fault to find if the deficiency of Horticultural Chemistry was less, and if the arrangement was more simple; the first fault is comparatively trifling; but the latter is of much greater importance, and I should like in a future edition to find it more luminous from a simplification of its arrangement.

1803. Viridarium; or Green-house Plants, containing fifty plates drawn and coloured from nature. By HENRIETTA, M. MORIARTY, London 8vo. Mrs M. has written several novels.

1805. Minutes on Agriculture and Planting, &c. London. 4to. By WILLIAM AMOS, Farmer at Brothertoft in Lincolnshire.

He had been Gardener and Bailiff to some Peer. He also was author of some works on the Drill Husbandry.

1805. A Complete Dictionary of Practical Gardening, London. 2 vols, 4to. by ALEXANDER MACDONALD, an assumed name by Dr. R. W. DICKSON, of Hindon in Middlesex, author of several Agricultural works.

Architectural Sketches. London. fol. No. 1. by G. J. PARKYNS, author of "Monastic Remains," and reputed author of the six designs for laying out grounds, published, 1793, with Soane's Designs for Villas.

1806. The Florist's Manual. London. 12mo. by a Lady, author of "Conversations on Botany." &c.

1807. The Practical Gardener. London. 8vo. by WILLIAM SHAW.

1808. A Treatise on the Culture of the Pine Apple. Newark. 8vo. by WILLIAM GRIFFIN, formerly Gardener to James Manners Sutton, Esq. at Kelham Hall, near Nottingham, and now to Samuel Smith, Esq. Wood Hall, Herts.*

1809. An Essay on the cultivation of the Plants belonging to the Order of Proteæ. London. 4to. by J. KNIGHT. F. H. S.

This work has been attributed to Mr. Salisbury, but is the production of Mr. Knight, who was Gardener to — Hibbert,

* Loudon's Encyclop. of Gardening. p. 1113.

Esq. of Clapton, whose collection of Plants he now possesses, and carries on the business of a Nurseryman.

1811. On the Mode of forcing the Vine in Denmark. London. 8vo. by PETER LINDEGAARD, Gardener to the King of Denmark, at Rosenburgh.

This work was published in the Danish language at Copenhagen. Mr. Lindegaard is a Corresponding Member of the London Horticultural Society, and is decidedly the first Horticulturist in Denmark; some of his writings will be found in the table of contents of the Horticultural Transactions.

THOMAS HAYNES, nurseryman at Arundel in Northamptonshire, is author of the following works.

1. Improved System of Nursery Gardening. London. 1811, 8vo.

2. Interesting Discoveries in Horticulture: being an easy, rational, and efficacious System of propagating all hardy American, and Bog Soil Plants, with Ornamental Trees and Shrubs of general description, Green-house Plants, including Botany Bay and Cape Plants; Herbaceous Plants, affording favourable shoots and Fruit Trees in every variety, by planting Cuttings chiefly in the warm months, without artificial Heat. London. 1811. 8vo.

3. A Treatise on the improved culture of the Strawberry, Raspberry, and Gooseberry. London. 1812. 8vo.

4. On collecting Soils and Composts and preparing them for use, &c. London. 1821. 12mo.

WILLIAM JACKSON HOOKER, L. L. D. F. R. S,

& L. S. &c. This excellent Botanist and Botanical Draftsman is the editor of the following works.

1. Pomona Londinensis; containing representations of the best Fruits cultivated in British Gardens; with descriptions. 1813—15. 4to. In parts.

2. Exotic Flora, containing figures and descriptions of new, rare, or otherwise interesting exotic Plants, especially of such as are deserving of being cultivated in our Gardens, &c. In parts 8vo. 1823—26.

3. The Botanical Miscellany—In Quarterly numbers. 1829.

Dr. Hooker in conjunction with Mr. Curtis, Horticulturist of Glazen Wood, Essex, is editor of the Botanical Magazine; which office he commenced in January 1827.

1812. The Exotic Gardener, &c. London. 8vo. 3rd Edition 1826. By J. CUSHING.

Mr. Cushing, was a native of Ireland. He was for many years foreman of the Forcing Department, in the Garden of Messrs. Lee and Kennedy at Hammersmith. He died in 1819 or 1820.

1812. Tranactsions of the HORTICULTURAL SOCIETY of LONDON. vol. 1.

PART I.
1809. 1. Introductory Remarks relative to the objects which the Horticultural Society have in view, by T. A. KNIGHT, Esq. 2. An attempt to ascertain the time when the Potatoe was first introduced into the United Kingdom, with some account of the Hill

Wheat of India. by Sir J. BANKS, Bart.* 3. On the cultivation of the Sea Kale. by Mr J.MAHER. 4. Some hints respecting the proper mode of inuring tender plants to our climate. by Sir J. BANKS, Bart. 5. On a variety of the Brassica Napus, or Rape, which has long been cultivated on the Continent. Mr. JAMES DICKSON. V. P. H. S.† 6. Observations on the method of producing new and early Fruits. by T. A. KNIGHT. Esq. 7. On the cultivation of the Polianthis Tuberosa, or Tuberose, with its Botanical description and figure. by R. A. SALISBURY, Esq. 8. On the revival of an obsolete mode of

---

* It would approach to ingratitude not to take more particular notice of this universal patron of the Arts and Sciences. SIR JOSEPH BANKS, was born at Revesby Abbey, the seat of his father in Lincolnshire, in 1743. He was educated at Eton and Oxford, which University he left in 1761, on the death of his father. He thus inherited an ample fortune, yet the active pursuit of Scientific Discoveries was more to his taste than literary ease. In 1763 he made a voyage to Labrador and Newfoundland. In 1768 he went round the world with Cook, and in 1772 he made a voyage to Iceland and the Western Isles of Scotland. Natural History was the favourite of his Scientific Studies, and every department of it was enriched by his researches. In 1771 he was elected L. L. D. at Oxford. In 1775 he was created a Knight of the Bath, and chosen to the Presidency of the Royal Society, and three years afterwards he was made a Baronet. He at first gave much dissatisfaction to some of the Members of the Royal Society, so as nearly to cause it to divide, but it gradually passed away, and from that time until his death, May 9th 1820, he was universally hailed as a munificent friend of Science and Literature.

† MR. JAMES DICKSON, F. L. S. was born at Kirk House, Peeblesbire, in 1738. He was first instructed in Gardening, in the Garden of the Earl of Traguhair; he afterwards was employed in the Brompton Nursery then kept by Mr Jeffery. He acted as head Gardener in several families until 1722, when he founded the herb and seed shop in Covent Garden so well known under the name of Dickson and Anderson. He was one of the first Members both of the Linnean and Horticultural Societies. Of the lat-

managing Strawberries. by Sir J. BANKS, Bart. 9. On raising new and early varieties of the Potatoe, by T. A. KNIGHT, Esq. 10. On the advantage of grafting Walnut, Mulberry, and Chesnut Trees. by T. A. KNIGHT, Esq. 11. An account of some new Apples. by Mr. A. BIGGS.

PART II.

1809. 12. On the cultivation of Common Flax, as an ornamental plant. By Mr. JOHN DUNBAR, Gardener to T. Fairfax Esq. 13. An account of the method of cultivating the American Cranberry at Spring Grove. By SIR J. BANKS, BART. 14. On a new method of training Fruit Trees. By T. A. KNIGHT, Esq. 15. Observations on the different species of Dahlia, and the best mode of cultivating them in Gt. Britain, By R. A. SALISBURY, Esq. 16. A Description of a forcing House for Grapes with observations on the best method of constructing them for other fruits. By T. A. KNIGHT, Esq. 17. A short Account of Nectarines and Peaches, naturally produced on the same Branch. by R. A SALISBURY, Esq. 18. An Account of a method of hastening the maturation of Grapes, by J. WILLIAMS, Esq.

ter he was one of the Vice-Presidents. He was a good Botanist, and more particularly devoted his attention to the Mosses. He died at Croydon, Aug. 14th, 1822 (Trans. Hort. Soc. of London. v. Append. i.)

His first publication commenced in 1785, being a Fasciculus of his "Plantarum Cryptogamicarum Britanniæ" which was completed in 1801. In 1793 he began publishing his "Hortus Siccus Britannicus" which was finished in 1802. He was a frequent guest at the table of Sir J. Banks and was very generally admired for his talents, and general integrity. He was twice married. His second wife, a sister of the celebrated Mungo Park, survives him.

PART III.
1809. 19. Observations on the culture of Dahlias in the north of Great Britain. by J. WEDGEWOOD, Esq. 20. Hints relative to the culture of Early Cape Brocoli. by Mr. J. JOHN MAHER. 21. An Account of the Burr-knot Apple. by the Rev. JOHN SIMPSON. 22. On the species of the Crocus and their cultivation. by A. K. HAWORTH, Esq. 23. On the Horticultural Management of the Sweet or Spanish Chesnut Tree. by Sir. J. BANKS, Bart. 24. On the construction of Hot-bed Frames, by T. A. KNIGHT, Esq. 25. A short account of a new Apple, called the Downton Pippin. by T. A. KNIGHT, Esq. 26. On the Forcing Houses of the Romans, and their Fruits now in our Gardens. by Sir J. BANKS, Bart. 27. On the management of the Onion, by T. A. KNIGHT, Esq. 28. An improved method of cultivating the Alpine Strawberry, by T. A. KNIGHT, Esq. 29. Observations on the form of Hot-houses, by the Rev. T. WILKINSON. 30. On some new varieties of the Peach, by T. A. KNIGHT. Esq.

PART IV.
1810. 31. On a mode of training Vines. By Mr. JOSEPH HAYWARD. 32. On some Exotics which endure the open air in Devonshire. By A. HAWKINS. Esq. 33. On a new variety of Pear. By T. A. KNIGHT Esq. 34. Some Account of the Ipomœa Tuberosa. By Mr. JOHN TURNER. 35. On Potatoes. By T. A. KNIGHT, Esq. 36. A new and expeditious mode of budding. T. A. KNIGHT, Esq. 37. On the Spring Grove Codling. By Sir J. BANKS, Bart. 38. On the best mode of constructing a Peach-house. By T. A. KNIGHT, Esq.

Part v.

1811. 39. On the cultivation of Horse-radish. By Mr. JOSEPH KNIGHT.* 40. On the culture of the Potatoe in Hot-beds. By T. A. KNIGHT Esq. 41. On the present mode of budding and Grafting. By Mr. J. WILMOT. 42. A concise view of the theory respecting Vegetation. By T. A. KNIGHT, Esq. 43. On raising young Potatoes in the Winter months. By A. SHERBROOK, Esq. 44. Account of some Apples and Pears, of which Grafts have been distributed. By T. A. KNIGHT, Esq. 45. Some Account of the red Doyenné Pear. By R. A. SALISBURY, Esq. 46. On the utility of Oxygen Gas in promoting Vegetation. By D. HILL, Esq. 47. On pruning and training standard Apple and Pear Trees. By Mr. J. MAHER.

APPENDIX:

i. Some objects for which the Society intends to present Premiums and Medals.

ii. Selections from French Horticultural Authors. By Sir J. BANKS, Bart.

iii. On the cultivation of the Jamrosade. Translated from the French of M. Thouin. By R. A. SALISBURY. Esq.

iv. On the Vegetation of high Mountains, translated from the French of M. Ramond, by R. A. SALISBURY, Esq.

v. On a Bank for Alpine Plants, from the French of M. Thouin, by R. A. SALISBURY, Esq.

* London's Encyclop. of Gardening. p. 1118.

1812. A concise and practical Treatise on the growth and culture of the Carnation, Pink, Auricula, Polyanthus, Ranunculus, Tulip, &c. London. 12mo. A plate. By THOMAS HOGG.

Mr. Hogg, was master of an Academy at Paddington, Middlesex, he is now a florist at the same place, where he has a collection of Carnations and Piccotees, perhaps the finest in the world. He is celebrated for his successful culture of them. He has more than seven hundred varieties of all prices from two to sixty shillings.

1812. Plans, Elevations, and Sections of Hot-houses, and Green-houses, an Aquarium, Conservatories, &c. recently built in different parts of England for various noblemen and gentlemen, &c. London. folio. By GEORGE TODD, Surveyor and Hot-house builder.

1813. 1. Observations on the barrenness of Fruit Trees; the means of prevention and cure. Edinburgh. 8vo. By PETER LYON, an Apothecary and Physic Gardener at Comely Garden, near Edinburgh. He also wrote,

2. A Treatise on the Physiology and Pathology of Trees, with observations on the barrenness and canker of Fruit Trees; the means of prevention and cure. Edinburgh. 1816. 8vo. 2nd Ed.

1813. 1. Account of some experiments to promote the improvement of Fruit Trees, by peeling the Bark. London. 8vo. By SIR JOHN SINCLAIR, Bart, The experiments were made by the Mr. Lyon just mentioned.

2. General Report of the Agricultural state, and Political circumstances of Scotland. Drawn up under the direction of Sir J. Sinclair, Bart. Edinburgh. 1814. 2 vols.

1814. LEONARD PHILLIPS, jun. Fruit Tree Nurseryman Lambeth, wrote the following.

1. A Catalogue of Fruit Trees for sale. London. folio.

2. Transactions in the Fruit Tree Nursery, Vauxhall. London. 1815. folio.

——————The Forcer's Assistant; or a treatise with useful hints on forcing, by a new device for the application of Frames to the culture of Melons, Pines, and other choice Fruit, from Dwarf Plants; and of the early Esculents usually in demand for the first Tables; including a few plain directions for forcing the Grape, Cherry, and Peach in houses: with an appendix describing the Patent forcing frame, and exhibiting some of its advantages; to which is prefixed an introduction connecting the principal parts of the Theory of Vegetation, with the practice of Horticulture. Chipping Norton, 8vo. By E. WEEKS, formerly Gardener to Lord Kirkwall, now of the Horticultural Repository. London.

1814. Memoirs of the CALEDONIAN HORTICULTURAL SOCIETY. vol. 1. 8vo.

1. On the Curl in Potatoes. MR. T. DICKSON.
2. On the same. By J. SHERIFF, Esq. 3. On employing Earthen-ware Tubes for flues in Hot-houses.

By C. LORIMER Esq. 4. On planting Asparagus By Mr. J. SMITH. 5. On cultivating French Pears in Scotland. By Mr. J. SMITH. 6. On Gooseberry Caterpillars and Onion Maggot. Mr. J. MACKMURRAY 7. On the same. By Mr. J. GIBB. 8. On the Wall Trees at Loanwells, near Kirkaldy. By Mr. E. Sang. 9. On the culture of Onions. By Mr, J. MACDONALD. 10. On covering the soil of Hot-beds, &c. By Mr. HENDERSON. 11. On the Scotch Fir. By Mr. G. DON 12. On Carrot Worms and preserving Cauliflowers. Mr. SMITH. 13. On removing insects, Mildew, &c. in Fruit Trees. Mr. D. WEIGHTON 14. On Hot-house flues. By R. STEVENSON, Esq. 15. On hastening the bearing of Fruit Trees, &c. By Mr. R. INGRAM. 16. On medicines from the Lettuce. By Dr. DUNCAN, Sen. 17. On the state of some Fruits in Scotland. by A. G. HUNTER, Esq. 18. On destroying the blue Insect in Wall Trees, By Mr. P. BARNET. 19. On transplanting old Fruit Trees. By Mr. T. THOMSON. 20. On destroying Caterpillars, &c. By Mr. J. KYLE. 21. On destroying Wasps. By Mr. J. MITCHELL. 22. On destroying the Green fly; and bringing Pear Trees to bear. By Mr. W. BEATTIE. 33. On Maggots that infest Shallots. By Mr. W. HENDERSON. 24. On moving large Fruit Trees. By Mr. J. STEWART 25. On preserving Apples and Pears. By Mr. J. STEWART. 26. On the Pine Bug. By Mr. A. MIURHEAD. 27. Receipts for making Currant Wine. 28. On the Currant Tree while ripening its fruit. By Mr. J. MACDONALD. 29. On the Canker. By Mr. J. SMITH. 30. On propagating by cuttings the Burr-Knot Apple. By Dr. DUNCAN

Sen. 31. On turning the branches of Fruit Trees over the Wall. By Sir J. BANKS, Bart. 32. On Clay Paint for Fruit Trees. By Mr. J. SCOUGAL. 33, On the Turnip fly. By Mr. A. GORRIE. 34. On pruning Fruit Trees, By the Hon. BARON HEPBURN. 35. On a medicine from the Lettuce. By Mr. J. HENDERSON. 36. On storing Vegetables for Summer use. By Mr. J. HENDERSON 37. On destroying Caterpillars. By Mr. R. ELLIOT 38, On planting Peach Trees on a north border. By Mr. MACRAY. 39. On the Gooseberry Caterpillar, and on the Onion and Carrot Worms. By Mr. J. MACKRAY 40. On retarding Fruit blossoms. by Mr. A. GORRIE. 41. On some tender plants cultivated in the open air at Guernsey. By Dr. MACCULLOCH. 42. On a rotation of crops: By Mr. T. KELLY. 43. On a small orchard in East Lothian. By Mr. J. SMITH. 44. On composts. By Mr. D. WEIGHTON. 45. On destroying a Gooseberry Caterpillar. By Mr. J. TWEEDIE. 46. On Sea Kale. By Sir G. S. MACKENZIE. On the Carse of Gowrie Orchards. By Messrs. MACRAY and GORRIE. 48. On the canker. By Mr. J. SMITH. 49. On the same. By Mr. E. SANG. 50, On preserving the blossom of Fruit Trees. By Mr. J. LAIRD. 51. On a new ground onion. By Dr. R. Cumming. 52. On the Lactucarium. By Mr. A. GORRIE. 53. On the Tree onion. By Mr. G. NICOL. 54. On Can flues in Hot-houses. By Dr. Duncan, sen. 55. On excluding Wasps from Hot-houses. By Mr. J. DICK. 56. On preserving Trees from Hares. By Mr, J. SMEALL. 57. On preventing Mildew in Peach Trees. By Mr. J. KIRK 58. On British opium. By J. HOWISON, Esq. 59. On the Carlisle and Keswick Codlins. By Sir

J. SINCLAIR, Bart. 60. On pruning old Apple and Pear Trees. By Mr. J. YOUNG. 61. An address from the Rubus Chamæmorus. By Mr. GORRIE. 62. On forcing Sea Kale. By Mr. W. GIBBS. 63. On renovating old Peach trees in Hot-houses: By Mr. A. HAY. 64. On the Carnation. By Mrs. J. MITCHELL. 65. On the same. By Mr. W. CRAWFORD. 66. On the Guernsey cultivation of the Parsnip. by Dr. MACCULLOCH. 67. On the Mangold Wurtzel. By Dr. J. C. LETTSOM. 68. On preserving Potatoes. By the Rev. A. DOW, D. D. 69. On cherry trees. By Mr. W. UNDERWOOD. 70. On a new pruning instrument. By Mr. W. MENZIES. 71. On Cast Iron Espalier rails. By Mr. J. MIDDLETON 72. On the Potatoe. By Mr. D. CRIGHTON. 73. On an increase of Manure. By Mr. T. BISHOP. 74. On preventing the Blight in Fruit Trees. Mr. G. SINCLAIR. 75. On pruning and training Pear Trees. By A. STEWART.

1816; A plain and practical treatise on the culture and management of the Auricula, &c. London. 12mo. By ISAAC EMMERTON.

Mr Emmerton was an enthusiastic admirer of the Auricula. He was a nurseryman and florist at Barnet.

1816. A Treatise upon Bulbous Roots, Green-house Plants, Flower Gardens, Fruit Trees, the culture of the Sea Kale, Destruction of Insects, &c.—Bath. 12mo. By J. SALTER, Nurseryman, &c. Wells-Road Nursery, Bath.

Mr. JAMES MEAN, head Gardener to Sir Abraham Hume Bart. edited in 1816, the two following works of Abercrombie

1. The Practical Gardener, revised with considerable additions. London 12mo. The 3rd Edition 1829.

2. The practical Gardener's Companion, or Horticultural Kalendar, containing the latest improvements in Horticultural practice. To which is annexed, on a plan never before exhibited, the Garden, Seed and Plant estimate; edited from an original MS. of J. Abercrombie. London. 18mo.

1. Hortus Gramineus Woburnensis, or an account of the Results of Experiments on the produce, &c. of Grasses and other plants. Instituted by John, Duke of Bedford. Folio. 2nd edition 8vo. 1825.

2. An Essay on the Weeds of Agriculture. London. 1825, 8vo.

3. Hortus Ericæus Woburnensis. London 1825. 4to.*

These works are by Mr. GEORGE SINCLAIR, F. L. S. &c. who for many years was Gardener to the Duke of Bedford, and is now of the firm of Cormack and Sinclair, Nurserymen, Newcross, near London. The above are excellent works, but the first contains the result of one of the greatest efforts to place the cultivation of plants upon an enlightened basis that has ever been written. It is the detail of patient, experienced practice, guided by Science—No educated cultivator of the soil should be without it.

1817. GEORGE BROOKSHAW, a teacher of flower painting, published the following works.

* This, for private distribution, was printed at the expence of the Duke of Bedford.

1. Pomona Britannica; or a collection of the most established Fruits at present cultivated in Gt. Britain; selected from the Royal Gardens at Hampton Court, and from the most celebrated Gardens round London, accurately drawn and coloured from nature. London. 2 vols. 4to.

2. The Horticultural Repository, containing delineations of the best varieties of the different species of English Fruits to which are added the blossoms and leaves, in those instances in which they are considered necessary, accompanied with full descriptions of their various properties, times of ripening, and directions for planting them, so as to insure a longer succession of fruit; such being pointed out as are particularly calculated for forcing. Part I. 8vo. 1821.

1817. Transactions of the HORTICULTURAL SOCIETY of London. Vol. 2.

Preliminary Observations. by A. CARLISLE, Esq.
 1. Account of the Elton Pear. By T. A. KNIGHT, Esq. 2. Account of a Walnut-Tree. By A. CARLISLE, Esq. 3. On the transplantation of Blossom Buds. By T. A. KNIGHT, Esq. 4. On an early variety of Grapes from Amiens. By T. A. KNIGHT, Esq. 5. On raising Lemons and Oranges from Cuttings. By A. HAWKINS, Esq. 6. On the good effects of watering the frozen branches of Peach and Nectarine Trees very early in the morning. By G. H. NOEHDEN, L. L. D. 7. On the proper stock for the Moor-park Apricot. By T. A. KNIGHT, Esq. 8. On destroying Slugs. By Mr. J. WILMOT, 9. On an insect occasionally very injurious to Fruit Trees. By W. SPENCE, Esq. 10. On inarching leafless branches of Peach Trees.

By T. A. KNIGHT, Esq. 11. On the cultivation of the Monopsis Conspicua and another species. By R. A. SALISBURY, Esq. 12. An account drawn up 100 years ago of several Pears then cultivated at Little Chelsea. By Mr. LUTTRELL. 13. Report of the Fruit Committee. By A. WILBRAHAM, Esq. 14. On the prevention of the Curl in the Potatoe. By T. A. KNIGHT, Esq. 15. On the culture of the Mulberry. By T. A. KNIGHT, Esq. 16. On the early puberty of the Peach Tree. By T. A. KNIGHT Esq. 17. On two Apples cultivated in Cornwall. By Sir C. HAWKINS Bart. 18. A plan of a Fruit Room. By Mr. JOHN MAHER. 19. On the culture of the Pear tree. By T. A. KNIGHT, Esq. 20. . On the prevention of the Mildew. By T. A. KNIGHT, Esq. 21. On the culture of the Mulberry, and on forced Strawberries bearing a second crop. By J. WILLIAMS, Esq. 22. Some account of the Snowberry. By the Secretary. 23. On the culture of the Shallot, &c. By T. A. KNIGHT, Esq. 24. Account of a new Strawberry. By Mr. M. KEENS. 25. A list of Apples and Pears exhibited to the Society with remarks. By Mr. J. MAHER. 26. Remarks on the Verdelho Grape of Madeira. By J. WILLIAMS, Esq. 27. On forcing Vines and Peaches. By J. WILLIAMS, Esq. 28. On propagating the Mulberry by Cuttings. By T. A. KNIGHT, Esq. 29. On a successful method of raising Onions. By Mr. FULLER. 30. On making Wine from the leaves of the Claret Grape. By H. S. MATTHEWS, Esq. 31. On the benefit of planting late ripened potatoes. By T. A. KNIGHT, Esq. 32. On liquid manure. By T. A. KNIGHT, Esq. 33. On the ill effects of excessive heat in forcing-houses during the night.

By T. A. KNIGHT, Esq. 34. On two varieties of Cherry raised at Downton. By T. A. KNIGHT, Esq. 35. On a new Peach. By T. A. KNIGHT, Esq. 36. A method of growing early forced Potatoes. By Mr. T. HOGG. 37. Remarks on pruning Gooseberry Trees. By Mr. J. MAHER. 38. On some vulgar errors respecting Insects being destroyed by cold. By W. SPENCE, Esq. 39. On the cultivation of Lobelia fulgens in Belgium. By J. B. VAN MONS. M. D. 40. Account of the Mellidora Pellucida. By the Secretary. 41. On the want of permanent character in varieties of Fruit, when propagated by Grafts and Buds. By T. A. KNIGHT, Esq. 42. On the first appearance of the Aphis Lanigera in this country. By Sir J. BANKS, Bart. 43. On the form which the glass of a Forcing-House ought to have. By Sir G. S. MACKENZIE, Bart. 44. On the propagation of the Lycoperdon cancillatum. By T. A. KNIGHT, Esq. 45. On the connection between the leaves and Fruit of Vegetables, &c. By A. CARLISLE, Esq. 46. On Fresh Vegetable Manure. By the Rev. J. VENABLES. 47. On the preservation of Fruits during the Winter and Spring, by T. A. KNIGHT, Esq. 48. On a remarkable property of the Hoya Carnosa By Mr. J. MAHER. 49. On the effects of different Stocks in grafting. By T. A. KNIGHT, Esq. 50. Account of a new North American Peach. By J. BRADDICK, Esq. 51. On three new Cherries, Elton, Black Eagle and Waterloo, By T. A. KNIGHT, Esq. 52. Of growing Mushrooms under Glass. By Mr. S. JEEVES. 53. On three new Peaches. By T. A. KNIGHT, Esq. 54. Observations on the above. By J. SABINE, Esq. V. P. 55. On the culture of Peaches and Apricots as Es-

proved. 62. On some improvements in Gardening, by Sir J. BANKS, Bart. 63. On ventilating forcing houses. By T. A. KNIGHT, Esq. 64. On the preservation of Fig Trees in Winter. By Mr. JAMES MEAN. 65. On the Jerusalem Cherry. By J. SABINE, Esq. 66. On the cultivation of the True Champion. By J. BRADDICK, Esq. 67. On the cultivation of Asparagus. By Mr. D. JUDD. 68. On the treatment and ripening the fruit in the open air of the Cactus Opuntia. By J. BRADDICK, Esq.* 69. On the original Moss Rose for Money. By T. HARE, Esq. 60. On a new method of forcing Vines and Nectarines. By G. ANDERSON, Esq. 65. On Wilmot's Bon Chretien Pear. By W. HOOKER, Esq. 66. On propagating from the seeds of old ungrafted Trees. By T. A. KNIGHT, Esq. 67. On the vegetable Marrow Gourd. By J. SABINE, Esq. 68. On blanching Gourd Rhubarb. By T. HARE, Esq. 69. On a new variety of Azalia Indica. By Mr. W. ANDERSON. 70. On improving the productiveness of Fruit Trees. By G. H. NOEHDEN, L. L. D. 71. On watering Fruit Trees early in Spring. By J. SOWERBY, Esq. 72. On seven double Pæonies. By J. SABINE, Esq. 73. On the cultivation of the Cucumber during the Autumn and Winter. By W. T. AITON, Esq.†

* Mr. Braddick died at his seat near Maidstone, April 14th, 1828, aged 68.

† ROBERT TOWNSEND AITON, is Gardener at the Royal Gardens of Kew and Kensington. To the first situation he was appointed in 1793 on the death of his father; to the latter in 1804, after the decease of Mr. Forsyth. William Aiton, the father of the above was born in 1731, near Hamilton in Lanarkshire. In 1754 he visited London in pursuit of employment as a Gardener, to which profession he had been brought up. Philip

74. On the Ord's Apple. By R. A. SALISBURY, Esq. 75. On giving Horticulture a scientific and systematic form. By G. H. NOEHDEN, L. L. D. 76. On the management of the Orange, Lemon and Citron Trees. By Mr. J. MEAN. 77. On some Apples imported by the Society from Rouen. By W. HOOKER, Esq. 78. Further particulars of the subject of No. 51. By J. SABINE. Esq. 79. On preserving Brocoli in Winter. By T. A. KNIGHT, Esq. 80. On different Plants grown as Winter Greens By Mr. W. MORGAN. 81. On the benefit of forcing by Steam. By Mr. J. BROWN. 82. Observations on the preceding. By T. A. KNIGHT, Esq. 83. On the Verdelho Grape. By T. A. KNIGHT, Esq. 84. On a method of ripening Grapes in a Common Hot-bed frame by means of Dung heat. By G. ANDERSON, Esq. 85. On promoting the early puberty of seedling Apples and Pears. By J. WILLIAMS, Esq. 86. On growing Mushrooms in houses. By Mr. J. OLDAKER. 87. On Tallies for Plants. By A. SETON, Esq. 88. On Sir G. Mackenzie's plan for Forcing-Houses. By T. A. KNIGHT, Esq. 89. On the most eligible Fences for Gardens, &c. By J. WILLIAMS, Esq. 90. On the tubers and cultivation of the Lathyrus Tuberosus. By Mr. J.

Miller discerned his abilities, and obtained for him a situation in the Royal Gardens, and in 1759, he was appointed Botanical Superintendant at Kew. In 1783 he obtained the charge of the Royal Kitchen and Pleasure Gardens. Six years afterwards he published a Catalogue of the plants, under the title of "Hortus Kewensis" 3 vols. 8vo. He died in 1793. W. T. Aiton has published an enlarged edition of the "Hortus Kewensis." London. 1810—13, in 5 vols 8vo. and an epitome in 1814, to which is added a selection of the esculent Vegetables and Fruits cultivated in the Royal Garden. It needs scarcely be remarked that the "Hortus Kewensis" is a work of first authority as regards Botanical nomenclature, &c.

DICKSON. 91. On a Method of forcing Asparagus. By Mr. W. ROSS. 92. On pruning the Peach Tree in cold situations. By ₁T. A. KNIGHT, Esq. 93. On the management of Fruit Trees to be forced very early in the ensuing Season. By T. A. KNIGHT, Esq. 94. On raising Mignonette in Pots throughout the year. By Mr. G. RISHON. 95. On Strawberries in Forcing Houses during the Winter and Spring. By Mr. W. MORGAN. 96. Account of the Roseberry Strawberry. By J. SABINE, Esq. 97. On ringing Fruit Trees. By G. H. NOEHDEN, L. L. D. 98. An improvement of the Stove for Plants By W. KENT, Esq. 99. On cultivating Strawberries in the open ground. By Mr. M. KEENS. 100. On a new method of cultivating Lobelia Fulgens. By Mr. W. HEDGES. 101. Condensed notices of communications.

APPENDIX.

i. An easy and infallible mode of forcing Trees to bear Fruit, Translated from the German of the Rev. G. C. L. Hempel, By G. H. NOEHDEN, L. L. D.

ii. On a stove for Tropical Plants. By J. SABINE, Esq.

iii. On the works of the Rev. J. V. Sickler, By G. H. NOEHDEN, L. L. D.

iv. On M. Noisette's mode of training Fruit Trees. By G. H. NOEHDEN, L. L. D.

1818, Short practical directions for the culture of the Ananas or Pine Apple. Warwick. 8vo. By THOMAS BALDWIN, Gardener to the Marquis of Hertford, at Ragley, Warwickshire.

1818. The Shrubbery Almanack—A single sheet.

——— A Treatise on Hedge Row Timber and Hedges. London. 12mo. By FRANCIS BLAIKIE, Steward to T. W. Coke Esq. of Holkham, Norfolk.

——— The science of horticulture. London: 8vo. Plates. By JOSEPH HAYWARD.

Mr. Hayward was originally a clothier in Yorkshire, but is now residing at Plumstead, in Kent, and pursues Horticulture as his amusement: In 1825 he published "the Science of Agriculture." London. 8vo.

1818. Page's Prodromus; or a general nomenclature of all the plants, indigenous and exotic, cultivated in the Southampton Botanic Gardens; arranged alphabetically as they are considered hardy or tender to the climate of Britain, under their different characters of Trees and Shrubs, Herbaceous, &c. The generic and specific names after the Linnæan system, with the English names, propagation, soil, height, time of flowering, native country, &c. also occasional hints for their cultivation. An Appendix containing selected lists of annuals; all the choicest fruits now in cultivation, with their characters, &c. and a short tract on the sexual system, from the Philosophica Botannica of Linnæus. London. 8vo. By W. B. PAGE, nurseryman, Southampton. His father-in-law, Mr. Kennedy of the Hammersmith Nursery, is considered to be the author of the above.

1818. MEMOIRS of the CALEDONIAN HORTICULTURAL SOCIETY. Vol. 2. 8vo.

1. On an economical Hot-house. By Sir J. S. MACKENZIE, Bart. 2. On the Guernsey mode of cultivating the Guernsey Lily, By Dr. MACCULLOCH. 3. On Wire Grates for excluding Wasps. By Mr. J. MACKRAY. 4. On Figs in Scotland. By Mr. J. SMITH. 5. On the blotches on the shoots of Peach Trees. By Mr. J. KINMENT 6. On the Orchards of Newburgh. By Mr. D. BOOTH. 7. On the insects on Peach, Nectarine and Cherry Trees, and on treating Gooseberry Bushes. By Mr. J. NAISMITH. 8. On straw Ropes for sheltering Blossoms. By Mr. J. LAIRD. 9. On a new Apple. By Sir J. S. MACKENZIE, Bart. 10. On Sea Kale. By Mr. T. BORTON. 11. On French Pears. By COLONEL SPENS. 12. On Hot-walls. By Mr. D. TROTTER. 13. On protecting Trees from Hares. By Mr. R. ELLIOT 14. On Bees. By Dr. J. HOWISON. 15. On Wine Making. By Dr. MACCULLOCH. On a Melon Pit. By Mr. W. SANDERSON. 17. On cultivating Fruit Trees. By Mr. J. SMITH. 18. On applying Lime to the stems of Fruit Trees, By Mr. T. BISHOP. 19. On propagating the double Rocket by cuttings. By Mr. D. ROBERTSON. 20. On the French cultivation of Asparagus. By Dr. MACCULLOCH. 21 Horticultural Gleanings. By Sir G. S. MACKENZIE, Bart. 22. On Brocoli. By Mr. W. WOOD. 23, On promoting fruitfulness in Fruit Trees. Mr. W. BEATTIE. 24. On forcing houses. By Sir G. S. MACKENZIE, Bart. 25. On Manure. By Mr. A. GORRIE. 26. On Celery. By Mr. J. WALKER. 27. On Hotbeds of Flax refuse. By Mr. P. BARNET. 28. On the scale in Fruit Trees. By Mr. T. THOMSON. 29. On the eve Apple. By Mr. A SMITH, 30.

On the Brown Apple of Burntisland. By Dr. DUNCAN, sen. 31. On Lactucarium. By Dr. DUNCAN, sen. 32. On applying oil to the stems of Trees, &c. By Sir G. S. MACKENZIE. Bart. 33. Report on the naturalization of Plants. By J. YULE, M. D. 34, On raising Mushrooms. By Mr. W. WOOD. It concluded with 3 Discourses by Dr. Duncan sen. on the 13 Dec. 1814. on the 4th Dec. 1815, and on the 3rd Dec. 1816.

ROBERT SWEET, F. L. S, &c. is author of the following works.

1. Hortus Suburbanus Londinensis; or a catalogue of Plants cultivated in the neighbourhood of London, arranged according to the Linnæan System; with the addition of the Natural Orders to which they belong, reference to books where they are described, their native places of growth, when introduced, time of flowering, and reference to figures. London. 1818. 8vo.

2. The Hot-house, and Green-house Manual, or Botanical Cultivator, giving full instructions for the management and best method of cultivating and propagating all the plants cultivated in the Hot-houses, Green-houses and Borders in the Gardens of Great Britain. London. 1820. 8vo. The second edition 1825.

3. Hortus Britannicus; or a catalogue of all Plants cultivated in the Gardens of Gt. Britain whether exotic or indigenous arranged according to the Natural Orders to which they belong, with references to the Linnæan Classes and Orders, &c. London. 1826. 8vo.

He is also editor of several periodicals we shall have occasion to mention.

ROBERT MONTEATH, Designer and Valuer of Woods, Plantations, &c. residing at Stirling, is author of the two following publications.

1. The Forester's Guide and Profitable Planter, &c. Stirling, 1819, 8vo. 12mo. Plates.

2. Miscellaneous Reports on Woods and Plantations, showing a method to plant, rear, and recover all Woods, Plantations, &c: Edinburgh, 1827. 8vo. Plates.

1820. Memoirs, Historical and Illustrative of the Botanic Garden at Chelsea, belonging to the Society of Apothecaries of London. London. 8vo. by HENRY FIELD, Apothecary.

———An Historical description of White Knights, a seat of the Duke of Marlborough. London. folio. Plates. By Mrs. HOFLAND.

Mrs. Hofland is the wife of the Landscape Painter, so well known. She is the author of several tales, &c. The engravings in the above work are by her husband.—To it is prefixed an Essay on Gardening from the classical pen of Mr. Hope, of Deepdene, near Godstone, so favourably known as the author of "Anastasius." He also published a magnificent work, on Household Furniture.

HENRY PHILIPS, F. H. S. was formerly a Schoolmaster at Bayswater, near London. He is publicly known as the author of the following works.

1. Pomarium Britannicum; or an Historical and Botanical Account of Fruits known in Gt. Britain. London, 1820. 8vo.

2. The history of cultivated Vegetables. London. 1822. 2 vols 8vo.

3. Sylva Florifera, the Shrubbery; containing an historical and botanical account of the flowering Shrubs and Trees which now ornament the Shrubbery, &c. 1823. London. 2 vols. 8vo.

4. Flora Domestica, or Portable Flower-Garden. London. 1823 and 1827. 8vo.

5. Flora Historica—London. 1824. 2 vols. 8vo.

1820. A short, plain Treatise on Carnations and Pinks, 8vo., By RICHARD PIGOTT, Florist at Sherdington, near Cheltenham.

———1. An Essay on the uses of Salt for agricultural purposes, and in horticulture. By CUTHBERT WILLIAM JOHNSON. London. 8vo. The second edition in 1821. The third in 1829.

2. Observations on the employment of Salt in Agriculture and Horticulture. By the same Author. London. 1825. It is now in its ninth edition.

I cannot trust myself, as the near relative of the author of the above, to give an opinion on their merits, but I must gratify myself by quoting the opinion of a far abler judge; "I have perused the essay, says Mr. G. Sinclair, the scientific and experienced author of the Hortus Gramineus Woburnensis, in a letter now before me, with very great pleasure, and I am sure there can be but one opinion of its great merit, as it unquestionably is superior to any publication that has yet appeared on the subject. Such a body of evidence, so ably arranged, and connected by such forcible reasoning, I have seldom had the fortune to peruse."

1820. Transactions of the HORTICULTURAL SOCIETY of LONDON. Vol. 3.

1. On a Peach Tree from the seed of an Almond. By T. A. KNIGHT, Esq. 2. On cultivating Mushrooms in exhausted Hot-beds. By the Rev. W. WILLIAMSON. 3. Of a method of training Vines under Glass. By A. SETON, Esq. 4. A method of conveying Water to Plants in houses. By Mr. G. LODDIGES. 5. On a Peach Tree at Cockfield Hall in Suffolk. By LORD ROUS. 6. On the cultivation of Rampion. By Mr. J. DICKSON. 7. On cultivating the Gloriosa superba. By Mr. J. SWEET. 8. Descriptions of several Aquatics, and their general management. By W. KENT, Esq. 9. On a mode of treating Fruit Trees. By Mr. C. HARRISON. 10. On the cultivation of Celery. By Mr. D. JUDD. 11. On growing young potatoes through the year. By G. H. NOEHDEN, L. L. D. 12. On the Aphis Lanigera, and its destruction—By Sir O. MOSLEY, Bart. 13. Notes on the above. By A. SETON, Esq. 14. On pruning and training the Mulberry against a wall in a cold climate. By T. A. KNIGHT, Esq. 15. On the cultivation and varieties of the Portugal Onion. By J. WARRE, Esq. 16. On Celeriac. By J. SABINE, Esq. 17. On cultivating Fig Trees in the open air. By the Right Hon. Sir. J. BANKS, Bart. 18. Upon the variations of the Red Currant raised from seed. By T. A. KNIGHT, Esq. 19. A method of producing Dwarf fruit bearing trees of Oranges and Lemons by grafting. By Mr. J.

NAIRN. 20. On the Esperione Grape. By J. T. AITON, Esq. 21. On retarding the ripening of Grapes in Hot-houses. By R. ARKWRIGHT, Esq. 22. On the purple fruited, edible, and other Passion flowers. By J. SABINE, Esq. 23. Condensed notices of Communications to the Society. 24. On the comparative produce of the Red Apple Potatoe grown in single or double drills or in beds. By Mr. J. DRUMMOND. 25. On the cultivation of the Balsam. By the Rev. W. WILLIAMSON. 26. On a new Hot-bed frame. By Mr. J. NAIRN 27. On propagating the Walnut by budding. By T. A. KNIGHT, Esq. 28. On cultivating Succory By Mr. J. OLDAKER. 29. On the original Ribston Pippin Tree. By Sir H. GOODRICKE, Bart. 30. On a method of forcing Rhubarb. By Mr. D. JUDD. 31. On a method of growing Cucumbers. By Mr. G. MILLS. 32. On the treatment of Pear Trees. By Mr. C. HARRISON. 33. On forcing Rhubarb in Pots. By T. A. KNIGHT, Esq. 34. On pruning and management of transplanted Standard Trees. By T. A. KNIGHT, Esq. 35. On the varieties of Brocoli and their cultivation. By Mr. H. RONALDS. 36. On the mealy Insect which infests the Larch. By Sir O. MOSELY, Bart. 37. Experiments on the cultivation, and on the production of Blue instead of Red flowers, on the Hydrangea Hortensis. By Mr. W. HEDGES. 38. On the cultivation of the Tree Mignonette. By J. SABINE, Esq. 39. On ripening seeds in a wet season. By J. LIVINGSTONE, Esq. 40. On the treatment of Amaryllis longifolia, and on hydrids, &c. By the Hon. and Rev. W. HERBERT. 41. Substance of a Memoir on Brussels Sprouts. By J. B. VAN MONS, M. D. 42. On the varieties of

Magnolia glauca. By J. SABINE, Esq. 43. On the variations of the Scarlet Strawberry when raised from the seed. By T. A. KNIGHT, Esq. 44. Of a new early Black Cherry. By T. A. KNIGHT, Esq. 45. On a new seedling Plum. By T. A. KNIGHT, Esq. 46. On the Species and varieties of Dahlia, and their culture. By J. SABINE, Esq. 47 On glazing Hot-houses, &c. By J. R. GOWEN, Esq. 48. On the Pitmanston White Cluster Seedling Grape By J. WILLIAMS, Esq. 50. On the Seckle Pear. Mr. D. HOSACK, M. D. 51. On preserving Fruit from Wasps. By T. A. KNIGHT, Esq. 52. On a select collection of apple trees, and on four new desert Apples. By J. SABINE, Esq. 53. On the species and varieties of Beets. By Mr. W. MORGAN. 54. Further account of a stove for Tropical Plants. By W. KENT, Esq. 55. On the causes of decay in Fruit Trees. By the Rev. W. WILLIAMSON. 56. On coverings for cucumber Frames. By A. SETON, Esq. 57. On the Loquat By LORD BAGOT. 58. On the cultivation of the Under-ground Onion. By Mr. J. MAHER. 59. On training the Fig-tree. By T. A. KNIGHT Esq. 60. On Apples exhibited to the Society. By Mr. J. TURNER. 61. On blackening Garden Walls. By Mr. H. DAWES. 62. On a species of Casuarina. By the GRAND DUKE of SAXE WEIMAR. 63. On the Vines at Valentines House in Essex. By Mr. G. LOWE. 64. Directions for raising Ferns from Seed. By Sir J. E. SMITH. P. L. S. 65. On the Tomato. By J. SABINE, Esq. 66. On a moveable Frame for training Vines in a House. By J. ELLIOT, Esq. 67. Condensed communications to the Society. 68. On the varieties of the Onion. By Mr. C. STRACHN. 69,

On the classification of Peaches and Nectarines, on their diseases, &c. By Mr. J. ROBERTSON. 70. On the superiority of scions taken from the trunks of Apple Trees. By T. A. KNIGHT, Esq. 71. On the best form of Garden Pots. By T. A. KNIGHT, Esq. 72. On Wilmot's new early Orlean's Plum. By W. HOOKER, Esq. 73. On two Mulberry Trees growing at Holkham Hall. By R. WILBRAHAM, Esq. 74. On the Downton Strawberry. By J. SABINE, Esq. 75. On the culture of the Guernsey Lily. By T. A. KNIGHT, Esq. 76. On the Culture of Onions, By J. WEDGEWOOD, Esq. 77 On the culture of the Impatiens Balsamia. By Mr. J. FAIRWEATHER. 78. On the culture of Figs on the back Walls of Vineries. By J. SABINE, Esq. 79. On raising varieties of the Iris Xiphioides. By Mr. W. MASTERS, Jun. 80. Description of the supposed true Welsh Onion. By Mr. T. MILNE. 81. On the difficulties of transporting Plants from China to England. By J. LIVINGSTONE, Esq. 82. Account of Count Zubow's Steam Pits at St. Petersburgh. By Mr. F. E. L. FISCHER. 83. Account of a Fig Tree planted in 1648, and growing at Oxford. By Mr. W. BAXTER. 84. On the varieties of Spring Radish. By Mr. C. STRACHN. 85. On the culture of the Guernsey Lily. By the Rev. W. WILLIAMSON. 86. On the best Irish Apples. By Mr. J. ROBERTSON. 87. On Martin's Nonpareil Apple. By J. WILLIAMS, Esq. 88. Effects of very high temperatures on some plants. By T. A. KNIGHT, Esq.

APPENDIX.

i. On the Genus Citrus, varieties, &c. cultivated in Italy. By G. H. NOEHDEN, L. L. D.

ii. On the use of the scoria of the Forge in Horticulture. From the French of M. Thouin. By Mr. J. TURNER.

iii. On the native country of the Apricot. From the French of M. Regnier. By R. A. SALISBURY, Esq.

WILLIAM COBBETT, the well known, inconsistent, political writer, is the son of a farmer who resided near Farnham. Cobbett was born there in 1776; he obtained employment in 1783 in a London Attorney's Office; but the following year enlisted, and went with his regiment to America, and was ultimately made a serjeant In 1792 he went to France, but proceeded thence, in the same year, back to America, where he continued employing himself in writing until 1801 when he came home to England. He again returned to America in 1816, but came back to his native country in 1820, and resides at Kensington, where he cultivates a large Garden, and strenuously recommends the growth of the American Locust Tree, Indian Corn, &c. Of his chameleon political works we have nothing to remark, but he requires to be noticed as the author of

1. The American Gardener; or a treatise on the situation, soil, fencing. and laying out of Gardens, on the making and managing of Hot-beds, and Green-houses, and on the propagation and cultivation of the several sorts of vegetables, herbs, Fruits and Flowers. London. 1821. 12mo.

2. , The Woodlands, or a Treatise on Planting. In 8vo parts, began 1826.

PATRICK NEILL. M. A. F. L. S. Secretary to the Natural History and Caledonian Horticultural Societies of Edinburgh. This scientific and excellent Gentleman is author of the following

Journal of a Horticultural Tour, through some parts of Flanders, Holland, and the North of France, in the Autumn of 1817, by a deputation of the Caledonian Horticultural Society. Edinburgh. 1823. 8vo.

Besides the above he has written several Essays which have appeared in the Edinburgh Encyclopœdia, Encyclopœdia Britannica, the General Report of Scotland, &c.

1821. Appendix to the Botanical Magazine and Botanical Register. By the Hon. and Rev. WILLIAM HERBERT, F. H. S. London. 8vo.

——— Outline of a General History of Gardening, London. 8vo.

1822. Transactions of the HORTICULTURAL SOCIETY of LONDON. Vol. 4.

1. On the means of giving strength to the stems of Plants growing under glass. By T. A. KNIGHT, Esq. 2. An improved method of planting Vines for forcing. By Mr. D. JUDD. 3. On the Alexandrian Ciotat Grape. By J. WILLIAMS, Esq. 4. On the varieties of Autumn and Winter Radishes. By Mr. W. CHRISTIE. 5. On the production of Hybrids. By the Hon. and Rev. W. HERBERT. 6. Condensed communications to the Society. 7. On the cultivation of the Granidilla. By Mr. R. CHAPMAN. 8. Plan for forcing Sea Kale. By Mr. T. BALDWIN. 9. On the best varieties of Apples cultivated in Norfolk. By Mr. G. LINDLEY. 10. Upon the cultivation of the Pine Apple without Bark; or other Hot-bed. By T. A. KNIGHT, Esq. 11. On the produce of Peaches at Wortley Hall

since 1808. By Mr. C. HARRISON. 12. On the glazing of Hot-houses. By J. SABINE, Esq. 13. On a screen for protecting Wall Trees. By R. HOLDEN, Esq. 13. On the advantages which trained Peach Trees derive from their roots penetrating the border on the north side of the Wall. By Mr. J. ROBERTSON. 15. On the management of Grapes in Vineries. By Mr. W. GRIFFIN.* 16. On destroying Wasps. By Sir. T. FRANKLAND, Bart. 17. On obtaining a succession of Neapolitan Voilets through the Winter. By Mr. I. OLDAKER. 18. On forcing Cherries. By Mr. T. TORBRON. 19. Experiments &c. in ringing the Bark of Trees and other plants. By J. SABINE, Esq. 20. Condensed communications to the Society. 21. On the cultivation of the Filbert. By the Rev. W. WILLIAMSON. 22. On the cultivation of the African Gladioli and other Cape Bulbs in open borders. By the Hon. and Rev. W. HERBERT. 23. On the most economical mode of heating the flues of forcing houses, as regards Fuel. By T. A. KNIGHT, Esq. 24. Physiological observations on Ringing Fruit Trees. By T. A. KNIGHT, Esq. 25. On the culture of Hyacinths. By the Hon. and Rev. W. HERBERT. 26. Account of the Rosa Banksiæ. By J. SABINÉ, Esq. and on its culture by Mr. T. OLDAKER. 27. On the Guernsey Lily, and other bulbs of the Genera, Nerine, Coburgia and Brunsvigia. By the Hon. and Rev. W. HERBERT. 28. On the Standard Fig Trees at Arundel Castle. By Mr. J. MAHER. 29. On the culture of early Melons. By Mr. P. FLANAGAN. 30. On a new mode of training Goose-

* See p. 262.

berry Bushes. By Mr. S. JEEVES. 31. Further account of the Downton Strawberry. By T. A. KNIGHT, Esq. 32. On the culture of Figs in the Stove. By T. A. KNIGHT, Esq. 33. On fruits ripened in 1819, and exhibited to the Society. 34. On an improved forcing pit. By Mr J. WEST. 35. On the Chinese mode of Dwarfing Trees, and Shrubs. By J. LIVINGSTONE, Esq. 36. On the Pitmanston Orange Nectarine. By J. WILLIAMS Esq. 37. On making the Roseberry Strawberry produce fru't late in the year. 38. On Mr. Walker's improved construction of Hot-house flues. By A. SETON Esq. 39. On the management of Parasitical Plants. By the Hon. and Rev. W. HERBERT. 40. On a hollow wall erected at the Earl of Arrans, Bognor, Sussex. 41. A method of managing Vines in a common Grapery. By Mr. J. MEARNS. 42. On a new hybrid Passiflora. By J. SABINE, Esq. 43. On the construction of the Piers and Copings of Garden Walls. By the Rev. T. G. CULLUM. 44. On some Flanders Apples and Pears exhibited to the Society. By Mr. J. TURNER. 45. On the Double Scotch Roses cultivated in England. By J. SABINE, Esq. 46. On the management of the Genus Citrus in the Garden at Shipley Hall, Derbyshire. By Mr R. AYRES. 47. On a new Psidium. By W. CATTLEY, Esq. 48. On a new Melon. By Mr. D. ANDERSON. 49. On the cultivation of the Cock's Comb. By T. A. KNIGHT, Esq. 50. On the classification of Plumbs. By Mr. J. ROBERTSON. 51. On the Chinese Chrysanthemums cultivated in England at present, &c. By J. SABINE, Esq. 52. On the cultivation of Pines in the Garden of the Port-

man Nursery, New Road. By W. HOOKER, Esq.
53. On Hybrids. By T. A. KNIGHT, Esq. 54.
On the Ranunculus and Anemone. By the Rev. W.
WILLIAMSON. 55. On the varieties of the Garden Carrot. By Mr. W. CHRISTIE. 56. On
the flowering of the Agave Americana in the open
air, in the garden of J. Yates Esq. near Salcombe,
Devonshire. By A. HAWKINS, Esq. 57. On
making Pines fruit within the year. By P.
MARSHLAND, Esq. 58. On the mode of cultivating Aquatic and Bog Plants, in the Botanic
Garden at Munich. By CHEVALIER F. de PAULA
SCHRANK. 59. On transporting Buds of Fruit
Trees to considerable distances. By T. A. KNIGHT
Esq. 60. On a Russian mode of training Apple,
Cherry, and Plumb Trees. By Mr. J. BUSCH.
61. Condensed communications to the Society.
62. On the Crinun Amabile, its management, &c.
By Mr. J. VERREL. 63. On training and pruning Plum Trees. By T. A. KNIGHT, Esq. 64.
On managing the Fig in the open air. By the Rev.
G. SWAYNE. 65. On a steam Apparatus. By
Mr. J. HAYWARD. 66. On managing Fruit
Trees in Pots. By T. A. KNIGHT, Esq. 67. On
some North American esculents. By R. A. SALISBURY, Esq. 68. On an improved method of
raising Early Potatoes in the open ground. By T.
A. KNIGHT, Esq. 69. On the cultivation of
Pinks. By Mr. T. HOGG. 70. On raising early
Cucumbers. By R. VACHELL, Esq. 71. On
the Ayrshire Rose. By J. SABINE, Esq. 72.
On the Steam Pits in the Imperial Gardens of Taurida at St. Peterburgh. By Mr. M. M. CALL.
73. On the cultivation of Mushrooms. By Mr. T. ROGERS. 74. On grafting the shoots of choice Dahlias

on the tubers of common ones. By Mr. T. BLAKE 75. On the cultivation of Strawberries, By the Rev. T. GARNIER. 76. On cultivating the American Cranberry in dry beds. By R. HALLETT, Esq. 77. On the New Zealand Spinach. By Mr. J. ANDERSON. 78, On grafting the Vine. By T. A. KNIGHT, Esq. 79. On a hybrid Amaryllis. By J. R .GOWEN, Esq. 80. On some standard Figs at Sompting, near Worthing, Sussex. By J. SABINE Esq. 81. On fruits exhibited to the Society as ripened in 1820. 82. On forcing Plums. By J. T. AITON, Esq. 83. On a pit for fruiting Pines and Melons, with observations on the production of Seeds of Pine Apples. By Mr. W. BUCK. 84. On the cultivation of the Water Cress. By Mr. W. BRADBERRY. 85. On the Pine apple By T. A. KNIGHT, Esq. 86. On flowering the Lilium Japonicum. By Mr. S. BROOKS. 87. Condensed notices of communications to the Society. 88. On the cultivation of Chinese Chrysanthemums. By Mr. J. WELLS.

———Hortus Anglicanus, or modern English Garden. London 12mo. 2 vols.

1823. A treatise on the culture and management of Fruit Trees. Sheffield. 8vo. By CHARLES HARRISON, F. H. S. Gardener to Lord Wharncliffe, at Wortly Hall, Yorkshire, without Walls or Glass.

———Plan for cultivating Grapes in the field. Liverpool. 8vo.

1824. The art of promoting the growth of the Cucumber and Melon in a series of directions for the best means to be adopted in bringing them to a complete state of perfection. London. 1824. By THOMAS WATKINS.

Mr. Watkins is Gardener to W. Knight, Esq. of Highbury Park; he was for many years previously foreman to Mr. Grange, Nurseryman, Hackney.

1824. A practical treatise on the growth and culture of the Gooseberry, including a catalogue of the most esteemed varieties. London. 12mo. By F. D. LEVINGSTON.

——— The Fruit Grower's instructor, or a Practical Treatise on Fruit Trees, from the Nursery to Maturity, and a description of all the best Fruits now in cultivation &c. London. 8vo. By G. BLISS—One of the most extensive Orchardist's in the kingdom.

1824. Transactions of the HORTICULTURAL SOCIETY of LONDON. Vol 5.

1. On the different species and varieties of Brassica. By M. A. P. de CANDOLLE. 2. On horizontal Espalier Training. By Mr. J. MEARNS. - 3. On the Chinese Horticulture and Agriculture. By J. LIVINGSTONE, Esq. 4. On the House management of Peaches and Nectarines. By Mr. P. FLANNAGAN. 5. On the accidental intermixture of character in certain Fruits. By Mr. J. TURNER 6. On new Hybrid Passifloras. By J. SABINE, Esq. 7. On the destruction of Caterpillars on Fruit Trees. By Mr. J. SWEET. 8. On tropical Fruits likely to be worth cultivating in England. By Mr. J. LINDLEY. 9. On some Pears received

from the Luxemburgh Garden. By Mr. J. TURNER.
10. On the cultivation of the Pine Apple. By T.
A. KNIGHT, Esq. 11. On a new variety of Ulmus
Suberosa, and on a method of grafting slender
scions. By T. A. KNIGHT, Esq. 12. On some
Chinese Chrysanthemums. By J. SABINE, Esq.
13. On the Fruit of Fig Trees. By Sir C. M. L.
MONCK, Bart. 14. Effects of ringing Fig Trees.
By Sir C. MONCK, Bart. 15. On some diseases
of Fruit Trees. By Mr. J. ROBERTSON. 16.
A method of training Standard Apple Trees. By J.
SABINE, Esq. 17. On the construction of Strawberry Beds. By W. ATKINSON, Esq. 18. On
packing living plants in foreign countries. By Mr.
J. LINDLEY. 19. On grafting Vines. By J.
BRADDICK, Esq. 20. On the Providence Pine
Apples grown at Ragley. By J. SABINE, Esq.
21. On fertilizing the blossoms of Pear Trees. By
the Rev. G. SWAYNE. 22. On Hot-house flues.
By Sir G. S. MACKENZIE, Bart. 23. A method
of Forcing Peaches and Nectarines chiefly by Dung-heat. By Mr. J. BREESE. 24. A Pine Pit. By
Mr. T. SCOTT. 25. A Melon and Pine Pit. By
T. A. KNIGHT, Esq. 26. On curvilinear Iron
Roofs to Hot houses. By T. A. KNIGHT, Esq.
27. On the variation in the colour of Peas, occasioned by the cross Impregnation. By Mr. J.
GOSS. 28. An improved mode of cultivating the
Melon. By T. A. KNIGHT, Esq. 29. Culture
of the Alpine Strawberry. By J. WILLIAMS, Esq.
30. On the native country of the Wild Potatoe, and
its cultivation in the Chiswick Garden. By J. SABINE, Esq. 31. Notices of Fruit. 32. On the
Flat Peach of China. By T. A. KNIGHT, Esq.
33. Culture of Mesembryanthemums. By Mr. W.

MOWBRAY. 34. Culture of the English Cranberry in dry beds. By Mr. T. MILNE. 35. To obtain good Cauliflowers in Winter. By Mr. G. COCKBURN. 36. Culture of Tetragonia expansa By the Rev. J. BRANSBY. 37. Method of securing the scion when fitted to the stock. By D. POWELL, Esq. 38. Injurious influence of the Plumb-stock upon the Moorpark Apricot. By T. A. KNIGHT, Esq. 39. On some Mule Plants. By T. KNIGHT, Esq. 40. On the Woburn Perennial Kale. By Mr. G. SINCLAIR. 41. On the culture of Horse Radish. By Mr. D. JUDD 42. Method of cultivating Mushrooms. By Mr. W. HOGAN. 43. On the fertilization of the female blossoms of Filberts. By the Rev. G. SWAYNE. 44. A Wash for fruit Trees. By J. BRADDICK, Esq. 45. Methods of forcing Peaches in Denmark and Holland. By Mr. P. LINDEGAARD. 46. Culture of Asparagus in Austria. By Mr. J. BAUMAN. 47. Notice of Seedling Amaryllis's presented by the Hon. and Rev. W. Herbert. By Mr. J. LINDLEY. 48. Improved method of obtaining Early Crops of Peas, after severe Winters. By T. A. KNIGHT, Esq, 49. Management of Fig Trees in the open Air. By Mr. S. SAWYER. 50. Culture of Melons in the open air. By J. WILLIAMS Esq. 51. Improved Steam Pit for Cucumbers, &c. By the Rev. W. PHELPS. 52. Description of of the Amaryllis Psittacinâ-Johnsoni. By J. R. GOWEN, Esq. 53. Method of protecting Cauliflowers, &c. through the Winter. By Mr. J. DRUMMOND. 54. Culture of the Yellow Rose, and tender Chinese Roses. By J. WILLIAMS, Esq. 55. Culture of Arachis hypogœa. By Mr. J. NEWMAN. 56. Culture of the Banyan Tree. By CAPT. P.

RAINIER, R. N. 57. Further Notes on Grafting Wax. (37) By D. POWELL, Esq. 67. On the supposed influence of the Pollen, in cross breeding upon the colour of the Seed Coats, &c. By T. A. KNIGHT, Esq. 59. On a new Plum (Downton Imperatrice) By T. A. KNIGHT, Esq. 60. On the effects of age on Fruit Trees. By T. A. KNIGHT, Esq. 61. On a Hybrid Amaryllis. By J. R. GOWEN, Esq. 62. Culture of the Pine Apple. By Mr. A. STEWART. 63. Reverse grafting of a Pear Tree. By Mr. W. BALFOUR. 64. Notices of Fruits exhibited to the Society. 65. On some new Pears. By Mr. J. TURNER. 66. On five new Chinese Chrysanthemums, and on the culture, &c. By J. SABINE, Esq. 67. On the Pears called Silvanges. By M. C. F. PIERARD, 68. Preparation of Strawberry Plants for forcing. By T. A. KNIGHT, Esq. 69. On transplanting Peas for early Crops. By Mr. D. JUDD. 70. On the edible Fruits of Sierra Leone. By J. SABINE, Esq. from the communications of Mr. G. DON. 71. The management of Hot-house fire-places. By W. ATKINSON, Esq. 72. Forcing grapes in Denmark. By Mr. P. LINDEGAARD. 73. Fig Trees in a house. By J. SABINE, Esq. 74. Condensed Communications. 75. Description of a Vinery and a mode of training in it. By Mr. W. BEATTIE. 76. A Pine House and Pits. By C. HOLFORD, Esq. 77. Apparatus for ventilating Hot-houses. By Mr. G. MUGLISTON. 78. On the protection of the blossoms of Wall-fruit. By T. A. KNIGHT, Esq. 79 Culture of Asparagus during the Winter. By Mr. P. LINDEGAARD. 80. Method of raising the seed of the Carrot, Turnip, and Radish in the East Indies. By W.

INGLEDON, Esq. 81. On an Elruge Nectarine. By Mr. J. BOWERS. 82. Classification of Peaches and Nectarines. By Mr. G. LINDLEY.

APPENDIX.

i. Memoir of Mr. Dickson.

ii. List of Pears cultivated in France and the Netherlands. By LE CHEVALIER J. PARMENTIER.

1824—Cottage Economy and Mansion Economy. Shrewsbury. 12mo.

1825. 1. Essays on Landscape Gardening, and on uniting Picturesque effect with rural Scenery, &c. London. 4to. Plates. By RICHARD MORRIS F. L. S. &c. Landscape Gardener.

2: Flora Conspicua; a selection of the most ornamental flowering, hardy exotic and indigenous Plants, 4to. Plates.

This elegant little work appeared in numbers which commenced in 1825, and ceased in September, 1826, when only fifteen numbers had appeared.

JOHN LINDLEY, F. L. S. Assistant Secretary to the London Horticultural Society, &c. Besides several papers which have appeared in the Transactions of the Society has published the following,

1. Report upon the new and rare Plants which have flowered at the Garden of the Horticultural Society. London. 4to.

2. Instructions for Packing Seeds and Plants for sending home from foreign countries. London. 8vo.

1825. A series of Facts, Hints, Observations, and Experiments on the different modes adopted for raising Plantations of Oak. London. 8vo. By WILLIAM BILLINGTON, M. C. H. S, and late Gardener to Lords Yarborough and Haddington.

―――Transactions of the HORTICULTURAL SOCIETY of LONDON. Vol. 6.

1. On climate considered with regard to Horticulture. By J. F. DANIELL, Esq. F. R. S, &c. 2. On the use of charcoal dust for Onions, and preventing clubbing in Cabbages, &c. By Mr. T. SMITH, Gardener to M. Bell, Esq. Woolsington, Northumberland. 3. On the plants growing near Constantinople. By the Rev. R. WALSH, L. L. D. 4. On the cultivation of the Madeira Vaccinium in the open air. By Mr. W. FOULK. 5. Plants flowered in the Chiswick Garden. By Mr. J. LINDLEY. 6. On the cultivation of Strawberries. By T. A. KNIGHT, Esq. 7. Management of Tigridia Pavonia during Winter. By Mr. J. D. PARKS. 8. Condensed notices of communications to the Society. 9. On a new seedling Grape (Tottenham Park Muscat) By Mr. H. BURN. 10. On a Lime Duster for Fruit Trees. By Mr. S. CURTIS. 11. On forcing Cucumbers. By Mr. T. ALLEN. 12. On the varieties of Endive. By Mr. A. MATTHEWS. 13. An instrument for fumigating with Tobacco. By Mr. J. READ. 14. On a self acting Ventilator for Hot-houses. By J. WILLIAMS, Esq. 5. On the varieties of Strawberry. By Mr. J. BARNET. 16. Green-house at Sir R Preston's, Bart, Valleyfield in Perthshire. By Mr. A. STEWART. 17. Benefits of protecting the stems of

Fruit Trees from frost in early Spring. By T. A. KNIGHT, Esq. 18. Method of obtaining early crops of the Fig and Grape. By T. A. KNIGHT, Esq. 19. Culture of the Pine Apple. By Mr. W. GREENSHIELDS. 20. On the Calville Rouge de Micoud, a new variety of Apple. By M. ANDRE THOUIN. 21. On Hot-house flues. By the Rev. G. SWAYNE. 22. Culture of Strawberries. By T. A. KNIGHT, Esq. 23. Culture of the Guernsey Lily. By T. A. KNIGHT, Esq. 24. Plants which have flowered in the Chiswick Garden. 25. On a disease to which Grapes are liable. By Mr. D. JUDD. 26. On the varieties of parsnip. By Mr. A. MATTHEWS. 27. Culture of Ginger in a glazed Pit. By Mr. C. DUFF. 28. On the Laws which govern the production of double flowers. By Mr. J. LINDLEY. 29. On grafting, budding, and cultivating Roses. By J. B. VAN MONS, M. D. 30. On some new chrysanthemums. By J. SABINE, Esq. 31. On the culture of Chinese chrysanthemums. By Mr. D. MUNRO. 32. On the forcing of Figs at Harewood House, Yorkshire. By J. SABINE, Esq. 33. On a late and early variety of Pear. By Mr. D. MONTGOMERRY. 34. On transplanting spindle-rooted Plants. By T. A. KNIGHT, Esq. 35 Experiments carried on in the Chiswick Garden. 36. Culture of the Passiflora Quadrangularis By Mr. W. MITCHESON. 37. On growing Asparagus in single rows. By Mr. A. DICKSON. 38. Of fruits ripened in 1823 and 1824. 39. Meteorological Observations in the Chiswick Garden during 1825. 40. Culture of hardy Orchidéous Plants. By Mr. S. MURRAY. 41. On obtaining a second crop of Melons. By Mr. C. HARRISON. 42. American Fruit Trees sent to the society. By Mr. M. FLOY. 43. Culture of Celeriac. By Mr. J. P. PETERSON. 44. Culture of Nelúmbium speciósum. By Mr. A. STEWART. 45. A Pit for Winter and early Spring Forcing. By Mr. A. STEWART. 46. Growth of some Cedars of Lebanon at Hopetoun House. By Mr. J. SMITH. 47. Effects a combination of Heat and Moisture has on Vegetation. By Mr. A. GORRIE. 48. Culture of plants in Moss. 49. A Pit and Stoves heated by Fire and Steam jointly. By Mr. W. MAC MURTRIE. —New Seedling Pears. By T. A. KNIGHT, Esq. 50. Culture of Hedychium. By Mr. J. COOPER, 51. On Blackening Walls. By Mr. C. HARRISON. 52. Forcing Vines in borders under Glass. By the Rev. B. COOPER, A. M. 53. On Glycine sinensis, now Wisteria Consequana. By J. SABINE, Esq. 54. On the Pœonia Moutan, (Tree Pœony) By J. SABINE, Esq. 55. On the effect of the frost of Apl. 29th 1826, on certain plants in the Chiswick Garden. By Mr. J. LINDLEY. 56. Propagation of Zamias. By Mr. F. FALDERMAUN. 57. Stoves for Melons and Cucumbers. By Mr. J. HAYTHORN. 58. Strawberries cultivated for Market in Scotland. By Mr. J. SMITH. 59. Culture of Fuchsias. By Mr. J. SMITH. 60. Vineries with arched, hanging Trellises. By Mr. W. SMITH. 61. On the qualities of newly raised Fruits exemplified in Plums. By T. A. KNIGHT, Esq. 62. On Tobacco Water for destroying insects. By Mr. J. HARRISON. 63. Culture of Nelumbiums. By J. CLARE, Esq. 64. Condensed communications to the Society. 65. The Siberian Bittersweet, a new and valuable cider apple. By T. A. KNIGHT, Esq. 66. On two varieties of

Mango. By J. SABINE, Esq. 67. On ten varieties of Persian Melon. By Mr. J. LINDLEY. 68. On some new esculent Vegetables in the Chiswick Garden in 1825—6.

1825. MEMOIRS of the CALEDONIAN HORTICULTURAL SOCIETY. Vol. 3. 8vo.

1. On the employment of Salt in Horticulture. By S. PARKES, Esq. 2. On some Russian Culinary Vegetables. By W. HOWISON, M. D. 3. On the management of Fruit Trees. By J. CARR, Esq. 4. On Steam for heating Hot-Houses. By Mr. J. HAY. 5. On Russian Chicory. By W. HOWISON, M. D. 6. On shallow Planting. By Mr. E. SANG. 7. On Medicines from the Lettuce. By J. YOUNG, Esq. 8. On the Soil for Peaches. By Mr. J. KIRK. 9. On grafting the Ribston Pippin. By Mr. J. DECK. 10. On forcing Sea Kale and Asparagus in a vinery. Mr. A. MELROS. 11. On regulating the Conservatory, &c. By Mr. J. MURRAY. 12. Horticultural Notices. By Mr. MURRAY. 13. Horticultural communications. By A. KEITH, Esq. 14. On preserving Trees from Hares; and Cauliflowers in winter. By Mr. W. BULL. 15. Horticultural Gleanings, By Sir J. S. MACKENZIE. 16. On the Ionian and Egyptian Melons. By J. HOWISON, Esq. 17. On the Potatoe Onion. By the Rev. J. M. ROBINSON. 18. On Mr. Knight's Doctrines regarding Fruit Trees. By Mr. NEILL. 19. On the Auricula and Polyanthus. By Mr. W. HENDERSON. 20. Hints for preserving foreign Plants, &c. during transmission. By J. HOWISON, Esq. 21. List of the Irises in the Garden of D. FALCONER, Esq. at Carlowrie. By A.

FORRESTER. 22. Remains of Ancient Orchards at Jedburgh. By T. SHORTREED, Esq. 23. On raising varieties of the Pink. By Mr. J. NICOL. 24. Horticultural communications from Mr. G. YOUNG. 25. On the Citrus tribe, the Camellia Japonica, Thea, and the Ericœ. By Mr. W. HENDERSON. 26. On Destroying Moths. By Mr. P. MUSGRAVE. 27. On a Pine Apple Pit at Edmonstone. By Mr. J. MACNAUGHTON. 28. On preparing Lactucarium, or Lettuce Opium, By F. G. PROBART, Esq. 29. Observations on Lactucarium, By A. DUNCAN Sen. M. D. 30. On a Vinery with three rows of parallel Trellises. By the Rev. H. WASTELL. 31. On varieties of Lolium perenne; and on transplanting Turf. By G. WHITWORTH, Esq. 32. On Exotics naturalising in East Lothian. By Mr. J. STREET. 33. Horticultural Gleanings (on the Alpine Strawberry and Asparagus and French Beans) 34. On Gooseberry and Currant Trees. By Mr A. BISSET. 35. On Potatoes, and a new variety, the Kilspindie Bloom. By the Rev. Dr. A. DOW. 36. On the Potatoe. By Sir G. S. MACKENZIE. Bart. 73. On forcing Rhubarb. By Mr. J. SMITH. 38. Report of the Society's Wine Committee. 39. On a new Vinery, and training the Vine. By Mr. A. REID.

1826. Camellia Britanica. London. 4to, 8 Plates. By CHANDLER and BUCKINGHAM, Nurserymen, Vauxhall.

———Catalogue of Plants in the collection of C. LODDIGES and SONS, Hackney. London. 12mo.

Such a collection of Plants as is in the possession of Messrs.

Loddiges, does not exist elsewhere in the world. The stock if sold at the retail prices is worth £200,000. A statement of it will afford a better criterion to judge of the state of our Horticulture, and the efforts made to increase the number of our Garden Plants than any other I can make. Altogether there are in their Gardens and Houses 8000 Species, exclusive of 2000 Varieties. To be more particular, of tender Exotics they have the following number of species, of the chief Genera Palmœ, 120. Acacia, 73. Bignonia, 25. Gardenia, 17. Passiflora, 33. Diosma, 38. Erica, 309. Ixia, 25. Eucalyptus, 31. Aloe, 68. Pelargonium, 136. Of Hardy Trees and Shrubs they have 2,664 Species part of which are as follows, Acer, 27. Andromeda, 16. Azalea, 19. Berberis, 10. Betula. 23. Clematis, 11. Cratægus, 47. Cytisus, 15. Fraxinus, 32. Ilex. 8. Juglans, 14. Juniperus, 21. Pinus, 40. Prunus, 39. Quercus, 40. Rhododendron, 14. Rosa, with its varieties 1459. Salix, 192. Vaccinium, 33. Ulmus, 20.*

1826. A Practical Essay on the culture of the Vine, and a treatise on the Melon. By an experienced Gardener. Royston. 8vo.

1827. Account of the different Gooseberry Shows in England during 1826, Manchester. 12mo.

Account of the different flower shows in England during 1826. Ashton-under-Lyne. 12mo.

———1. A Memoir on the Planting and Rearing of Forest Trees. By W. WITHERS Jun. Esq. Solicitor, Holt, Norfolk. Holt. 8vo.

2. A Letter to Sir Walter Scott, Bart. exposing cer-

* Gardener's Magazine, v. i, p. 318.

tain fundamental errors in his late Essay on the Planting of Waste Land, &c. By the same Gentleman. Holt. 1828. 8vo.

————Catalogue of Fruits cultivated in the Garden of the Horticultural Society of London, at Chiswick. London. 8vo.

The number of varieties enumerated in this work amount to 3825, and then nearly 1000 more doubtful ones in the Garden. There are 1205 varieties of Apple. 246 of Cherry. 73 of Melons, &c. but I shall have occasion to give a fuller list, at the conclusion of this chapter.

1827. Ten minutes advice to my neighbours on the use and abuse of Salt as a manure. By W. COLLYNS, Esq. Surgeon of Kenton, near Exeter. This has passed through four Editions.

1828. 1. Half a dozen Hints on Picturesque, Domestic Architecture. London. 4to. 2nd Edition. Plates.

2. Designs for Parsonage Houses, &c. London. 4to. Plates.

These two works are by T. F. HUNT, Architect, St. James's Palace, London.

1828. The Art of promoting the growth of the Cucumber and Melon. By T. WATKINS, Gardener to W. Knight. Esq. Highbury Park, and many years foreman to Mr. Grange of Hackney. London. 8vo.

————Dendrologia; or a treatise of Forest Trees, with Evelyn's Sylva revised, &c. London. 8vo. By J. MITCHELL, Stanstead, Sussex.

————The Planter's Guide, or a practical Essay on the best method of giving immediate effect to Wood, by the removal of large Trees and Underwood, &c. Edinburgh. 8vo. Plates. 2nd edition 1829. By Sir HENRY STEUART, Bart. L. L. D. F. R. S. &c.

1828. Transactions of the Botanical and Horticultural Society of Durham, Northumberland and Newcastle-upon Tyne. Vol. 1. Part 1. Newcastle. 8vo.

————On the culture and use of Potatoes. By Sir JOHN SINCLAIR, Bart, &c. Edinburgh. 8vo.

————The Practical Gardener and Modern Horticulturist. Part 1. To be completed in about fourteen monthly parts. London. 8vo. By CHARLES MAC'INTOSH, C. M. C. H. S. late Gardener to the Earl of Bredalbane, &c.

————Practical Instructions for the formation and culture of the Tree Rose. London. 12mo. Anonymous.

The Kitchen Garden Directory, for such vegetables as are grown in the open air. By JOHN SAUNDERS. London. 12mo.

————1. On the portraits of English Authors on Gardening. London. 8vo. By S. FELTON, Esq. Author of "Miscellanies on Ancient and Modern Gardening." &c.

2. Gleanings on Gardens, chiefly respecting those of the ancient style in England. 1829. 8vo.

————The Domestic Gardener's Manual, being an Introduction to Gardening or philosophical Principles. By a Horticultural Chymist. Part 1. 8vo.

1829. A Treatise on the Insects most prevalent on fruit Trees, and Garden produce; Recipes for their destruction, &c. By JOSHUA MAJOR, Landscape Gardener. London. 8vo.

———— An Inaugural address delivered at the first meeting of the Glamorganshire and Monmouthshire Horticultural Society, on the 22nd September, 1828. By H. MOGGRIDGE, Esq. Cardiff. 8vo. Plates.

I have thus brought to a close the Literary Catalogue of the first eight-and-twenty years of the present Century, the chief characteristic of which is an union of scientific and practical knowledge demonstrated in the works it enumerates. Besides these Standard Works there are many periodicals which deserve our notice.

THE BOTANICAL MAGAZINE, or Flower Garden displayed, is the longest established of the periodicals relating to Horticulture, and is perhaps more ably conducted than any. It was commenced in 1787 by the late William Curtis (see p.244.) At first it appeared very irregularly, but its sale soon became so extensive as to insure more attention on the part of the Publishers. Upon the death of Mr. Curtis, in 1799, the editorship was given to Dr. Sims; but this gentleman latterly not giving satisfaction, his share was purchased in 1827, and it is now conducted by Dr. Hooker, assisted by Mr. W. Curtis, Horticulturist, of Glazen Wood, Essex, a relative of the original Editor. The drawings were originally by Mr. Sowerby, afterwards by Mr. Sydenham Edwards, and now by Dr. Hooker. It has extended to fifty-five volumes.

THE BOTANICAL REGISTER, on a similar plan as the preceding, for giving figures of Exotic Plants cultivated in this country, was commenced in 1815 and has reached the fourteenth volume. It was edited by J. B. Ker, Esq. who for some time assisted the Botanical Magazine by his scientific attainments. The plates by Mr. Sydenham Edwards. It is now conducted by John Lindley, Esq.

THE BOTANICAL CABINET, on a similar plan was established in 1817 by Messrs. Loddiges and Sons, Nurserymen, of Hackney. It has reached the twelfth volume.

THE BOTANIC GARDEN, is edited by Mr. B. Maund, a very intelligent man, residing as a bookseller, at Bromsgrove. It is beautifully executed as regards the drawings; and the literary part is correct, and contains much information. It has attained to its third volume.

THE GERANIACÆ, or drawings of the natural Order of Geraniums, commenced in 1820; THE BRITISH FLOWER GARDEN. 1822; THE CISTINEŒ, or Natural Order of Cistus, in 1825; THE FLORA AUSTRALASICA, or plants of New Holland and the South Sea Islands, in 1827; The FLORIST'S GUIDE and CULTIVATOR'S DIRECTORY, or drawings of the choicest Florist's flowers, 1827. Are all edited by Mr. Robert Sweet. (see p. 303.)

THE GARDENER'S MAGAZINE, commenced in 1826, and is now in its fifth volume. It has changed its periods of publication several times, but has settled into a bimensial periodical, appearing in months alternating with the Magazine of Natural History. They are both edited by Mr. Loudon. It is a very cheap publication, and collects into its pages from every source whatever appears that is interesting to the Gardener. It is rather prejudiced and visionary in some of its antipathies and the schemes |which it advocates.

THE POMOLOGICAL MAGAZINE, or figures and descriptions of the best varieties of Fruit, commenced at the close of 1827. It is edited by "Two gentlemen intimately connected with the Horticultural Society of London."

Of the transactions of the London and Edinburgh Horticultural Societies, I have given the contents in the order in which each volume appeared. I shall now proceed to sketch the rise of their parent Societies.

The Horticultural Society of London, had its origin in 1804 from a few individuals of wealth and talent who associated for the improvement of the Art in which they delighted. Their views soon enlarged, and on the 17th of April, 1809, they were incorporated into the above named Society: The Charter states the Society to be for the improvement of Horticulture in all its branches, ornamental as well as useful, though the President, Mr. Knight, declares their attention to be chiefly confined to the latter. This exclusion of all writings that relate to Landscape Gardening from their Transactions has been blamed by some persons, I think inconsiderately, for nothing new can be stated upon its general Principles; and particular details can be of comparatively little service; for the genius of every place, and the taste of every proprietor differs.

The original corporation of the Society consisted of George, Earl of Dartmouth; Edward, Earl Powis; Brownlow, Bishop of Winchester; John, Lord Selsey; Charles Greville, Esq.; Sir Joseph Banks, Bart; W. T. Aiton; John Elliot; T. A. Knight; C. Miller; R. A. Salisbury; J. Trevelyan, Esqrs, and J. Dickson; T. Hoy; and W. Smith, Gardeners.

The Society has power to purchase lands, &c. and is liable to be sued, and able to sue; to have a common Seal; an indefinite number of Fellows, the power of naming which was to be in any five of the above-named original members before the first of May 1809, but afterwards to be in the power of any seven or more Fellows. The Society is to have a Council of fifteen Fellows, a President, Treasurer, and Secretary. The first President to be the Earl of Dartmouth; Charles Greville, first Treasurer; R. A. Salisbury, first Secretary. New ones to be elected annually. The president is every year to appoint four Vice-Presidents from among the Members; three of the council to go out annually, and three other Fellows elected to their places. Vacancies in the council, &c. are to be filled up within two months. When Bye Laws are made or altered, which must be at a General Meeting, a majority at least of two-thirds of the Fellows present is required, and those present must amount to seven.

At the first establishment of the Society, and for a few years afterwards the number of its Fellows amounted to not more than three or four hundred; but in 1822 they had increased to 1520, in the two preceding years 660 fellows having been elected. In 1824 the fellows amounted to 2197. In 1826 the number was 1984; In 1827, it was 2044.

In 1821 they founded a garden at Chiswick, covering thirty-three Acres, which they have on a lease renewable for ever, of the Duke of Devonshire. To the formation of this Garden, which is confessedly one of the most extensive in the World, the King, and the greater part of the Fellows, contributed and none but Subscribers participate in its benefits. Some object to subscribe on the plea that the original members ought not to be called upon for fresh subscriptions having originally subscribed with the impression that they should be benefitted by every after proceeding of the Society. That this plea is fallacious is demonstrated by the simple fact that without farther Subscriptions the funds of the Society were not sufficient to found a Garden; and surely those who do subscribe additionally ought to have some additional priviliges, provided they do not infringe upon the rights of original Fellows.

Of the arrangement, richness of contents, and management of the Garden I can speak most favourably. I might have arranged some of the departments differently, had I been concerned; but persons would be found to say the like of the most perfect Garden that could be devised. Taste and Judgement differ in every one. The most censorious must agree that the stock of Plants in the Chiswick Garden is splendid, and that their management is an illustration of the best Horticulture of our day. To enrich their Garden no pains have been spared, the whole pecuniary power of the Society, and the personal interest of the Fellows has been employed to render it as perfect as possible. In 1821 the Society sent out to Bengal and China Mr. John Potts, and to the latter country Mr. J. D. Parks in 1823. Mr. John Forbes in the last named year was sent to the eastern shore of Africa; Mr. D. Douglas to the United States, and in 1824, the same Gardener proceeded to Colombia, as did Mr. J. M'Rae to the Sandwich Islands, all for the purpose of collecting new plants. The result of their researches has been most gratifying. Besides these especial collectors the Society has numerous Corresponding Members in every quarter of the globe, who from time to time have much forwarded the views of the Society.

Of the President of the Society I have already spoken, and concurrent praise is due to its Secretary, Mr. Sabine, than whom no man has laboured more assiduously or more effectually to promote the interests of the Society. Of the benefits he has conferred upon Horticulture his papers in the Transactions of the Society are ample testimonies. Being only in his sixtieth year, the Society and our Country may hope to profit for many years yet by his labours.

Having no immediate interest in the Society, much less being its deputed advocate, it does not come within the intention of this work to defend it under the complaints that have occasionally been brought against it. I must however say that those I have read of, or listened to, have been founded upon false reasoning, upon personal pique for some fancied wrong, or the parties have been the first aggressor. To say the Society never took [an injudicious step, would be to say that it is perfect beyond all Human Institutions; but to say that it has hitherto been conducted upon liberal principles, and that it has fulfilled the intention for which all such Institutions are founded, the general benefit of its particular Art, by the agency of its members, for these naturally deserve to be first served, is certainly saying of it no more than it merits.

One fundamental objection however I must pause to refute; it is that which urges that Scientific Societies of this kind, if not injurious to the Art they profess to improve, are at least useless; for all the grand discoveries of Science, have arisen from the labours of isolated individuals.

It is true that the genius of Bacon, Galileo, Newton, Hervey and many others, carried those giants of intellect and research through every opposition whether arising from neglect, from poverty, or from persecution. They arose unassisted by any Institutions, and stand like the Eastern Pyramids, monuments of greatness, amid plains barren and pathless. But what of this? have not Lavoisier, Linnæus, Banks, Knight, Davy and many others, been nurtured amid Institutes of modern days? Let it be marked that those who consider a Society is to be valued only as extraordinary, and science-convulsing discoveries emanate from it, by no means have a just idea of the sphere of utility of such Institutions. Societies are useful as being centres towards which minor discoveries and improvements naturally flow and are concentrated, to be again communicated more at large by their members, their publications, and their lectures. Discoveries naturally thus flow to them because they hold out rewards and distinctions to which every generous mind aspires. Added to this there is a great benefit in the association of individuals of kindred minds, for it is certain that to every person who follows a liberal Art or Science professionally, there are a hundred who delight in it purely for amusement. This is especially the case among those of hereditary distinction and wealth, persons who thence have a power to forward every pursuit they may be attached to. Their example and opinions, are dictatorial in the habits and tastes of a nation; and it is only by bringing them in contact, by means of Public Institutions, with their equals in Society and in their Pursuits, that they can be enlisted in the cause of science. The discoveries of every Member of the Royal and of the Horticultural Societies would have been beneficial in their individual capacities, but they could never have been so generally diffused as they have been by means of the Meetings and Transactions of those Societies; Mr. Knight might have been the same excellent Horticulturist as now; and Sir H. Davy as admirable a Chemist; but would their example, their writings, have been so widely beneficial if not diffused by the means of the various societies to which they belong.

Again Societies have a command of interest and money that enables them to follow plans which would be ruinous to or unattainable by individuals. Where is the individual could have introduced the hundreds of new plants which the Horticultural Society has?

No individual ever had such a Laboratory as the splendid one of the Royal Institution; and this was the nursery of Davy's discoveries which constitute a new era in Chemistry.

His career of research began in the Scientific Institute at Bristol; it was perfected in those of London.*

* Whilst writing the above I see by the Public Papers that this distinguished man is dead. The benefits he has conferred upon the Arts of cultivating the Soil by his "Elements of Agricultural Chemistry," entitle him to more than the above brief notice.

SIR HUMPHREY DAVY, was born Dec. 17th, 1779, at Penzance in Cornwall of an ancient family' but of the middle class—His education commenced at the Grammar Schools of Penzance and Truro. At the former place he resided at the House of Mr. John Tomkin, Surgeon. He was always a distinguished boy, wrote poems at the age of nine, and continued to court the Muses until 15 when he became a pupil of Mr. (since Dr.) Borlase of Penzance, intending to graduate as M. D. at Edinburgh—At eighteen by his own application he had acquired the rudiments of Botany, Anatomy, Physiology, the simpler Mathematics and Metaphysics, but Chemistry soon obtained his sole attention—His first experiments were upon the air disengaged by Sea Weeds from the Water of the Ocean—The communication of them induced a correspondence with Dr. Beddoes, who persuaded the embryo Philosopher of 19 to give up his views of going to Edinburgh for the uncontrolled superintendance of a series of experiments on factitious Airs at Bristol—Residing with Dr. Beddoes and constantly employed in Chemical pursuits, at the age of 21 he gave their results to the Public in "Researches Chemical and Philosophical"—a work so well received by the scientific World as to lead to his being appointed Professor of Chemistry in the Royal Institution. His first experiments were directed to the improvement of the process of Tanning, the results of which obtained from him the candid avowal that practice had done so much for the Art as to leave little expectation of improvement from any known Theory—Galvanism was at the same period an object of his experiments—In 1802 he commenced his Lectures before the Board of Agriculture which he continued for 10 years. The course is before the Public in his "Elements of Agricultural Chemistry"—In 1803 he was elected F. R. S.—in 1805 Member of the Royal Irish Academy. By his talents and urbanity he had acquired the friendship of most of the Litterati and Philosophers of the Metropolis. Sir J. Banks—Cavendish—Hatchett—Wollaston—Babington—Children—Tennant, &c. and corresponding with the principal Chemists of Europe.—In In 1806 he delivered the Bakerian Lecture of the R. S.—taking for his subject some new electrical discoveries of his own. Soon afterwards he stamped an

For the purpose of forming a Horticultural Society at Edinburgh, a meeting of several gentleman was held at the house of Mr. T. Dickson near that city, on the 25th of November, 1809, and a still more numerous meeting occured on the 5th of December, when the Society was formed; the Earl of Dalkeith being chosen President; Sir J. Hall, Dr. Rutherford, Dr. Coventry and Mr. Hunter, Vice-Presidents, and Mr. W. Nicol and Mr. P. Neil, Secretaries. A general Quarterly Meeting was then determined on the 6th of March, 1810, on which day the Laws and Regulations of the Society, which had been previously drawn up by a committee, were revised and adopted. Those

---

Epoch in Chemistry by the decomposition of the fixed Alkalies Potass and Soda. About the same time he became Secretary to the R. S.—In 1808 he received a prize from the French *Institute*, an honourable token of merit, bestowed by minds superior to national prejudices—From this time until the greater part of 1810 was elapsed he was employed in experiments on Oxymuriatic Acid, the simple nature of which he discovered—At the close of this year he delivered a course of Lectures before the Dublin Society—and in its last month received the honorary degree of L. L. D. from Trinity College of that City. In 1812 he was united to Mrs. Apreece, widow of S. A. Apreece, Esq.—a lady of talent, amiability, and fortune. A few days previously he was knighted by his present Majesty in his capacity of Regent—In 1815 he gave safety to Miners in the Lamp which bears his name, his attention being first drawn to the subject by Dr. Gray, a member of a Committee at Sunderland which had been formed for the purpose of enquiring into the causes of the frequent explosions and the means of prevention.—The Coal Owners of Tyne and Wear presented him with a service of Plate worth £2000 as a token of gratitude and sense of the benefit. In 1813 he was elected Corresponding Member of the French Institute—In 1817 one of the eight associates of the Royal Academy—In 1818 he was created a Baronet and during the succeeding years his name has been added to the list of members of most of the learned bodies of Europe. His travels for the advancement of Science have been to different parts of Europe—to investigate the causes of Volcanic Phenomena—to instruct Miners in the use of the Safety Lamp—to examine the remains of the Chemical Arts of the Ancients, especially their preparation of colours—and to attempt the unfolding of the Herculanean MSS. He was employed upon these last at the close of 1818 and the commencement of 1819. On his return to England in 1820, Sir J. Banks died, and Davy was elected P. R. S. in his place—His friend Drs

regulations declare that the Society shall be called THE CALEDONIAN HORTICULTURAL SOCIETY; to be constituted of Ordinary, Honorary, and Corresponding Members. To have a President, four Vice-Presidents, two Secretaries, a Treasurer, twelve Counsellors, an Experimenter, and Painter. One Vice-president and two Counsellors to be changed annually and the President to be elected every two years. Twelve members to form a quorum of the Society, and three a quorum of the Council. The Secretaries prepare the Transactions, of which every member must purchase a copy. Every new regulation or alteration of any previous one to be made at a Quarterly Meeting. The objects of the society are the promoting and improving the cultivation of Fruits, Flowers, and Culinary Vegetables.

In January 1812 the total number of Members were 179.

Wollaston, who was considered worthy of contesting with him for the highest seat in the English Court of Science, declining to be a candidate after his friend had been nominated.—A slight opposition was made by some unknown persons who proposed Lord Colchester, but, Sir Humphrey was hailed as President by a majority of nearly 200 to 13. Ill-health obliged him to resign the Presidency and he died whilst trying the influence of a milder climate, at Geneva, on the 29th of May, 1829.

In private this illustrious individual was esteemed for his virtues, his amiability, his warmth of friendship and his sincerity.—In tracing his public progress, the truth, which cannot be too strongly maintained, is evidenced, that he who advances with steady pace along the path of Analysis, aiming at the demonstration of facts, rather than the illustration of previously formed Theories must always be a permanent Benefactor of Mankind whatever may be his pursuit—Such was Cavendish, such was Davy—With an equal love of Science, with patience equally exhaustless, and with perseverance equally unsubduable—their text and illustrations were furnished by the Laboratory—The few theoretical Inductions they have given us are the results from facts they had previously discovered—as such they are among the few immutables of Science—like all Truth, they will descend unimpaired amid the discoveries of ages—and if Chemistry ever becomes a perfect Science, will take their places in the structure incapable of illustration, or improvement by the master hand that guides the arrangement.

In 1815 they were 418. In this year it was proposed to raise subscriptions of an extra guinea from the Members, for the purpose of sending a deputation on a Horticultural Tour in Flanders and Holland which was carried into execution and the results of the observations then made were published by Mr Neil in 1823. In 1816 a plan for a Garden was submitted to the Society by Mr. Hay, and adopted, but from want of means it was not commenced until 1824. It is now completed and is excellently conducted. In 1819 the members amounted to 637 The Duke of Buccleugh and the Earl of Roseberry have been their Presidents.

I shall now proceed to enumerate the various Plants at present cultivated in our Gardens, accompanying the chief of them with slight historical notices. I shall commence with the fruit

AMELANCHIER, 3 Varieties.

Introduced during the last Century from America. They are allied to the Medlar,

ALMOND, 10 Varieties.

We know from the Scriptures that the Almond is a native of Syria, and it has been observed wild by most modern Travellers in Eastern countries. It was cultivated by the Greeks, and from thence was made known to the Romans, who however had it not in their Gardens in the time of Cato. It is said to have been first planted in England in 1548.

CUSTARD APPLE. 2 kinds.

These are natives of Tropical Climates. One was cultivated here by Tradescant in 1656. The other by Miller in 1739.

ARCTOSTAPHYLOS—2 kinds. APRICOT. 64 varieties.

Pliny is the first writer to mention this fruit by name. Whether it is the Armenian Plum of Columella admits of doubt. Theophrastus had only heard of it. It is a native of China, &c. It is an unwarranted assumption of M. Regneir that it cannot be a native of so mountainous a country as Armenia, since Mr. Buckingham says they abound in that country. It is said to have been first introduced into this country in 1524.

BERBERRY. 10 Varieties

A native of this country.

PINE APPLE. 95 varieties.

A native of the torrid zone in South America. It was first made known in England from China in 1657. (Evelyn's Diary) but was not fruited here until the reign of Charles the 2nd. (vide p.112 and 136.)

PRICKLY PEAR. 1.

CHESNUT. 32 varieties.

The Chesnut is said to have been brought to Europe by the Greeks from Asia Minor; and that the Romans obtained it from Castanea, a Greek Town of Thessaly. Some writers have considered it as a native of this Island. But I am much rather inclined to think it was introduced by the Romans for its present name is a corruption of the Roman name, and there is no synonyme for it in the language of the ancient Britons.

CHERRY. 246 varieties.

The Cherry is a native of Pontus, in Asia, whence it was introduced to the Romans by Lucullus 68 years before the birth of our Saviour: In less than 26 years says Pliny, they were grown in Britain.

BIRD CHERRY. 2 kinds.

CAROB. 1 kind.

CITRUS family, including Lemons, Oranges, and Limes, 24 varieties, though foreign authors mention 169.

The above are all natives of Asia. The Lemon was well known to the Romans, but Pliny says they could not succeed in cultivating them. They were grown here in the reign of James the 1st: The Orange was like the Lemon known to the Romans but they failed in cultivating it. It was first grown in modern Europe at Lisbon in 1548, being brought thither by Juan de Castro. Evelyn in his Diary informs us that they were first cultivated in England about 1580. The Citron was introduced into Italy by Palladius in the second Century. When it was first cultivated in England is unknown.

CORNELION CHERRY. 2.

NUT AND FILBERT. 32.

The Hazel Nut is a native of this country. The Cob Nut was introduced into Europe by David, Baton of Zorneck from Constantinople in 1583. John Rea first cultivated them in England in 1665. Filberts were obtained by the Romans from Pontus and were known at first as Pontic Nuts, but being chiefly cultivated at Avella, they were afterwards called Avellan Nuts. They probably introduced them to this country.

CRATŒGUS, including the Medlar, Hawthorn, &c. 38.

The Medlar was known both to the Greeks and Romans, being mentioned by Theophrastus and Pliny. If not a native of of this country it was known as early to its inhabitants as the time of the Romans.

MELON. 73.

This fruit was introduced to the Romans from Armenia, where it is a native, by Lucullus. It was first grown in this country in 1520; Gough was decidedly wrong in stating they were common here in the time of Edward the 3rd, the melons of those days are synonymous with our pompions

QUINCE. 8.

The Quince grows wild in Germany, but was introduced to Rome from the Isle of Crete. When it was first cultivated here is unknown but probably at a very early period.

DATE. 2.

This was a native of Syria, as we learn from the Sacred Writings. It was known to the Romans.

OLEASTER. 1.

CROWBERRY. 4.

ERIOBOTRYA. 3.

ROSE APPLE. 2.

EUPHORIA. 3

FIG. 75.

The Fig has always been highly esteemed among the Eastern Nations. We learn it was amongst the chief food of the Isrealites, from the Holy Scriptures, The Athenians were so choice of theirs that they would not permit them to be exported, and Saturn one of the Roman Deities, was represented as crowned with new Figs. So much attention did they pay to it that in the time of Pliny they had twenty-nine varieties. The Fig was introduced to this country by the Romans. We have seen that it was cultivated here in 1257. The Marseilles variety may have been first introduced by Cardinal Pole in the reign of Henry 8th, but other varieties were known much earlier

STRAWBERRY. 121—22 worthy of cultivation.

The strawberry is a native of most temperate climates. It is scarcely noticed by ancient writers. The Red wood Strawberry and the Hautboy are both natives of this country; as the Scarlet is of Virginia and was introduced to England about 1625. The Chili was brought from America by M, Frazeir into France, and into England by Miller in 1727. The Alpine is a native of Germany and was first grown here in 1768.

GAULTHERIA. 1.

GLYCOSMIS. 1

WALNUT. 11.

The Walnut is a native of the northern parts of China, and Persia, from whence it was obtained by the Greeks, and from the Greeks it was brought to the Romans by Vitellius just previous to the death of the Emperor Tiberius. They are supposed to have been introduced here from France, and that our common name is a corruption of the original Gaul-nut. It is certain they were here before Tusser wrote in 1557.

MACLURA. 1.

MANGO. 3.

MULBERRY. 6.

The Mulberry Tree is a native of Asia. It is mentioned in the Scriptures. It was introduced to Greece and Rome from Persia. It is said to have been first planted in England at Sion House in 1548.

OLIVE. 1.   CRANBERRY. 3.   GRANADILLA. 4.
PEACH. 224.

The Peach is a native of Persia. They were not common in Greece, when Pliny lived, just previous to whose time they had been introduced to the Romans but did not succeed well. They were introduced to this country in the early part of the reign of Henry the 8th.

NECTARINE. 72

This native of Persia was introduced into England about the year 1524. It is not certain whether the Romans were acquainted with it. If they were they considered it merely as a variety of the Peach.

PINUS. 1

PISTACHIA. 3.

PLUM. 298.

It is impossible to state with any thing like precision when the several Plums we now possess were first introduced or by whom. They are natives of every quarter of the globe, and varieties have been raised in every Country. Pliny, Columella, &c. mention that an immense number were known to the Romans.

The Damascene or Damson is a native of Damascus and was imported to Rome about 114. B. C. The Orleans Plum was first raised near the town of that name in France. The Green Gage, is properly the Reine Claude, being raised in France, during the reign of Francis the first, and so named in honour of his queen Claude. It was called the Green Gage, by the Gardener of the Gage family at Hengrave Hall, the tree coming to him from France without any title affixed. The Perdrigon was brought to England from Italy by Lord Cromwell in the reign of Henry the seventh.

GUAVA. 4:

POMEGRANATE. 1.

This fruit is a native of Africa and Asia. It is mentioned in Scripture as being one of the products of Canaan. The Greeks cultivated it much. The Romans first obtained it about a century before the Christian Æra from Carthage.

CRAB. 30.

APPLE. 1205.

The Apple has been a favourite fruit through all ages and in every climate where it will grow. It is mentioned as one of the choicest by Solomon. The Greeks had many varieties of it, and the Romans still more. It was probably known to the Britons even before the invasion of the Romans (vide p. 33.) Pippins were introduced into England in the 16th year of the reign of Henry the 8th. The Golden Pippin is said to be a native of Parham Park, in Sussex. It is universally allowed to be an English Apple. The Ribston Pippin was accidentally raised at Ribston Park in Yorkshire in the beginning of the last Century. The Siberean Crabs were first known here in 1758 and 1784, the small variety in the latter year.

PEAR. 630.

The Pear like the Apple is a general, and from the earliest ages has been a favorite fruit. The Greeks were very fond of it, and it was consecrated by them to Minerva before the Olive. The Romans had many varieties in their earliest state as a nation, and continually were increasing their varieties; they probably introduced it to this country, our name for it being a corruption of the Roman name. It was cultivated before the time of King John.

SERVICE. 13.

This fruit is a native of England and many other parts of Europe. It was much esteemed by the Romans.

CURRANT. 35.

GOOSEBERRY. 185.

These fruits are natives of England and other parts of Northern Europe. They were unknown to the ancients. It was not until the 16th Century they were much attended to either on the continent or this country, since then no fruit has been more benefitted by cultivation.

ROSE. 8, with edible fruit.

RASPBERRY. 23.

This fruit was known to the Greeks and Romans, but was

not much esteemed by them. The Red Raspberry is a native of this country; but was little attended to until the close of the 16th Century. The large Varieties both red and yellow were brought to us from Antwerp.

BRAMBLE. 21.

ELDER. 3.

WATER CALTROPS. 1.

TRIPHASIA. 1.

WHORTLEBERRY. 23.

VARRONIA. 1.

VIBURNUM. 2.

GRAPE VINES. 167.

ZIZYPHUS. 3.[*]

Of culinary vegetables we cultivate the following

CABBAGES, CAULIFLOWERS, and other Brassicas. 58.

This tribe was in the greatest esteem among the Greeks and Romans. It has been known to us from the earliest ages.

PEAS. 25.

[*] For the number of varieties of each fruit in the above Catalogue I am indebted to that of the Chiswick Garden published by the London Horticultural Society.

This Vegetable, at least some of its varieties, have been known from the earliest ages. The best varieties of our Garden Pea originated in France and were introduced in the middle of the 16th Century, to this country from thence. The Rouncival appears to be our oldest variety.

BEAN. 15.

This was a chief article of food among the Greeks and Romans. It has been long known in this country being mentioned by some of our oldest Authors. Many varieties of course have been introduced within the last two Centuries. We had the Mazagan, from a Portugese settlement of that name on the coast of Morocco.

KIDNEY BEAN. 18.

This is believed to have been a native of Turkey and other parts of Eastern Europe. It is mentioned by Pliny. When first introduced here I find no mention, but Henry Compton, Bishop of London, first made us acquainted with several varieties in the latter part of the 17th Century.

POTATOES. 27.

This most valuable of Roots was introduced from the colony settled in America by Sir Walter Raleigh about the year 1586. It is a native of the continent of South America. It was first cultivated on Raleigh's Estate in Ireland; but never came into general use until the commencement of the present Century. It was considered as a delicacy in the time of James the 1st, for in 1619 a small quantity is mentioned as bought for the Queen's use at one shilling per pound. They were recommended in 1662 by the Royal Society to be more extensively planted; but even in 1718 Bradley mentions them as a root of "little note." This late period of their coming into general use has been used as an argument against the belief that Sir W. Raleigh introduced them, the futility of this is demonstrated by the fact that they are only just becoming abundant at Bengal. "At first, says Bishop Heber they were unpopular as elsewhere, now (1826) they are much liked"*

JERUSALEM ARTICHOKE. 1.

This is a native of Brazil, but introduced by the French from Canada, and into this country in 1617. It soon became very common.

TURNIP. 13.

This is believed to be an indigenous plant improved by culture, but it is not confined to this country it having been grown by the earliest Romans; as well as by the Greeks before them.

CARROTS. 9.

Carrots are mentioned by Pliny and long before him by Theophrastus, both of them agreeing that the best were grown in Greece and its Islands. The Garden Carrot is probably a variety of the Wild Carrot, which is a native of several parts of Europe.

PARSNIP. 4.

This is a native of our country improved by cultivation.— The Greeks as well as the Romans cultivated it. The finest

* Narrative of a Journey in the Upper Provinces of India. v. i. p. 13

in the time of the latter Emperors were grown in Germany, whither, Pliny tells us, Tiberius was accustomed to send for them.

BEETS. 11.

The Greeks and Romans estimated this root very highly.—It was introduced into this country in 1548. The white variety from Portugal in 1570.

SKIRRETS. 1.   SCORZONERA 1.   SALSIFY. 1.

RADISHES. 15.

The Radish is said to be a native of China; if so it was imported into the East of Europe very early, for the Greeks admired and cultivated it in their earliest ages. In their oblations to Apollo at Delphos they offered the Radish made of Gold, whilst the Beet was formed of Silver, and Turnips only in Lead They were much admired by the Romans, and were a very general accompaniment of their meals. There were four kinds cultivated here by Gerarde in the reign of Queen Elizabeth.

SPINACH. 3.

This was unknown to the ancients. It is believed to be a native of Spain. It was not cultivated here much before 1568, for Turner in that year mentions it as lately introduced

ORACH. 6.   Introduced before 1548.

NEW ZEALAND SPINACH. 1.   Introduced by Sir Joseph Banks.

SORREL. 2.

These are both natives of Europe. The Romans were very

fond of them with their other meats, as the French are at present. They are little noticed now in England though in the time of Henry the 8th they were in almost every garden.

ONIONS, 18.

Onions have been admired from the earliest ages. The Israelites murmered for them in the wilderness. Theophrastus among the Greeks wrote a treatise upon them. The Egyptians worshipped them. The Romans cultivated them extensively. They have been cultivated here immemorially. The Welsh Onion was brought here from Siberia in 1629.

LEEKS. 3.

The Leek is said to be a native of Switzerland which is very doubtful. The Romans had the best from Egypt; they were first brought into esteem among them by the Emperor Nero. They have been known in this country from a very early age. They were common in the days of St. David who died about A. D. 544.

CHIVES. 1. ROCHAMBOLE. 1.

GARLIC.

This was detested by the politer Greeks and Romans. It was cultivated here at the time of Henry the 8th.

SHALOT.

This is a native of Palestine; it was introduced to Rome from Ascalon in Syria, of which the present name is a corruption. It was first cultivated in England in 1548.

ASPARAGUS. 2.

This is a native of England as well as of Eastern Europe and Asia. It was in great esteem among the Romans. It was cultivated here in the time of Queen Elizabeth, but how defective the cultivation was is demonstrated by Gerarde who says it was of "the size of a Swan's quill."

SEA KALE.

This is a native of England, and has been sought after, by those living near the Sea Coasts where it is found, immemorially, but its culture was not attempted until the close of the last Century.

ARTICHOKE. 3.

The Artichoke appears to be a native of northern Africa. The Greeks and Romans obtained it from thence. The latter esteemed it more than any other culinary plant, perhaps on account of the expense attending its importation, for as it does not succeed in the climate of Italy, they were dependant upon Sicily and other moist climates for their supply. They paid annually about 6,000 000 sesterces for them. It was brought into this country, about 1548, and grows finer in our climate than in any other part of Europe.

CARDON. 4.

Was first cultivated here in 1683 by Mr. John Sutherland. Parkinson mentions them in 1629, as not being known how to be managed in this country.

RAMPION.

ALISANDER.

HOP.

BLADDER CAMPION.

LADY THISTLE. COTTON THISTLE.

LETTUCES. 19.

The Lettuce is a native of many parts of Europe. It was eaten as a sallad herb both by the Greeks, and Romans. So fond were the later Romans of them that Pliny says they devised means of having them throughout the year. Their cultivation is first noticed in this country in 1562.

ENDIVE. 12.

Endive was a sallad herb of the Romans. It appears to have been introduced into England about 1548. They preserved it through the Winter in earth. Queen Elizabeth in her last illness eat little but Succory Pottage.

DANDELION.

CELERY. 5.

Celery is a native of this country, but its cultivation was taught us by the Italians, not more than half a Century since.

MUSTARD. 2.

The Romans used mustard seed in Medicine, and the young plants stewed. The seeds were first made known for using when in powder with other meat, in the reign of Elizabeth. Tusser mentions it as a sallad herb.

RAPE. LAMBS LETTUCE. GARDEN AND AMERICAN CRESS. 4. WATER CRESS. 3. BROOKLIME. GARDEN ROCKET. SCURVY GRASS. BURNET. WOOD SORREL.

PARSLEY. 3.   2 Y

The Romans always added it to their pottages. It was cultivated here in 1548.

PURSLANE. 2. TARRAGON.

FENNEL AND DILL. 4. Fennel was much used by the Romans as a seasoning to their dishes. It is a native of this country, and has been employed in cookery immemorially.

CHERVIL.

This is a native of England and other parts of Europe. It was cultivated by the Greeks and Romans as it was in this country as early as the time of Gerarde.

HORSE-RADISH.

This native of England was used in Gerarde's time as it is now with meat. It does not appear to have been known to the ancients.

NASTURTIUM. 3.

The minor variety of this native of Peru was brought to Europe by the Spaniards in 1580; and Gerarde mentions cultivating it a few years after. The major variety was not known in Europe until 1684.

MARIGOLD. 4.

This native of southern Europe was known to the Romans being mentioned by Columella, but I think not as an object of culture. It was cultivated in this country previous to the publication of Dodoen's Herbal in 1573.

THYME. 2;

Thyme was cultivated by the Romans for medicine and the use of their Bees. It has been used immemorially here as a seasoning.

SAGE. 4. CLARY. 1.

Garden Sage appears to have been first cultivated here about 1573, and Clary about ten years previously.

MINTS. 3.

Pliny says every meat of the Roman husbandmen was seasoned with Mint. It has been in use with us as far back as our records reach.

MARJORAM. 4.

Marjoram is a native of southern Europe. The Candia Marjoram was brought to us in 1551. The Sweet from Portugal in 1573, and the Pot Marjoram from Greece in 1759. It was used by the Romans in medicine.

SAVORY. 2.

Savory which is a native of southern Europe, was used by the Romans as a condiment. They probably introduced it to this country. It is mentioned as a standard garden product in our oldest Herbals.

BASIL. 2.

Southern Europe is the native habitat of this plant. The Romans had many prejudices against it, yet cultivated it, and used it. They believed the more it was cursed the better it thrived. It was cultivated here in 1548, but has been chiefly valued as a medicinal plant. In the days of Mary and Elizabeth it was cultivated in pots as a fragrant herb for ladies.

ROSEMARY. 3.

Rosemary, is a native of many parts of Europe. It was employed by the Roman Physicians. It was cultivated in this country in 1548.

LAVENDER. 2.

Lavender is a native of many parts of Europe. It has been cultivated in the earliest ages for its fragrance. Spikenard (Essential oil of Lavender) is mentioned in Scripture. The Greeks and Romans cultivated it, and it was in our Gardens early in the reign of Henry the 8th.

TANSY. 3. COSTMARY.

RHUBARB. 3.

This native of Asia was known as a Medical Plant to Dioscorides, who lived about the time of the Christian Era. Its leaves were boiled as a sauce for meat here in the time of Gerarde. It is not mentioned as being so employed however by Switzer or any of his contemporaries; and the use of its stalks for Tarts, &c. appears to be an introduction of the present Century.

POMPIONS.—GOURDS—6.

These are natives of southern climates in every quarter of the globe. They were boiled and eaten by the Romans as now by us, and were probably brought to this Island by them. They were common when our oldest Herbals were written.

The Vegetable Marrow Gourd was introduced in 1819 from the East Indies.

ANGELICA. ANISE. CORIANDER.

CARRAWAY.

Though now found wild in this country, Carraway was doubtless imported to us by the Romans, who obtained it from Caria. The early Greeks as well as Romans employed it as a condiment, &c.

RUE.

This plant is a native of England and many other parts of Europe. It was much employed as a seasoning and mendicament by the Greeks and Romans. The former made of it as well as of Parsley borderings for the compartments of their Gardens. It has been in esteem here as far back as our records go.

HYSSOP.

This has been used as a medicinal Herb ever since the days of Moses. It was cultivated here in 1548. The Greeks and Romans employed it in medicine.

CHAMOMILE. 2.

This has been used as a stomachic, as far back as the time of the early Romans.

ELECAMPANE.

LIQUORICE.

WORMWOOD, 4.

Was known as a medicinal herb to the early Greeks and Romans. It was cultivated in our Gardens in Tusser's time.

BALM.

This was a mendicament of the Greeks and Romans; it was "much sowen in Gardens" in Gerarde's time.

TOMATOS. 7

EGG PLANT. 3.

This is much cultivated on the continent as an esculent. It is a native of Africa, and was introduced before Gerarde wrote in 1596.

CAPSICUMS. 12 at least.

This native of South America was introduced to Europe by the Spaniards. They were cultivated here in the reign of Henry the 8th.

SAMPHIRES. 3.

Samphire was used as a culinary Plant by the Romans, though we do not know that they ever attempted to cultivate it. It was similarly employed by us in Gerarde's time, but was never cultivated in our Gardens until the commencement of the present century.

MUSHROOM. I am not aware that the Greeks ate of this vegetable. The later Romans were very fond of it.

The increase of the inhabitants of our Pleasure grounds within the last few years, places the taste and patronage which are bestowed on Gardening in a very conspicuous point of view. Of Stove Plants we now cultivate about 1800 species and varieties. Of Green-House Plants nearly 3000. Of hardy Trees and Shrubs nearly 4000. Of hardy Perennial Flowers nearly 3000. Of Biennial and Annual Flowers together about 800. To particularize the different genera of these would exceed the limits I have prescribed to this work. I have not included the varieties of Florist's flowers in the above general list. They are more than proportionably numerous. Of Hyacinths we have about 300 varities, whereas in 1629, Parkinson mentions but 50. The passion for this flower however has much abated, for Miller in the early part of the last Century says the Dutch gardeners had 2000 sorts. Of tulips we have nearly 700 varieties. The cultivation of this flower has declined of late years. It was at its height both in this country and in Holland towards the middle of the 17th Century. In Holland nearly £600 was agreed to be given for a single root. Of the Ranunculus we have nearly 500 varieties. Of the Anemone about 200. Of Dahlias (now Georginas) between 200 and 300. Narcissi 200. Auriculas more than 400. Pinks 300. Carnations about 350. Of Roses included in the list we have given of hardy Trees and Shrubs there are more than 1450. Another instance of the progress made in increasing the number of our cultivated plants is furnished by the genera Erica. But five kinds of Heath were described by Miller as known in England about 60 years since; we now cultivate nearly 350.

Mr. Loudon makes the number of plants cultivated by Gardeners at present amount to 13,140. Of these 1400 are natives of Gt. Britain; 47 were Exotics introduced previous to, and during the reign of Henry the 8th—Seven during that of Edward the 6th. 533 during that of Elizabeth. In that of James the 1st, twenty. Charles the 1st, 331. Ninety-five during the Usurpation. Charles the 2nd, 152. James the 2nd, 44.

William and Mary, 298. Anne, 230. George the 1st, 182. George the 2nd, 1770. George the 3rd, 6756. During the first sixteen years of this century on an average 156 plants were annually introduced. The ardour of research is not the least abated now.

If we consider the present state of our Horticulture as regards its practical details, there is every reason to be satisfied with its improved state over that of any other period of our History. The progress has not been, perhaps cannot be, marked by any extraordinary discovery, but the improvement has been gradual, and though few new practices have been introduced, old ones have been improved, and are now certainly better understood, and more correctly performed. This is owing to the more general diffusion of Scientific information among our Gardeners. As a demonstration of this Mr. Loudon's Encyclopædia of Gardening may be compared with any standard Work on the same Art, of previous Centuries. The constitution of Soils; the mode of operation of different manures, and their economical management; the operation of the Air upon the roots as well as other parts of plants, and the consequent necessity for not sowing or planting at an indiscriminate depth; the importance of pulverizing the Soil; rotation of Crops; rendering the natural heat afforded by the Sun of the greatest possible benefit by darkening the colour of enclosures, &c. the very great variety of Tools and engines the gardener has offered to him, are all evidences of improvement. The art of Training and Pruning so as to check over vigorous Trees, and promote the strength of the more weak are equally improved. Though grafting and budding have been improved; it is yet to be regretted that the question whether grafts may be inserted successfully upon stocks of a contrary species, has not been set at rest by a course of extensive experiments. It justifies those who maintain an affirmative opinion upon this point, that such men as Pliny and Lord Bacon, declare they have seen Nuts, Grapes, Figs, Apples, &c. growing on one stem, and an Apple on a Colewort stock. In the highest department of our Art improvement continual and continuing is not wanting. Forcing which we have seen arose under the Emperors of Rome, and was revived in England about the time Parkinson lived, has ever since gradually advanced towards perfection ; for perfection in forcing is obtaining the fruits of warm climates in as great a state of excellence in those which are colder as when cultivated in their native soils. Though on common Hot-beds Bell Glasses were sometimes used in Parkinson's time, yet the usual protection for plants forced upon them was simply straw, or mats supported from them by sticks. Evelyn more than fifty years after mentions no other protection than Bell Glasses. In the sixth edition of the Complete Gardener in 1717, London and Wise mentions no other more extensive protection ; but Mr. Lawrence in 1723, in the third edition of his *Gentleman's Recreation*, makes mention of Frames, for the purpose of recording an improvement, without alluding to them as a late invention. The improvement he mentions, is having a fixed wire bottom to the frame, which being filled with the earth may be moved to a fresh hot-bed when the heat declines in the first, or whilst any necessary stirring, &c. of the Dung is being performed. Pits of various forms have been invented since. Another improvement for the constant supply of fresh Air to plants in Frames, was by the celebrated Dr. Hales in 1741. on the principal that warm air ascends. A pipe bent in the form of the letter L, is buried in the dung of the bed, with one orifice communicating with the exterior air, the other open in the frame, at the top of the frame a hole is bored with an Augur, the impure heated air is constantly flowing from this, and fresh warmed air is constantly rising through the pipe to supply its place. The next improvement worthy of notice was proposed by Mr. Knight, P. H. S. in 1809. It consists of having the sides of the frame of an equal height all round, and building the bed with the requisite slope, thus presenting every part of the contained plants at an equal distance to the glass.

3 A

Of Forcing Houses, Conservatories and other structures of the kind, we have seen that they were known to the Romans, and in this country in the seventeeth, if not at the close of the sixteenth Century. At first they were merely heated sheds, without windows for the admission of light. In the *French Gardener* Evelyn mentions their being constructed with windows. These structures were rudely heated by burning charcoal in holes made in the floor of the house. This continued as late as the middle of the seventeenth Century. In the first years of the 18th Century regular structures with glass roofs were introduced. Between the middle and close of that century Speechley erected the magnificent Pineries at Welbeck; Aiton and Sir W. Chambers raised the plant stoves at Kew; and Abercrombie, Nicol, Kyle, &c. proportionably contributed to the improvement of such structures. They continued however chance-directed edifices until the commencement of the present century. In 1809 Dr. Anderson and the President of the London Horticultural Society in 1806, roused the attention of Gardeners to the subject; the first by his philosophical reasoning; the latter by the same united to the voice of experience. Mr. Knight directed his remarks chiefly to demonstrate the proper angle for glass roofs of Hot-houses; they gave rise to the patent structures of Stewart, Jordan and others; and these were still farther improved on the firm basis of mathematical demonstration in 1815 by Sir G. Mackenzie, who shewed what is now confirmed by practice, that an hemispherical glass roof admits the most rays of light. This was further advocated by Mr. Loudon in 1817.

Another improvement, also a birth of the present Century, is forming the frames of the houses of Cast Iron instead of Wood. The plan of heating Hot-houses by flues is owing to the Duke of Rutland about 1717. Steam was first employed for the same purpose by Mr. Wakefield of Liverpool in 1788; and more effectually by Mr. Butler, Gardener to the Earl of Derby at Knowle near Liverpool, in 1792. It did not begin to be generally adopted until about 1816; and this appears to be likely to be superceded by employing hot Water, which was first strenuously advocated in 1828, though first proposed and adopted by A. Bacon Esq. of Elcot in Berkshire, in 1821.

The style in which our grounds are usually laid out may be characterized in one sentence. Convenience is endeavoured to be rendered as attractive as possible, by combining it with the beautiful, and appropriate. The convenience of the inmates of the mansion is studied by having the kitchen and fruit Gardens near the house, fully extensive enough to supply all their wants, and kept in the appropriate beauty of order and neatness; without any extravagant attempt at ornament by the mingling of useless trees, or planting its Cabbages, &c. in waving lines. In the Flower Garden which immediately adjoins the house—dry walks, shady ones for Summer, and sheltered, sun-gladdened ones for the more intemperate seasons, are conveniently constructed. Their accompanying borders and parterres, are in forms, such as are most graceful, whilst their inhabitants distinguished for their fragrance are distributed in grateful abundance; and those noted for their elegant forms and beautiful tints, are grouped and blended as the taste of the Painter and the harmony of colours dictate. The Lawn from these glides insensibly into the more distant ground occupied by the Shrubberies, and the Park. Here the genius of the place dictates the arrangement of the levels and of the masses of Trees and Water. Common sense is followed in planting such trees only as are suited to the soil. A knowledge of the Tints of their foliage, guides the Landscape Gardener in associating them, and aids the laws of Perspective in lengthening his distant sweeps. If gentle undulations mark the surface, he leads water among their subdued diversities and blends his trees in softened groups, so as to form light glades to harmonize with the other parts. If high, and broken ground has to be adorned; the designer mingles Water falls with broader masses of darker foliaged trees, and acquires the beauty peculiar to the abrupt and the grand, as in the former he aimed at that which is secured by softer features.

To enter into minute details does not come within the scope of the present work, and therefore for more particulars I must refer to the works of Wheatly, Knight, Repton, Loudon, and others, before mentioned,

From the preceding tables and statements but one inference can be drawn, if we consider them as data whereby to judge of the future prospects of our Art. It is that as far as the strictly practical parts of Gardening are concerned, no mere empirical experience can much improve them. There is no Fruit, no Culinary Vegetable, no Flower or Ornamental Plant, whether exotic or indigenous that cannot be obtained in its most desired state, at any period of the year. I of course do not mean to say that in any Horticultural establishment such perfection is positively and regularly obtained, but that any flower may be obtained in sucession through the year, any fruit or culinary Vegetable in a state of perfection similarly continuously if it is required of a first rate Gardener of the present day; he has the knowledge which would enable him to effect it.† The Gardeners of the present day then have to look for improvement in those Sciences which may guide to a more judicious conducting of their present practices, and to the discovery of new modes of treatment. Of those Sciences Botany in its most comprehensive form, and Chemistry are the chief. Of the importance of Botanical knowledge to the Horticulturist no one can rationally doubt. It is to the researches of Botanists that

---

* This opinion is also that of the President of the Horticultural Society. In a letter now before me he says: "Physiological knowledge can alone now divert the Gardener to improvement! for he possesses all that mere practice is likely to give."

we owe the chief or rather nearly the whole of the Flowers which adorn our Gardens; it is to information first drawn from their discoveries that we are indebted for our numerous varieties of Fruits and Culinary Vegetables; their science is the best system of Mnemonics for retaining the names of the numerous cultivated objects of the Gardener's care; their Science aids him to an enlightened practice, and to an intelligible language. The same observations apply to Chemistry; the nature of Soils, of Manures, of the food and functions of Plants would all be unknown but from the analyses which Chemists have made for the benefit of the Cultivators of the Soil. Without a knowledge of it, many of the gardener's simplest operations must be unintelligible to himself, and consequently be casually performed; for they are learnt by rote or stumbled upon by chance. We know that every plant has a particular temperature in which it thrives best ; a particular modification of food ; a particular degree of moisture; a particular intensity of light; and those particularities vary at different periods of their growth. It is certain that Plants are subject like all organized bodies to various influences. Acids are injurious to some; alkalies to others; the excess of some of their constituents, and the deficiency of others insure disease to the Plants to which such irregularities occur. Disease is accompanied by decay more or less extensive and rapid; and if these cannot be checked by salutary applications and treatment, death ultimately ensues.

Now if it was possible for any Science or Sciences to teach the cultivator of Plants, how to provide for them all the favourable contingencies, all the appropriate necessaries above alluded to, and to protect them from all those which are noxious to them, the art of cultivation would be far advanced to perfection—Now such Sciences are Botany and Chemistry. I do not mean to assert that these Sciences, as at present known are capable of supplying all the desiderata I have alluded to, but they can many of them. Besides, these Sciences have not reached their present state in a day. They are the structures of ages and daily improving. Neither have they been the creations of single minds, but have been gradually raised by many intellectual labourers, from the the time of the Greek Philosophers and Arab Alchemists until now. Let it not be argued that the cultivator of the Soil should wait for others to make discoveries, and that he need only take advantage of them. Who is so well calculated for making discoveries in an Art, as he who is constantly practising it? Should the Physician be ignorant of Pharmacy, and confining himself merely to detect diseases, leave to the Pharmaceutist to prescribe appropriate remedies? As absurd is it to assert that, though Botany and Chemistry are the best aids of Horticulture, the Gardener should leave their application to others.

If it was true, which the preceding parts of this work will demonstrate it is not, that the cultivation of the Soil has not improved during the last two-thousand years, such an argument *ex ignorantiâ* would avail nothing against the possibility of improvement.

No one can argue that Botany has done nothing for the Gardener; the immense and continual increase of the species of Plants cultivated by him—the improved varieties of Mr. Knight and others alone may prevent such an assertion. I am perfectly willing to grant, and lament that facts justify the admission, that Chemistry has not been brought to the illustration and improvement of the agricultural arts so successfully as to the Arts of manufacture. This is chiefly owing to the insensibility of Cultivators, but not entirely so. It partly arises from the great difficulty and intricacy of Vegetable Chemistry. " If the exact connection of effects with their causes, says Kirwan, has not been so fully and extensively traced in this as in other subjects, we must attribute it to the peculiar difficulty of the investigation. In other subjects, exposed to the joint operation of many causes, the effect of each, singly and exclusively taken, may be particularly examined, and the experimenter may work in his laboratory, with the object always in his view; but the secret processes of vegetation take place in the dark, exposed to the various and undeterminable influences of the Atmosphere, and require, at least, half a year for their completion." Such difficulties are only so many powerful reasons for increasing the number of labourers in this field of Science; and when these have gone on collecting observations and facts, some mastermind will arise, in an age perhaps not very distant, and render the whole more luminous, by arranging them in the magic order of System. Science can never supersede the necessity of a practical education for the cultivator; can never supersede the use of the Dunghill, the Plough, the Spade, and the Hoe; but it can be one of their best guides; can be a pilot even to the most experienced.

As proof of what can be effected by a combination of scientific and practical knowledge in the cultivation of the Soil, the example of Lavoisier may be quoted. He was one of the most illustrious Chemists of his day. He cultivated two hundred and forty Acres in La Vendée, for the purpose of demonstrating to his countrymen the importance of sustaining the art of cultivation on scientific principles. In nine years his produce was doubled. His crops afforded one third more than those of ordinary cultivators.

These observations will be rendered daily more and more needless; for the rising generation of Gardeners are really men of Science. The necessity for this was seen during the closing of the last century, and such conviction has effected the reformation. Some persons are still bigots enough to oppose such an improved education for Gardeners, but the intollerant worshippers of Antiquity are gradually becoming silent, if they will not confess to conviction of error. We ought to rejoice to observe the gradual suffusion of education and the mole hills of prejudice, and the multitude of the exclusionists and of the self-sufficient, diminishing in the same ratio. Our Gardens are no longer under the direction of men who retain their profession as unaltered as the New Zealand savages do the religion of their forefathers; with as much bigotry, and as unenlightened.

Our Gardeners are now men of Science, and friends of improvement; the present state of our Horticulture affords us overwhelming testimony of the benefits gained by this revolution. Such a diffusion of Scientific information must become still more general, and every friend of his country will endeavour to promote it. It is the readiest, the most unfailing mentor that can accompany practice; and without it the Cultivators of the Soil will never attain their object—which is the obtaining the best crops of certain plants, at certain times, and at the least possible expense.*

Of the encouragement by public patronage which Gardening receives, and which is necessary to the progress of every Art; Gardening has no reason to complain. The Horticultural Societies of London and Edinburgh, contain among their members a large proportion of the Talent of both countries; but it is not alone among the sons of Genius that the Art finds friends; for the wealth and the aristocracy of the country afford their equally powerful aid for its encouragement. Garden produce is now part of the necessaries of life; consequently a garden, is one of the first required appendages to the Cottage, as well as to the Palace. Less than two centuries ago neither vegeta-

* In the above I have paraphrased and quoted from some of my writings in the Gardener's Magazine, v. iii. 130. v. v. 130. &c.

is new part of the necessaries of life; consequently a Garden is one of the first required appendages to the Cottage as well as to the Palace. Less than two Centuries ago neither Vegetables or Fruits were much sought after. Gross animal food was the sustenance of the lower Classes, and choicer kinds of it formed the repasts of the higher members of the community. In the old Household Books of great families, Fruits are rarely mentioned, Culinary Vegetables still more seldom; but now Bread and Vegetables form a chief part of a poor man's diet; as the latter are among the choicest dishes at the tables of the wealthy, and in the desserts which close their feasts they are emulous to excel. Flowers are equally highly prized and sought after, among the most generous of their fosterers stand pre-eminent our fair countrywomen.

Such are the encouraging auspices under which Gardening is now flourishing, and such are the equally bright promises of its future progress. Some persons, without sufficient consideration, have expressed their opinion that it is now as perfect as any Art can be, and therefore like all other human institutions it must now decline, since in them decay commences as soon as improvement ceases. That the History of the Arts and Sciences warrants the conclusion that they never stand still, but are ever on the advance or decline, I cannot deny, but I do deny that Gardening is capable of no further improvement. This I have already pointed out, and until the Vegetable Tribes of other climes are no longer capable of furnishing any thing new, and until the researches of the Chemist and Phisiologist are perfect, Horticulture has yet better things to hope for, and aim at. A second class of despondents are those who in the general diffusion of knowledge and liberal principles, see nothing but threatened convulsions and revolutions, the ruin of the Arts, the destruction of social order, if not the conclusion of Time. Such persons are opposed to education being imparted to Gardeners.

I have already expressed my opinion upon the benefits likely to accrue from our Gardeners being men of scientific acquirements, and see no necessity to revert to particulars. I would however observe generally that as human knowledge on which our institutions are founded must continue to improve, or must deteriorate, few persons will be found to argue that the latter is desirable—Let us improve as long as we can. Those who in a diffusion of knowledge see our social order endangered argue perversely. Whilst education is partial, those blessed with it may be proud of their distinction, and obtain undue notions and power by their superiority, but when education becomes general such distinction must cease.

He is no philosopher who neglects a certain present good, for fear that in some future period it may be abused; but in the encouragement of Gardening whilst an immediate good is obtained, there is no fear of its perversion in after days. Its diffusion among the poorer classes is an earnest, or means of more important benefits, even than the present increase of their comfort. The labourer who possesses and delights in the garden appended to his Cottage is generally among the most decent of his class; he is seldom a frequenter of the ale-house; and there are few among them so senseless as not readily to engage in its cultivation when convinced of the comforts and gain derivable from it. When the lower order of a state are contented, the abettors of anarchy cabal for the destruction of its civil tranquility in vain, for they have to efface the strongest of all earthly associations, home and its hallowed accompaniments, from the attachment of the labourer, before he will assist in tearing them from others, in the struggle to effect which, he has nothing definite to gain, and all those flowers of life to lose.

The same reasoning applies with undiminished force to the higher classes.—Every thing that tends to endear to a man his home, attaches him with proportionate force to his country that contains it.

Gardening is a pursuit adapted alike to the gay and the recluse, the man of pleasure, and the lover of science. To both it offers employment such as may suit their taste, all that can please by fragrance, by flavour, or by beauty; all that Science may illustrate; employment for the Chemist, the Botanist, the Physiologist, and the Meteorologist. There is no taste so perverse as that from it the Garden can win no attention, or to which it can afford no pleasure. He who greatly benefitted or promoted the happiness of mankind in the days of Paganism was invoked after death and worshipped as a deity; in these days we should be as grateful as they were without being as extravagant in its demonstration; and if so we should indeed highly estimate those who have been the improvers of our Horticulture, for as Socrates says " it is the source of health, strength, plenty, riches, and of a thousand sober delights, and honest pleasures" " It is the purest of human pleasures" says our own Verulam. It is amid its scenes and pursuits that "life flows pure, the heart more calmly beats."

THE END.

White, Printer, Eye.

INDEX.

A

	PAGE
Abdalonimus.	1
Abercrombie (J.)	219
Acanthus	87
Acacia	326
Academy of Gardeners	134
Academus	7
Acer	326
"Acetaria"	107
"Account of some experiments on the Barking of Fruit Trees"	289
"Account of the Gooseberry shews"	326
"Account of the Emperor of China's Gardens"	205
Account of Mr. Cowell's Aloe	188, 198
Aconite	87, 151
"Account of a Stone producing Mushrooms"	209
"Adam armed"	267
"Adam's Luxury and Eve's Cookery"	203
Addison, (J)	260
Adonis	7, 87
African Bulbous Plants	312
Agave Americana	314

	PAGE
Aged Fruit Trees	319
Agricola	35
Agriculture	31
Aiton, R. T.	298, 307, 315
Aiton, W. T.	298
Alcinous	6
Alexandrian Ciotat Grape	311
Allen, (T.)	321
Almond	3, 17, 55, 92, 339
Alisander	88, 182, 352
Aloe	4, 188, 326
Alpine Strawberry	287, 317, 325
Alpine Plants	288
Amaryllis Psittacinâ Johnsoni	318
Amaryllis	315, 318, 319
Amaryllis Longifolia	307
Amaranthus	87, 131
Amelanshier	339
America	66
American Fruits	322
American Plants	131
American Cranbury	286, 315
"American Gardener"	310
"American Physician"	110
Amos, W.	28
Anatolius	8
"Ananas, or a Treatise on the Pine Apple"	226
"Anastatius"	304
Anderson, D.	313
Anderson, W.	298
Anderson, G.	298, 299
Andilly, R. A. d'	107
Andromeda	326

	PAGE
Anemonies	84, 87, 314, 359
Angelica	68, 90, 179, 357
Anne, Queen,	139, 145, 360
Annise	68, 72, 170, 357
"Anecdotes of Painting in England"	241
Aphis Lanigera	297, 306
Apiarium	113
"Apopiroscopy"	158
Apple, 4, 6, 7, 16, 17, 33, 35, 40, 55, 92, 74, 126,	129
133, 180, 273, 286, 287, 288, 293, 296, 299,	302
303, 308, 309, 311, 313, 314, 317, 322, 323,	324
327, 345,	
"Appendix to the Botanical Magazine and Register"	311
"Approved Experiments touching Fish and Fruit"	77
Apples, to preserve	291
Apricot, 17, 55, 57, 92, 129, 136, 180, 295, 297,	310
318, 339	
Aquatics	306, 314
Arachis Hypogea,	318
Arboriculture	164
"Arborum Plantatione"	46
Arbutus	92
Archer, C.	257
"Architectural Sketches"	282
Arctostophylos	339
Argyle, Duke of	16
Aviaries	
Arkwright, R.	307
"Arnold's Chronicle"	47
Arpinum	21
"Art and manner how to Graft and Plant"	69
"Art of Planting the Vine"	236
"Art of Gardening"	252

	PAGE
"Art of promoting the growth of the Cucumber and Melon"	315, 327
"Art of Making Cider"	116
"Art's Improvements"	156
"Art's Mistress"	94
Artichoke	68, 72, 89, 90, 131, 352
Asarabacca	99
Ashmole, Elias	99
Asparagus	13, 68, 72, 89, 138, 291, 297, 300, 302, 318, 319, 322, 324, 325, 351.
Asphodel	87
Association of Plants	74
Astley, F. D.	257
Atkinson, Wm.	317, 319
Auricula	87, 213, 289, 293, 324, 358
Aurora	7
Austen, Francis	93
Austen, Ralph	96
Avallonia	23
Ayres, R.	313
Ayrshire Rose	314
Azalea	325
Azalea indica.	296

B

Babylon, Hanging Gardens of,	4
Bacon, Lord	65, 140
Bagot, Lord	306
Baldwin, T.	301, 311
Balfour, W.	219
Balsam	307
Balsam Apple	87

	PAGE
Balm	68, 90, 179, 358
Bank for Alpine Plants	288
Banks, Sir J.	285, 286, 287, 288, 292, 297, 306
Banquetting Rooms	143
Banyan Tree	318
Barberry	55, 92, 181, 340, 326
Barnet, J.	321
Barnet, P.	291, 302
Barren Wort	87
Barton, T.	302
Basil	[13, 72, 89, 178, 179, 308, 350
Batchelor's Buttons	68, 84
Bauman, J.	414
Baxter, W.	309
Bay	92
Bay Cherry, Laurel	84
Beacon's Field	143
Bear's foot	90
Bear Ears	84
Beale, Dr. John	101
Beans	8, 13, 90, 153, 182, 348
Beattie, W.	291, 302
"Beauties of Flora displayed"	328
"Beauties of Stowe"	205
Becket House	143
Bedford, Lucy Countess of	145
Bee	302
"Bee, The"	237
Beets	13, 68, 72, 89, 178, 179, 308, 359
Belvoir Castle	152
Bell flower	84
Bell Glasses	89, 361
Bellingham, C.	70

	PAGE
Betula	326
Bickman, G.	205
Biggs, A.	286
Biguomia	326
Billingsly, S.	115
Billington, W.	321
Bird Cherry	341
Bishop, T.	293, 302
Bisset, A.	325
Black Eagle Cherry	297
Blackening Walls	323
Bladder Campion	352
Bladder Nut	93
Blagrave, Samuel.	115
Blaikie, F	301
Blake, Stephen.	110
Blake, T.	314
Blenheim	125, 146, 233, 265, 268
Blessed Thistle	68, 92
Blight	181, 273, 293, 297
Bliss, G.	316
Blite	89, 179
"Blood of the Grapes"	98
Blood wort	89
Blossom Buds, transplanting	295
Blue Insect	291
Blue Bottle	87
"Boke of Husbandry"	47
"Boke of Surveying, &c."	48
"Booke of Regarde"	51
Balfours	63
Bollar, Nicholas.	46
Bonfeil, J.	78

	PAGE
Boothby, Sir B.	298
Borage	68, 87, 89, 179
Borderings	83
Borecole	178, 182
Botany its benefit to Gardening	62, 147, 364
Botanic Gardens	62, 63
"Botanic Garden"	241, 330
Botanists at the Close of the 17th Century	148
"Botanical Tracts"	209
"Botanists and Gardeners new Dictionary"	217
"Botanical Dictionary"	232
"Botanical Magazine"	155, 245, 284, 311, 329
"Botanical Cabinet"	330
"Botanist's Companion"	273
"Botanist's Repository"	274
"Botanical Miscellany"	284
"Botanical Register"	330
Boutcher, W.	234
Bowers, J.	320
Box	23, 82, 93
Braddick, J.	298, 317, 318
Bradberry, W.	315
Bradley, Richard	154, 182
Bramble	347
Bransby, J.	316
Brassica	178, 316, 347
Bray, John.	46
Breese, J.	317
Bridgeman,———.	261
"Brief Discoveries," &c.	95
Brithnod	39
"British Flower Garden"	330
"British Fruit Garden"	222

	PAGE
"British Housewife and Gardener's Companion"	188
"British Gardener's Director"	206
Brocoli	178, 181, 287, 299, 302, 307
Brompton Nursery	116, 123
Brooks, S.	315
Brookshaw, G.	294
Brooklime	353
Broom	88
Browne, R.	248
Brown, L.	265
Brown, J.	299
Brown, Sir T.	103, 132
Brown Apple of Burntisland	303
Brulles, —,	250
Brunsvigia	312
Brussel's Sprouts	307
Bryant, C,	248
Buck, W.	315
Bucknall, T. D.	257
Budding (see *Inoculation*)	
Bugloss	68, 72, 87, 89, 179
"Bulbous Roots flowering in water bottles"	195
Bulbous-rooted Violet	86
Bull, W.	324
Bullace	55
Bulleyn, William,	51, 56
"Bulwarke of Defence,"	53
Burch, J.	314
Burleigh, Lord,	141
Burleigh House	268
Burn, H.	321
Burnet	90, 353
Burr-knot Apple	287, 291

C

	PAGE
Cabbages, 13, 72, 88, 89, 131, 182, 178,	321
Cactus Opuntia	298
Call, M.	314
"Calendarum universale,"	187
Caledonian Horticultural Society,	337
Calcoensis, Henry	46
Caligula's Nest	22
Camellia Japonica,	325
"Camellia Britannica,"	325
Camphor,	4
Campions,	68
Cambridge Botanic Garden,	151
Campanula,	87
Canada Potatoes,	90
Candolle, A. P. de.	316
Candy tuft,	88
Canker,	291, 192
"Capilarium de villis,"	40
Caprification,	40
Campsicum,	358
Carduus benedictus,	179
Carlisle, A.	295, 297
Carlisle Codlin,	292
Carse of Gowrie Orchards,	292
Carr, J.	324
Carrots, 13, 33, 72, 88, 90, 314, 317,	349
Carrot-Worms,	291
Carob,	341
Caracalla's Garden,	26
Carnations, 68, 85, 86, 111, 132, 289, 293, 305,	359
Carpenter, —.	190
Carter, D.	227
"Caractacus,"	235
Carraway,	90, 179, 357
Cashiobury,	136, 141, 143

3 D

	PAGE
Castle Howard,	146
Castel, Robert	195
Castle-hill,	268
Casuarina,	308
Cassidony,	90
"Catalogue of Trees, &c."	195
"——— Seeds, &c."	187
"——— Trees and Shrubs,"	202
"——— Hot-house and other Plants,"	205
"——— Seeds and Roots,"	205
"——— Plants, &c."	217
"——— Green-house Plants, &c."	232
"——— Trees, Shrubs, &c."	232
"——— Plants in the Garden of J. Blackbourne, esq."	238
"——— Fruit Trees,"	290
"——— Lodiges and Son's Plants,"	235
"——— Fruits in the Chiswick Garden," 327,	332
"——— British Medical and other Plants,"	245
"Catalogus Plantarum Angliœ,"	148
"——— Plantarum officinalium in Chelseiano,"	195
"——— Arborum Fructicumque,"	199
"——— Arborum, &c."	76
Caterpillars,	87
Cato,	13
Cattley, Wm.	313
Cauliflower, . 89, 131, 153, 291, 318,	324
Can-flues,	292
Caville rouge de micoud Apple,	322
Cedar, 4,	323
Celer,	26
Celery, 302, 306,	353
Celeriac, 181, 306,	323
Celandine,	90
"Certain Miscellany Tracts in Scripture of Gardens,"	103
Ceres,	7

	PAGE.
Chamber, Sir W.	211
Chamomile,	87, 90, 179, 357
Chandler & Buckingham,	325
Change of Seed,	175
Chardon,	90, 181, 352
Charles 1st.	134, 142, 359
Charles 2nd.	108, 112, 120, 135, 142, 359
Charter of the Gardener's Company	133
Chapman, R.	311
Chatsworth,	143
Chelsea Garden,	63, 64, 150, 304
Cherries,	17, 35, 40, 55, 50, 57, 92, 129, 136, 180, 293, 297, 298, 299, 302, 308, 312, 314, 327, 340
Chesnuts,	17, 55, 74, 92, 111, 286, 287, 340
Chervill,	72, 80, 182, 384
Chemistry applied to Horticulture,	150, 305
Chicory,	324
Child, R.	97
Chinese Horticulture,	313, 316
Chinese Roses	318
Chiswick Garden,	321, 322, 327
Chivalry,	41
Chives,	351
Christianity, its Introduction,	36
Christie, W.	311, 314
Christmas Flower,	84, 151
Christ's Thorn,	93
Chrysanthemum,	313, 314, 115, 317, 319, 322
Churchy, G.	77
Chuz,	6
Cicero,	21
Cinnamon	4
Cis Chervill,	89
Cistus,	88
"Cistineæ,"	330

Citizen's Gardens,	26, 41
Citron,	17, 299
Citrus genus,	309, 313, 325
"City Gardener,"	191
Clare, J.	323
Clair Voye'es	144
Claret Grape, Wine from its leaves,	296
Clarke, G.	158
Clary,	89, 355
Clady Paint,	291
"Clergyman's Recreation,"	156
Clematis,	88, 326
Climate, as influencing Horticulture,	321
Cobbet, W.	310
Cobham, Lord	264
Coburgia,	312
Cockburn, G.	318
Cock's Comb,	313
Cockle Strewer,	143
Cole,	72
Cole-wort,	13, 72, 89
Columella,	13
Columbkill,	37
Columbine,	68, 84, 87
Collins Samuel	190
Collyns, W.	327
"Collection of Husbandry," &c.	117
Commerce,	43, 66
"Complete Husbandry, &c."	97
" ———— Gardener's Practice,"	110
" ———— Vineyard,"	110, 115
" ———— Gardener,"	117, 125
" ———— Planter and Ciderdist,"	122
" ———— Body of Husbandry,"	188, 208
" ———— Modern Husbandry,"	201

	PAGE.
"Complete Seedsman's Monthly Calendar,"	202
" ———— Florist,"	204
" ———— Body of Planting and Gardening,"	214
" ———— Farmer,"	218
" ———— Forcing Gardener,"	222
" ———— Wall-tree Pruner,"	223
" ———— Kitchen Gardener,"	223
" ———— Dictionary of Practical Gardening,"	282
Compton, Bishop Henry 137, 202, 204,	348
"Compendious method of raising Italian Brocoli, &c."	181
"Composition des Paysages,"	267
"Comparative view of Curvilinear & other Hot houses,"	279
Composts, 283, 292,	293
"Concerning the effects of English Husbandry,"	97
"Concise and Practical Treastise on the Culture of the Carnation, &c."	289
"Connection between the leaves and fruit,"	297
" ———— of certain parts of a Tree with the Fruit,"	102
"Construction of Timber, &c."	200
Conservatory,	324
Constantinople Plants,	321
Convolvolus,	87
Cooke, Moses 115,	136
Cooper, J.	323
Cooper, B.	323
Cornet plums,	55
Cornell, 84, 92,	341
Coriander, 72, 179,	357
Costmary, 89, 90, 179,	356
"Cottager's Companion,	274
"Cottage Economy and Mansion Economy,"	320
Cotton, Charles	55
Cotton Thistle,	353
"Country Housewife,"	205
" ———— Gentleman's Companion,"	182

"Country Gentleman's and Farmer's Director,"	187
"———————— vade mecum,"	190
"Countryman's Jewel,"	69
"Country Housewife's Garden,"	79
"Countryman's Recreation,"	94, 98
Coventry, Francis	205
Coverings for frames,	308
Cowell, John	198
Cowley, Abm.	148
Cowley, —.	122
Cowslip,	84, 87
Crab,	345
Cranes Bill,	87
Cratœgus,	326
Cranbury,	315, 318, 344
Crawford, W.	293
Cress,	72, 90, 353
Cresinus, C. F.	14
Crighton, D.	293
Crinum Amabille,	314
Crocus,	84, 87
Crowberry,	342
Crown Imperial,	84, 86
Cromwell, Thomas, Lord	57
Cromwell, Oliver	135, 142, 359
Cucumber,	3, 13, 14, 54, 72, 89, 90, 153, 177, 200, 253, 298, 307, 314, 315, 321, 323
Cuckow-flower,	88
Culinary Vegetables,	13, 56, 88, 90, 347
"Cultu Hortorum Carmen,"	114
"Culture of Forests,"	248
Cullum, T. G.	313
Cullum, Sir D.	122
Cummingham, Dr. R.	292
Cummin,	72
Curtis, W.	244, 329

Curtis, S.	321, 329
Curl,	290, 296
"Curious and Profitable Gardener,"	198
"——— experiments in Gardening,"	203
"Curiosities of Art and Nature, &c."	128
Currants, 17, 56, 92, 181, 291, 306,	325, 346
Currant Wine,	291
Cushing, J.	284
Custard Apple,	339
Cyclamen,	84, 87
Cypress,	7, 92
Cyrus,	4

D

Daffodils,	84, 86
Dahlia, 286, 287, 308,	314, 359
Daisies,	85, 87
"Daily Assistant in English Gardening,"	223
Damascene or Damson,	55, 345
Damask Rose,	57
Danes,	38
Danby, Earl of	63
Dandelion,	353
Daniel, J. F.	321
Dawes, H.	308
Darwin, E.	241
Date,	342
Davy, Sir H.	336
De Lille, J.	230
Deck, J.	324
Democritus,	8
"Dendrologia, a Treatise on forest Trees,"	327
"Description of a Patent Hot-house,"	237
"——— certain methods of Planting, &c.	247
"——— eleven thousand Plants,"	249
"Designs for Parsonage Houses,"	327
"——— for Chinese Buildings, &c."	211
"Design for Plenty,"	97
Destruction of Rome,	29

	PAGE
Dethycke, H.	67
Devonshire, Exotics in	287
"Dialogue on the distinct Characters of the Picturesque, &c.	254
"———— upon the Gardens of Lord Cobham,"	205
Dick, J.	302
Dicks, J.	320
Dickson, A.	322
Dickson, J. 285, 290, 299, 306, 320,	337
Dickson, R. B.	282
Dickson and Co,	205
"Dictionarum Botanicum,"	186
"———— Rusticum,"	127
"Dictionary of all sorts of Country Affairs, &c."	127
"———— of the Ornamental Trees, &c. in Gt. Britain,"	243
Dill, 68, 72, 90, 179,	354
"Different modes of cultivating the Pine Apple,"	279
Diosma,	326
"Directions of certain methods of Planting, &c."	247
"———— for the culture of Crambe Maritima,"	245
"———— for cultivating Vines in America,"	205
"Discourse of Husbandry used in Brabant, &c."	95
"Discourses concerning the growth of Plants,"	188
"Discourse on the History of Trade and Navigation,"	106
"Dissertation on the true Cytisus, &c."	182
"———— on Cyder, &c."	198
"———— on the growth of Wine in England,"	248
"———— on Oriental Gardening,"	212
"Distinguishing properties of a fine Auricula,"	213
Deseases of Trees, &c. 91, 302, 308, 317, 321,	322
Dittany,	7
Dodoens Rembert,	53
Dog's Grass,	7
——— Tooth Voilet,	87
"Domestic Gardener's Manual,"	328

		PAGE.
Donaldson, —.		122
Dan, G.	291,	319
Double Flowers,	86, 209,	322
———— Blossomed Cherry,		88
Apple,		88
Peach,		88
Dow, Rev. A.	290,	325
Downton Hall,	253,	271
———— Imperatrice Plum,		319
———— Strawberry,	318,	319
———— Pippin,		287
Doyenne Pear,		288
Dragons,		90
"Draughts for Gardeners,"		78
Drope, Francis		115
Druids,		32
Drummond, J.	307,	318
Ducket, Thos.		103
Dufresnoy,		260
Duff, C.		322
Duhilhier, N. F.	122,	152
Dunbar, J.		206
Duncan, Dr. senr.	291, 292, 312,	325
Dung-heat,		299
Dunstable Monastery Gardens,		40
"Dutch Garden,"		130
"———— Horticulture,"		132
"———— Florist,"	213,	217
Dwarf Fruit Trees,		135
Dyvers Soyls for Manuring,		

E

Earthenware Flues,	290
East Indies,	66
East Lothian, Exotics in,	325

	PAGE.
East Lothian Orchards,	292
Eastern Nations,	10
"Eden, or a Complete body of Gardening,"	208
Edger Hall,	124, 146
Edgings,	83
Edinburgh Botanic Garden,	63
Edward the 3rd.	45
——— the 6th.	359
Effects of high Temperatures,	309
Egg Plant,	358
Egyptian Melon,	324
Eighteenth Century,	147
Elder,	357
Elecampane,	179, 357
"Elemènts of Agricultural Chemistry,"	336
"——————— Agriculture,"	196
"——————— Modern Gardening,"	244
"Elfrida,"	235
Elizabeth, Queen	132, 133, 141
Elliot, R.	292, 302
Ellis, Wm.	201
———, T.	236
Elruge Mectarine,	320
Elton Pear,	295
——— Cherry,	297
Ely, its Wine,	39
Emmerton, I.	293
Emmerich, A.	248
"Encyclopædia of Gardening,"	279
Endine,	13, 68, 72, 89, 321, 353
Eucalyptus,	326
"England's happiness increased,"	113
"——————— Improvement,"	108
"English Improver improved,"	96
"——————— Vineyard,"	105, 112

'English Seed of some Plants, best,"	88
"―― Herbal, &c."	130
"―― Botany,"	249
"―― Garden,"	235
"―― Gardener,"	117
―― Gardening, passim,"	31
―― Flora,	148
"―― Husbandman,"	79
"Engravings of Heath's,"	274
"Enrichments of the Weald of Kent,"	79
Envil,	237, 268
Epicurus,	8
Epigram,	208
"Epistle to Richard Boyle,"	260
"Epitome of Husbandry,"	115
Ericœ,	325, 326, 359
Eriobotrya,	342
Ermenonville,	243
Esculents,	324, 347
Esher,	233, 264
Espalier,	26
―― Rails,	293
Esperione Grape,	307
"Essay on the Elements of Architecture,"	80
"―― on Timber Trees,	96
"―― on the 1st Book of Lucretius,"	105
"―― concerning the best methods of Pruning,"	200
"―― on Planting,"	214
"―― on the theory of Agriculture,"	217
"―― on the natural situations of Gardens,"	236
"―― on design in Gardening,"	229
"―― on Landscapes,"	243
"―― on Gardening,"	251
"―― on the Picturesque,"	254
"―― on Imagination,"	260

	PAGE.
"Essay on Packing Plants,"	274
"——— on the culture of the Proteœ,"	282
"——— on the weeds of Agriculture,"	294
"——— on the uses of Salt as a Manure,"	305
"——— on Coral,"	113
"——— on Harmony,"	202
"Essays on Landscape Gardening,"	320
"——— on Husbandry,"	117
"——— on Agriculture,"	216
"Essay on the preservation of the health of Agriculturists, &c."	244
Euphoria,	342
Eve Apple,	302
Evelyn, Charles	190
———, John 65, 103, 112, 136,	154
"Every Man his own Gardener,"	222
Exotics in Devonshire,	287
———, 131, 133, 151,	359
"Exotic Flora,"	284
"——— Gardener,"	284
"Expert Gardener,"	95
"Experiments and Observations on Vegetation, &c."	102
"Experimental Husbandman and Gardener,"	188
Exton Hall,	146
Eyre, —.	202

F

Fairchild, Thos.	191,	199
Fairweather, J.		300
Falconer, W.		243
Fallowing,	188,	191
"Family Dictionary,"		186
Family Genius,		104
"Farmer's Instructor,"		202

	PAGE.
"Farewell to Husbandry,"	79
Faulderman, F.	323
Featherfew,	87, 90
Felton, S.	245
Fennel,	13, 68, 78, 89
Fennugreek,	179
Fern,	308
Ferme ornee,	264
"Few minutes advice to Gentlemen of landed Property,"	256
Feudal System,	58
Field, H.	304
Fig, 3, 4, 6, 16, 17, 40, 56, 92, 126, 181, 298, 302, 306, 308, 309, 312, 313, 314, 315, 317, 318, 319, 322, 342	
"Figures of Plants,"	196
" ——— English Fungi,"	250
Filberts, 17, 55, 92, 131, 181, 312, 318,	341
Finochio,	181
"Finibus Virtutis Christianæ,"	110
First Suggester of Landscape Gardening,	250
Fischer, F. E. L.	300
Fitzherbert, Sir A.	48
"Five hundred points of good Husbandry,"	50, 55
Flanagan, P.	312, 316
Flat Peach of China,	317
Flax,	287, 361
Flea-berries,	92
Fleetwood, Wm.	127
Flemish Worsted Manufacturers,	132
"Flora, Ceres, and Pomona,"	171
"Flora Conspicua,"	320
" ——— Australasica,"	330
" ——— Domestica,"	305
" ——— Historica,"	305

	PAGE.
" Flora Londinensis,"	245
"—— Diœtetica,"	243
"—— Rustica,"	277
" Flora's Paradise beautified,"	75
"Florists' Manual,"	282
"—— Directory,"	251
"—— Delight,"	250
"—— Feast,"	132
"—— Vade mecum,"	119
"—— Guide and Cultivator's Directory,"	330
Florence Cherry,	298
Floriculture,	85, 132, 359
Floy, M.	323
" Flower Garden,"	83, 111
"—— displayed,"	201
"—— for Ladies' and Gentlemen,"	200
Flower amoure,	68
"—— Petilius,	68
"—— Gentle,	84
Flowers,	359
Fonthill,	268
Forcing, 14, 18, 119, 152, 257, 286, 287, 288,	296,
299, 300, 311, 313, 323, 361	
" Forcer's Assistant,"	290
"Forester's Guide,"	304
Forester, A.	324
Forest Laws,	42
"—— Pruner,"	276
Forsythe, W.	250 273
Fora Holitorum,	11
Forms of Stoves for Forcing Houses,	257
" Foure Bookes of Husbandrie,"	71
" Four Books of Plants,"	148
Foulk, W.	321

		PAGE.
Fountains,	4, 24, 82,	166
Fowler, —.		153
Fox Glove,		87
Frames,	287, 307,	361
Frankincense,		4
Frankland, Sir T.		312
"Fragments on the theory and practice of Landscape Gardening,"		256
Fraxinus,		326
"French Gardener,"		105
——— Gardening,		138
——— Horticultural Writers,		288
Fresh Vegetable Manure,		297
Frost, its effects,		323
——— Injury to Blossom prevented,		181
"Fruit Gardener,"		227
Fruit Garden,	15, 92, 74, 111,	180
Fruit Trees, in Pots		314
" ——— Grower's Instructor,"		316
" ——— Walls Improved,"		122
" ——— Garden Kalander,"		156
Fruit Room,		296
Fruits' in Jacob's time,		3
" ——— of the Romans,"		17
" ——— for every Month,"		200
——— New and Early to produce,		285
"Fruiterers' Secrets,"		77
Fructiculture, 16, 75, 91, 180, 302, 306, 314, 315, 316, 318, 321, 222, 323, 324		
"Frugum Historia,"		54
Fulham Palace,		57
——— Nursery,		202
——— Gardens,	137,	204
Fuller, —.		296

	PAGE.
Fulmer, S.	242
"Fumifugium,"	105
Fumigating,	321
Furber, Robert	199, 200
Fuschia,	323
Future Progress of Gardening,	364
Gandon, James	158
"Gardens, The,"	257
———— of Cyrus	102
———— of the Greeks and their Gardening,	6, 7, 8
"Garden, or art of laying out Grounds,"	230
"———— Mushroom, its culture,"	222
———— Geta's,	26
———— Pots,	309
"———— of Epicurus,"	121
"———— of Eden,"	70
———— Architecture,	24, 167
———— Statuary,	24, 167
———— Designers,	24, 146
———— Buildings, Ornamental,	143
———— Produce, now in request,	368
Gardenia,	326
Gardiner, James	190
Garnier, T.	315
Garlic,	3, 17, 72, 89, 90, 351
Garrick, David	208
Garton, J.	230
Gardeners at the present time,	368
"———— and Planters Kalendar,"	231, 232
"———— Magazine,"	330
"———— Pocket Kalendar,"	232, 236, 396
"———— Alphabetical Kalendar,"	232
"———— Kitchen Garden,"	77

	PAGE
" Gardener's Remembrancer"	253
" ———— Pocket Dictionary"	223
" ———— Vade Mecum"	223
" ———— Pocket Journal"	224
" ———— Catalogue of Hardy Trees, &c."	215
" ———— Pocket Book"	209
" ———— New Kalendar"	209, 214
" ———— Universal Kalendar"	196
" ———— Kalendar"	196, 275
" ———— and Florist's Dictionary"	151, 193, 194, 196
" ———— Almanack"	119
" ———— Labyrinth"	66, 67
———— Company	133, 134, 217
Gaultheria	343
" Gentle Gardener"	127
Gelder Rose	88
" General Report, &c. of Scotland,"	290
" ———— Treatise on Gardening"	239
" ———— Advertisement concerning Cider"	102
" Generatione Arborum, &c."	46
Gentian	87
" Gentleman Gardener's Director"	204
" ———— Farmer"	196
" ———— Gardener Instructed	190
" ———— and Gardener's Kalendar	187
" ———— Recreation"	156
" ———— and Farmer's Architect"	224
" General Treatise of Husbandry"	185, 187
" ———— Natural History"	207
Gendre, ———	103
George the First	360
———— Second	360
———— Third	360
Gerarde, John	62, 75
Germander	83

	PAGE
"Geraniaceæ"	330
Gibson, J.	122
Gibb, J.	291
Gibbs, W.	293
Gidde, W.	78
Gifford, Humphrey	67
Gilbert, Samuel	119
Giles, J.	228
Gilliflower	68, 84, 86, 87, 90, 132
Gilpin, W.	227, 268
Ginger	322
Girardin	267
Gladiolus	67
Glass	15, 89
Glastonbury Thorn	196
"Gleanings on Gardens"	245
Gloriosa superba	306
Glycosmis	342
Glycine Sinensis	323
Goat's Beard	87, 90
Goldilocks	87
Golden Pippin	345
Goodricke, Sir H.	307
Gooseberry	17, 55, 72, 92, 131, 181, 283, 291, 297, 302, 313, 316, 325, 346, 326
Gooseberry Caterpillar	291, 292
Googe, Barnaby	77
"Good Housewife's Hand-mayde"	68
Gorhambury	132
Gorrie, A.	298, 302, 323
Goss, J.	317
"Government of Cattle"	69
Gower, J. R.	308, 315, 318, 319
Grafting	8, 16, 74, 91, 119, 180, 288, 317, 318, 319, 360
Granadilla	311, 344

Grapes	55, 57, 92, 126, 136, 286, 295, 296, 299, 306, 311, 312, 315, 319, 321, 322, 347
Gray, Christopher	202
"Great Improvements of Commons, &c."	200
Green Fly	152, 321
———— Gage	345
———— Houses	291
Greenwich Palace	141, 142
Grindal, Bishop of London	57
Griffin, W.	282, 312
Grœffer, J.	248
Groshede, Bishop of Lincoln	47
Ground Onion	292
"Grove Hill"	242
Guava	345
Gubbins, ——	262
Guernsey, Plants at	292
Gyllenborg	216
Gypsum	232

H

Haddington, Earl of	216
Hadrian's Garden	26
Hafod	268
Hagley	233, 237, 266, 268
Haines, R.	55
Hall, J.	95
Hallet, R.	351
Hales, Dr.	361
"Half-a-dozen Hints on Picturesque Architecture"	327
Ham	6
—— House	144
Hampton Court	142, 143, 144, 146, 295
Hanbury, W.	214

	PAGE
Hand-glasses	89, 361
Harrison, C.	306, 312, 315, 322, 323
Hare, T.	298
Harte, W.	213
Hartlib, Samuel	93, 95, 96
Hardy Plants	359
Hastening Fruitfulness	291
Hatfield House	141
Hawkins, A.	287, 295, 314
Hawkins, Sir C.	296
Hawarth, A. H.	252, 287
Hawthorn	84, 91, 341
Hay, A.	293
Hay, J.	324
Haynes, T.	283
Haythorn, J.	323
Hayward, J.	287, 301, 314
Heart's Ease	68
Heaths	274
"Heathery, or Monograph of the Genus Erica"	274
"Heat and Cold of Hot-houses"	210
Hedges, W.	300, 307
Hedge-row Trees	3, 84, 174
Hedychium	323
Heeley, J.	237
Hellebore	87
Hempel, G. C. L.	300
Henderson, J.	292
Henderson, W.	291, 324, 325
Henry the Eighth	55, 57, 359
Hentzner	59
Hepburn, Baron	292
Hepatica	84, 87
"Herbarium Synonyma"	47
"Herbarium Belgicum"	54

Herb Fluellin	68
—— Grace	68
—— Mastick	179
—— Sticas	68, 179
Herbert, W.	307, 311, 312, 313, 318
"Hereford Orchards"	101, 189
Heresbach, Conrad	70
"Heroic Epistle to Sir W. Chambers"	213
"Heroic Postscript"	213
Hesiod	9
Hesperides	7
Hill, or Hyll, T,	68
——, Aaron	205
——, Sir J.	207
——, D.	288
"Hints to Planters"	257
"Hints for the Management of Hot-beds"	250
" —— to the Proprietors of Orchards"	274
" —— on the Formation of Gardens"	278
"History of Cultivated Vegetables"	305
" —— of Gustavus Adolphus"	218
" —— of Gardening"	161
" —— of the propagation and improvement of Vegetables	110
"Historical Description of White Knights"	304
" —— View of the Taste for Gardening"	214
"Historia Plantarum Succulentarum	183
Hitt, T.	209
Hogg, T.	289, 297, 314
Hogan, W.	318
Holland	132, 136
Holland House	141
—— its Gardening	56, 153
——, Mrs.	304
Holford, C.	319
Hollow Root	87

	PAGE
Hollihock	85, 87
Holden, R.	312
Homer	6
Honesty	87
Honeysuckles	84, 88
Hooker, W. J.	283, 298, 299, 309, 329
Hope, ——	304
Hops	67, 72, 188, 352
Horse-radish	72, 90, 287, 318, 354
Horman, William	46
Horticulture its Origin and Progress	2, 258, 359
Horticultural Society of London	193, 270, 273, 320, 331
————Edinburgh	270
————Science and System	299
" ————Repository "	205
————Tour	57
" Hortus Siccus Britannicus"	286
" ————Anglicanus"	315
" ————Britannicus"	303
" ————Gramineus Woburnensis"	294
" ————Uptonensis"	242
" ————Ericæus Woburnensis	294
" ————Suburbanus Londinensis"	303
" ————Kewensis"	299
Hosack, D.	308
" Hot-house and Green-house Manual"	313
" ————Gardener"	223
————Flues	291
Hot-houses	18, 73, 92, 119, 122, 129, 135, 137, 153, 181, 237, 289, 290, 292, 297, 298, 302, 308, 312, 313, 317, 319, 321, 322, 323, 362.
Hot Walls	152 181, 237, 302
——Beds	14, 89, 119, 291, 302, 361
——Water for heating forcing houses	303
Houghton, ——	107, 117

	PAGE
Houghton	262
Howison, J.	292, 302, 324
———W.	324
Hoya Carnosa	297
Hughes, Wm.	111
Hunt, T. F.	327
Hunter, A. G.	291
Hunting	42
Hurtil Berries	55
"Husbandry anatomized"	122
"Husbandry and Trade improved"	107
"Husbandman's Magazine"	127
Hyacinths	84, 87, 133, 206, 212, 359
Hybrids	307, 314, 315, 316, 317, 318, 319
Hydrangea hortensis	307
"Hydriotaphia"	102
Hyssop	72, 83, 88, 179, 357

I

"Icnographia Rustica"	160
"Idea of a Botanical Garden"	209
" ———of the perfection of Painting"	106
Ignorance of Gardeners	56, 139
Ilam	233, 268
Ilex	326
Iliffe,———.	115
Ill effects of excessive heat in forcing-houses at night	296
Improvement of Gardening	57, 61, 65, 131, 146, 151, 298, 359
Improvement of the productiveness of Fruit Trees	298
" ————to the Art of Gardening"	110
"Improved System of Nursery Gardening"	283
Importation of Garden Produce	56, 153
Impatiens Balsamea	309
"Inaugural Address to the Glamorganshire Horticultural Society"	329

	PAGE
Indian Fig	88
———Reed	87
Influence of the Stock	297
"Influence of the Passions on Disorders"	243
Ingledon, W,	320
Ingram, R.	291
Inoculating	16, 91, 287, 288
Insects to destroy, &c.	291. 292, 293, 295, 297, 302, 307, 316, 321, 323, 325, 329
"Inspector"	207
"Instruction very profitable for Gardening &c."	70
"Instructions sur les Jardins Fruitiers".	109
"—————for packing Seeds, &c."	320
"—————for collecting Insects"	244
"—————how to plant and dress Vines, &c."	78
"Introduction to Gardening"	200
"—————to a general system of Hydrostatics, &c.	182
"—————to Botany"	216
"—————to the knowledge and practice of Gardening"	256
"Interesting discoveries in Horticulture"	283
Invasion, effects of	38
Ionian Melon	324
Ipomæ tuberosa	287
Iris	9, 84, 87, 324
Iris Xiphioides	309
Iron Scoria	310
Israel, Gardening in his time	3
Ivy	93, 256
Ixa	326

J

Jacob,———	100
James the First of Scotland	58
James the First	131, 133, 141, 359
——————Second	120, 137. 35_9_
James,———	139
Jamrosade	288

	PAGE.
...mine,	84, 88
...burgh Orchards,	325
...ves, S.	297, 313
...usalem Artichokes,	90, 349
"Jewel House of art and Nature,"	70
...hnson, C. W.	305
...nquil,	84
"Journal of a Horticultural Tour,"	311
...idas Tree,	88
"Judgment of Hercules,"	219
"Judica de varis Incontinentiæ, &c."	110
Judd, D. 298, 306, 307, 311, 318, 319,	322
...glans,	326
...ustice, J.	206
...uno,	7
Juniper,	83, 326
Jupiter,	7

K

Knapweed,	87
Kalendarium Horteuse,	106
Kaleidscope,	184
Keen's Seedling Strawberry,	296
Keen, M.	296, 300
Keith, A.	324
Kelly, T.	292
Kennedy, —.	236, 301
Kent, W.	262, 300, 306, 308
Kensington Gardens,	145, 264
Keswick Codlin,	292
Kew Gardens,	150, 211, 212
Kiddleston,	268
Kidney Beans, 13, 90, 153, 178,	325, 348
Kilspindie Bloom Potatoe,	325
Kinment, J.	302
Kirk, J.	292, 324
Kitchen Garden,	11, 15, 88, 126

3 G

	PAGE.
"Kitchen Garden Directory,"	328
"Kitchen and Flower Garden complete,"	205
Knight, T. A. 271, 284, 285, 286, 287, 288, 295, 296, 297, 298, 299, 300, 306, 307, 308, 309, 311, 312, 313, 314, 315, 317, 318, 319, 321, 322, 323, 361	
Knight, J.	282, 288
Knight, R. P.	252, 269
Knowle Park,	141
Kyle, J.	291
—— T.	246

L

Laburnum,	88
Labyrinths,	41
Lactucarium,	292, 303, 325
Lady Thistle,	353
Ladies Slipper,	87
"Lady's Recreation,"	156, 190
"—— Gardener's Companion,"	252
—— Bower,	84
Laird, J.	292, 302
"Landscape,"	252
—— Gardening,	139, 254, 259, 265, 363
"Landed Man's Assistant,"	158
Langley Batty,	197
Langford, T.	117
Lange de beefe, Ox tongue,	89
Larkspurs,	84, 85, 87
Larch,	93, 111
Laurentine Villa,	23
Lauristinus,	84, 88
Lavender,	84, 88, 179, 356
—— Gentle,	68, 83, 84, 88
Lawrance, Anthony	117
Lawrence, John	155
Lawson, W.	76
Layers,	16

	PAGE.
Leasowes, 219, 233, 237, 267,	268
Lectures, Fairchild's	191
Le Blond, 130,	197
"———'s Theory and practice of Gardening,"	197
Le Notre,	138
Lee, J.	216
Leeks, 3, 72, 88, 90,	351
Leeswold	144
"Legacy, or an enlargement of the discourse of Brabant Husbandry,"	97
"Legum Rusticarum,"	71
Lemon, 55, 78, 131, 295, 299, 306,	341
Lettuces, 13, 68, 72, 88, 89, 131, 179, 182,	353
Lettuce Medicines 291, 292, 303,	324
"Letter to U. Price, Esqr."	255
"——— H. Repton, Esqr."	254
"——— Sir W. Scott, Bart. on Planting,"	326
"Letter on the Blight and on raising late crops of Peas,"	273
"Letters on the beauties of Hagley, &c."	237
"——— about the improvement of Nurseries, &c."	102
Lettsom, J. C. 242,	293
Leucoium,	84
Levingston, F. D.	316
Lewis the fourteenth, 108, 109,	138
"Life of Sir J. Reynold's,"	246
Lightoler, J.	224
Lilacs, 60,	88
Lily, 4, 7, 68, 84,	86
——— of the Valley	87
Lilium Japonicum,	315
Lime, 93,	341
——— to fruit Trees,	302

	PAGE.
Lime duster,	321
Lindley, J. 256, 311, 316, 317, 318, 319, 320, 321, 322, 323, 324, 330	
Lindegaard, P.	283, 318, 319
Linnæus,	147
"Linnæan Transactions,"	251
Linaria,	87
Linacre,	57
Liquid Manure,	206
Liquorice,	72, 90, 367
Lister, Dr. M.	90
Lisle, l'abbé de	243, 257
Lisle, E. and T.	210
Literature of Gardening	45
Livingstone, J.	307, 300, 313, 316
Loanwells,	291
Loble, Matthew,	134
Lobelia, Fulgens,	297, 300
Locke, J.	224
Lodiges, G.	306, 326, 330
Lolium Perenne,	325
"London Gardener,"	216
"——— Garden's in 1691,"	122
———, George	123, 137, 145
Loquat,	308
Lorimer, C.	291
Lote,	92
London, J. C.	277
Love Apple,	87, 308, 358
——— everlasting,	87
Lavoisier,	367
Lowe, G.	308
Lucullus	20
Lungwort,	87
Lupines	72, 87

	PAGE.
Luttrell, —.	296
Lychnis,	87
Lycoperdon cancillatum,	297

M

Macnaughton, J.	325
Macdonald, J.	291
———, A.	282
Maclura,	344
Macculloch, Dr.	292, 293, 300
Mackmurray, J.	291
Mackray, J.	292, 302
Mackenzie, Sir G. S.	292, 297, 302, 303, 317, 324, 325
M'Phail, J.	253
Mac Murtrie, W.	323
Macray and Gorrie,	292
Macintosh, C.	328
Maddock, J.	251
Magnolia glauca,	308
——— grandiflora,	292
Maher, J.	285, 287, 288, 296, 297, 308, 312
Maidenhair,	7
"Maison Rustique,"	79
Major, J.	329
Malthus, —.	243
Mall in St. James's Park,	143
Mallows,	13, 72, 89
Mandrakes,	87
Mango,	324, 344
Mangolt Wurtzel,	243, 293
Manures,	8, 173, 297, 302, 305
Manufactures,	42, 132

	PAGE
"Management of Orange Trees,"	120
"Manner of raising, &c. Forest and Fruit Trees,"	116
Marigold, 68, 84, 85, 87, 89, 179,	354
Marjorum, 68, 72, 83, 88, 89, 179,	355
Market Gardens,	38
Marle,	32
Martial, 13,	18
Martagon,	84
Martyn, Professor 194,	277
Martyn, T.	277
Mary, Queen 138, 144,	360
Marsham, R.	215
Marshall, W.	246
————, C.	256
Markham, G.	78
Marshland, P.	314
Martin's Non Pareil Apple,	309
Marvel of Peru, 84,	87
Masters, W. junr.	309
Masterwort,	90
Maschal, Leonard	69
Mason, G.	209
————, W. 214, 234, 256,	257
Matthews, H. S.	296
————, A. 321,	322
Martius,	22
Maund, B.	330
Maudlin,	90
Mawe, T.	220
Maxwell, R.	213
Mazagan, Bean,	348
Meader, J.	234
Meadow Saffron, 84,	87
Meager, Leonard	117

		PAGE.
Mean, J.	224, 293, 297,	299
Mealy Insect,		307
Mearns, J.	313	316
Medlars,	17, 55, 91, 92, 181,	341
Medica,		87
Melros, A.		324
Mellidora, Pellucida,		297
Melons, 3, 54, 57, 89, 90, 131, 153, 176, 302, 312, 313, 315, 317, 318, 322, 323, 324, 326, 327, 342
"Memoirs, Illustrative and Historical of the Botanic Garden, at Chelsea,"		304
"———— of the Caladonian Horticultural Society,"		290
301, 324
"———— on the planting of Forest Trees,"		326
Menzies, W.		293
"Merlin,"		201
Mesembryanthemum,		317
Meteorological Observations,		322
"Method to preserve Peach and Nectarine Trees, &c."		248
"———— of raising some Exotic Seeds"		195
"———— of producing double Flowers,"		209
"———— of raising Trees from Leaves,"		208
"———— of cultivating Madder,"		196
Middleton, J.		293
Middle Ages,		41
Mignonette,		300
Milton,		259
Mills, G.		307
Milne, T.	309,	318
——— C.		232
Mills, J.		215
Miller, Philip	147, 150, 192,	199
———— his Dictionary,	151, 193,	277
Mildew in Trees	291, 292,	296

	PAGE.
"Minutes on Agriculture,"	221
Minerva,	7
Mint, 68, 72, 89, 179,	355
Mineral Springs	102
"Miscellaneous Reports on Woods,"	304
"——— Observations on the effects of Oxygen,"	257
"——— Tracts, &c. relating to Natural History,"	244
"Miscellanies on Ancient and Modern Gardening,"	245
"Miscellany Tracts,"	103
Mitshel, J. 291, 293,	327
Mitcheson, W.	322
Mizraim,	6
"Mode of forcing the Vine in Denmark,"	283
"Modern Gardener," 210,	234
"——— Eden,"	227
"——— Gardening,"	241
Moggridge, H.	309
Moly,	87
Monastic Remains, 37,	292
Montolieu, Mrs.	257
Monopsis conspicua,	296
Monteath, R.	304
Monch, Sir C. M. L.	317
Monopoly,	194
Montgomery, D.	322
"Monthly Register of new Experiments in Husbandry,"	185
Moore, Sir Thos.	200
Moor Park, 121,	145
——— Apricot,	318
Morris, R.	320
Morgan, W. 299, 300,	306
Moriarty, H. M.	281
Moracoc,	88

	PAGE
Mortimer, John	138
———, Cromwell	129
Mosley, Sir O.	306, 307
"Most Easy way of making Cyder"	113
Moss, Plants in	323
——— Rose de Meaux	298
Moths	325
Mountains, Vegetation of	288
Mount Edgecumbe	263
Mountain, Didymus	66, 67
Mouse Ear	87
Mowbray, W.	318
Muglester, G.	319
Muirhead, A.	291
Mulberries	17, 55, 74, 78, 92, 181, 217, 286, 296, 306, 307, 344
Mullein	87
Munro, D.	322
Munay, S.	322
———J.	324
———Sir Alex.	201
Murcian Kale	182
Mustard	13, 72, 90, 353
Mushrooms	13, 179, 182, 200, 204, 209, 222, 297, 303, 306, 314, 318, 356
Musk Grape Flower	84
"Museum Tradescantianum"	99
" ———Rusticum et commerciale"	218
Musgrave, P.	325
Myrtle	7, 18, 135
"Mystery of Husbandry"	119
Mythology	7

N

Naiads	7
Nairn, J.	307

	PAGE
Naismith, J,	302
Narcissus	7, 9, 84, 86, 359
Nasturtium	87, 354
" Nature, &c. of planting a Vinerard"	200, 201
"Naturalization of Plants	303
"Natural and Chemical Elements of Agriculture"	216
"Navelwort	87
Naven	72
Neat Houses (Cotarii)	39
Neale, A.	238
Neapolis	20
Neapolitan Violets	312
Nectarine	92, 129, 180, 246, 248, 286, 295, 298 302, 309. 316, 317, 320, 344
Neglect of Gardening	56
Neil, P.	310, 324
Nelson, Lord	249
Nelumbium	323
——————speciosum	322
Nep	89
Nerine	312
Nero's Garden	25
" New, Art of Gardening"	118
"———invented Stove"	122
"———System of Agriculture"	156
"———Improvements of Planting, &c.	184
"———Principles of Gardening"	198
"———Experiments, relative to the generation of Plants"	188
'———Treatise of Husbandry, &c.	202
'———Gardener's Dictionary"	229
"——— Orchard and Garden"	76
"———Book of good Husbandry"	77
"———Directions for planting, &c. Timber"	78
'———and Complete system of practical Husbandry"	215
"———Zealand Spinach	315, 318, 350

	PAGE
Newburg Orchards	302
Newman, J.	318
Nicol, G.	292
———W.	274
———J.	325
Nigella	72, 87
Nineteenth Century	270, 360
Noah	3
"Noblemen, Gentlemen and Gardener's Recreation"	161
Noehden, G. H.	295, 298, 299, 300, 306, 309
Noisette, W.	300
Nonsuch Palace	57, 59
————Flower	84
Norbury,	268
North,———.	215
North of England Gardening	136
————American Esculents	314
Norman's	38
Norwich Floriculture	132
"Nourse's discourses of the new improvement of Husbandry"	127
"Numismata"	107
Nuneham	267, 268
"Nurseries, Orchards, &c. encouraged"	117
Nurseryman	154, 199
Nuts	3, 4, 16, 55, 181, 341

O

Oak	7, 92, 326
Oatlands	264
"Observations, &c. Œconomical"	114
"————on Agriculture"	199
"————and Improvements"	94
"————on Husbandry"	210
"————on the River Wye"	228
"————on the Western Parts, &c."	228

	PAGE
Observations on the Coasts, &c.	229
"———— on several parts, &c.	229
"———— on Modern Gardening"	233
"———— on the diseases &c. of Trees"	250
"———— towards a method of preserving Seeds during Voyages"	217
"———— relative to Picturesque Beauty"	228
"———— on the barrenness of Fruit Trees"	289
"———— on the formation, &c. of Ornamental Plantations"	278
"———— on the employment of Salt"	305
"———— on the growth of the Vine and Olive"	225
"———— on the Changes in Landscape Gardening"	255
"———— On the Theory and Practice of Landscape Gardening"	255
"———— on the Genus Mesembryanthemum"	252
"———— on the laying out the Public Squares"	278
"Œconomical Surveys"	246
"Œconomicks of Xenophon"	183, 188
"Officiis secundum Humanœ"	110
Oil to Trees	303
Oldaker, J.	307, 312
"Old thrift newly revived"	78
Oleander	84, 88
Oleaster	342
Olives	3, 6, 7, 15, 19, 225, 344
"On Gardening"	243
"—Landed Property"	247
"—collecting Soils and Composts"	283
"—the supposed effects of Ivy on Trees"	256
"—the Introduction of Indian Architecture"	255
"—Sir F. Bacon's Natural History"	93, 102
Onions	3, 13, 54, 72, 88, 90, 287, 291, 292, 296, 306, 308, 309, 321, 324, 351

	PAGE
Onion Maggot	291
Opium British	292
Orach	68, 72, 89, 179, 350
Orange	17, 74, 92, 126, 135, 197, 295, 299
Orchard	15, 74, 91, 101, 274, 302, 325
"Orchardist, the"	257
Orchis	87
Orchideœ	322
Ord's Apple	299
Organy	68
Origin of Gardening	2
———— and production of proliferous Flowers	209
Orleans Plum	345
Ornamental Gardening	19, 58, 81, 121, 169, 126, 138, 140, 257
Orpheus	9
"Outline of a general History of Gardening"	311
Oxe-eye	87
Oxford Botanic Garden	63
Oxygen Gas to Vegetation	288

P

Page, W. B.	301
"Page's Prodromus"	301
Pageant	132
Painsbill	233, 264
Palms	325
Pansy	85, 87
"Paradise of Flora"	70
"———si in sole, &c."	82, 93
"———Regained"	156
"———Retrieved"	190
"Parallel of Ancient and Modern Architecture"	106
Parasitical Plants	313
Parsley	13, 68, 72, 89, 179, 353
Parsnips	13, 72, 88, 90, 293, 322, 349

Parks	33, 40
Parks, J. D.	321, 333
Parkes, S.	324
Parkyns, G. J.	282
Parkinson, John.	83, 93, 135
Parmentier, J.	320
Parliamentary Grant	250
Passion Flower	88, 307, 313, 316, 324, 326
Passiflora quadrangularis	322
Patience	89
Patents of Royal Gardeners	136
Patrons of Gardening	132, 133, 136, 154, 368
Pear	6. 16, 17, 40, 55, 74, 92, 126, 129, 180, 273 287, 288, 290, 293, 295, 296, 298, 299, 302, 307 308, 313, 316, 317, 319, 320, 322, 323, 346
Pears (to preserve)	291
Pear Trees to make bear	291
Peas	13, 72, 90, 133, 153, 182, 273, 317, 318, 319, 347
Peach	17, 55, 92, 126, 129, 136, 246, 248, 286 287, 292, 293, 295, 296, 297, 300, 302, 306, 309 311, 312, 316, 317, 318, 319, 324, 344
Peiresc	65
Pelargonium	326
Pellitory	87
Pennyroyal	72, 89
"Penshurst"	205
Peony	68, 85, 87, 298
Peppermint	179
Perfect, T.	209
Permanent character of budded grafted fruit	297
Persian Melon	324
Perewinkle	88
Perdrigon	47, 135
"Perfite platforme of a Hoppe Garden	67
Peter the great of Russia.	104

	PAGE
Peters, M.	231
Peterson, J. P.	323
Phelps, W.	318
Philips, H.	304
———— L.	290
"Philosophical account of the works of Nature"	184
"——— ——— ———treatise of Agriculture"	185
Physic herbs	90
Physical Botany	149
Phytologia	241
Piccotes	289
Piercefield	233, 268
Pierre, L. de St,	236
Pierard, C. F.	319
Pigot, R.	305
Pimpernal	72
Pine Tree	4, 92
———— Bug	291
———— Apple	112, 136, 152, 153, 206, 226, 230, 239
	279, 282, 300, 311, 313, 314, 315, 317, 319
	322, 325, 340
Pinus	326, 344
Pink	68, 85, 87, 289, 305, 314, 325, 359
Pistachia	344
Pitmanstone Orange Nectarine	313
———— ———— ———— Grape	308
"Plan for cultivating Grapes in the field"	313
"Plan of Mr. Pope's Garden, &c.	203
"———— ———— —an Orchard"	256
"Plans, &c. of Kew"	212
"———— &c. of ForcingHouses"	252, 289
"Planter's Kalendar"	275
"———— Manual	115
"———— Guide	234, 328
, Planting	180, 234

	PAGE
"Planting and Gardening"	346
"————and rural Ornament"	247
"Plantarum Cryptogamicarum Britanniœ"	286
Plants grow by Night	6
Plane Tree	8
Platt, Sir Hugh.	69
Plattes, Gabriel.	93, 116
"Plain and full Instructions to raise Fruit Trees"	117
"Plain and practical Treatise on the Auricula" &c.	293
Pleasure Grounds . 19, 55, 81, 121, 140,	363
Pliny, the Elder	13
————the younger	23
Plums 16, 17, 40, 55, 57, 92, 126, 129, 180,	308
309, 313, 314, 315, 323, 326, 344	
Plunket, Dr.	138
Pluto	7
"Pocket Kitchen Gardener"	282
"————Flower Garden"	232
"Poetical Epistle"	205
Polyanthus	289, 324
"Polymetus, &c."	212
"Pomona"	106, 107
"————Britannica"	295
"————Londinensis"	284
"————Herefordiensis"	272
"Pomarium Britannicum"	304
"Pomological Magazine"	331
"Pomona, or Fruit Garden illustrated"	198
Pomegranates 4, 6, 16, 17, 78, 88,	345
Pompions 54, 72, 89, 90,	356
"Pompey the little"	205
Pontey, W.	276
Pope	261
Poppy 7, 72, 85, 87,	179

	PAGE
Portraits 69, 76, 80, 93, 100, 112, 119, 191, 193, 204	
208, 210, 211, 213, 214, 219, 224, 226,	
231, 235, 240, 242, 277	
" ———— of English Authors on Gardening"	328
" ———————————————— "	245
Portugal Laurel	88
" Posie of Gillie Flowers "	67
Potatoes 90, 103, 129, 200, 234, 286, 287, 288, 290	
293, 296, 297, 306, 307, 314, 317, 325	
328, 348	
Potatoe Onion	324
Powell, A.	230
———, D.	318, 319
" Practical Husbandry improved"	94
" ———— Discourses concerning the four Elements"	186
" ———— Geometry"	
" ———— Observations on the British Grasses"	
" ———— Farmer or Herefordshire Husbandman"	227
" ———— Gardener and Modern Horticulturist"	328
" ———— Gardener"	238, 282, 294
" ———— Treatise on Planting"	252
———— Husbandman"	213
———— Treatise on Husbandry"	215
———— Gardener's Companion"	294
———— Planter"	275
———— Kitchen Gardener"	176
———— Planter of Fruit Trees"	117
———— Fruit Gardener"	180
———— Essay on the Vine"	326
———— Hints on domestic and rural Economy"	240
———— Gardener and Gentleman's Dictionary"	230
———— Treatise on the culture of the Gooseberry"	
———— Instructions for the culture of the Tree B	
" Practice of Gardening"	

	PAGE
Prague, Battle of	95
Present state of Gardening	360
Preservation of Fruit, &c.	297, 319
Preserving Blossom	292, 302, 312
Premiums of the London Horticultural Society	283
Prickly Pear	340
Price, Sir U.	254, 268
Primrose	84, 87
Privet	84, 88, 92
Probart F. G.	326
"Profitable Planter"	276
"———— Intelligencer"	94
"———— Arte of Gardening"	68
Professor of Botany	46, 82, 134
Propagation of Trees	164
"———— and Botanical arrangement of Plants"	223
Propagating from old roots	298
Promoting the early puberty of Seedlings	299
Proposals for the improvement of Waste Lands	188
"Proceedings concerning the improvement of all-manner of Lands, &c.	103
Providence Pine Apple	317
Protection from Hares	302, 324
Pruning	292, 293, 307
———Instrument	293
Psidium	314
"Public employment and an active life preferred"	106
Pullein S.	217
Purslain	72, 89, 354
Pyracantha	84, 92

Q

Quinces	16, 17, 55, 92, 181, 342
"Quintinie's Treatise of Orange Trees"	107
Quintinie, J. de la	108

R

Radishes	18, 72, 88, 90, 182, 309, 311, 319, 350
Raineir, Capt. P.	319
Raisins	78
Ramond, W.	288
Rampion	8, 9, 306, 352
Ranunculus	84, 87, 289, 314, 359
Rape	72, 285, 353
"Rapin of Gardens"	190
"Rairities of Richmond"	201
Raspberries	17, 65, 72, 92, 181, 283, 346
"Rational Farmer"	231
Rawdon, Sir Arthur	148
Ray, John.	148
Rea, John.	111, 119
Read, J.	321
"Recreatio Agricolæ"	94
"Recreations in Agriculture"	237
Red Spider	248
——Apple Potatoe	307
Reformation in Gardening	260
"Reformed Husbandman"	97
Regneir, W.	310
Reid, A.	325
——, J.	120
"Remarks, &c. on Virgil"	213
" ——————— on Hot-Houses"	278
" ——————— on Forest Scenery"	223
" ——————— on the Vinetum Britannicum, &c."	102
"Report of a Committee of the Horticultural Society of London"	273
" ———— of a Fruit Committee of the London Horticultural Society"	296

	PAGE
"Report of new and rare plants flowered in the London Horticultural Society's Garden"	320
"Re Rustica"	46, 47, 71, 218
Retarding Blossoms	292
"Retired Gardener"	125, 190
Reverse Grafting	319
"Review of Plants in the Botanist's Repository"	274
"—— of the Landscape"	237
Rhododendron	326
Rhodon and Iris	132
Rhubarb	90, 170, 293, 307, 325, 356
Ribston Pippin	307, 324, 346
"Riches of a Hop Garden"	188
Richmond Garden	202
Richardson, Richard	114
"Right manner of ordering Fruit Trees, &c."	103, 107
Ringing Fruit Trees	300, 312, 317
"Rise and Progress of the present taste in planting, &c."	226
Ripening Seeds	307
Robert of Gloucester———	39
Robertson, D.	302
————, J.	300, 312, 313, 317
Robinson, J. M.	324
————, ——.	257
Roch Abbey	268
Rochambole	351
Rocket	60, 72, 90, 302, 357
Rocque, B.	206
Rogers, T,	314
Roman Gardening	11, 27, 29
———Patronymies	12
———Estates in every province	21, 27
———Settlers	36

Ronalds, H.	307
Rosa Banksia	312
Rose 7, 9, 57, 84, 85, 88, 91, 120, 131, 132, 298,	312
313, 314, 322, 326, 328, 346, 359	
—— Campions	84
—— Plantain	87
—— Apple	342
——, John	112, 135
Rosemary	60, 84, 88, 89, 356
Roseberry Strawberry	300, 313
Ross, W.	300
Rotation of Crops	292
Rouncival Peas	348
Rous, Lord	306
Royal Herbalist	134
——— Gardener	230
——————— Patents	136
Rubus Chamœmorus	293
Rue	68, 72, 90, 179, 357
Rules for Landscape Gardening	261
"Rural Improver"	276
"——— Recreation"	276
Russian Esculents	324
Rutter, J.	227
Rye, G.	199

S

Sabine, J.	296, 297, 298, 299, 300, 306, 307, 310, 312
	314, 316, 317, 319, 322, 323, 324, 333
Saffron	4, 72, 87
Sage	72, 84, 88, 90, 179, 355
Salt	305, 324, 327
Salter, J.	293
Salmon, Wm.	30

	PAGE
Sallads	56, 89, 131, 200
Sallust	21
Salsafy	350
Salisbury, W.	273, 282
———, R. A.	285, 286, 288, 296, 299, 310, 314
Salix	326
Samphire	298, 358
Sanderson, W.	302
Sanicle	87
Sang, E.	291, 292, 324
Satin Flower	87
Saunders, J.	328
Savine	93
Savory	68, 72, 83, 89, 179, 355
Sawyer, S.	318
Saxe-Weimar, (Grand Duke of)	308
Saxons	36
Sayes Court	104
St James's Park	105, 142
Scabious	87
Scale in Fruit Trees	302
Scallions	90
Scarlet Strawberry	308
"Schoolmistress"	219
Schrank, F. de P.	314
Scite of a Garden	13, 80, 161, 180
Scions	309, 318
Science promoted by Commerce, &c.	42
" ——— of Agriculture"	301
" ——— of Horticulture"	301
" ——— of Good Husbandry, &c."	188
Scougal, J.	292
Scott, Reynold,	67
"Scot's Gardener"	120
" ————'s Director	206

	PAGE
Scott, T.	317
" Scotch forcing Gardener"	275
———— Fruits, state of	291
———— Fir	291
———— Roses	313
———— Gardeners	158
Scorzonera	87, 350
Scurvey Grass	179, 353
Sculptura	105
Sea Kale	245, 285, 292, 293, 302, 311, 324, 352
Seckle Pear	308
Senna	88
" Series of facts upon planting the Oak"	321
Services	16, 55, 92, 161, 186
Sercy, C. de	95
" Sermons on relative Duties"	128
Seton, A.	306, 308, 313
Severus	26
Shaw, J.	252
———, W.	287
Shallots	290, 291, 351
Shallot Maggots	291
Sharronck, Rt.	110
Sherbook, A.	288
Sherard (Drs. J. and W.)	149
Sheriff, J.	290
Shenstone, W.	219, 267
" Short, plain Treatise on Carnations and Pinks"	305
" ——— Practical Directions for the culture of the Anana"	309
" ——— and sure guide, &c, for ordering Fruit Trees"	115
" ——— Instructions for Gardening and Grafting"	68
" ——— Treatise on improved Hot-Houses"	278
" Shubbery Almanack"	301
Shuckborough	268
Siberian Bittersweet Apple	323

	PAGE
Siberian Crab	346
Sickler, J. V.	300
Siege of Troy in Kensington Gardens	145
Silvange Pear	319
Simpson, Rev. J. 289, 292,	328
Sinclair, G. 293, 294,	318
———, Sir J. 289, 292,	328
"Sketch of a plan for making the new Forest a real Forest"	247
"Sketch from " the Landscape" "	256
"Sketches of curvilinear Hot-Houses"	279
"———,——— and Hints on Landscape Gardening"	255
Skirrets 90,	350
Sloann, Sir Hans	153
Sloping Walls 152,	181
Smallage 72,	90
Smeall, J.	292
Smith, Sir J. E.	308
——— T.	321
———. A.	302
———, J. 291, 292, 302, 323,	325
———, John,	106
———, —.	127
———, W.	323
Smoke injurious to Plants	83
Snow, T.	158
Snowberry	296
Society of Gardeners	199
Soils	283
Solomon 3, 4,	6
——— Gardening in his time	4
"Solitary or Carthusian Gardener"	127
"Some doubts relative to the efficacy of Mr. Forsyth's Plaister"	273
"——— thoughts on Building, &c."	243

	PAGE
"Some account of the Emperor of China's Gardens"	213
Sorrel	68, 72, 89, 179, 350, 353
Sotian	8
Southernwood	84
Southcote, P.	264
Sowerby, J.	249, 296
Spanish Potatoes	90
Spence, W.	295, 297
———, J.	212
Spens, Col.	302
Sperage, Asparagus	68, 89
Speed, Adam	97
Speechley, W.	238
Spinach	68, 72, 89, 350
Spiderwort	84, 87
Spring Gardens	143
——— Grove Codlin	287
Spurge,	90
Spurge Olive	88
Star Flowers	84
——— of Bethlehem	87
Starwort	87
Statuary	24, 167
Stafford, Hugh,	190
Standish, A.	78
Steam for Forcing	299, 309, 314, 318, 323, 324, 362
Steele, R.	251
Stephenson, David,	204
Stevenson, R.	291
———, Henry,	190
Stewart, Sir H.	328
———, A.	293, 319, 321, 323
———, J.	291
Stirring the Soil	16
"Stirpium Historiæ Pemptades"	54

		PAGE
Stocks		84
Storing Vegetables		292
Stove		300, 308
——— Plants		131, 137, 359
Stowe		205, 233, 263, 264
Strachn, C.		308, 309
Straw Ropes for sheltering Blossom		302
Strawberries,	17, 55, 68, 72, 90, 181, 283, 286, 287 296, 300, 307, 309, 315, 317, 319, 321 322, 323, 325, 343	
Strawing Floors		83
Strawberry Hill		268
Stramonium		87
Street, J.		325
"Strictures on the absurd Novelties introduced in Gardening"		206
Studley		268
Style of Gardening		19, 40, 58, 140, 146
Succory		89, 307
Sugar		56
Sumach		83
Sun-flower		84, 85, 87
Sunk Fences introduced		262
Superstitions		10, 14, 72, 119, 154
"Supplement to Chamber's Cyclopœdia"		207
"Survey of Ancient Husbandry and Gardening"		188
"——— of Husbandry"		96
"Surveying and Book of Husbandry"		49
"Sure Method of improving an Estate by planting		196
Swayne, G.		314, 317, 322
Sweet Briar		84
———, Flag		4
———, John		68, 85, 87
———, Peas		87
———, William		85, 87

	PAGE
Sweet, R.	303, 330
———, J.	306, 316
Swinden, N.	238
Switzer, Stephen,	158
Sycamore	93
"Sylva"	105
" ——— Florifera, the Shrubbery"	305
"Synopsis Herbaria"	46
" ——— methodica Stirpium Britannicarum"	148
" ——— Plantarum Succulentarum"	252
Syringa	84
"Systema Agriculturæ"	113, 117
" ——— Horticulturæ"	113
"System of Botany"	207
" ——— of Agriculture"	247

T

Talende, Henry	152
Tamarisk	57, 82
Tansy	90, 179, 356
"Tancred"	80
Tapiary work	22, 24, 60, 136, 140, 145
Tarragon	68, 90, 354
Tarquin	12, 19
Tasso	259
Taverner, J.	77
Taylor, A.	230
Tea Tree	135
Temple, Sir Wm.	120, 136, 145
"Ten minutes advice on Salt as a Manure"	327
"Terra"	106
Tetragonia expansa	318
Thalictrum	87
Thea	325
"Theatrum Botanicum"	82
"Theophrastus on Gems"	207

	PAGE
"Theory and Practice of Gardening,"	130
Theobalds	60, 141
Thistle	87, 90
Thouin, M.	288, 310, 322
Thomson, I.	291, 302
Thompson, J.	243
"Thoughts on Planting"	236
"Three Essays on the picturesque, &c."	228
Thrift	83
Thyme	83, 88, 89, 179, 354
Tibur	22
Tigridia Pavonia	321
"Timber Tree improved"	201
Tobacco	87, 90
———— Water	323
Todd, G.	289
Tomato	87, 308, 358
Toppinghœ Hall	129
Torch Thistle	198
Torbron, T.	312
Tottenham Park Muscat Grape	321
Tradescant, John	98, 131, 204
"Tractatus de Agricultura"	51, 77
Transplanting	92, 310, 322
"Traité des Jardins Fruitiers"	109
"Tracts on Alabaster or Gypsum"	232
"———— on practical Agriculture and Gardening"	231
"Transactions of the London Horticultural Society"	284
295, 306, 311, 316, 321	
"———————— in the Fruit Tree Nursery"	200
"———————— of the Botanical and Horticultural Society of Durham"	328
Transplanting old Trees	291
Transporting plants, &c.	309, 314, 317, 320, 324
Training	286, 288, 292, 300, 306, 308, 314, 316
317, 319	

	PAGE
Transplanting Turf	325
"Tracte profytable for Husbandmen"	47
Trees, to preserve from Hares	292
Trees	315
Tree Rose	328
—— Mignonette	307
—— Onion	292
—— Trefoil	88
"Treatise on Husbandry"	94, 113, 210
" —— on Fruit Trees"	97, 101, 112, 210
" —— on Orange Trees"	107
" —— on Husbandry and Gardening"	185
" —— on Fallowing, &c."	188, 191
" —— concerning the Husbandry and Natural History of England"	203
" —— on the Hyacinth"	206
" —— on Civil Architecture"	212
" —— on Grapes and the Norfolk Willow"	215
" —— on Forest Trees"	216, 234
" —— on the culture of Peach Trees"	229
" —— on the Anana"	230
" —— on planting and Gardening"	236
" —— on forcing early Fruits, &c."	237
" —— on the cultivation of the Pine Apple	239, 282
" —— on the culture of the Vine"	239
" —— —— management of Peach and Nectarine Trees"	246
" —— —— Culture, &c. of Fruit Trees"	251, 315
" —— —— of the Cucumber"	253
"Treatise on Mulberries"	78
" —— on the Culture of the Apple and Pear"	273
" —— on forming, &c. Country Residences"	278
" —— on the improved culture of the Strawberry Raspberry, and Gooseberry"	283
" —— on Physiology and Pathology"	289

	PAGE
"Treatise upon Bulbous Roots, Green-House Plants, &c,"	293
" ———— on Hedge Row Timber"	301
" ———— on Insects most prevalent on Fruit Trees"	329
Trentham	268
Triphasia	347
Tropical Fruits	316, 319
Trotter, D.	302
Trowell, Samuel	202
Truffles	179
Trussler, J.	251
Tube-Rose	285
Turf	167
Tulip	84, 86. 111, 132, 133, 289, 359
Turnips	13, 33, 72, 88, 90, 319, 349
Turnip-fly	292
Turner, J.	287, 306, 310, 313, 316, 317, 319
———, Dr.	63, 64
Tusser, Thomas	49, 54
Tuscan Villa	23
Tweedie, J.	292
Twickenham	268
"Two Appendixes to an Essay on Design in Gardening"	254

U

Ulmus	326
———— suberosa	317
"Unconnected thoughts on Landscape Gardening"	219
Underdown, W.	293
Underground Onion	306
"Universal system of Water and Water works, &c."	162
" ———— Gardener and Botanist"	222
" ———— Gardener's Kalendar"	223
" ———— Botanist and Nurseryman"	231

V

Vaccinium	321, 32

	PAGE
Vachel, R.	314
Valerian	68, 87, 90
Van Campen	217
Van Mons, J. B.	297, 307, 322
—— Oosten	130
Varro	13
Varronia	347
Variegated Grass	88
Varieties from Seed	5, 6
Vauxhall	143
Vegetable Chemistry	149
——————— Marrow Gourd	298, 356
——————— Phisiology	149
——————— System, &c.	209
Vegetation, Theory of	288, 323, 324
Venables, Rev. J.	297
Ventilation	319
Venus	7
Verdelho Grape	296, 290
Verrel, J.	314
Versailles	142
Villas	19
" —— of the Ancients"	197
" Villa Garden Directory"	275
" Village Memoirs"	267
Vine 3, 4, 5, 6, 15, 17, 35, 37, 78, 92, 112, 180, 225	
239, 283, 287, 296, 298, 306, 308, 311, 313	
315, 317, 319, 323, 325, 326, 347	
Vineyard	3, 92, 200
" ——— The"	187, 197
" Vinetum Britannicum"	113
Violets	9, 84, 87
Virginian Creeper	68
——————— Silk	88
——————— Vine	93

	PAGE
"Viridarium or Green-house Plants"	281
"Vitruvius Britannicus"	157
Vispre, F. X.	248

W

Walnuts	17, 55, 74, 92, 181, 286, 295, 307, 343
Walter de Henly	46
Wall-flowers	84, 87
Waller, Edmund,	143
Walls	4, 8, 181, 308, 313
Walks	167
Walker, Dr.	151
———, J.	302
Walpole, (H. Earl of Oxford,)	240
Walsh, R,	321
Wanstead House	124, 146
Wardens	55
Ware Park	81
Warre, J.	306
Wasps	291, 292, 302, 308, 312
Wastell, H.	325
Watering Fruit Trees	298
——— Plants	162, 306
Watson, Sir Wm.	203
Watkins, T.	316, 327
Water Caltrops	347
——— Cress	315, 353
"Way to get Wealth"	79
Webb, W.	205
Wedgewood, J.	287, 309
Weeks, E.	290
"Weekly Miscellany for the improvement of Husbandry &c."	188
Weighton, D.	291, 292
Welsh Onion	309
Wells, J.	315

	PAGE
West, J.	313
Westminster Hall, Gardener's Stalls in	158
Weston, Sir R.	95
———, R.	231
Whateley, T.	233
Wheeler, J.	217
Whitworth, G.	325
White Knights	304
Whitaker, ———.	98
Whitmill, Benedict.	196
"Whole Art of Husbandry"	129
Whortleberry	347
Wilbraham, R.	309
——————, A.	296
William the Third	120, 138, 144, 360
——— of Malmsbury	39
Williams, J.	286, 296, 299, 308, 309, 311, 317, 318, 321
Williamson, W.	306, 307, 308, 309, 312, 314
Willow flower	87
Wilson, W.	237
Wilton	268
Wilkinson, T.	287
Wilmot, J,	288, 295
Wilmot's Orlean's Plum	309
———— Bon Chrétien Pear	298
Wildman, —	229
Wine, its discovery	3
——— making	302, 325
Windsor Castle	58, 146
Winter-Cherry	88, 90
————-Greens	209
Wise, Henry,	124, 145, 146
Wisteria Consequana	323
Withers, W.	326

	PAGE
Woburn Farm	264
———— Perennial Kale	318
Wolf's Bane	84
Wolfe, C. J.	158
Woolf	57
Wood, W.	302, 303
Woodward, Henry,	208
Woodstock	40
"Woodlands, or a Treatise on Planting"	310
"Works and Days"	9
Worlidge, John,	113
Wormwood	179, 357
Wotton, Sir H.	80, 131
Wreshill-Castle	58
Wright, ——.	264

X

"Xenophon's Treatise"	49

Y

Yellow Rose	318
"Yconomia, sive Housbrandria"	46
Yew	83, 93
"Young Gardener's Director"	189
"———————— best Companion"	242
Young, J.	283, 324, 325
Yule, J.	303

Z

Zamia	323
Zephyrus	7
Zizyphus	347
Zoroaster	6
Zubow's Steam Pits	309

ADDITIONS.

THOMAS HILL, (see p. 68.) His portrait, inscribed T. H. Æt. 42, is prefixed to his work on "Physiognome." 1571. It is an oval wood cut. Without engraver's name. 12mo.

SIR HENRY WOTTON. (p. 60.) There are two engraved Portraits of him one by W. Dolle, prefixed to his "Life" by Walton. 1670. 8vo. The other by P. Lombart, in Walton's "Reliquiæ Wottonianæ. 1654. 12mo.

WALTER BLYTHE. (p. 96.) His portrait, a small figure, is in his "English Improver Improved."

SIR T. BROWNE. (p. 103.) There are four engraved Portraits of him, One, in 8vo, Printseller's name Banc. Another prefixed to his "Vulgar Errors," Printseller's name Hove, 1672. 4to. A third by R. White, prefixed to his "Works" folio, 1686; and a fourth prefixed to his "Religio Medici." 1663, folio.

JOHN EVELYN. (p. 103.) There are the following portraits of him. 1. Prefixed to his "Sculptura," by J.

Worlidge, 1755, 8vo. 2. Prefixed to his translation of "Lucretius," drawn from life R. Gaywood, sc. 1654, 8vo. 3. Prefixed to his "Sylva," 1664. R. Nanteuil, del et sc. folio. 4. In Walpole's "Anecdotes of Painting," by A. Bannerman. 5. Prefixed to Hunter's 4to. Edition of the "Sylva," 1776.

J. DE LA QUINTINIE. (p. 108.) There are two Portraits engraved of him. One by W. Elder, and the other, prefixed to his "Traité des Jardins," by Picart.

CHARLES COTTON. (p. 115.) His Portrait by P. Lely, engraved by Ryland, is prefixed to his "Life," 1770, 8vo.

SIR W. TEMPLE (p. 120.) Lely painted his Portrait in 1679, the four first of the following were engraved from it. 1. A folio plate, Printseller, Banc. 2. In Birch's "Lives," folio, by Houbrahen. 3. Prefixed to his "Works" in 1720, folio, G. Vertue, sc. 4. Prefixed to his "Letters," 1700, 8vo. R. White, sc. 5. Prefixed to his "Life," by Boyer, 1714.

BISHOP FLEETWOOD (p. 127.) There is a Portrait of him prefixed to his "Sermons," 1717, 8vo. by V. Gucht. Another by Simon, from a painting by J. Richardson in 1702. There is a third mentioned by Bromby, by R. White, when Fleetwood was M. A.

ANDRE LE NÔTRE, or NOSTRE. (p. 138.) This celebrated man in our Hortulan Annals seems to deserve a more particular notice. He was born in 1613 and being educated an Architect it was not until his fortieth year, and then accidentally that his tase for the magnificent in Garden designing became known

He first displayed it in the Garden of Vaux le Vicompte, now Vaux Praslin. Louis the 14th struck with its style, reckless of expence, immediately made him Comptroller General of Buildings and Director of Gardens; created him a Knight of St. Michael, gave him a patent of Nobility, and wealth to support it. In 1678 he went to Italy and to England about 1682, but his presence was not required to infect the gentry of his age with a mania for his style. All Europe adopted it in different degrees. Its effect in this Country has been detailed pp. 140—146. He died in 1700. There are two engraved Portraits of him. One by J. Smith, 1699; the other by A. Masson, both after a painting by C. Marat.

LEONARD MASCHAL. (p. 69.) He was farrier to James the first. There is another Edition of his "Government of Cattle," dated 1662, if Bromby is a good authority.

GERVASE MARKHAM. (p. 79.) Bromley says he died in 1636.

RICHARD BRADLEY. (p. 188.) The work numbered 28 was published under the name of "Martha Bradley, late of Bath."

P. 141. Insert after line 4 from the top. Lord Bacon in 1612, gives the following list of Trees, Flowers, &c. which deserve a place in the Pleasure Garden; distinguishing the months in which they are in their greatest beauty. In January and Feburary, Mezereon; Crocus, yellow and grey; Primrose; Anemonies; Early Tulip; Oriental Hyacinth; Chamairis; Fritillaria. In March, Voilets; Daffodil; Daisy; Almond; Peach; Cornelian; Sweet Briar. In April, Double white

Voilet; Wall-Flower; Stock Gillyflower; Cowslip; Iris; Lilies; Rosemary; Tulip; Peony; Pale Daffodil; French Honeysuckle; Cherry; Plums; White Thorn; Lilac. In May and June, Pinks; Roses; Honeysuckles; Strawberries; Bugloss; Columbine; French Marigold; Flos Africanus; Currants; Fig; Raspberry; Vine; Lavender; White sweet Satyrion; Herba Muscaria; Lily of the Valley; Apple. In July, Gillyflowers; Musk Rose; the Lime or Linden; Jennetin and Codlin Apples. In August, Pears; Apricots; Barberries; Filberts; Musk Melons; Monks-hoods. In September, Grapes; Apples; Poppies; Peaches; Melo-cotones; Nectarines; Cornelians; Wardens; Quinces. In October and November, Services; Medlars; Bullaces; Holyoaks. December and January, Holly; Ivy; Bay; Juniper; Cypress; Yew; Pines and Firs; Rosemary; Lavender; Perewinkles (white, purple and blue;) Germander; Flags; Orange and Lemon Trees, " *if stoved*" and Sweet Marjoram.

p. 52. insert before line ten from the bottom. The following Fruits, Culinary Vegetables, &c. are mentioned by Tusser. Peas, Hastings for early Crops. Grey and Rouncivals. Garlick. Beans. Rosemary. Apples. Nuts. Apricots. Barberries. Bullace, black and white. Cherries, red and black. Chesnuts. Cornet Plums. Damsons, white and black, Filberts, red and white. Gooseberries. Grapes, white and red. Green or Grass, Pear, and Wheat Plums. Hurtle Berries. Medlars, or Marles. Mulberry. Peaches, white and red. Pears of all sorts. Quinces. Respis, or Raspberries, Raisins. (Currants.) Services, Strawberries, red and white. Walnuts. Wardens, white and red. Box. Bay. Hawthorn. Prim. Roses. Leeks. Avens. Betony. Beets. Betony. Bloodwort. Bugloss. Burnet. Borage. Cabbage. Coleworts. Clary. Cress. Endive. Fennel. French Mallows. French Saffron. Lang de beefe *(ox tongue.)* Lettuce. Lung-

wort, Liverwort. Marigolds. Mercury. Mints. Nep.
Onions. Orache, or Arache, red and white. Patience.
Parsley. Penuyroyal. Primrose. Poret. Sage, red and
white. English Saffron. Summer Savory. Sorrell. Spinage.
Succory. Seithes. Tansy. Thyme. Voilets of all sorts.
Alexanders. Artichokes. Blessed Thistle. Cucumbers.
Mustard, Musk Million, (Melon.) Purslane. Radishes.
Rampion. Rocket. Sea-holy. Sperage. Skirrets. Tarragon. Carrots. Citrons, Pompions and Gourds. Navew.
Parsnips. Rape. Turnip. Basil. Balm. Chamomile.
Costmary. Cowslips and Paggles. Daisies. Sweet Fennel.
Germander. Hyssop. Lavender. Lavender Spike. Lavender Cotton. Marjoram. Maudeline. Pennyroyal. Winter
Savory. Batchellor's Buttons. Bottles, blue, red and tawney.
Columbines. Campions. Daffodils, or Daffodondillies. Eglantine or Sweet Briar. Featherfew. Flower Armoure.
Flower de Luce. Flower gentle, white and red. Flowernice.
Carnations. Holyoaks, red and white. Indian Eye. Lark's
foot. Laus Tibi, Lilium convallium. Lilies, red and white.
Marigold double. Nigella Romana. Ponsies, or Heart's ease.
Paggles, green and yellow. Pinks of all sorts. Queen's Gilliflowers. Rosemary. Boxes of all sorts. Snapdragon. Sops-
in-wine. Sweet Williams. Sweet Johns. Star of Bethlem.
Star of Jerusalem. Stock Gilliflowers of all sorts. Tuft Gilliflowers. Velvet flowers, or French Marigold. Violets, yellow and white. Wall Gilliflowers of all sorts. Eyebright.
Famitory. Saxifrage. Woodroffe. Anise. Archangel.
Chervil. Cinquefoil. Cummin. Dragons. Dittany, or
Garden Ginger. Gromwell. Hartstongue. Horehound.
Loveage. Mandrake. Liquorice. Mugwort. Peony. Poppy.
Rue. Rhubarb. Smallage. Savin. Stitchwort. Valerian.
Woodbine. The above list he gives in alphabetical sections
"Fruit"—"Seeds and Herbs for the Kitchen." "Herbs and
Roots for Sallads and Sauce." "Herbs and Roots to boil, or
to butter." "Strewing herbs of all sorts." "Herbs, Branches

and Flowers for windows and pots." "Herbs to still in Summer" and " Herbs for Physic."

From the same author we learn many of the Garden practices of the age in which he lived. The above list of plants, drawn up as appropriate for any country garden, demonstrates sufficiently how extended was the practice of Gardening. As at Rome the Garden was under the care of the housewife. He recommends it to lie open to the south and west. Arbours made of Hawthorn were formed in it; the walks made with Saw Dust, Brick Dust, or Ashes. He mentions Capers, Lemons, Olives, Oranges, and Rice as things to be bought as sauce for meat.

p. 70. line 7 from the top. FLORAES PARADISE, beautified and adorned with sundry sorts of delicate fruites and flowers. By the industrious labour of H. P. Knight. With a remedy for fever, &c. 1600. London. 12mo. Another edition 1608, which is the only one I have seen.

The introductory pages of this work are mystical in the extreme; but the remainder of the work is replete with excellent directions, demonstrating by their variety, and the numerous gentlemen who communicated them, how extensively the taste for Gardening was spread among the higher classes of Society.

It contains many anticipations of what was advocated in subsequent years. As budding Double Roses upon Briars, Sloping Walls, Grafting Wax, Moving Trees when full grown, &c.

CORRECTIONS.

PAGE.	LINE.	
8	11 from the bottom, for *bring* read *hung*.
29	5 ———— erase the word *and*
41	13 ———— place the comma after the word and not before
42	2 from the top read *of* instead of *or*
65	19 ———— read *discovered*
72	12 from the bottom read *tastes* instead of *tarts*
83	9 ———— erase *to be used*
84	9 ———— read *Laurustinus*
87	4 from the top, read *Cyclamens*
89	17 ———— erase the note of interrogation
88	9 ———— erase the hyphen between *Tre——— Trefoil*
90	3 ———— do the same between *Clove* and *Gillyflower*
93	7 ———— erase the word *that*
94	11 ———— for *as* read *thus*
97	2 ———— for 1651 read 1652
105	4 from the bottom for *Sculture* read *Sculptura*
134	5 from the top erase the word *by*
169	7 ———— read *inexperience*
215	1 ———— for *five* read *four*
222	2 & 3 from the bottom is merely a repetition on the work numbered 3 in the list
227	7 & 8 from the bottom will be found mentioned under Mr. George Mason's name
236	2 from the top read *Episode*
244	1 from the bottom for 1779 read 1799
264	6 from the top read *edges*
274	3 ———— read 1516
281	3 ———— for *or* read *of*
307	4 from the bottom read *hybrids*
328	Erase the two works of Mr. Felton they are mere repetitions of what has been previously stated
352	8 from the bottom read *Chardon*

FINIS.

Printed in the United States
151353LV00003B/16/A